鋼の錬金術師

FULLMETAL ALCHEMIST

14

荒川弘

HIROMU ARAKAWA

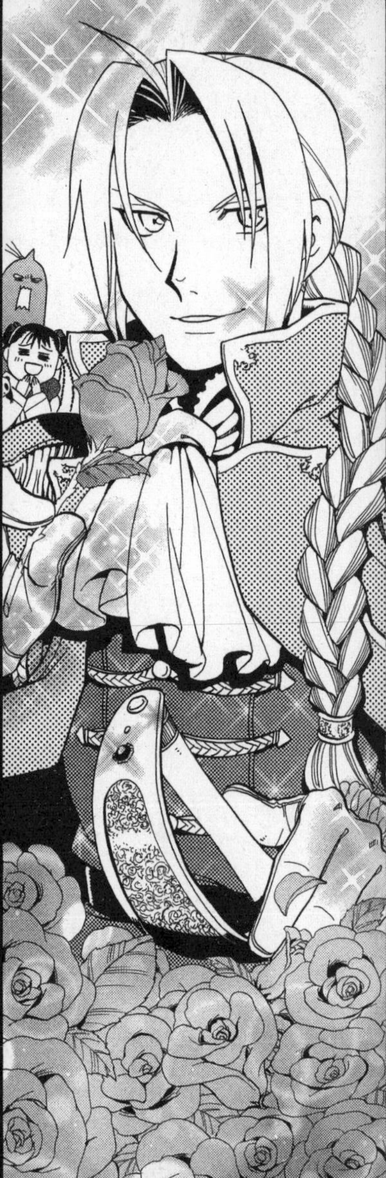

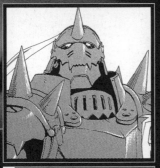

■ アルフォンス・エルリック

Alphonse Elric

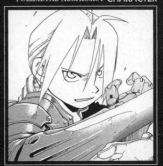

■ エドワード・エルリック

Edward Elric

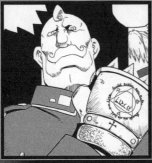

■ アレックス・ルイ・アームストロング

Alex Louis Armstrong

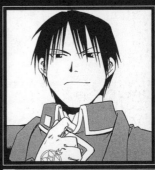

■ ロイ・マスタング

Roy Mustang

OUTLINE
FULLMETAL ALCHEMIST

The Elrics' plan to capture and interrogate Gluttony, one of the evil and nigh-invulnerable homunculi, goes awry when his "sibling" Envy crashes the party. Gluttony reveals his true bestial form and, in a rage, swallows Ed, Lin, and Envy, sending the three of them into a dark void eerily containing a large amount of rubble and…blood. Al, fearing his brother lost forever, demands that Gluttony take him to the mysterious "father" of the homunculi…

Meanwhile, Roy Mustang returns to Central City armed with the secret that President Bradley is actually a homunculus; however, when Mustang is summoned to meet with the top echelons of the military command, he is shocked to learn his intelligence is not as privileged as he thought. As Scar and May fight their way into the labyrinthine lair of the Homunculi which lies beneath Central, an unexpected reunion is at hand...

鋼の錬金術師
FULLMETAL ALCHEMIST

CHARACTERS
FULLMETAL ALCHEMIST

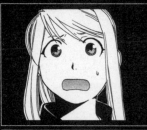

◻ ウィンリィ・ロックベル

Winry Rockbell

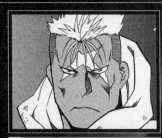

◻ スカー

Scar

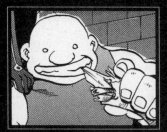

◻ グラトニー

Gluttony

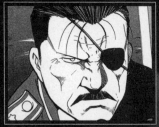

◻ キング・ブラッドレイ

King Bradley

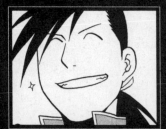

◻ リン・ヤオ

Lin Yao

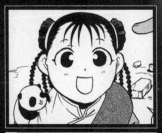

◻ メイ・チャン

May Chang

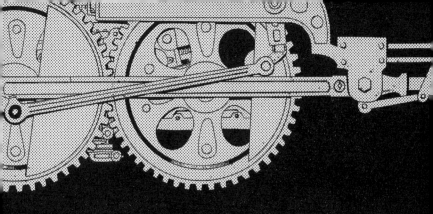

CONTENTS

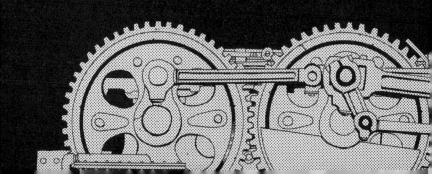

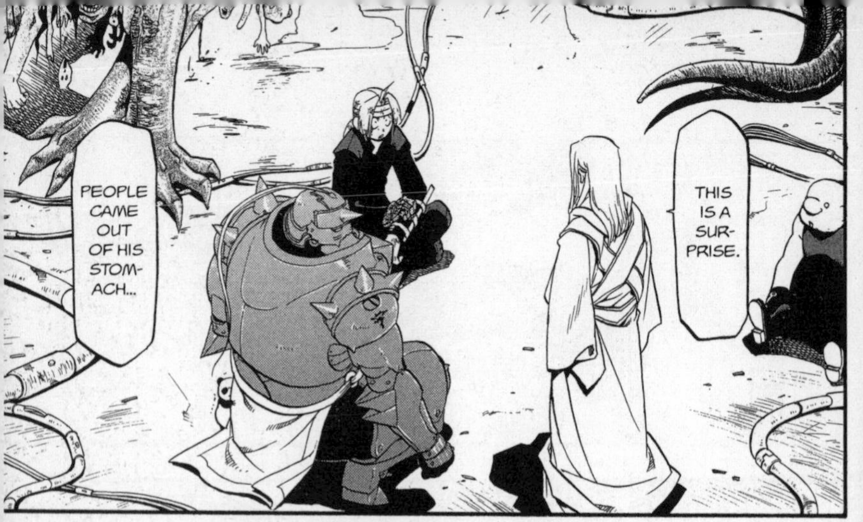
THIS IS A SURPRISE.
PEOPLE CAME OUT OF HIS STOMACH...

Chapter 54 The Fool's Struggle

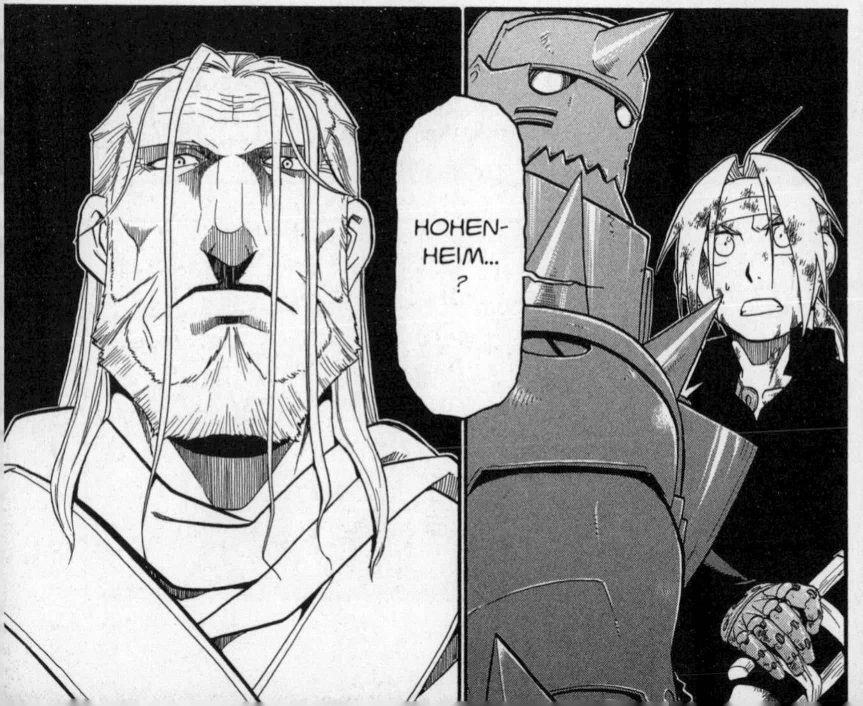
HOHENHEIM...?

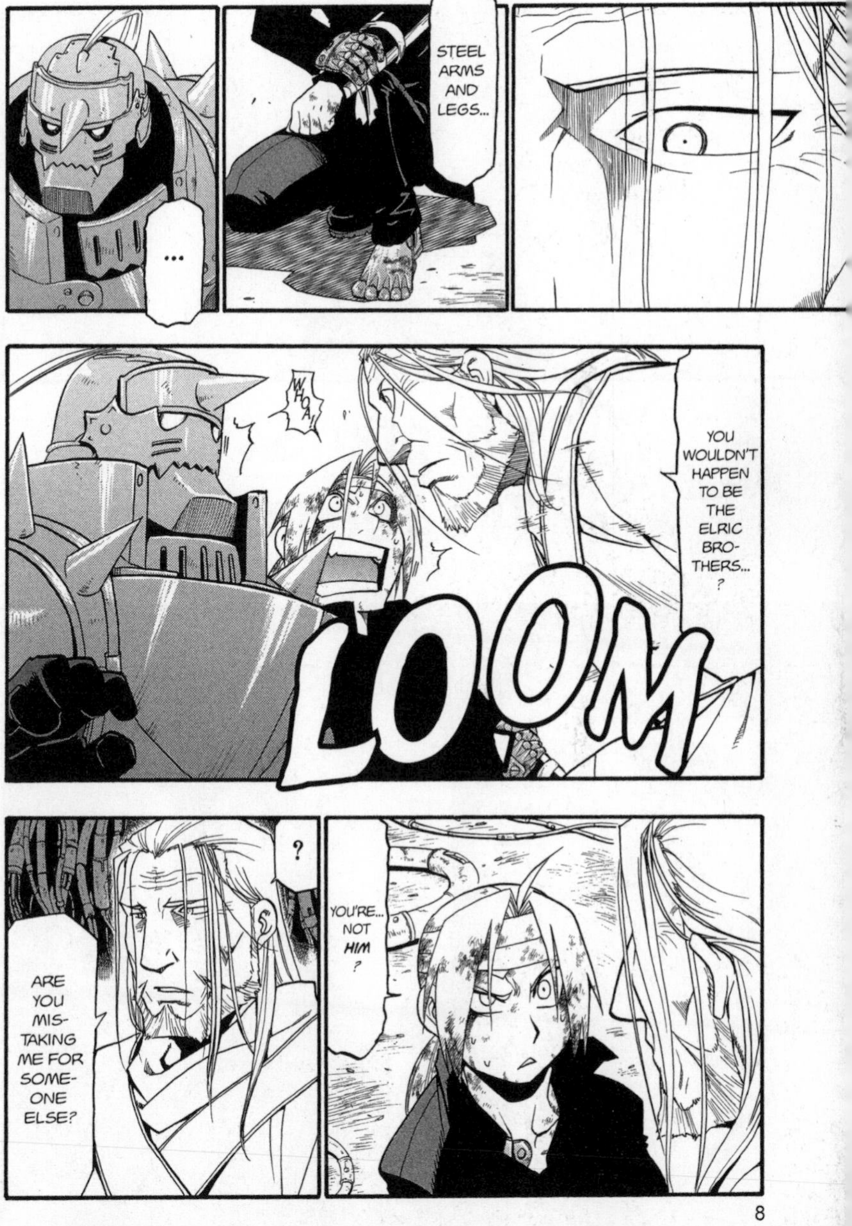
STEEL ARMS AND LEGS...
...
YOU WOULDN'T HAPPEN TO BE THE ELRIC BRO-THERS...?
WHOA!
LOOM
YOU'RE... NOT *HIM*?
?
ARE YOU MIS-TAKING ME FOR SOME-ONE ELSE?

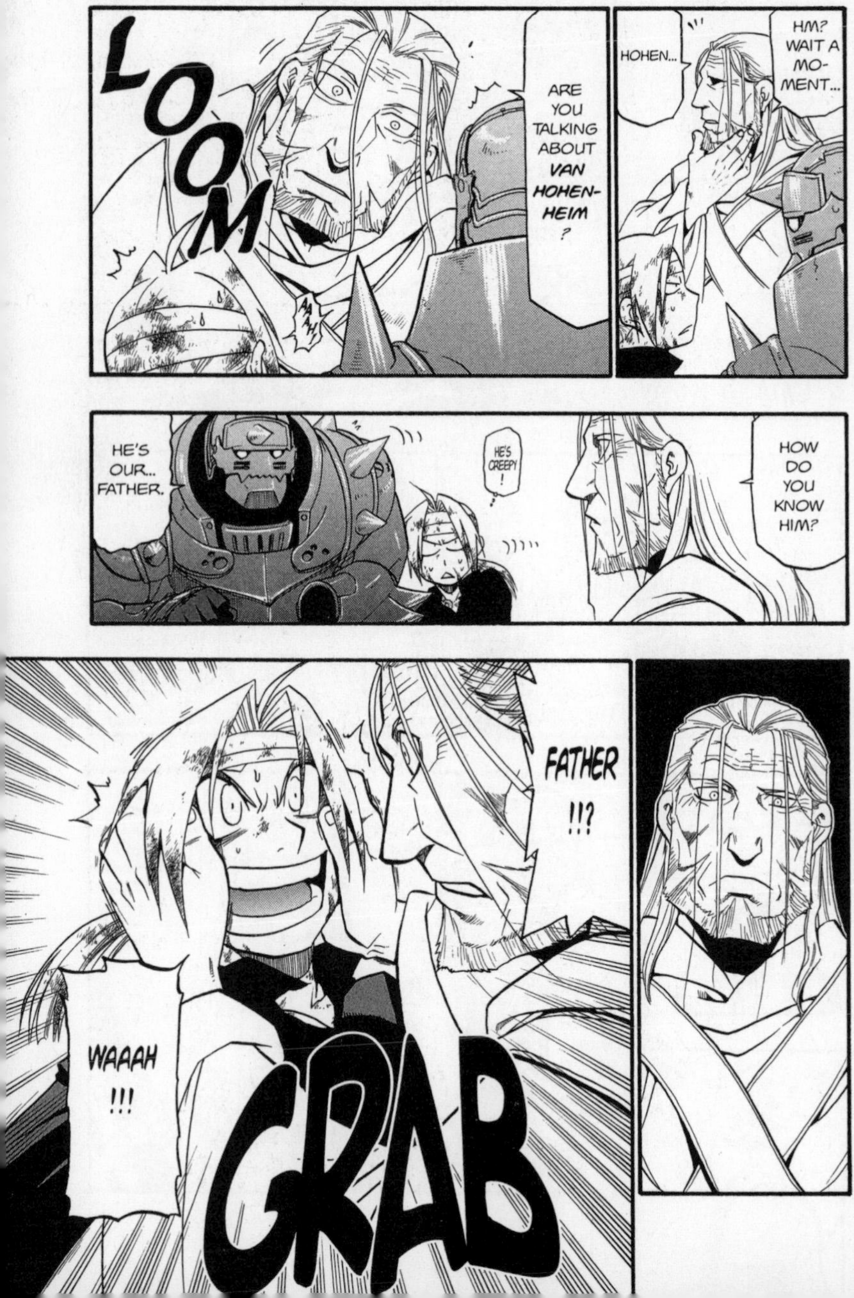

HM? WAIT A MO-MENT...
HOHEN...
ARE YOU TALKING ABOUT VAN HOHEN-HEIM?
LOOM
AAAH
HOW DO YOU KNOW HIM?
HE'S CREEPY!
HE'S OUR... FATHER.
FATHER!!?
WAAAH!!!
GRAB

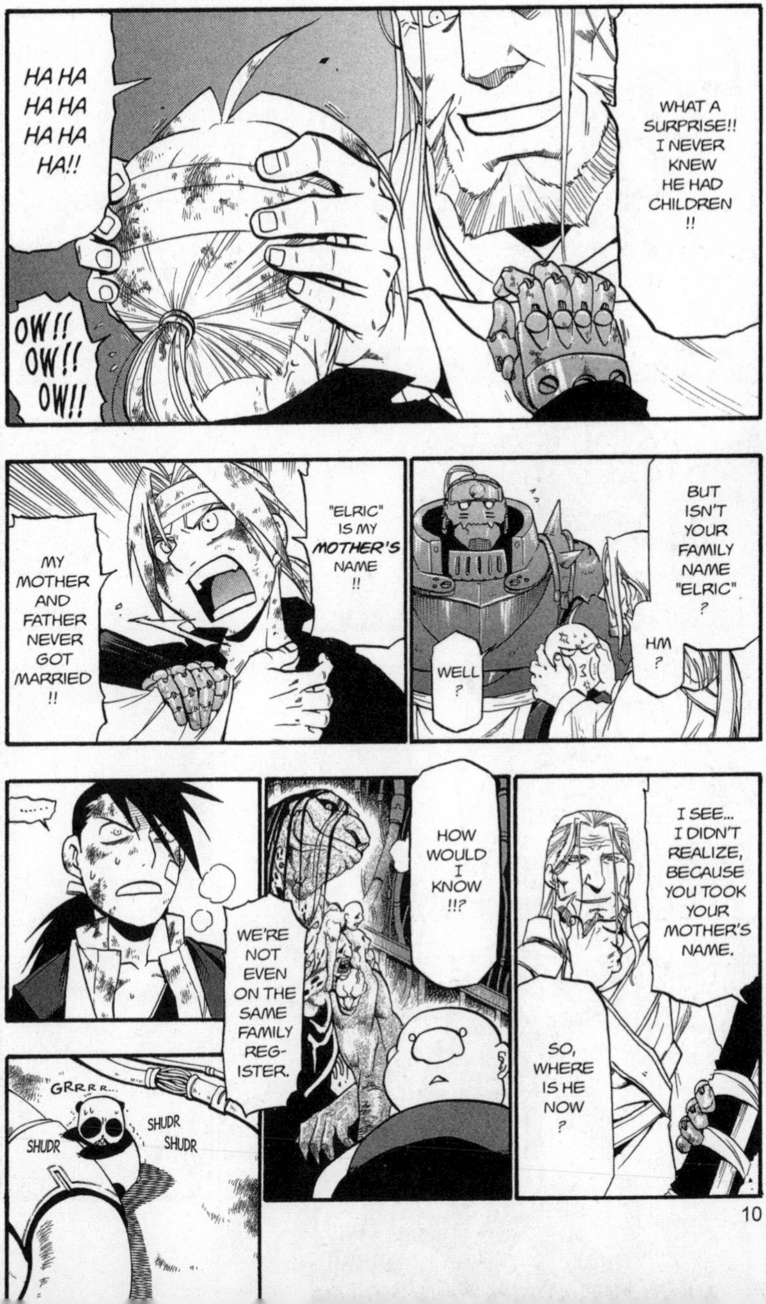
WHAT A SURPRISE!! I NEVER KNEW HE HAD CHILDREN!!
HA HA HA HA HA HA HA!!
OW!! OW!! OW!!
BUT ISN'T YOUR FAMILY NAME "ELRIC"?
HM?
WELL?
"ELRIC" IS MY MOTHER'S NAME!!
MY MOTHER AND FATHER NEVER GOT MARRIED!!
I SEE... I DIDN'T REALIZE, BECAUSE YOU TOOK YOUR MOTHER'S NAME.
SO, WHERE IS HE NOW?
HOW WOULD I KNOW!!?
WE'RE NOT EVEN ON THE SAME FAMILY REG-ISTER.
......
GRRRR...
SHUDR
SHUDR
SHUDR

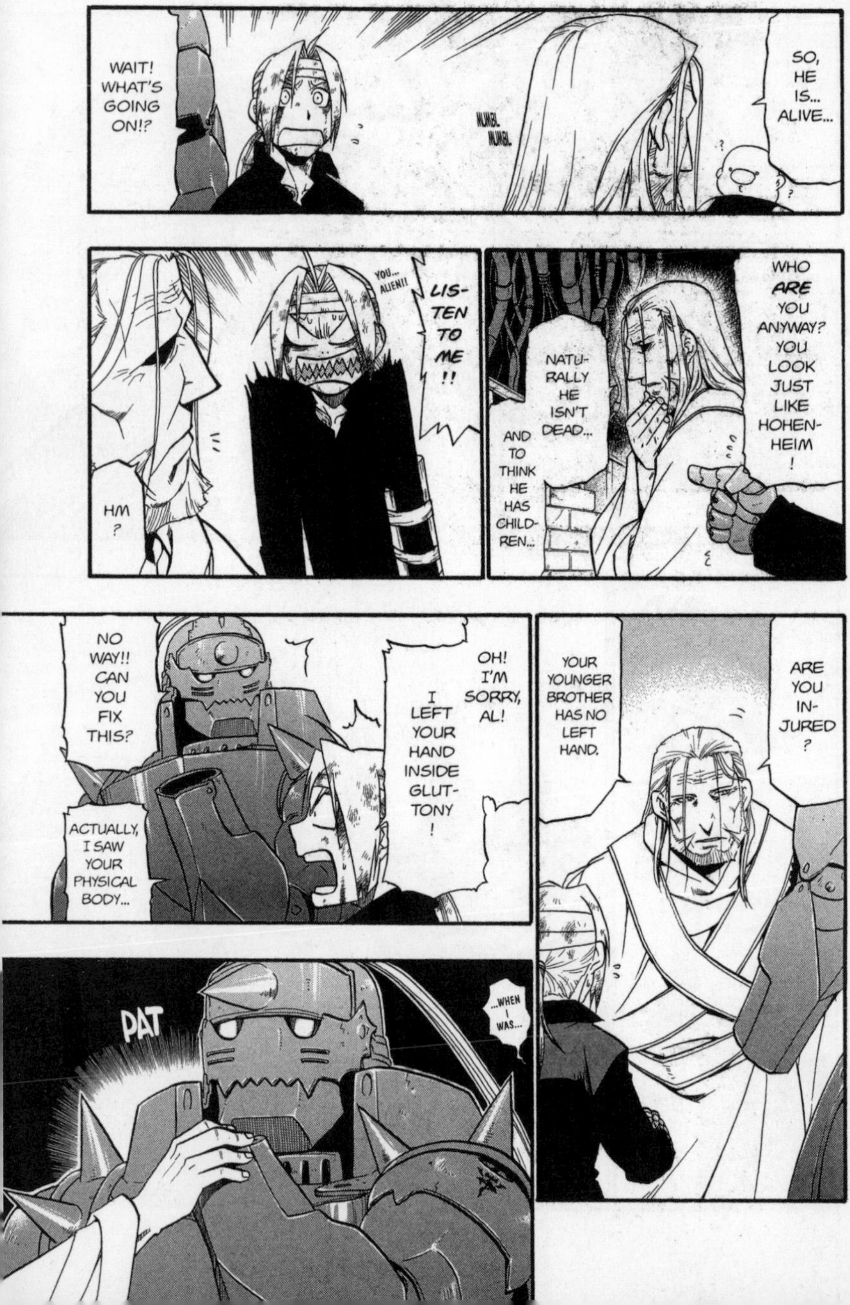
SO, HE IS... ALIVE...
MUMBL MUMBL
WAIT! WHAT'S GOING ON!?
WHO ARE YOU ANYWAY? YOU LOOK JUST LIKE HOHENHEIM!
NATURALLY HE ISN'T DEAD...
AND TO THINK HE HAS CHILDREN...
LISTEN TO ME!!
YOU... ALIEN!!
HM?
ARE YOU INJURED?
YOUR YOUNGER BROTHER HAS NO LEFT HAND.
OH! I'M SORRY, AL!
I LEFT YOUR HAND INSIDE GLUTTONY!
NO WAY!! CAN YOU FIX THIS?
ACTUALLY, I SAW YOUR PHYSICAL BODY...
...WHEN I WAS...
PAT

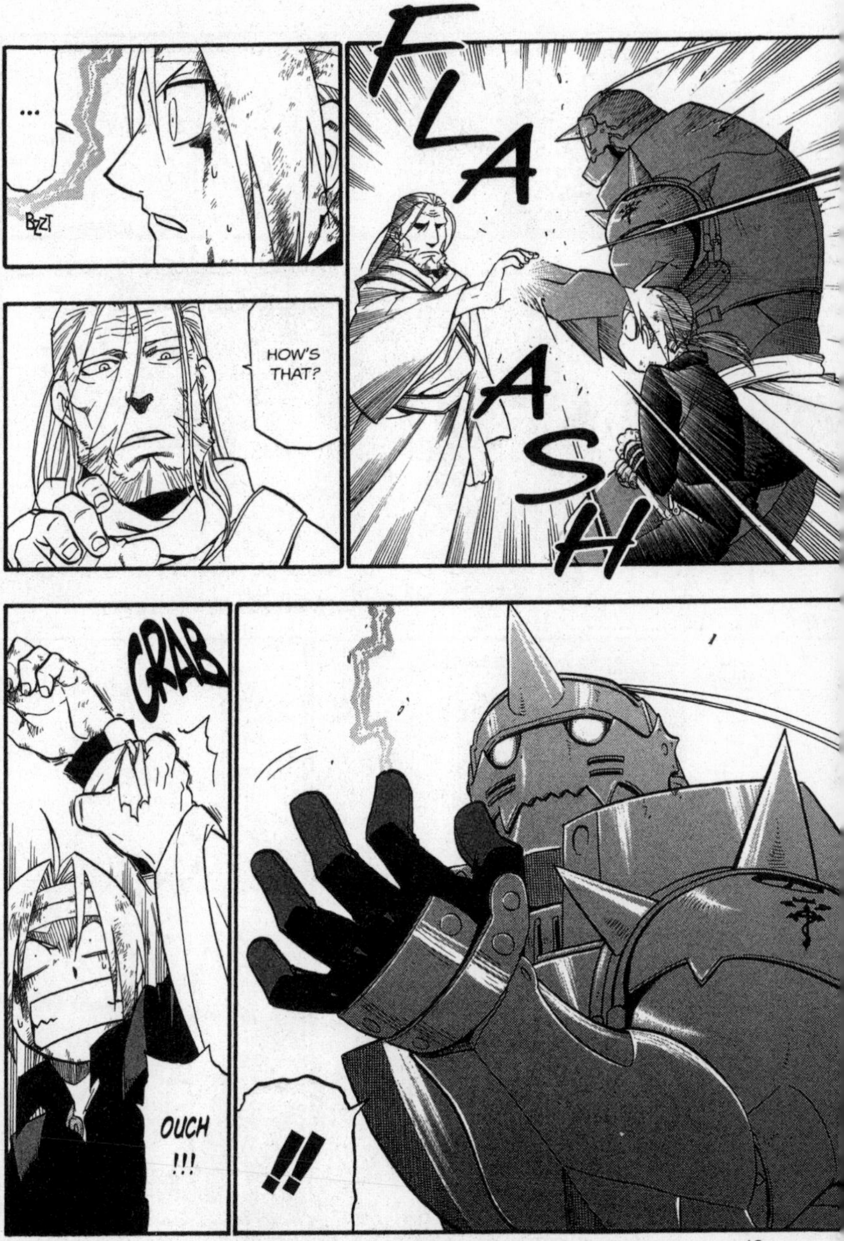
FLASH
...
BZZT
HOW'S THAT?
!!
GRAB
OUCH !!!

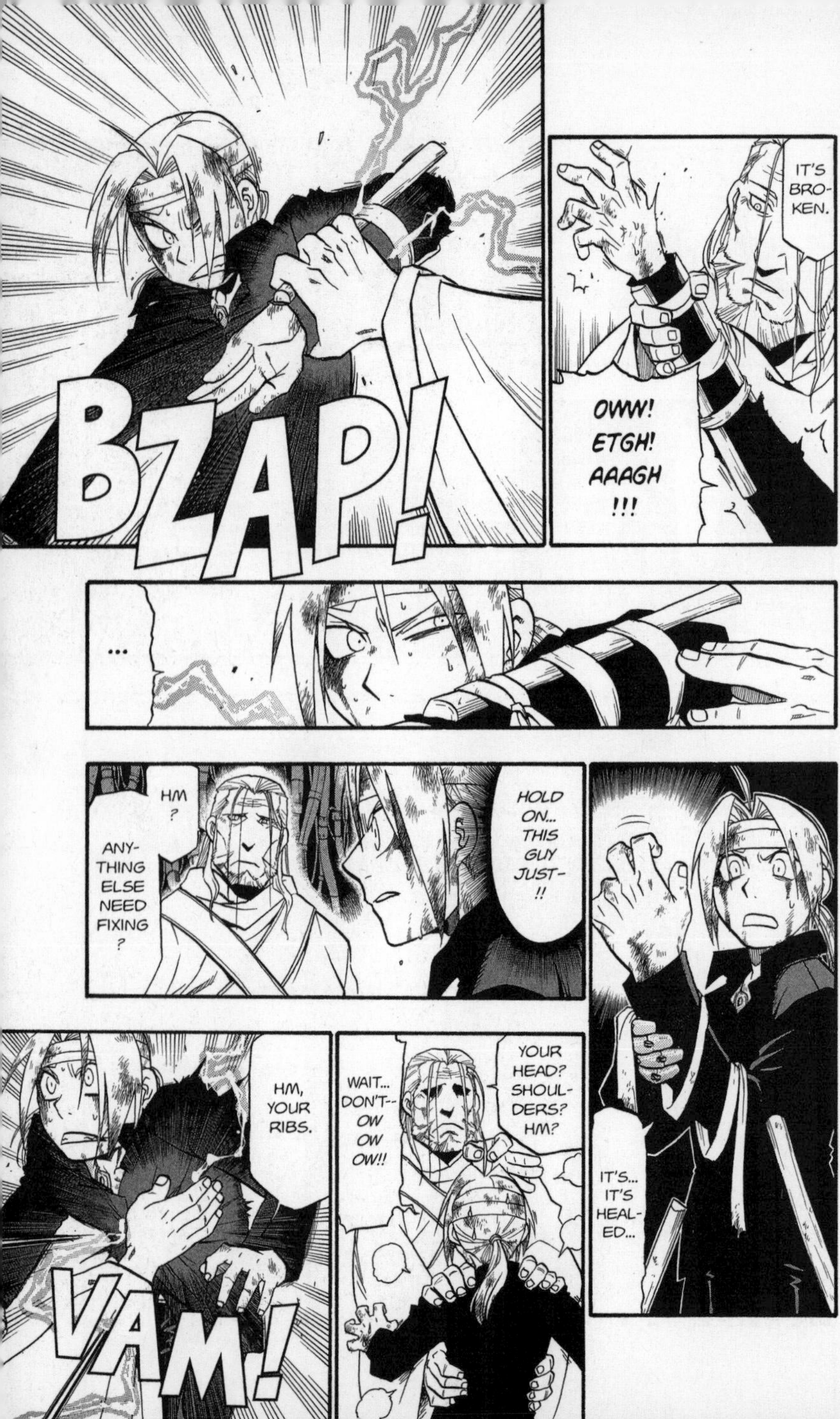
IT'S BROKEN.
OWW! ETGH! AAAGH !!!
BZAP!
...
IT'S... IT'S HEALED...
HOLD ON... THIS GUY JUST- !!
HM ?
ANYTHING ELSE NEED FIXING ?
YOUR HEAD? SHOULDERS? HM?
WAIT... DON'T-- OW OW OW!!
HM, YOUR RIBS.
VAM!

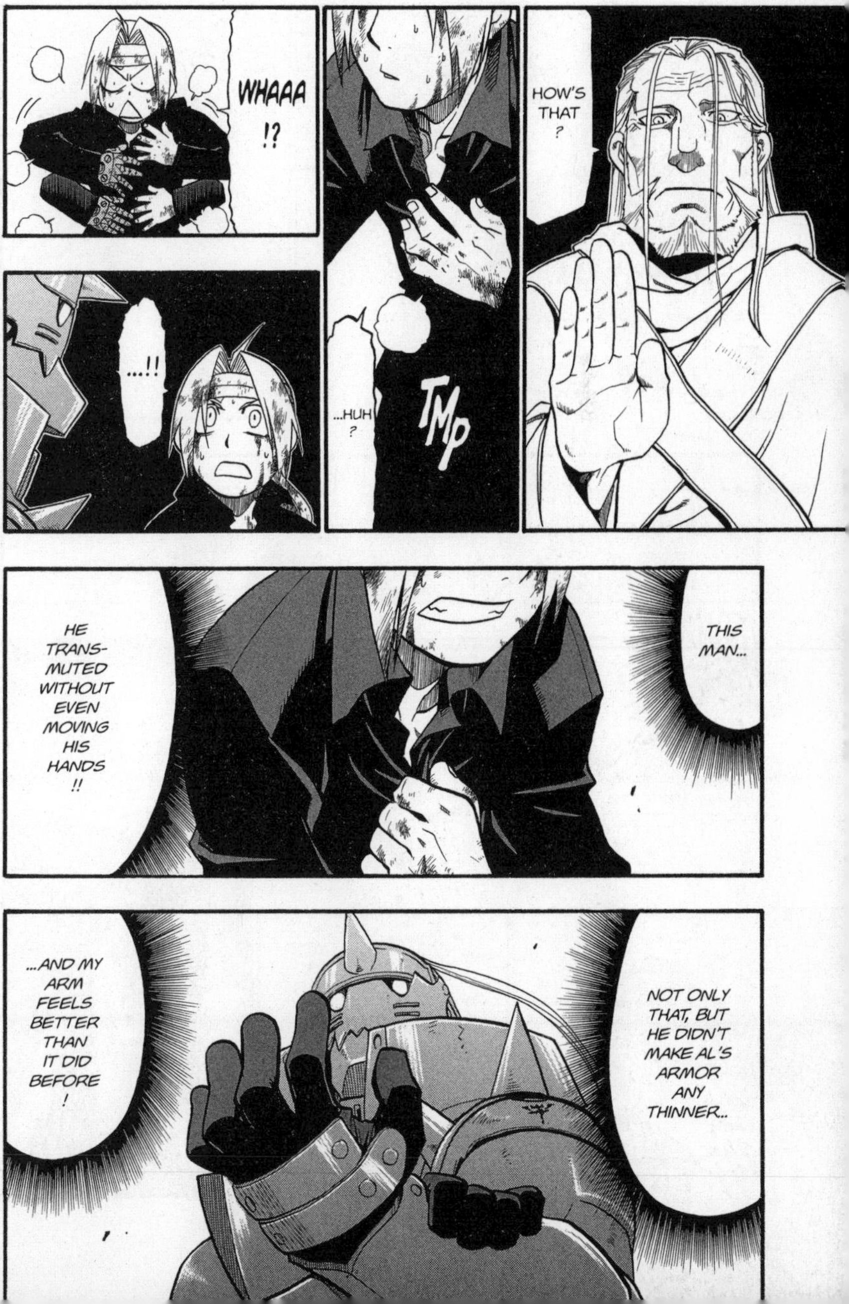
HOW'S THAT?
...HUH?
TMP
WHAAA!?
...!!
THIS MAN...
HE TRANSMUTED WITHOUT EVEN MOVING HIS HANDS!!
NOT ONLY THAT, BUT HE DIDN'T MAKE AL'S ARMOR ANY THINNER...
...AND MY ARM FEELS BETTER THAN IT DID BEFORE!

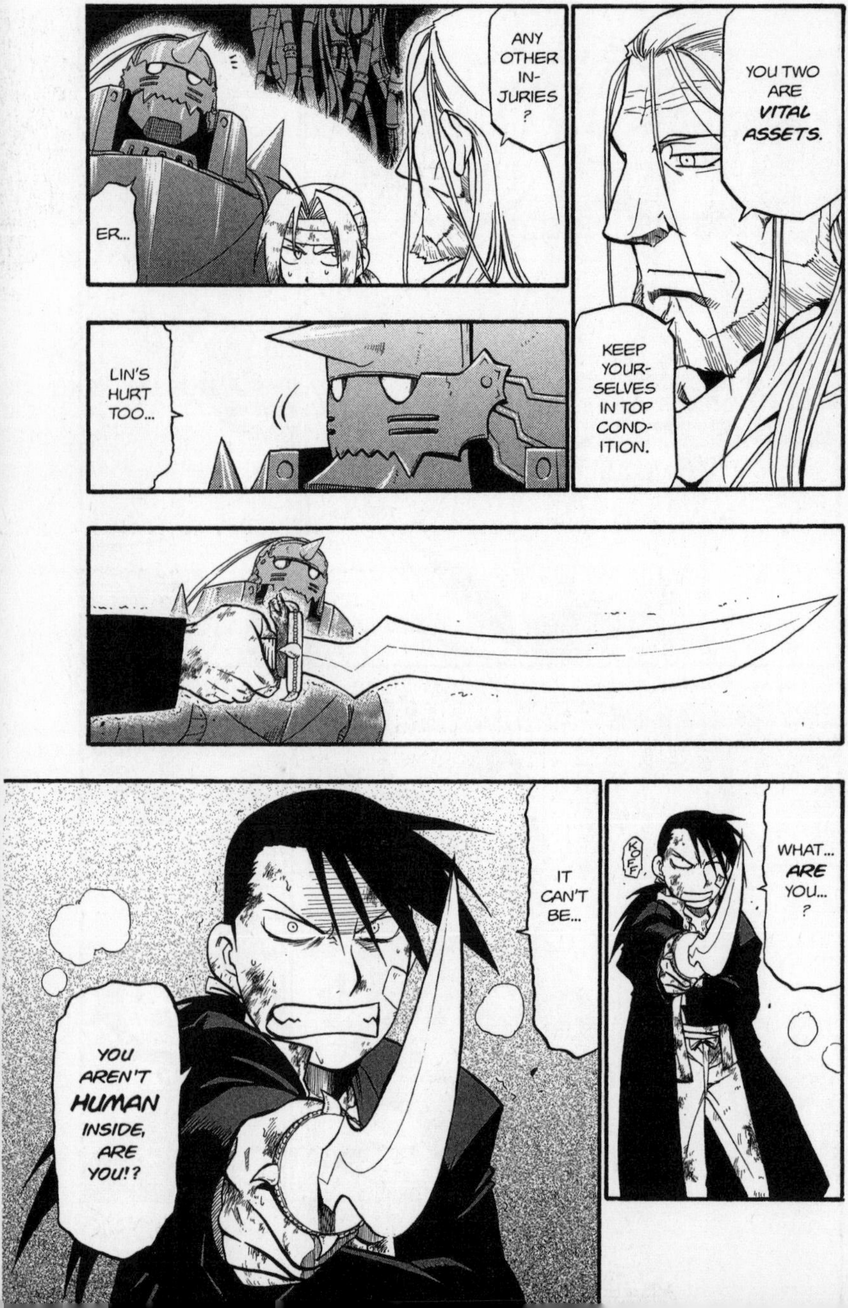
YOU TWO ARE VITAL ASSETS.
KEEP YOURSELVES IN TOP CONDITION.
ANY OTHER INJURIES?
ER...
LIN'S HURT TOO...
KOFF
WHAT... ARE YOU...?
IT CAN'T BE...
YOU AREN'T HUMAN INSIDE, ARE YOU!?

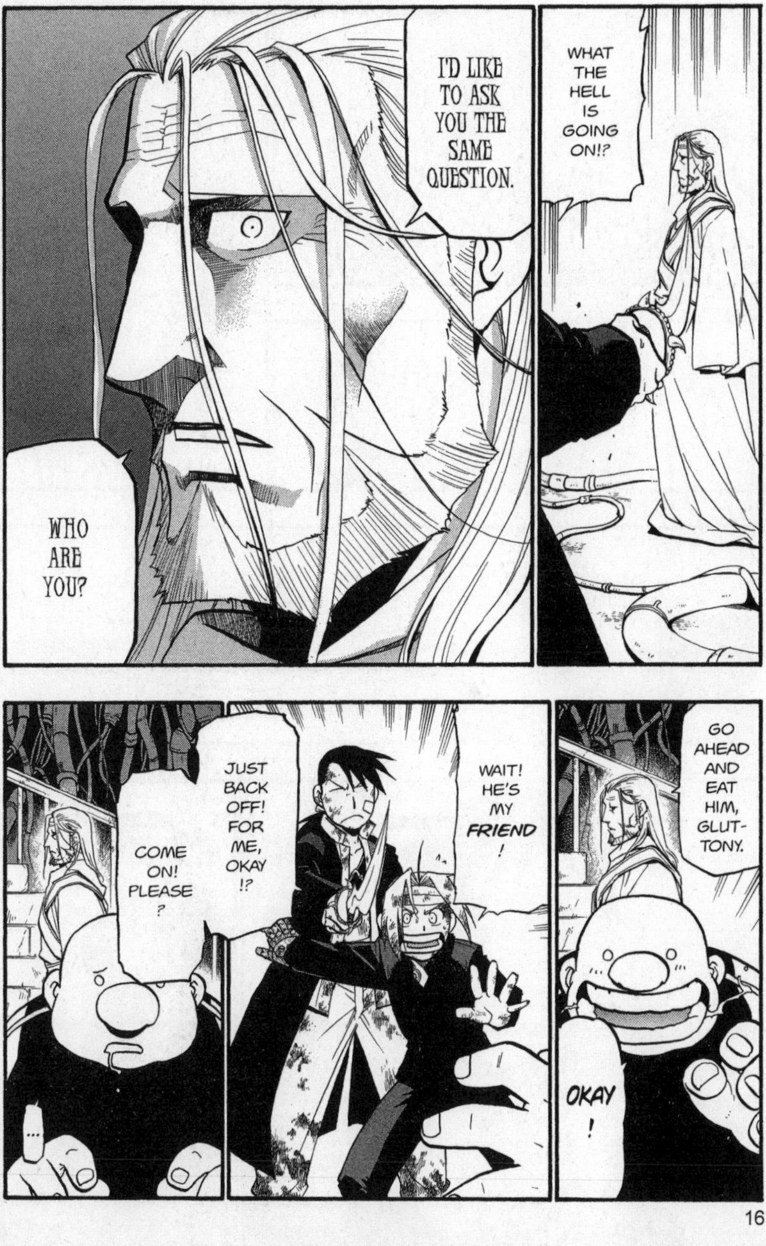
WHAT THE HELL IS GOING ON!?
I'D LIKE TO ASK YOU THE SAME QUESTION.
WHO ARE YOU?
GO AHEAD AND EAT HIM, GLUTTONY.
OKAY!
WAIT! HE'S MY FRIEND!
JUST BACK OFF! FOR ME, OKAY!?
COME ON! PLEASE?
...

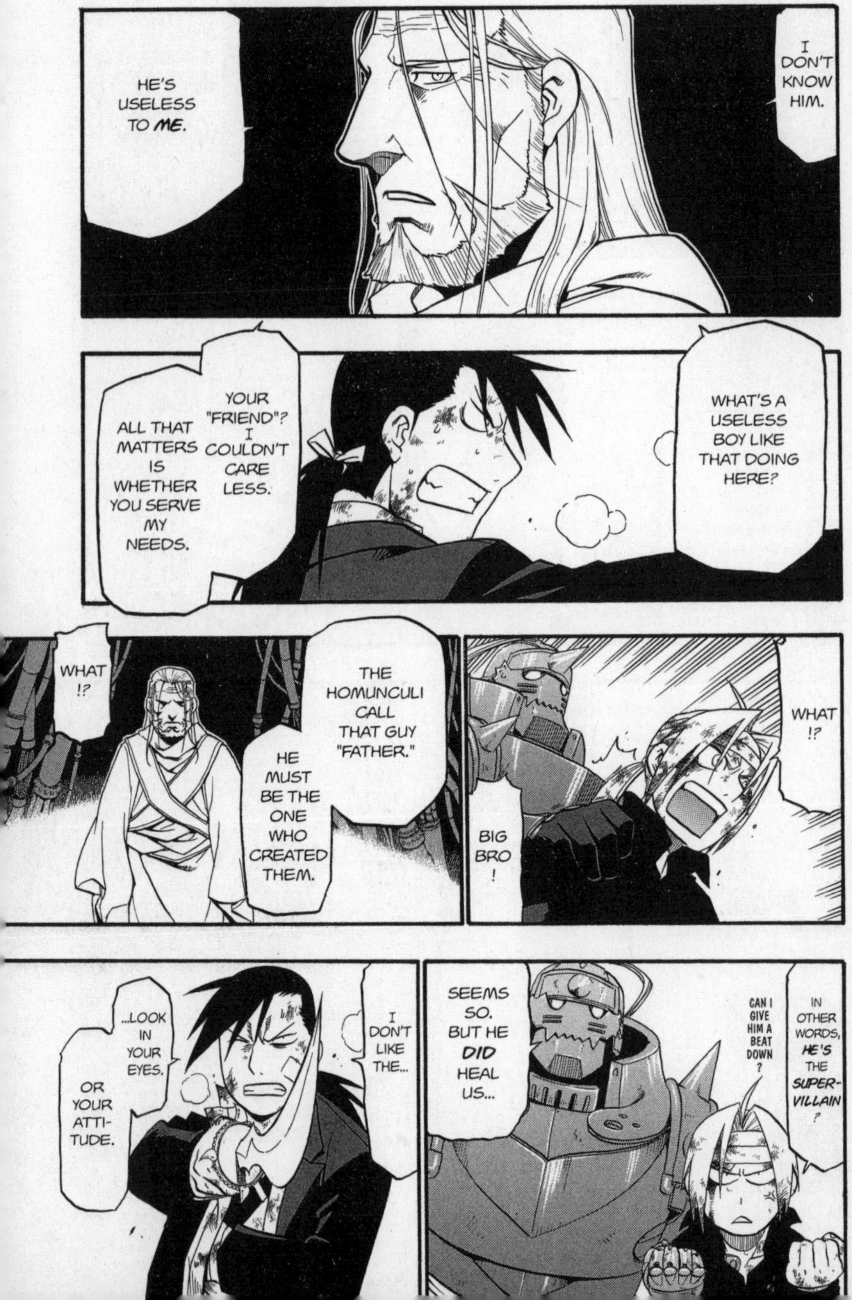

I DON'T KNOW HIM.
HE'S USELESS TO ME.
WHAT'S A USELESS BOY LIKE THAT DOING HERE?
YOUR "FRIEND"? I COULDN'T CARE LESS.
ALL THAT MATTERS IS WHETHER YOU SERVE MY NEEDS.
WHAT!?
BIG BRO!
THE HOMUNCULI CALL THAT GUY "FATHER."
HE MUST BE THE ONE WHO CREATED THEM.
WHAT!?
IN OTHER WORDS, HE'S THE SUPER-VILLAIN?
CAN I GIVE HIM A BEAT DOWN?
SEEMS SO. BUT HE DID HEAL US...
I DON'T LIKE THE...
...LOOK IN YOUR EYES.
OR YOUR ATTITUDE.

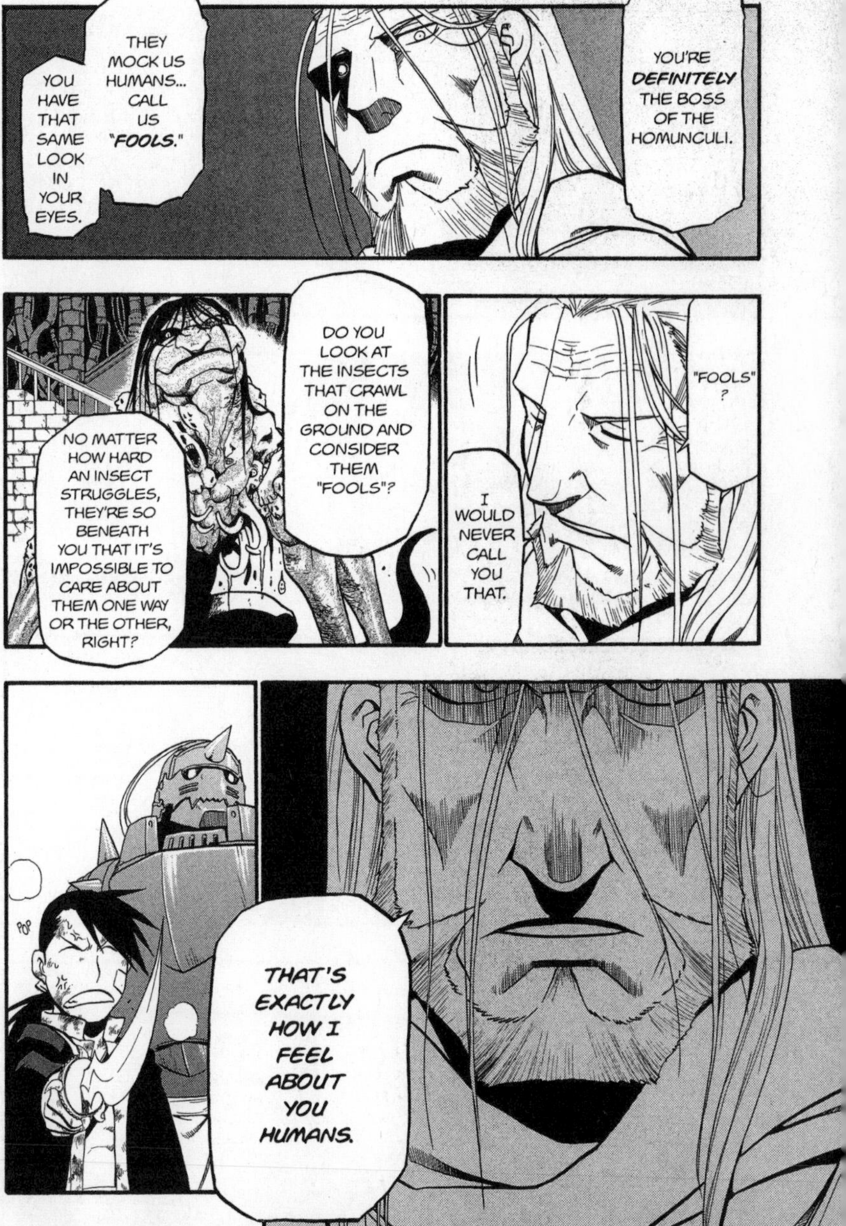
YOU'RE DEFINITELY THE BOSS OF THE HOMUNCULI.
THEY MOCK US HUMANS... CALL US "FOOLS."
YOU HAVE THAT SAME LOOK IN YOUR EYES.
"FOOLS"?
I WOULD NEVER CALL YOU THAT.
DO YOU LOOK AT THE INSECTS THAT CRAWL ON THE GROUND AND CONSIDER THEM "FOOLS"?
NO MATTER HOW HARD AN INSECT STRUGGLES, THEY'RE SO BENEATH YOU THAT IT'S IMPOSSIBLE TO CARE ABOUT THEM ONE WAY OR THE OTHER, RIGHT?
THAT'S EXACTLY HOW I FEEL ABOUT YOU HUMANS.
POP

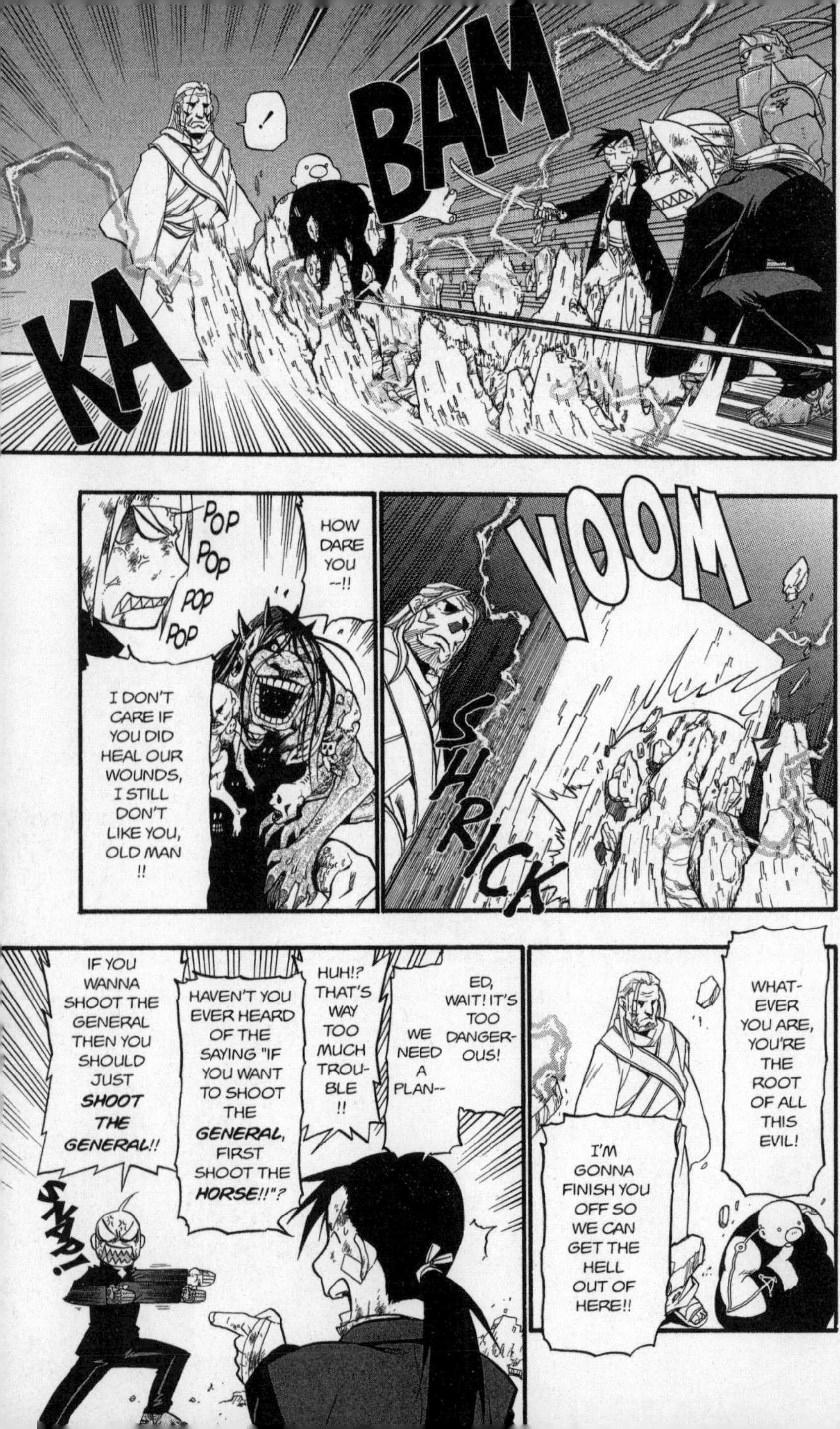
BAM
!
KA
VOOM
SHRICK
POP POP POP POP
HOW DARE YOU --!!
I DON'T CARE IF YOU DID HEAL OUR WOUNDS, I STILL DON'T LIKE YOU, OLD MAN!!
WHAT-EVER YOU ARE, YOU'RE THE ROOT OF ALL THIS EVIL!
I'M GONNA FINISH YOU OFF SO WE CAN GET THE HELL OUT OF HERE!!
ED, WAIT! IT'S TOO DANGER-OUS!
WE NEED A PLAN--
HUH!? THAT'S WAY TOO MUCH TROU-BLE!!
HAVEN'T YOU EVER HEARD OF THE SAYING "IF YOU WANT TO SHOOT THE **GENERAL**, FIRST SHOOT THE **HORSE**!!"?
IF YOU WANNA SHOOT THE GENERAL THEN YOU SHOULD JUST **SHOOT THE GENERAL**!!
SNAP!

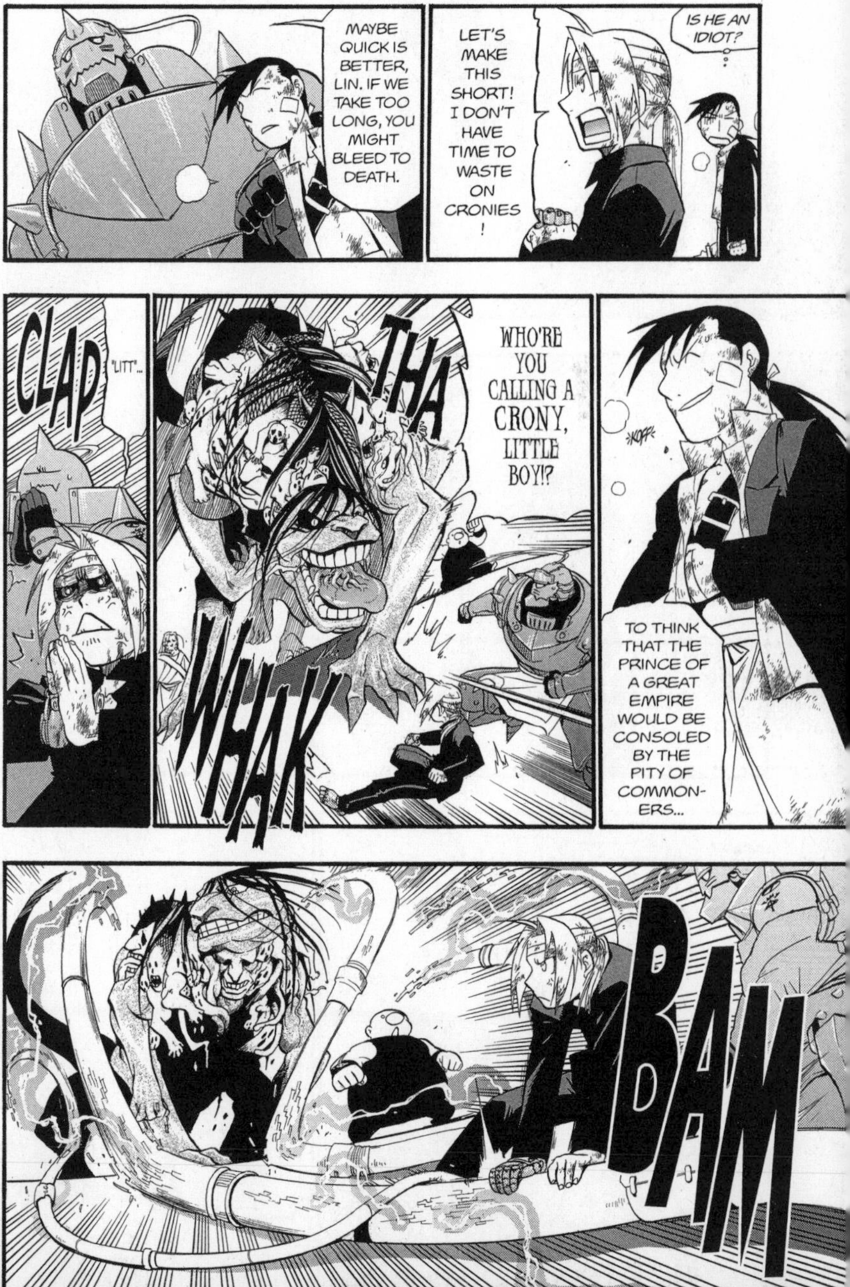
LET'S MAKE THIS SHORT! I DON'T HAVE TIME TO WASTE ON CRONIES!
IS HE AN IDIOT?
MAYBE QUICK IS BETTER, LIN. IF WE TAKE TOO LONG, YOU MIGHT BLEED TO DEATH.
KOFF
TO THINK THAT THE PRINCE OF A GREAT EMPIRE WOULD BE CONSOLED BY THE PITY OF COMMONERS...
WHO'RE YOU CALLING A CRONY, LITTLE BOY!?
THA
WHAK
CLAP
"LITT"...
BAM

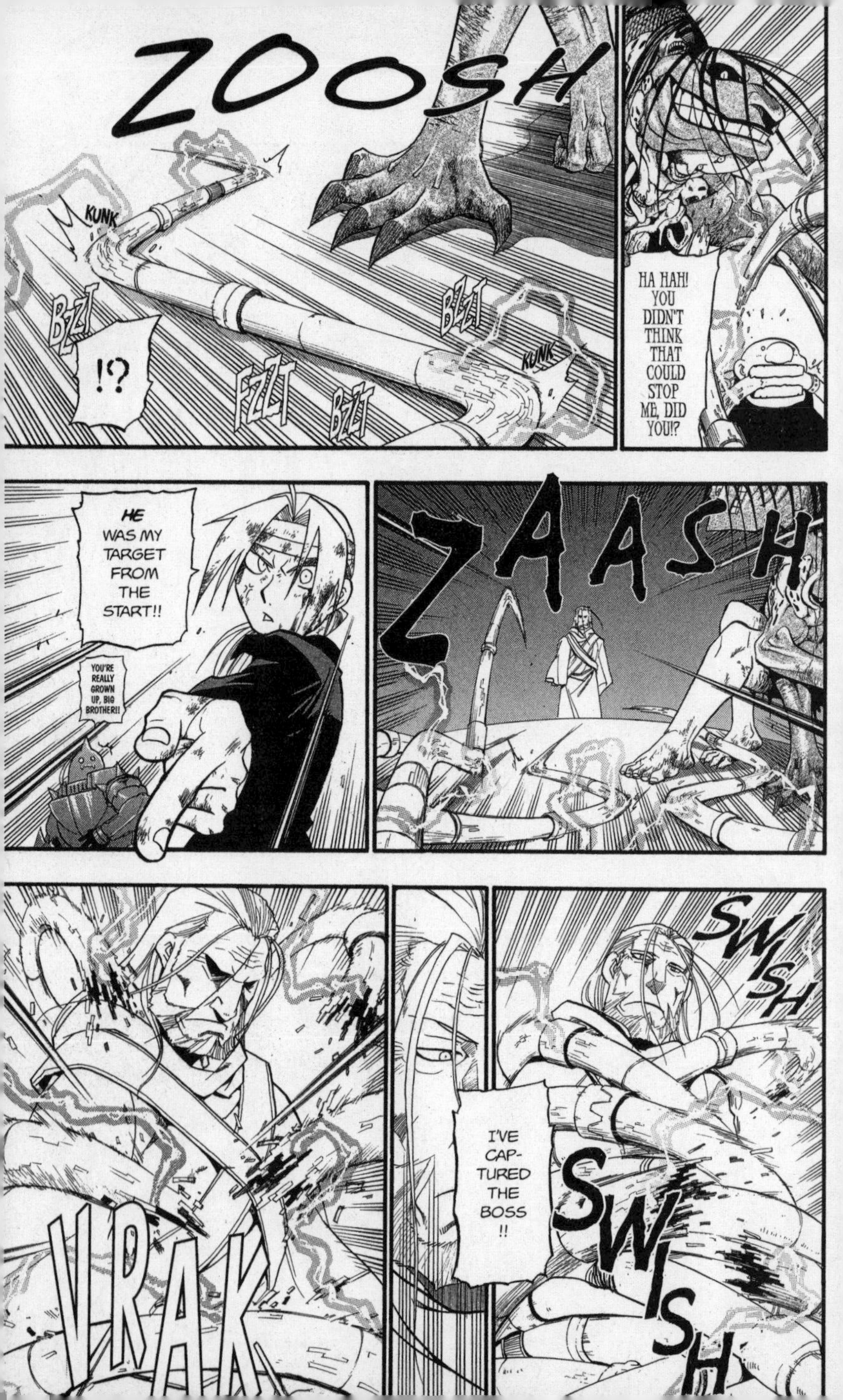
HA HAH! YOU DIDN'T THINK THAT COULD STOP ME, DID YOU!?
ZOOSH
KUNK
BZZT
!?
FZZT
BZZT
KUNK
BZZT
ZAASH
HE WAS MY TARGET FROM THE START!!
YOU'RE REALLY GROWN UP, BIG BROTHER!!
SWISH
I'VE CAP-TURED THE BOSS !!
SWISH
VRAK

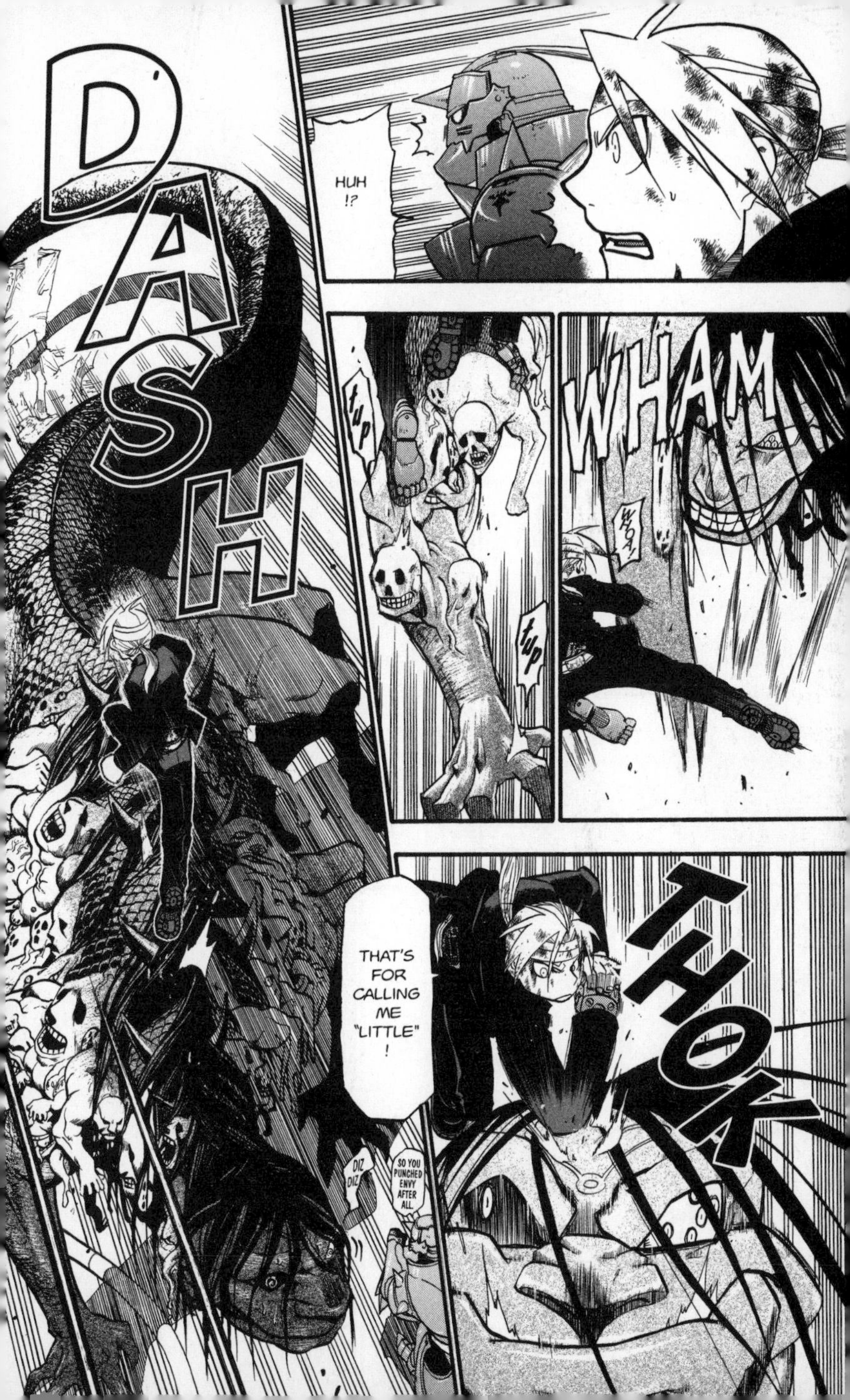
HUH !?
DASH
WHAM
WHOA!
tup
tup
THOK
THAT'S FOR CALLING ME "LITTLE" !
SO YOU PUNCHED ENVY AFTER ALL.
DIZ DIZ

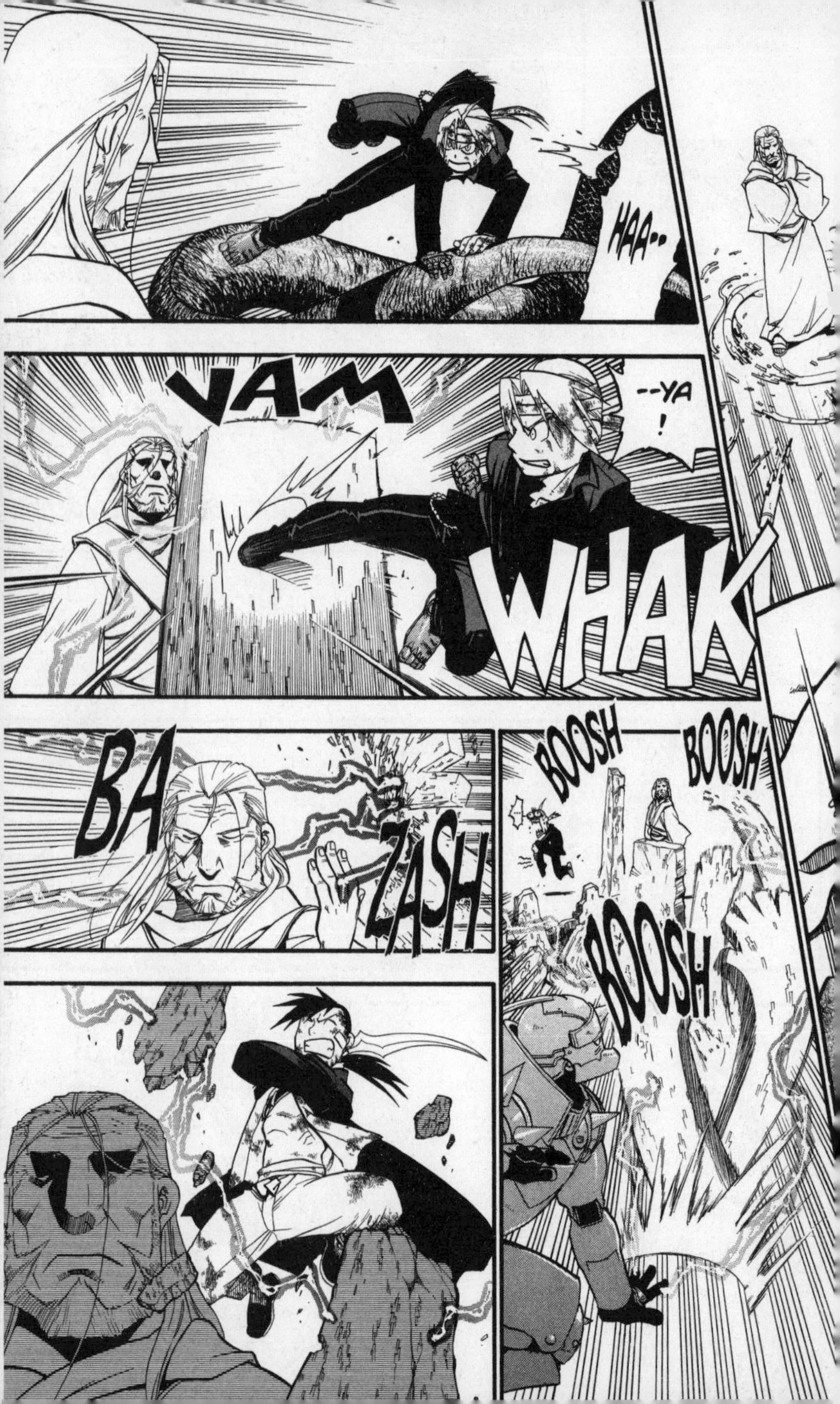
HAA..
--YA !
VAM
WHAK
BOOSH
BOOSH
BOOSH
BA
ZASH

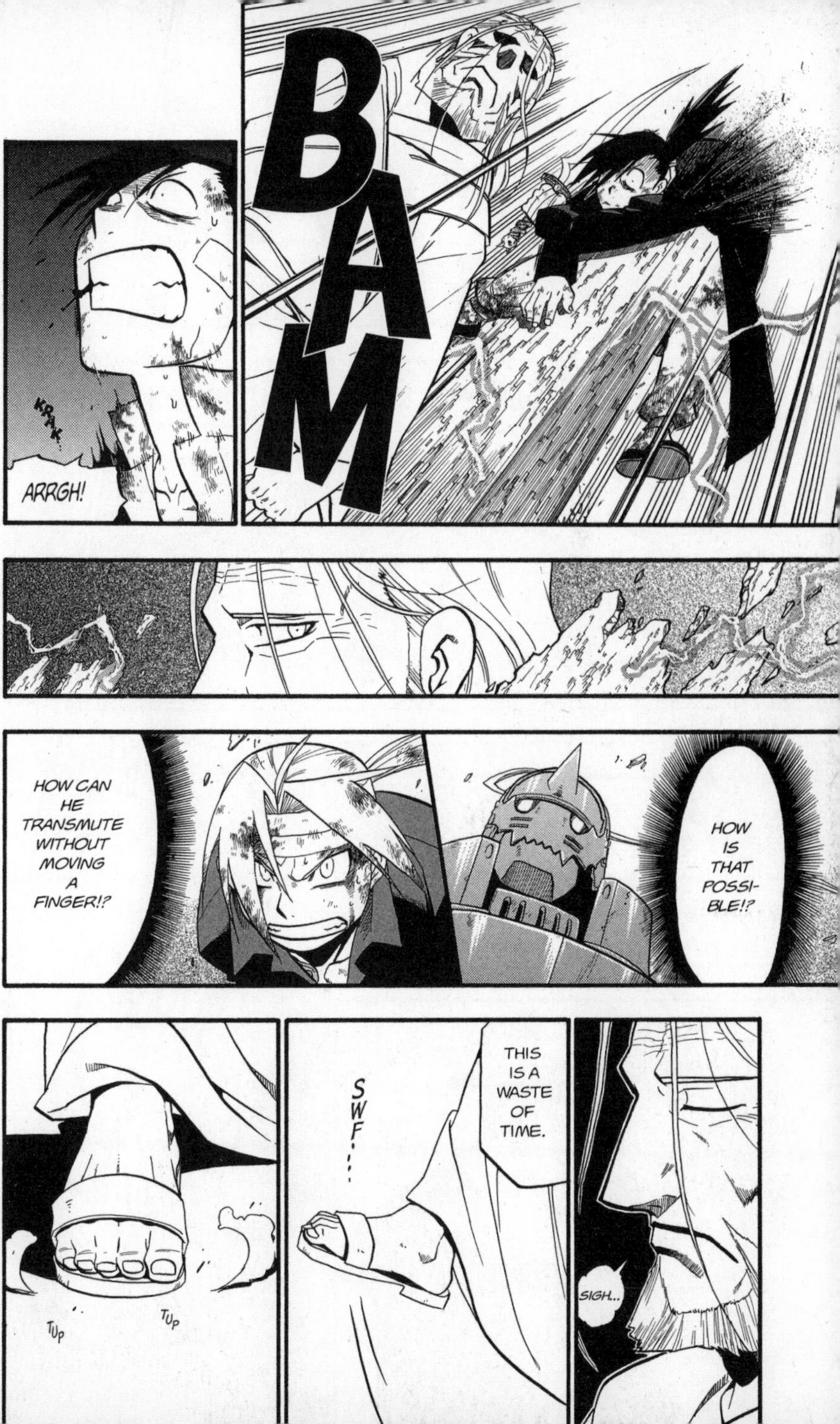
BAM
KRAK
ARRGH!
HOW IS THAT POSSI-BLE!?
HOW CAN HE TRANSMUTE WITHOUT MOVING A FINGER!?
SIGH...
THIS IS A WASTE OF TIME.
SWF...
TUP
TUP

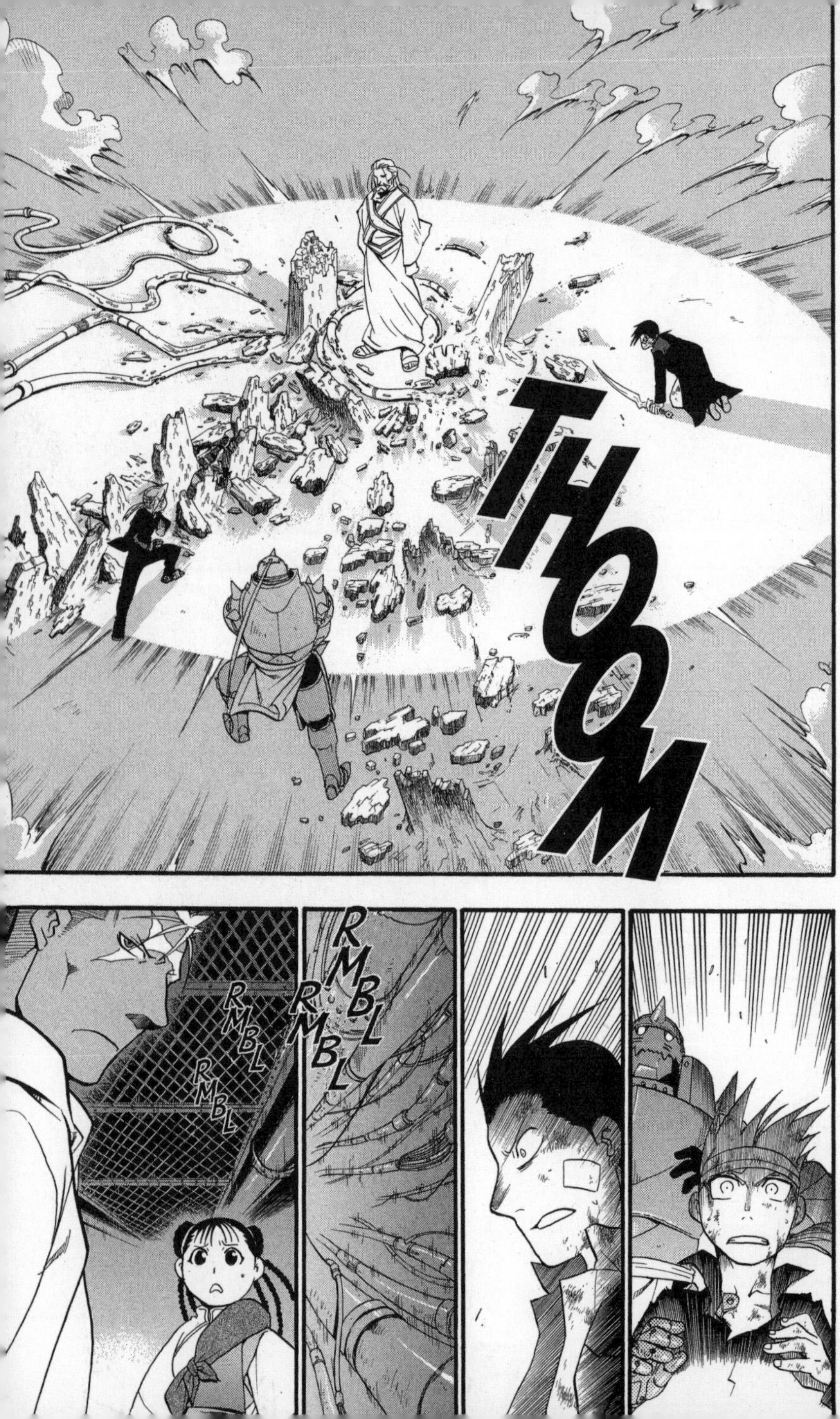
THOOM
RMBL
RMBL
RMBL
RMBL

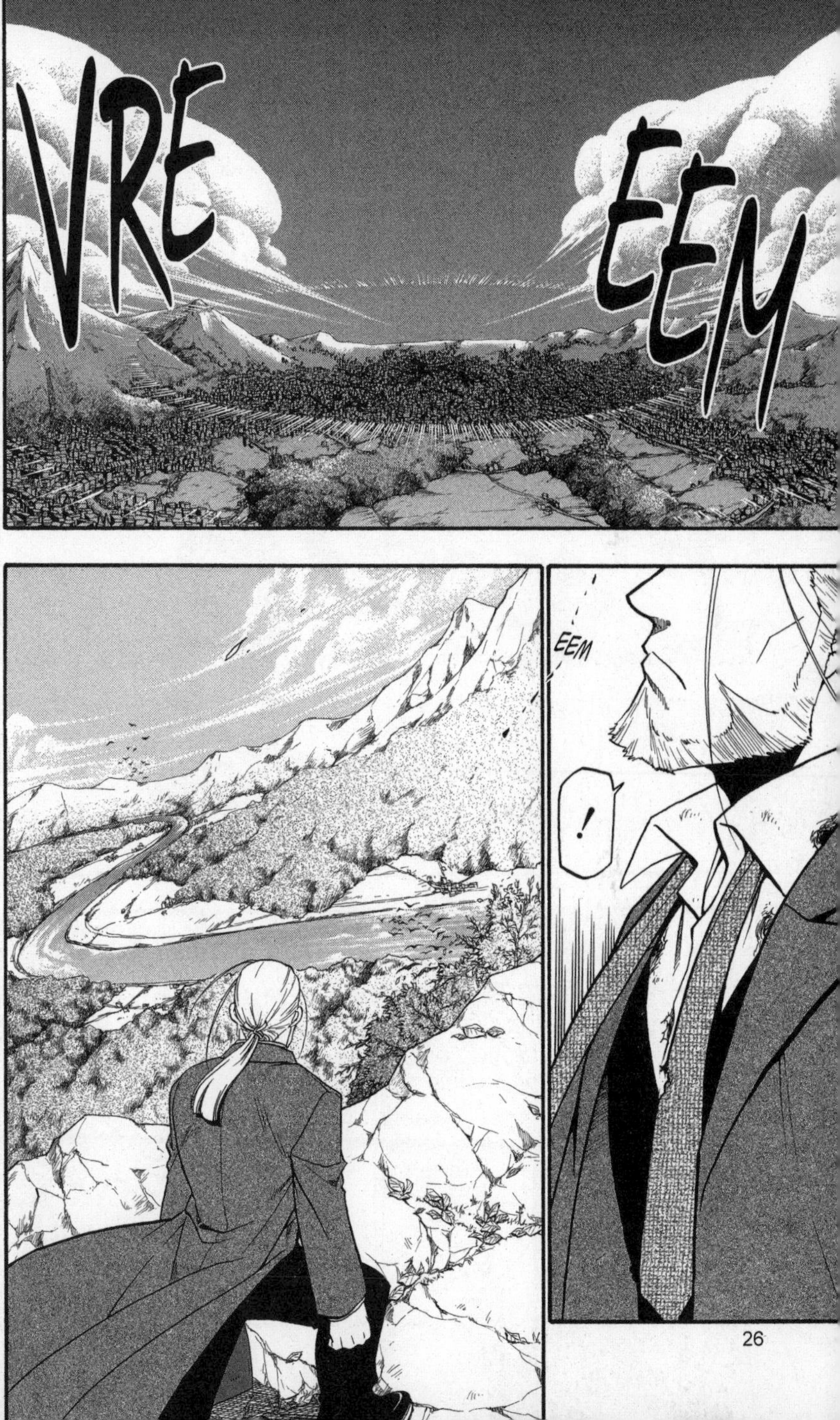
VREEEM
EEM
!

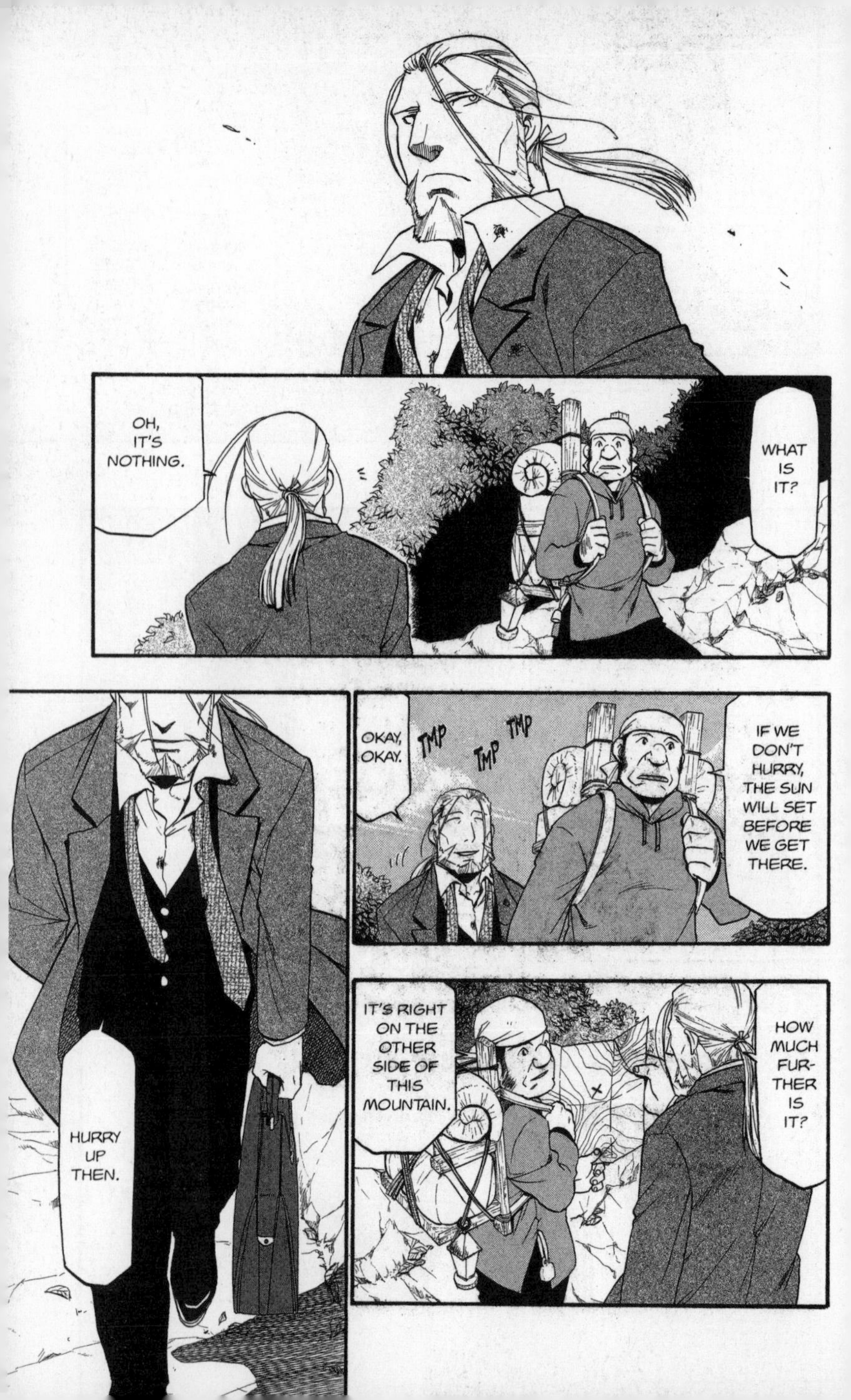
WHAT IS IT?
OH, IT'S NOTHING.
IF WE DON'T HURRY, THE SUN WILL SET BEFORE WE GET THERE.
TMP TMP TMP
OKAY, OKAY.
HOW MUCH FUR-THER IS IT?
IT'S RIGHT ON THE OTHER SIDE OF THIS MOUNTAIN.
HURRY UP THEN.

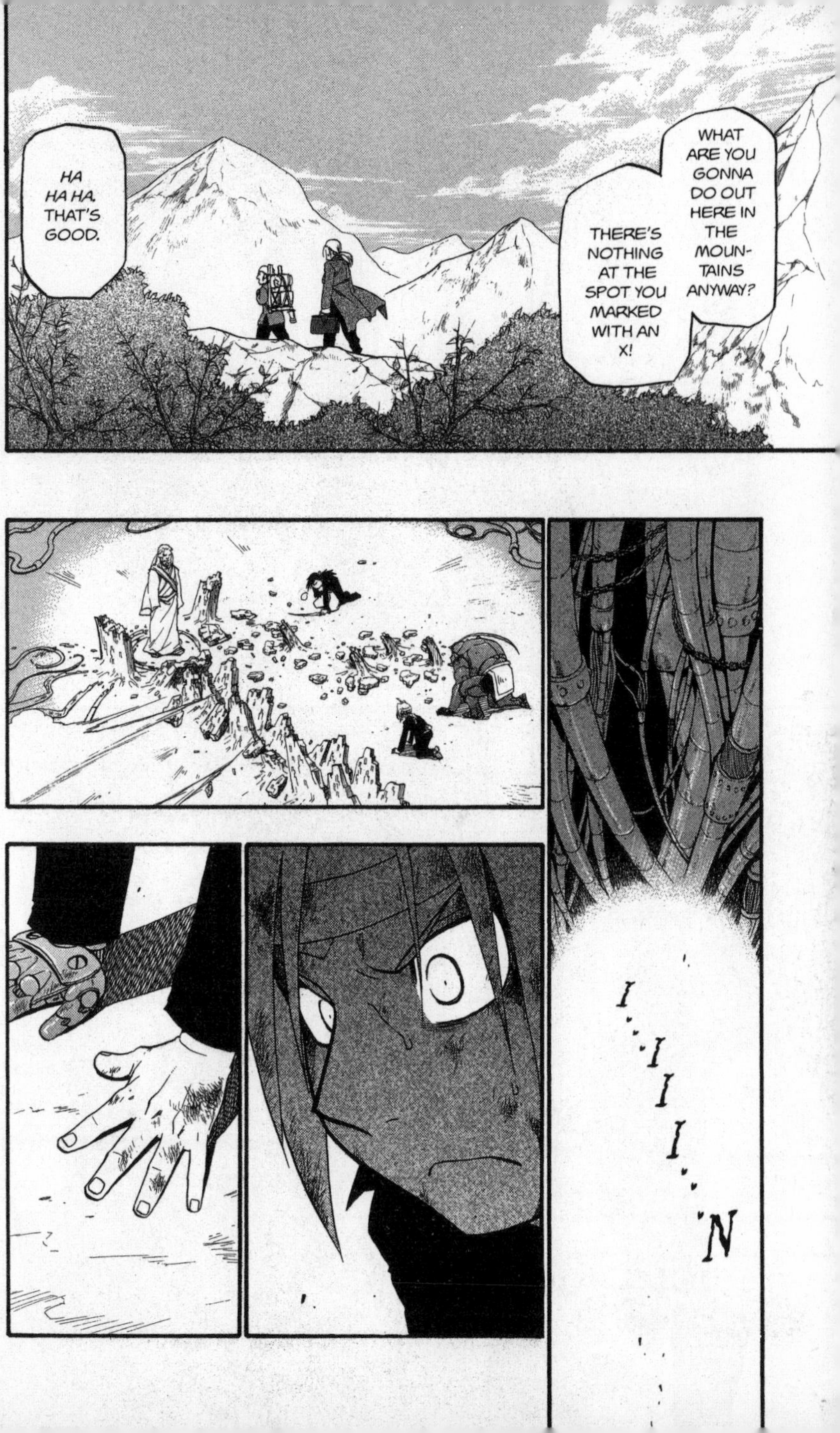
WHAT ARE YOU GONNA DO OUT HERE IN THE MOUN-TAINS ANYWAY?
THERE'S NOTHING AT THE SPOT YOU MARKED WITH AN X!
HA HA HA. THAT'S GOOD.
I...I...I...N

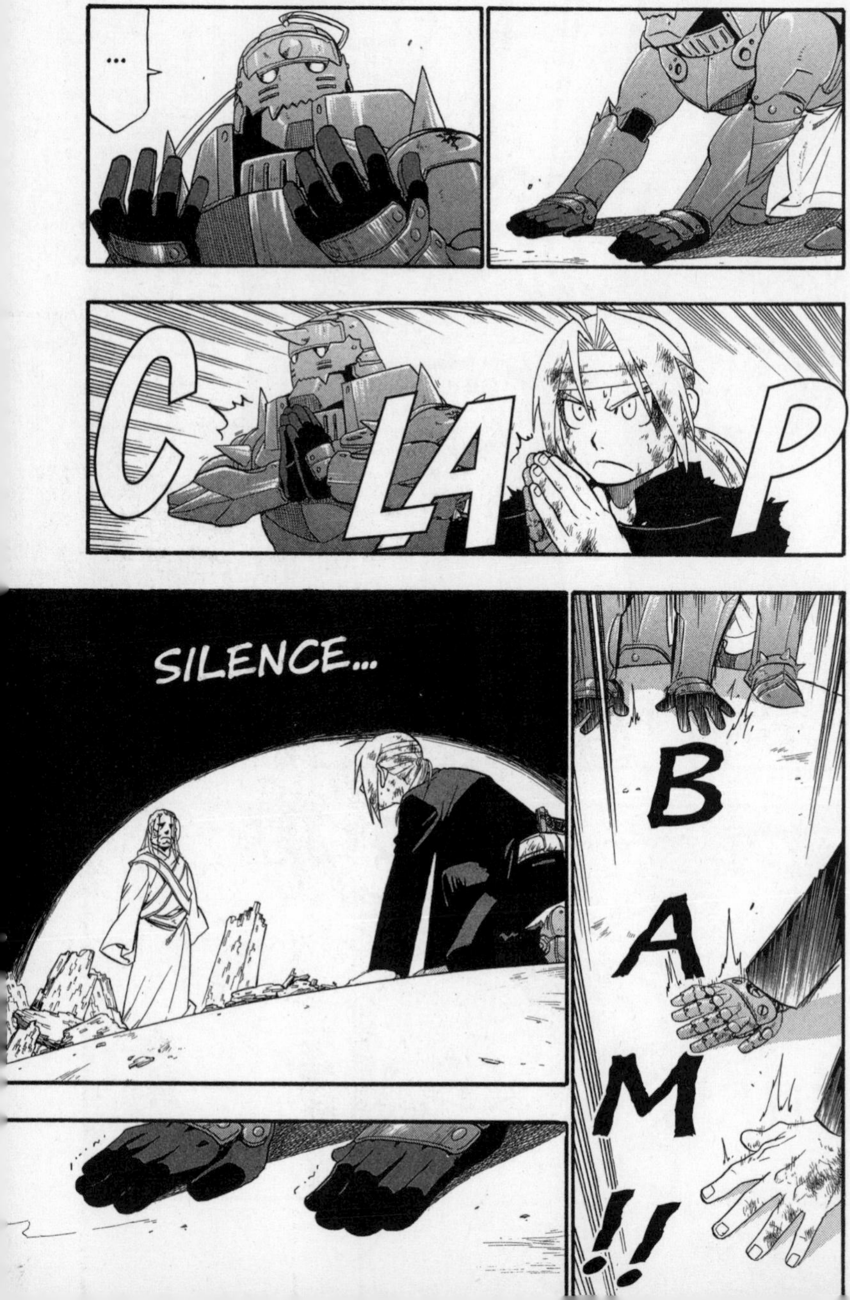
...
CLAP
BAM!!
SILENCE...

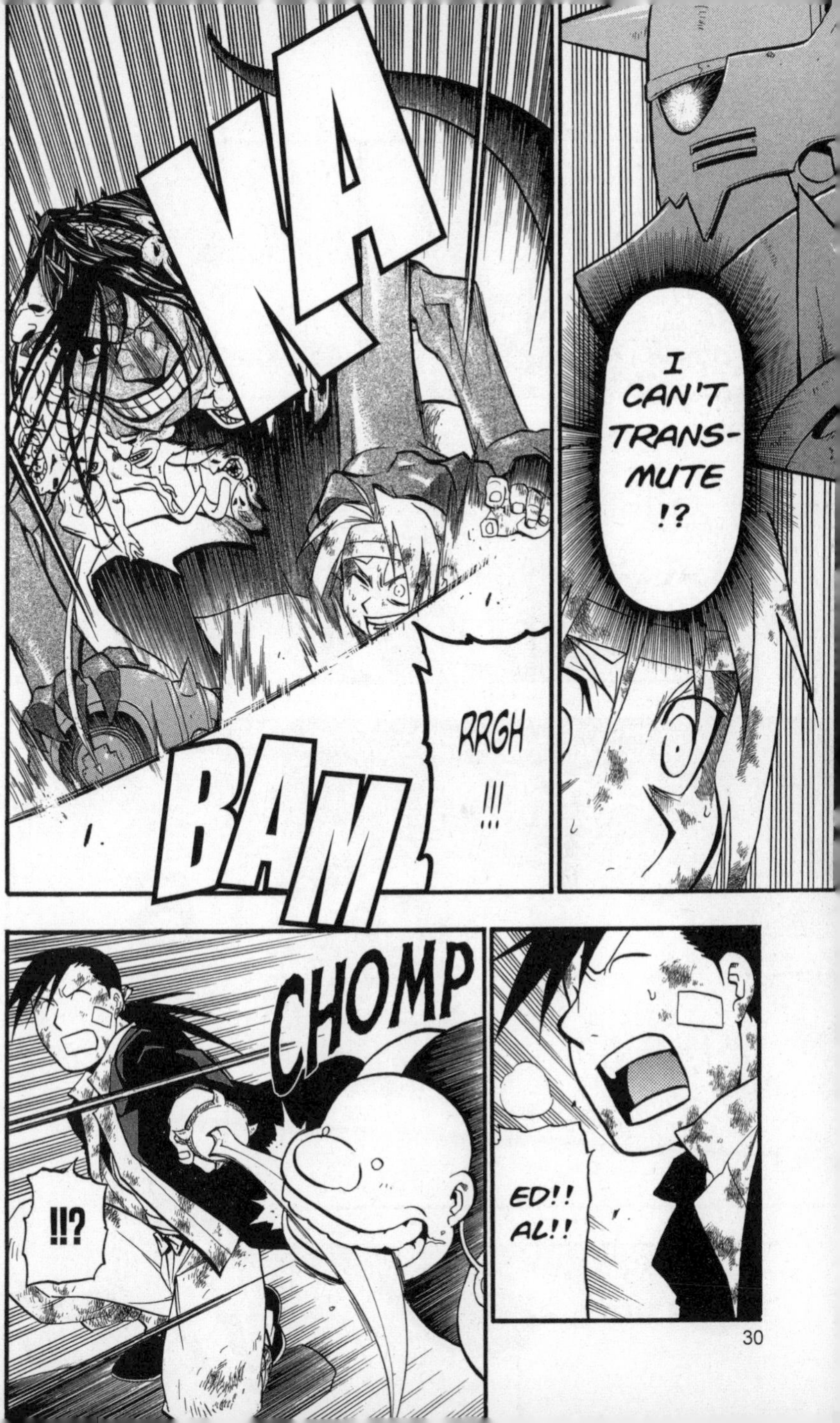
I CAN'T TRANSMUTE !?
KA
RRGH !!!
BAM
ED!! AL!!
CHOMP
!!?

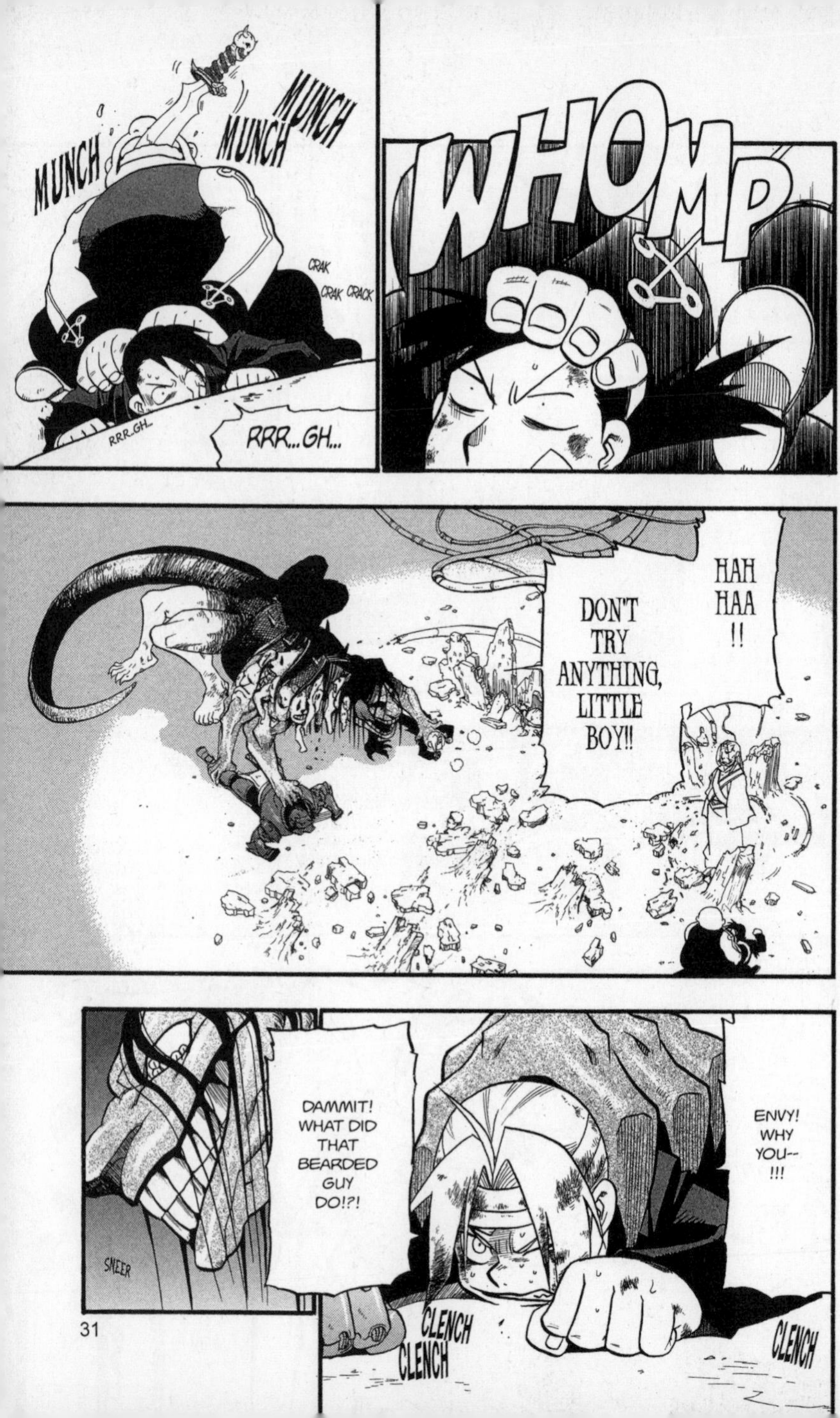
WHOMP
MUNCH
MUNCH
MUNCH
CRAK
CRAK CRACK
RRR...GH...
RRR...GH...
HAH HAA !!
DON'T TRY ANYTHING, LITTLE BOY!!
ENVY! WHY YOU-- !!!
CLENCH
CLENCH
CLENCH
DAMMIT! WHAT DID THAT BEARDED GUY DO!?!
SNEER

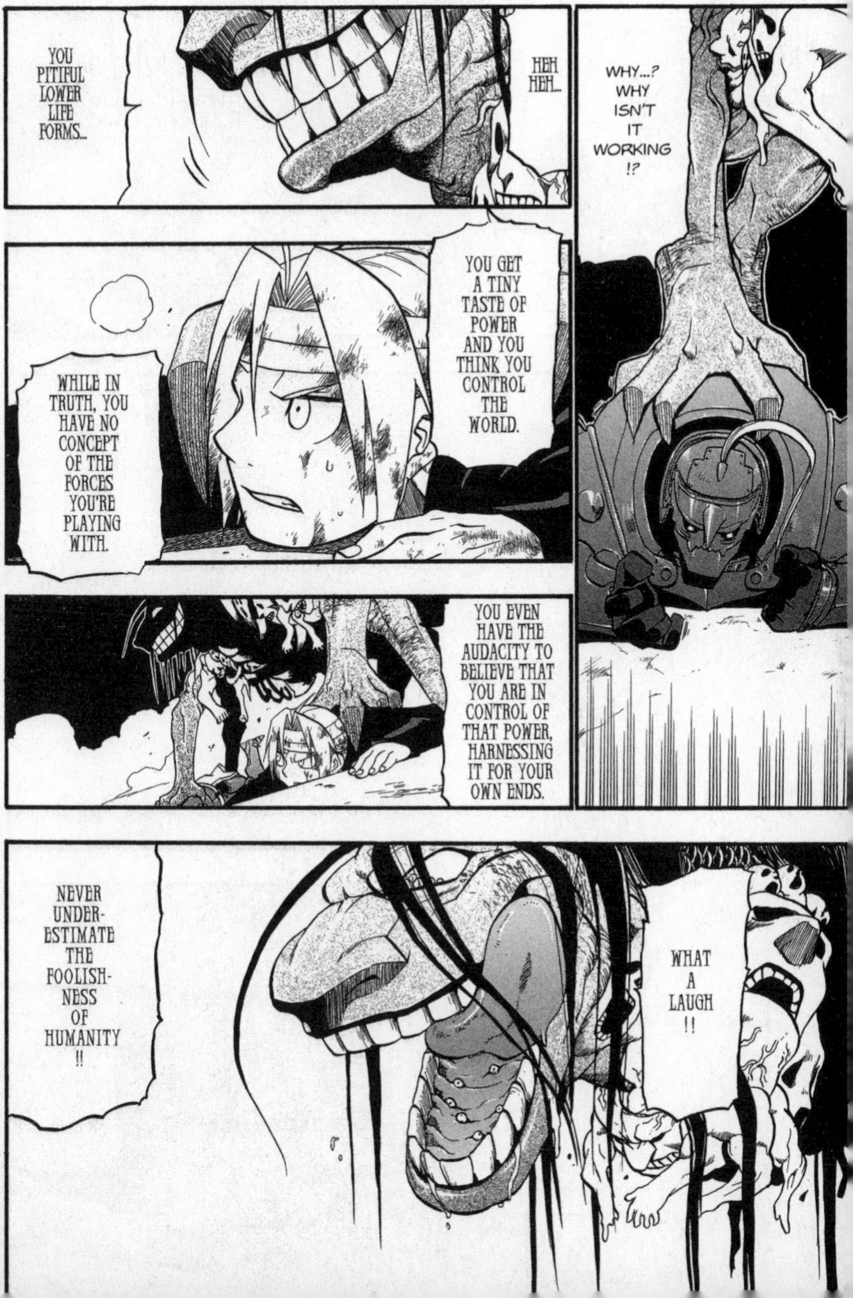
WHY...? WHY ISN'T IT WORKING!?
HEH HEH...
YOU PITIFUL LOWER LIFE FORMS...
YOU GET A TINY TASTE OF POWER AND YOU THINK YOU CONTROL THE WORLD.
WHILE IN TRUTH, YOU HAVE NO CONCEPT OF THE FORCES YOU'RE PLAYING WITH.
YOU EVEN HAVE THE AUDACITY TO BELIEVE THAT YOU ARE IN CONTROL OF THAT POWER, HARNESSING IT FOR YOUR OWN ENDS.
WHAT A LAUGH!!
NEVER UNDER-ESTIMATE THE FOOLISH-NESS OF HUMANITY!!

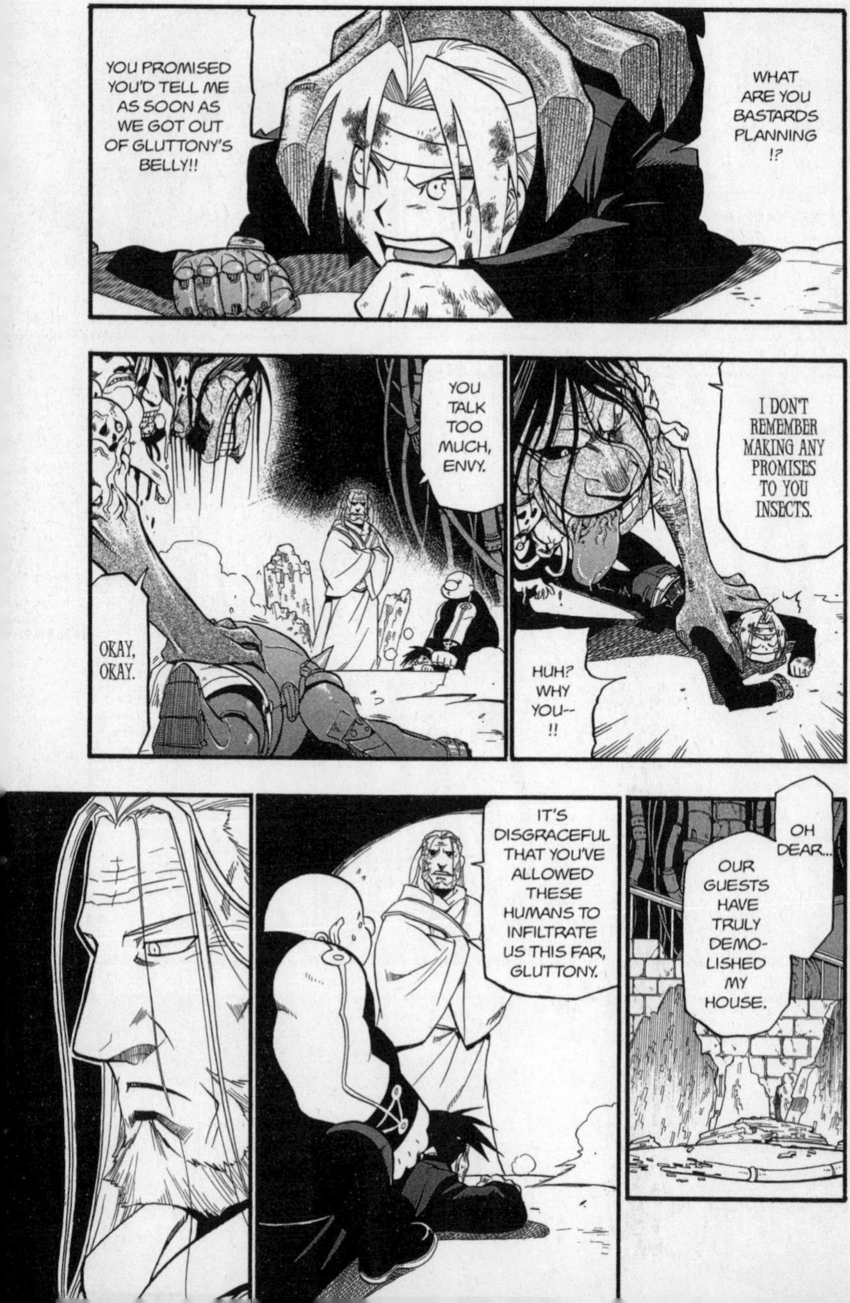
WHAT ARE YOU BASTARDS PLANNING !?
YOU PROMISED YOU'D TELL ME AS SOON AS WE GOT OUT OF GLUTTONY'S BELLY!!
I DON'T REMEMBER MAKING ANY PROMISES TO YOU INSECTS.
HUH? WHY YOU-- !!
YOU TALK TOO MUCH, ENVY.
OKAY, OKAY.
OH DEAR...
OUR GUESTS HAVE TRULY DEMO-LISHED MY HOUSE.
IT'S DISGRACEFUL THAT YOU'VE ALLOWED THESE HUMANS TO INFILTRATE US THIS FAR, GLUTTONY.

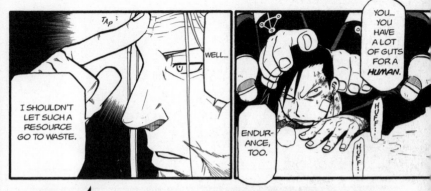

YOU... YOU HAVE A LOT OF GUTS FOR A *HUMAN*.
ENDUR-ANCE, TOO.
HUFF...
HUFF...
TAP
WELL...
I SHOULDN'T LET SUCH A RESOURCE GO TO WASTE.
YOU'D MAKE A GOOD *PAWN*.
BA
GAH
GLUB
GLUB
GLUB
GLUB
GLUB
GLUB

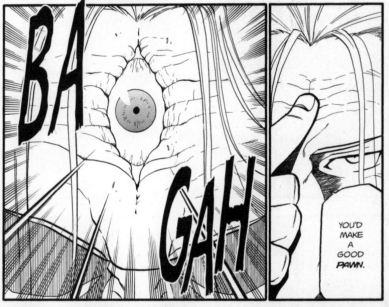

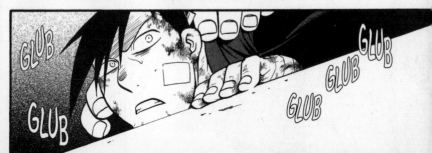

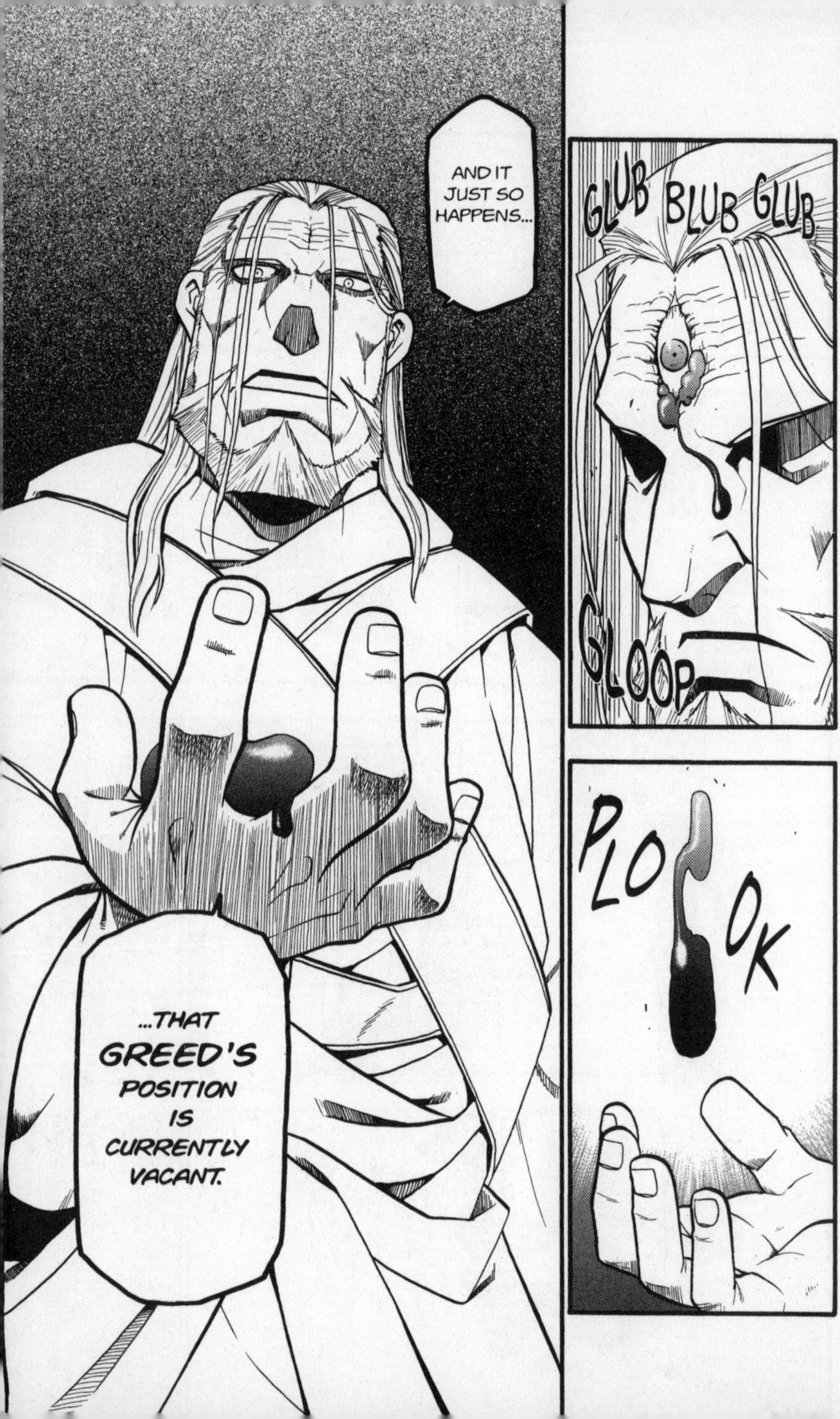
GLUB BLUB GLUB
GLOOP
PLOOK
AND IT JUST SO HAPPENS...
...THAT GREED'S POSITION IS CURRENTLY VACANT.

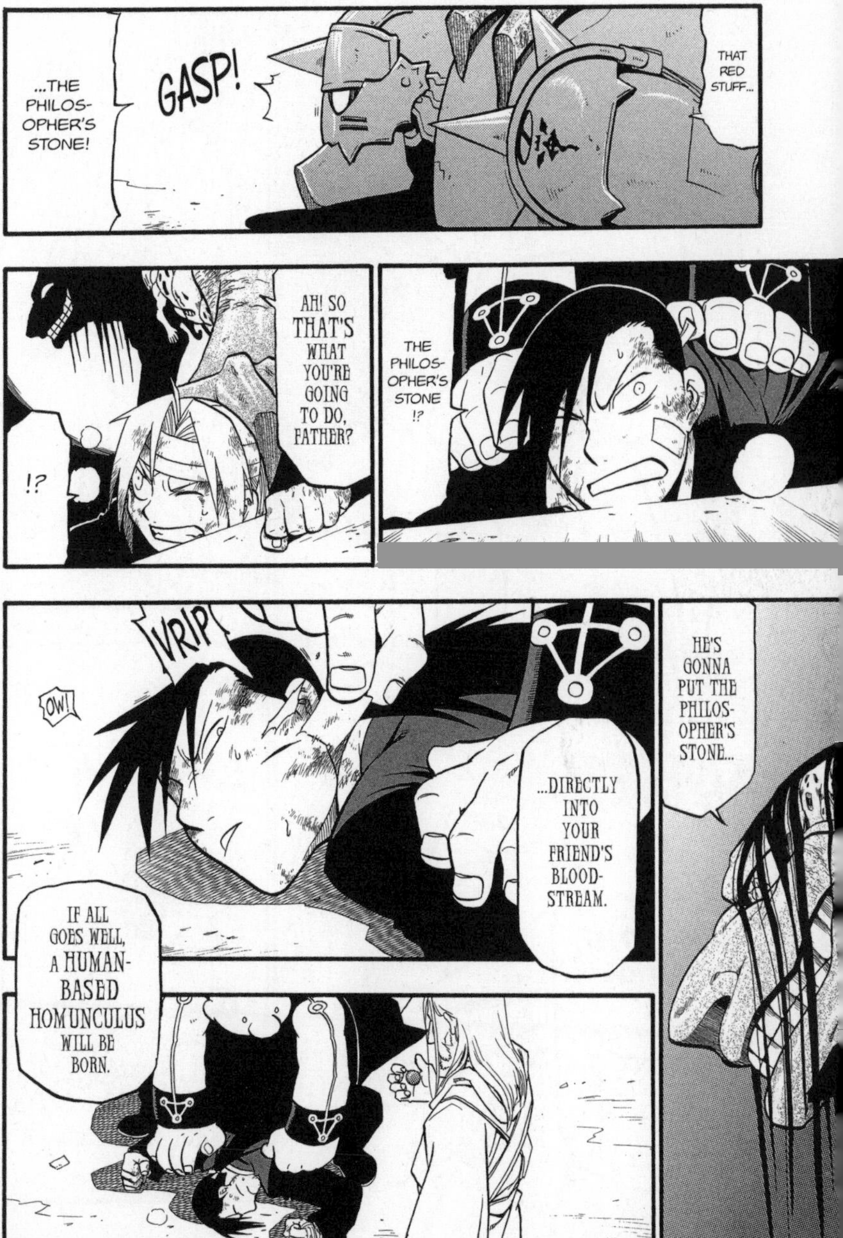
THAT RED STUFF...
GASP!
...THE PHILOS-OPHER'S STONE!
THE PHILOS-OPHER'S STONE !?
AH! SO THAT'S WHAT YOU'RE GOING TO DO, FATHER?
!?
HE'S GONNA PUT THE PHILOS-OPHER'S STONE...
VRIP
OW!
...DIRECTLY INTO YOUR FRIEND'S BLOOD-STREAM.
IF ALL GOES WELL, A HUMAN-BASED HOMUNCULUS WILL BE BORN.

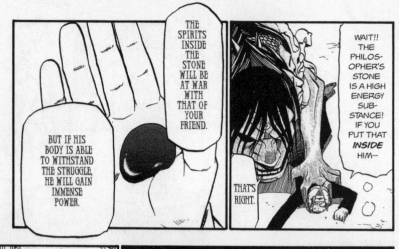

WAIT!! THE PHILOSOPHER'S STONE IS A HIGH ENERGY SUBSTANCE! IF YOU PUT THAT *INSIDE* HIM—

THAT'S RIGHT.

THE SPIRITS INSIDE THE STONE WILL BE AT WAR WITH THAT OF YOUR FRIEND.

BUT IF HIS BODY IS ABLE TO WITHSTAND THE STRUGGLE, HE WILL GAIN IMMENSE POWER.

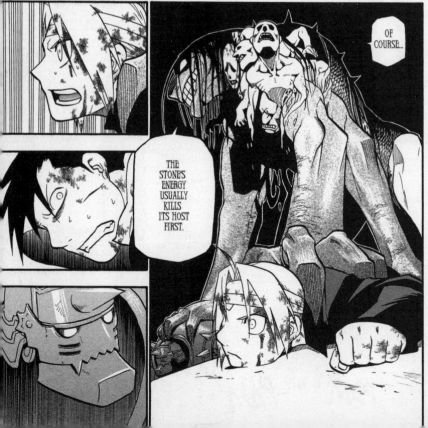

OF COURSE...

THE STONE'S ENERGY USUALLY KILLS ITS HOST FIRST.

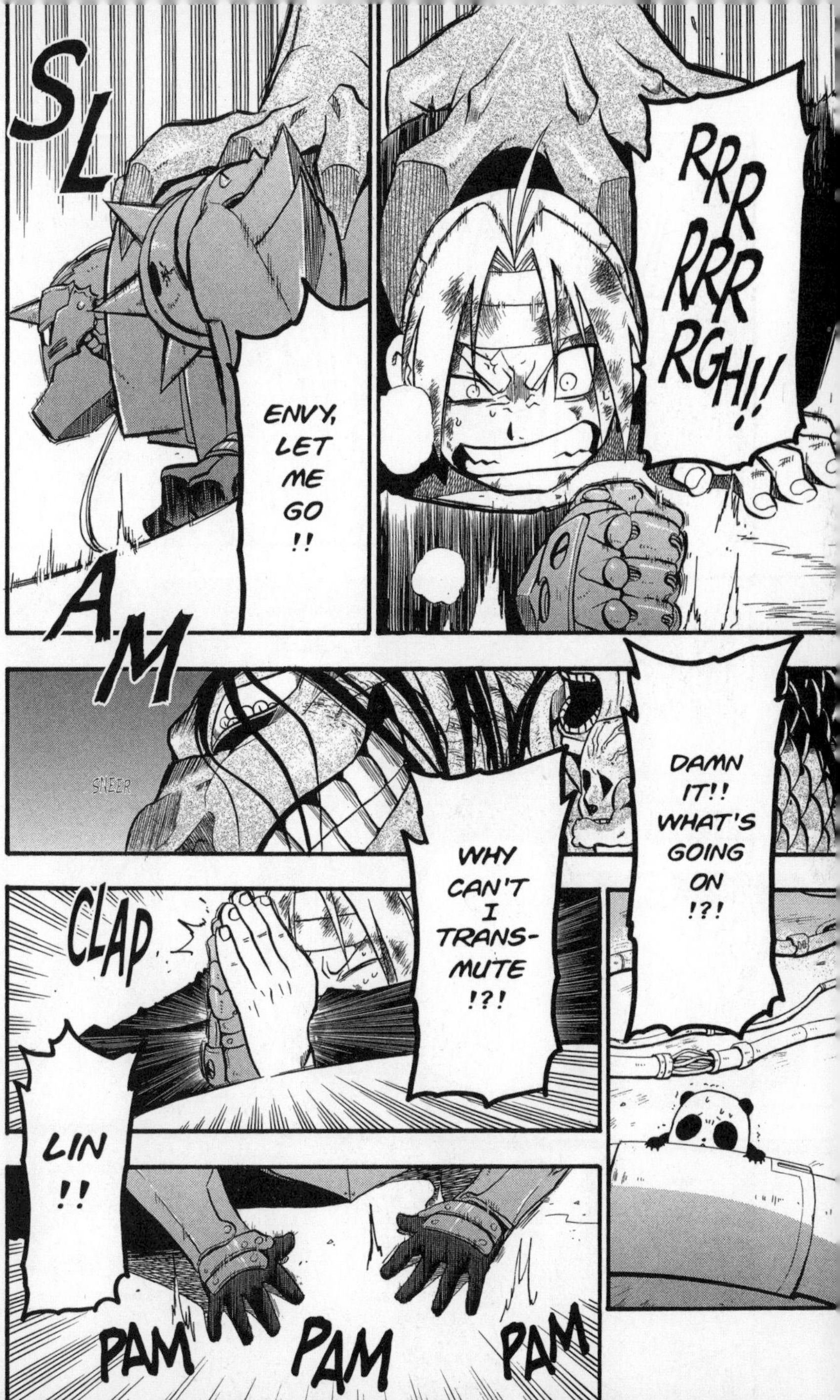
RRRRRRRGH!!
ENVY, LET ME GO!!
SLAM
DAMN IT!! WHAT'S GOING ON!?!
WHY CAN'T I TRANSMUTE!?!
SNEER
CLAP
LIN!!
PAM PAM PAM

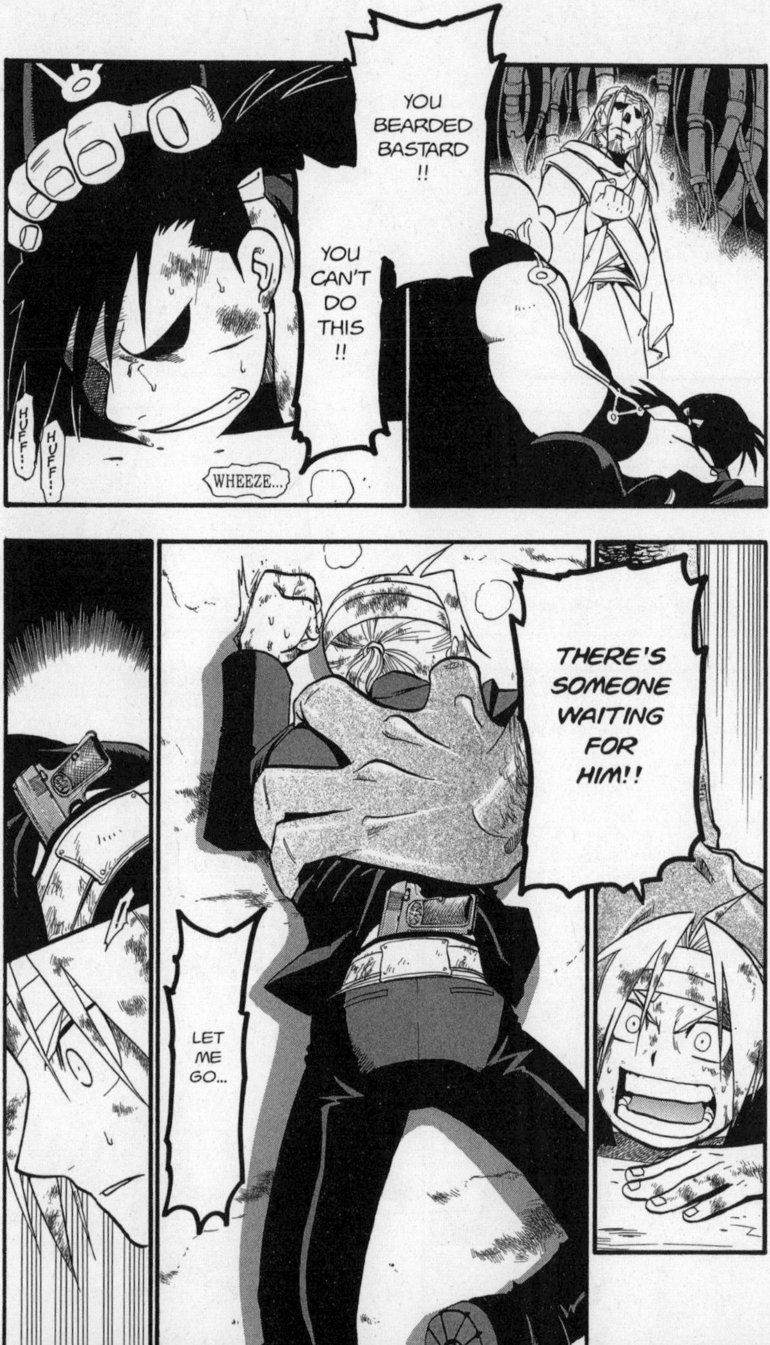
YOU BEARDED BASTARD !!
YOU CAN'T DO THIS !!
HUFF... HUFF...
WHEEZE...
THERE'S SOMEONE WAITING FOR HIM!!
LET ME GO...

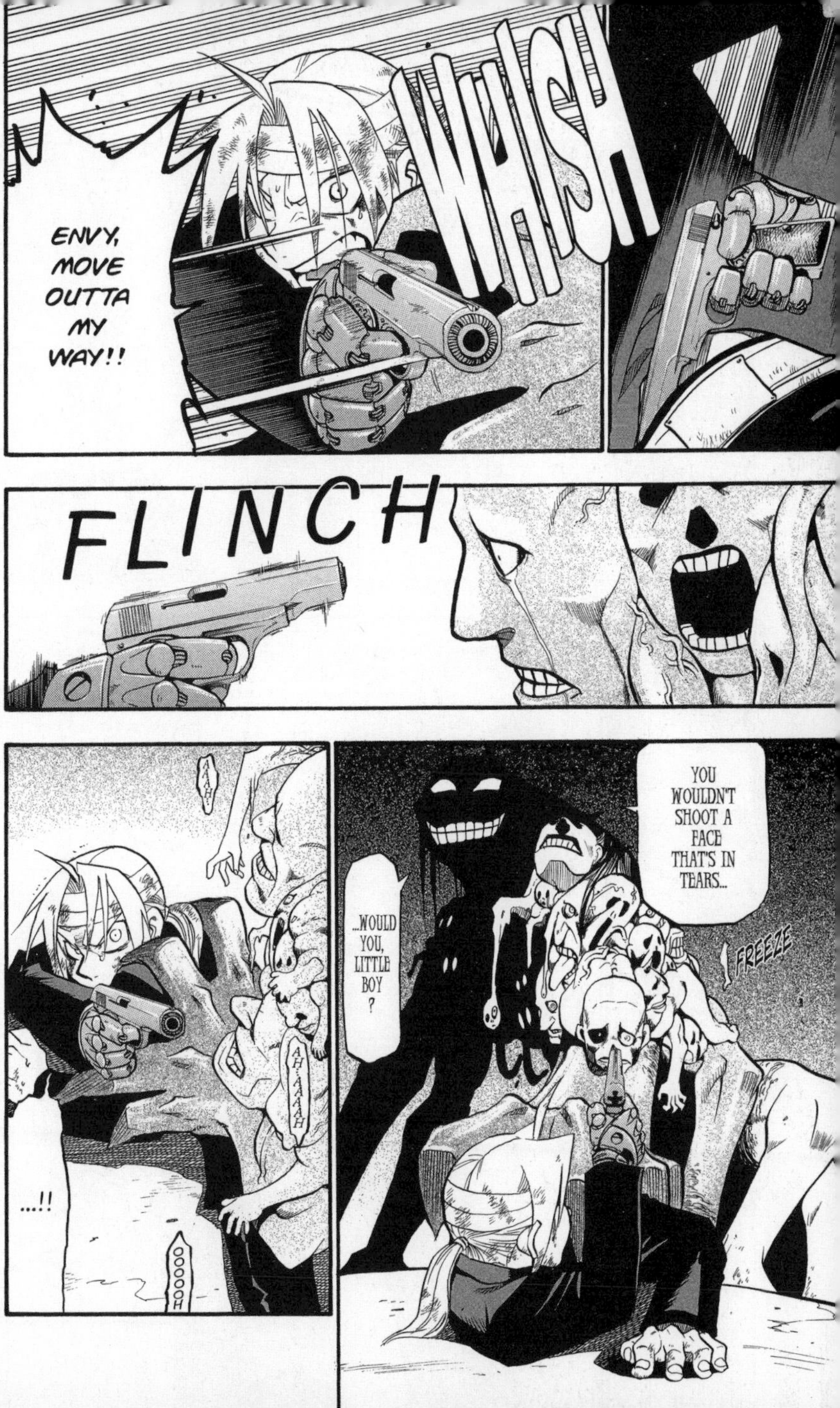
WHISH
ENVY, MOVE OUTTA MY WAY!!
FLINCH
YOU WOULDN'T SHOOT A FACE THAT'S IN TEARS...
...WOULD YOU, LITTLE BOY?
FREEZE
AAAH...
AH! AAAAAH
...!!
OOOOOH

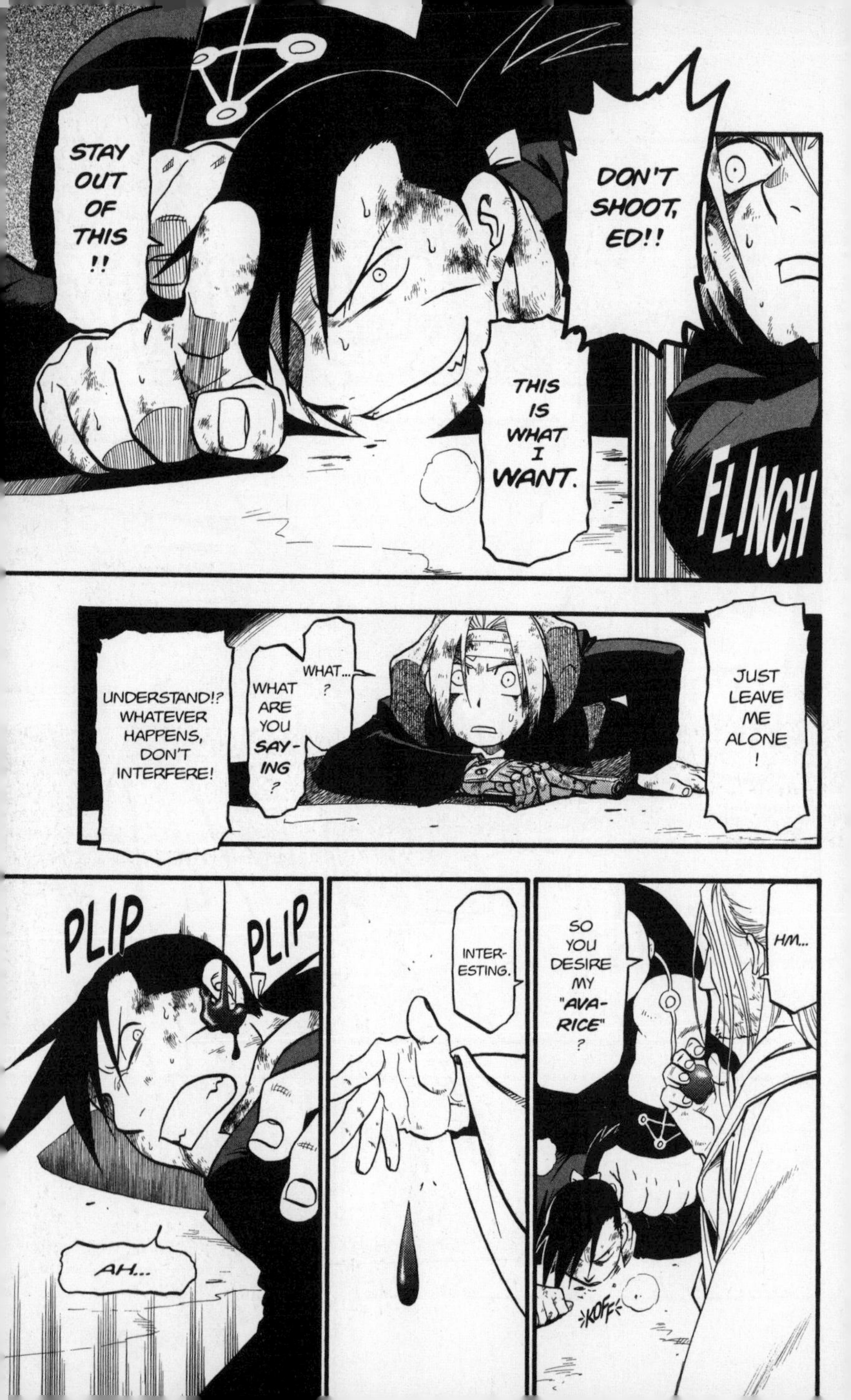
DON'T SHOOT, ED!!
FLINCH
STAY OUT OF THIS!!
THIS IS WHAT I WANT.
JUST LEAVE ME ALONE!
WHAT...? WHAT ARE YOU SAYING?
UNDERSTAND!? WHATEVER HAPPENS, DON'T INTERFERE!
HM...
SO YOU DESIRE MY "AVARICE"?
KOFF
INTERESTING.
PLIP PLIP
AH...

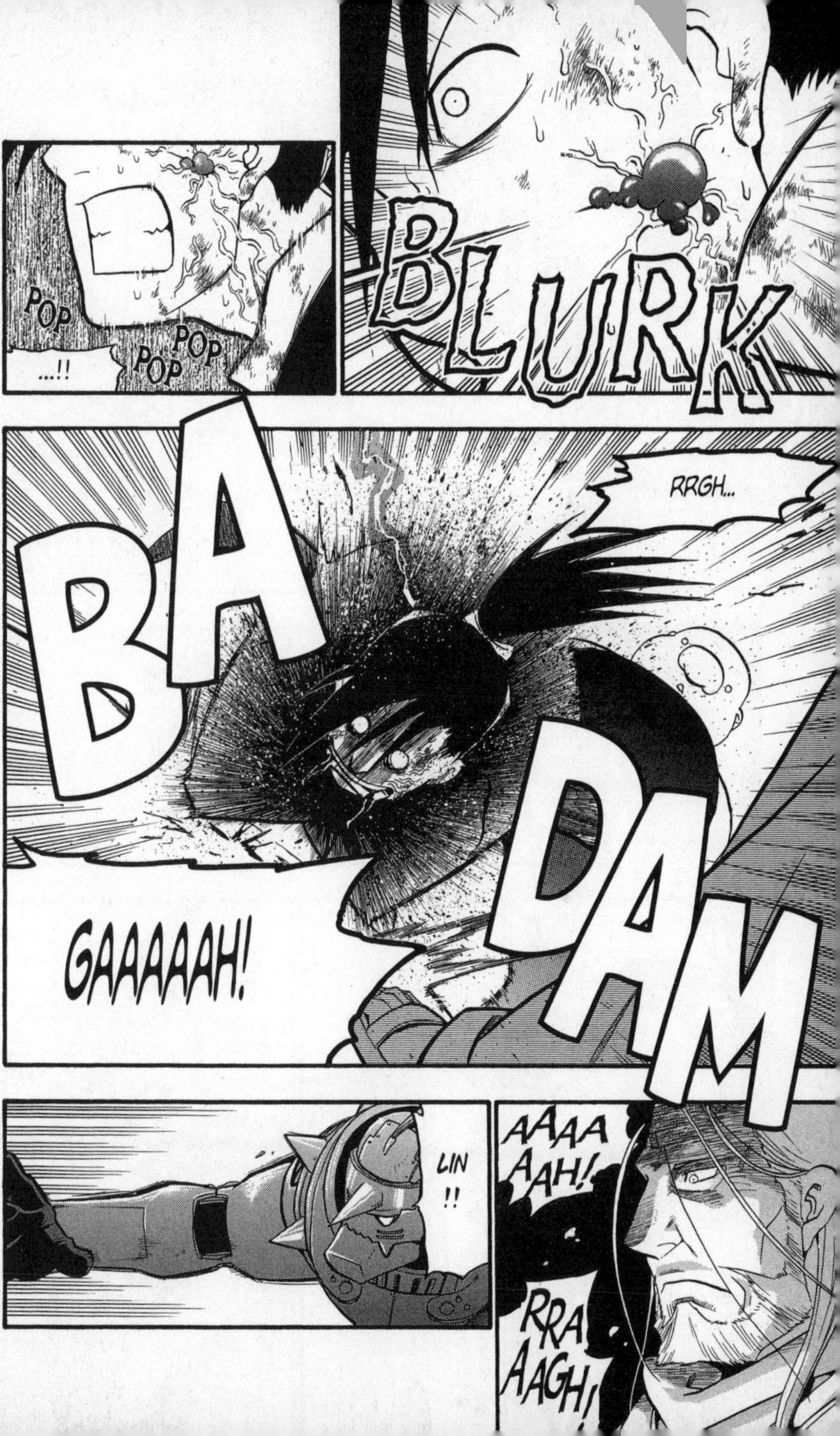
BLURK
POP
POP
POP
...!!
RRGH...
BADAM
GAAAAAH!
AAAAAAH!
RRAAAGH!
LIN!!

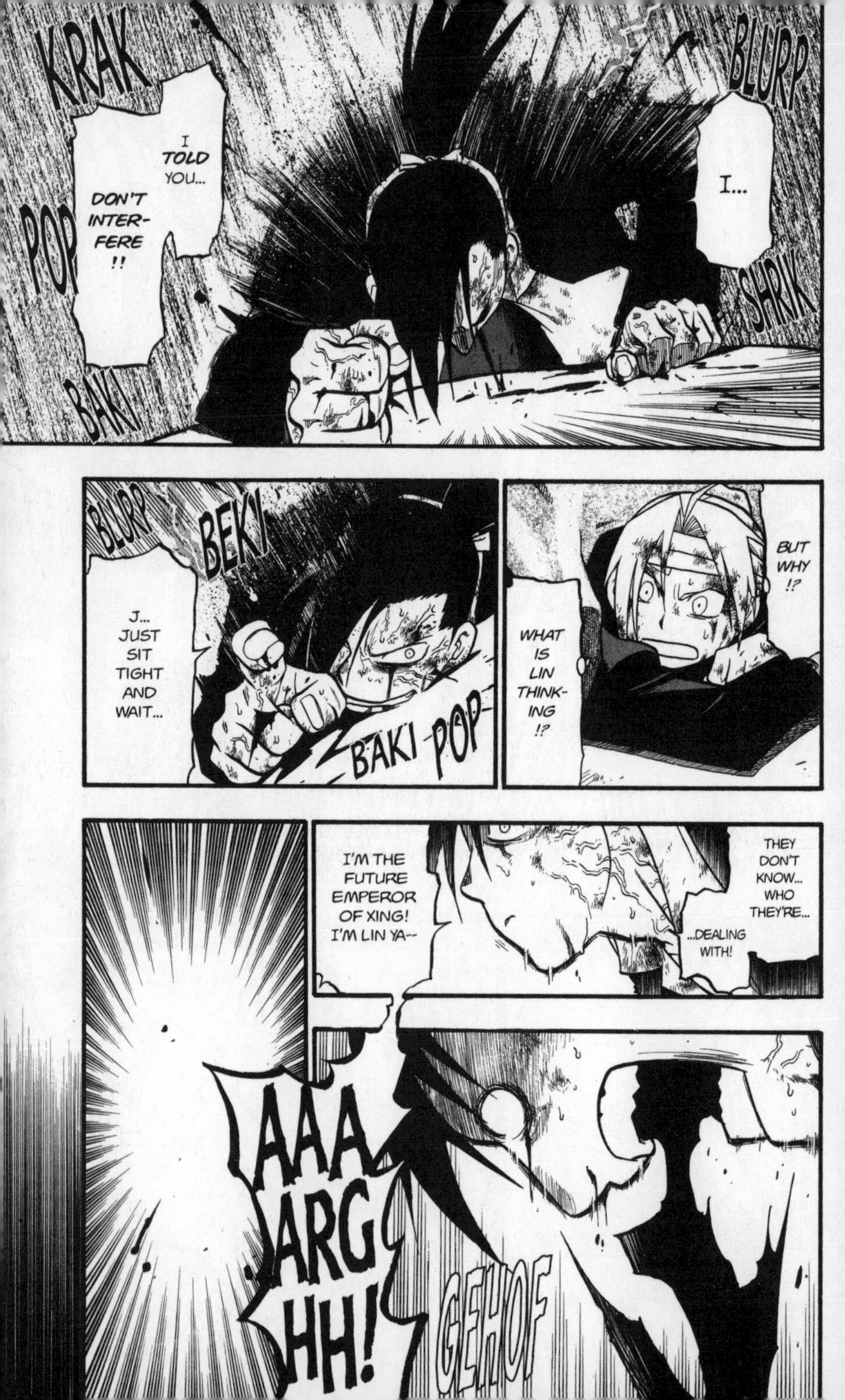
BLURP
I...
SHRIK
KRAK
I TOLD YOU...
DON'T INTERFERE!!
POP
BAKI
BUT WHY!?
WHAT IS LIN THINKING!?
BLURP
BEKI
J... JUST SIT TIGHT AND WAIT...
BAKI POP
THEY DON'T KNOW... WHO THEY'RE...
...DEALING WITH!
I'M THE FUTURE EMPEROR OF XING! I'M LIN YA--
GEHOF
AAAARGHH!

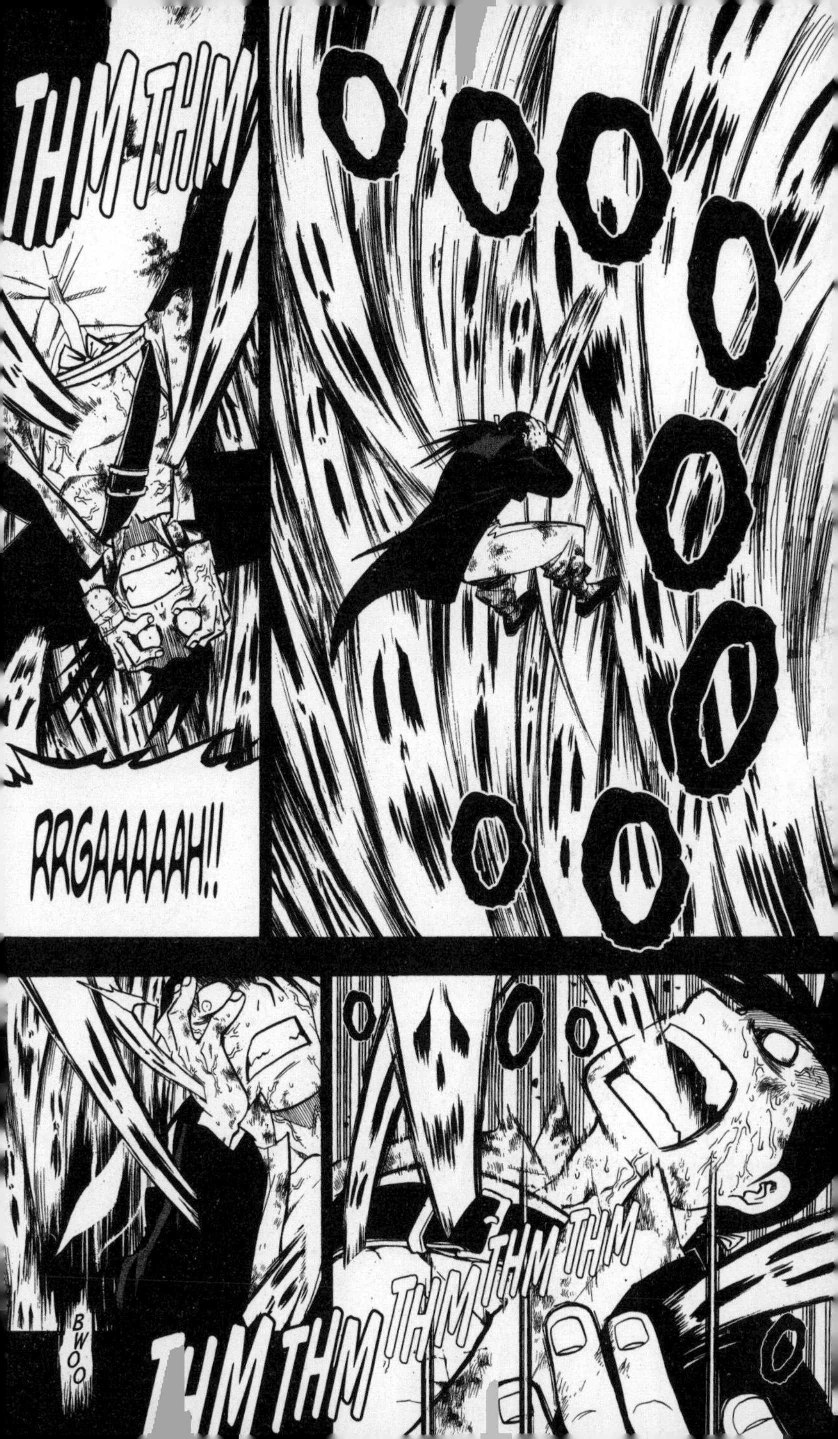
THM THM
RRGAAAAAH!!
THM THM THM THM
THM THM
BWOO

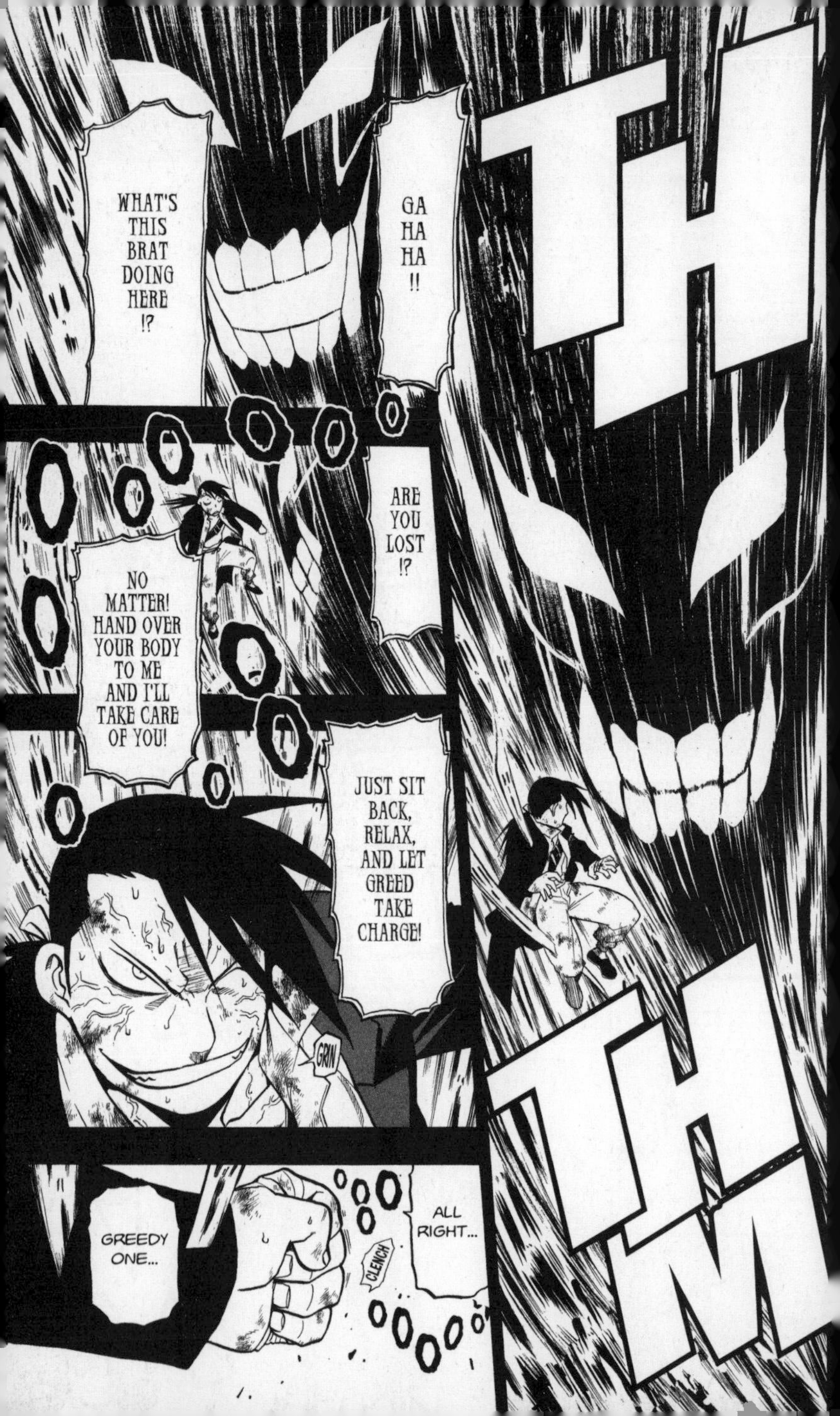
TH
THM
GA HA HA!!
WHAT'S THIS BRAT DOING HERE!?
ARE YOU LOST!?
NO MATTER! HAND OVER YOUR BODY TO ME AND I'LL TAKE CARE OF YOU!
JUST SIT BACK, RELAX, AND LET GREED TAKE CHARGE!
GRIN
ALL RIGHT...
CLENCH
GREEDY ONE...

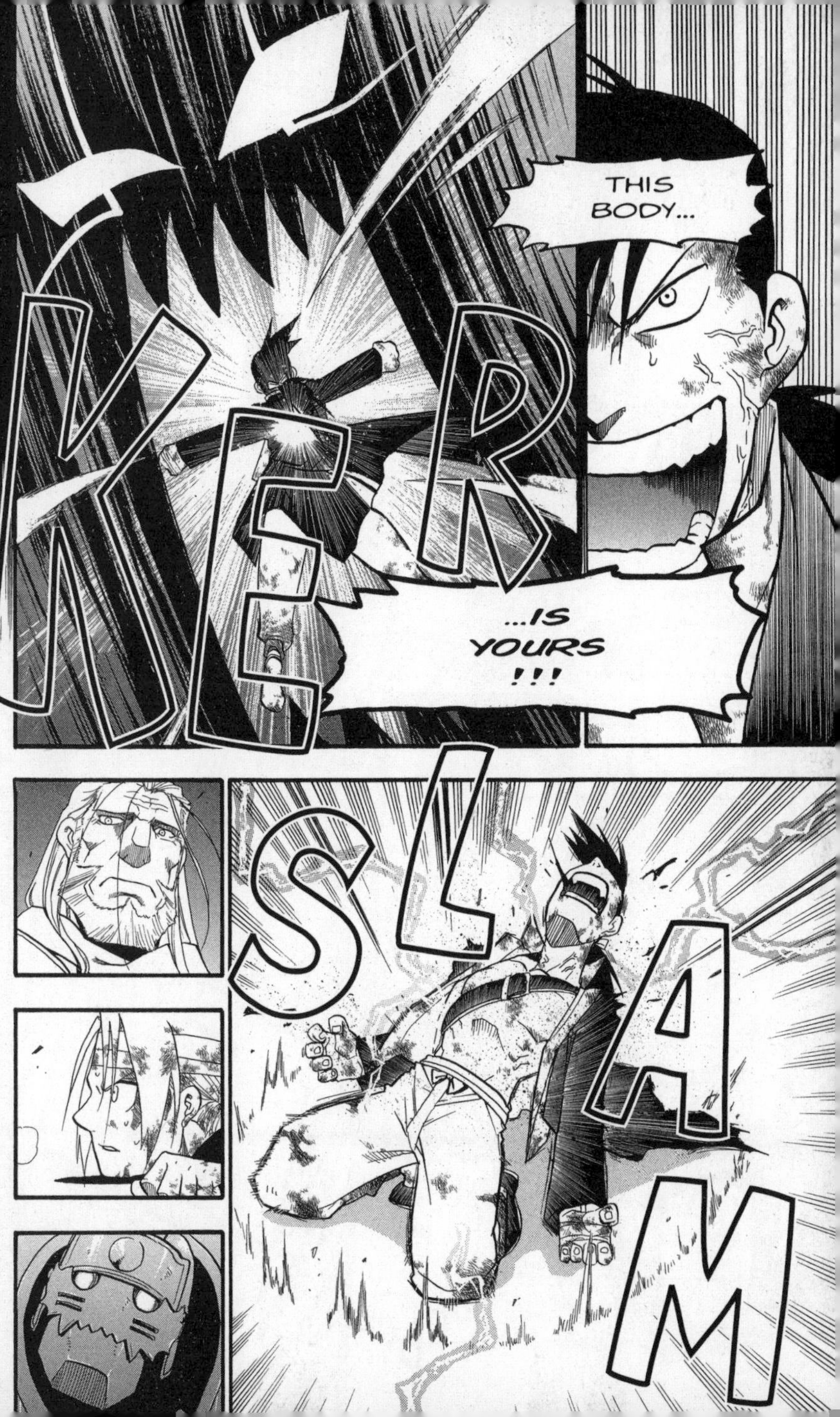
THIS BODY...
KRR
...IS YOURS !!!
SLAM

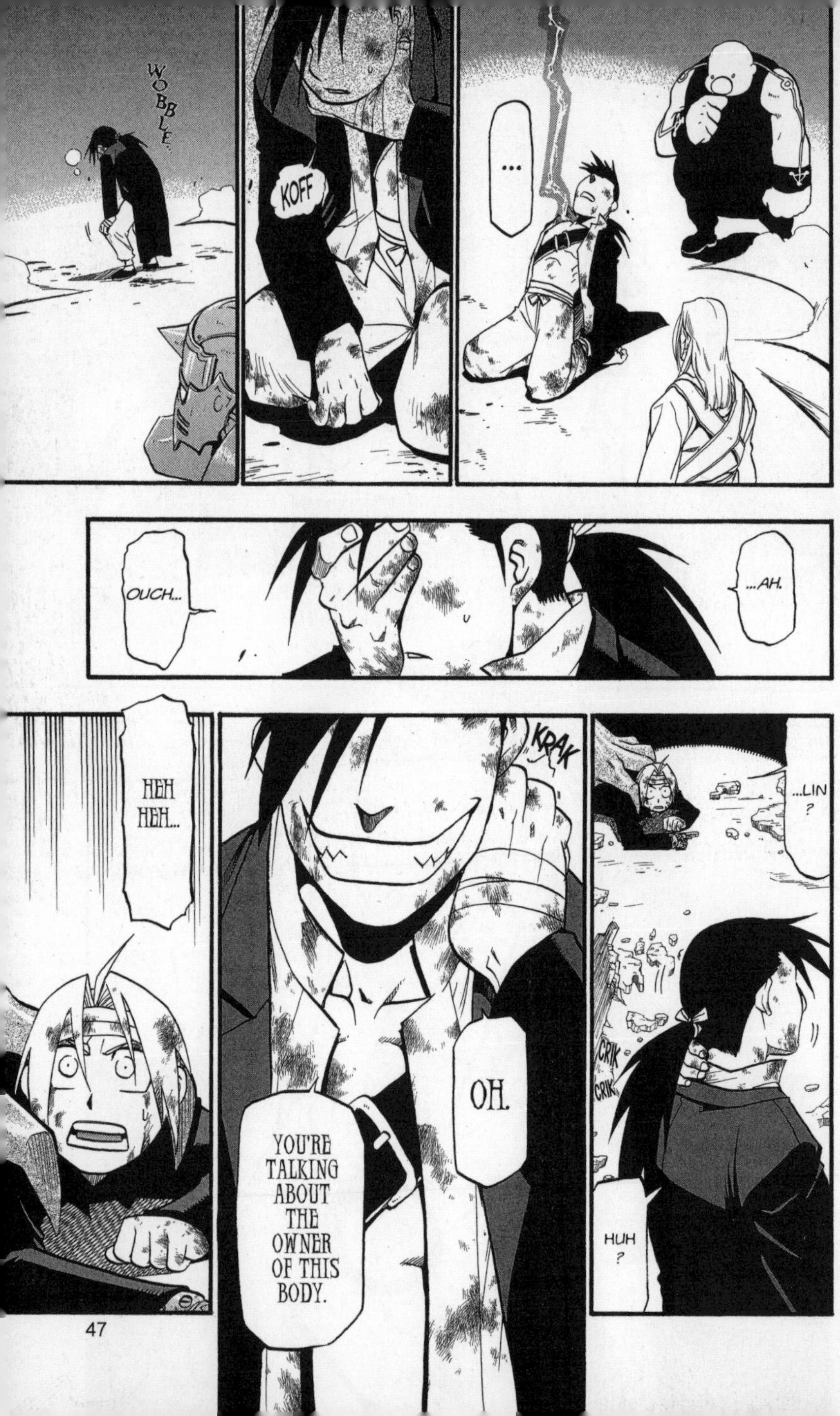
...
KOFF
WOBBLE...
...AH.
OUCH...
...LIN ?
KRAK
CRIK CRIK
HUH ?
OH.
YOU'RE TALKING ABOUT THE OWNER OF THIS BODY.
HEH HEH...

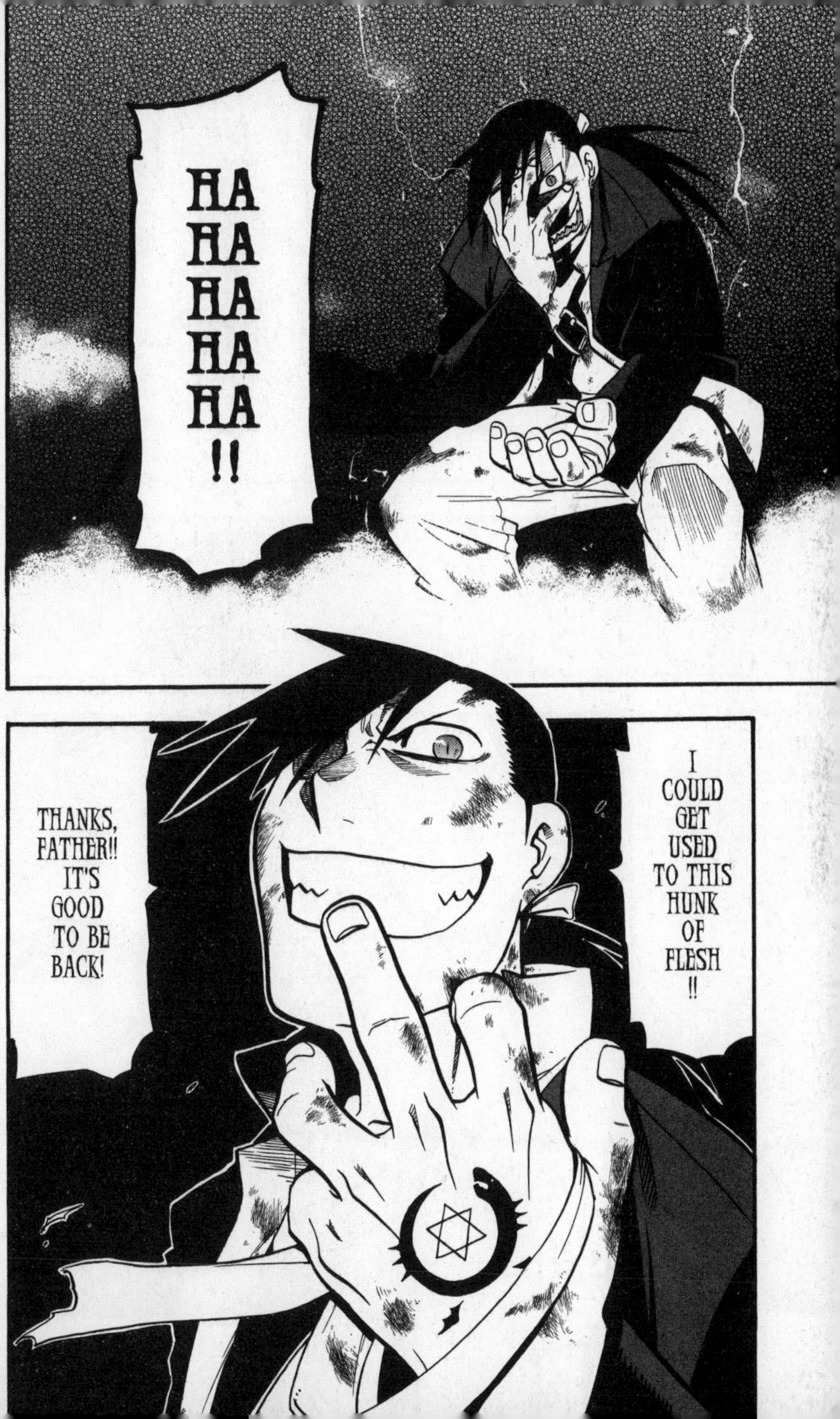
HA HA HA HA HA!!
I COULD GET USED TO THIS HUNK OF FLESH!!
THANKS, FATHER!! IT'S GOOD TO BE BACK!

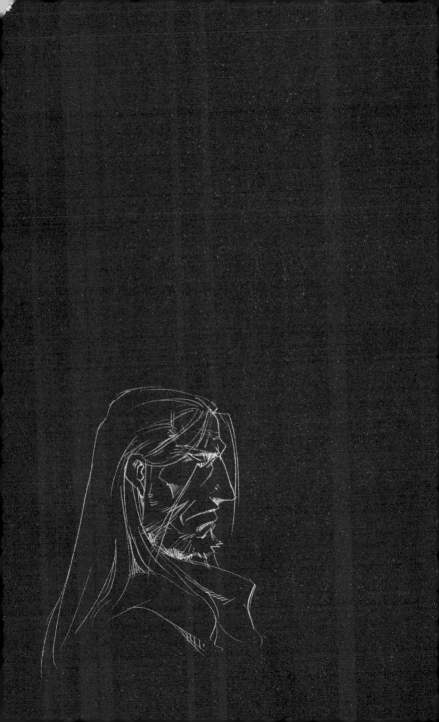

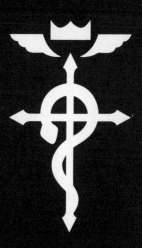

FULLMETAL
ALCHEMIST

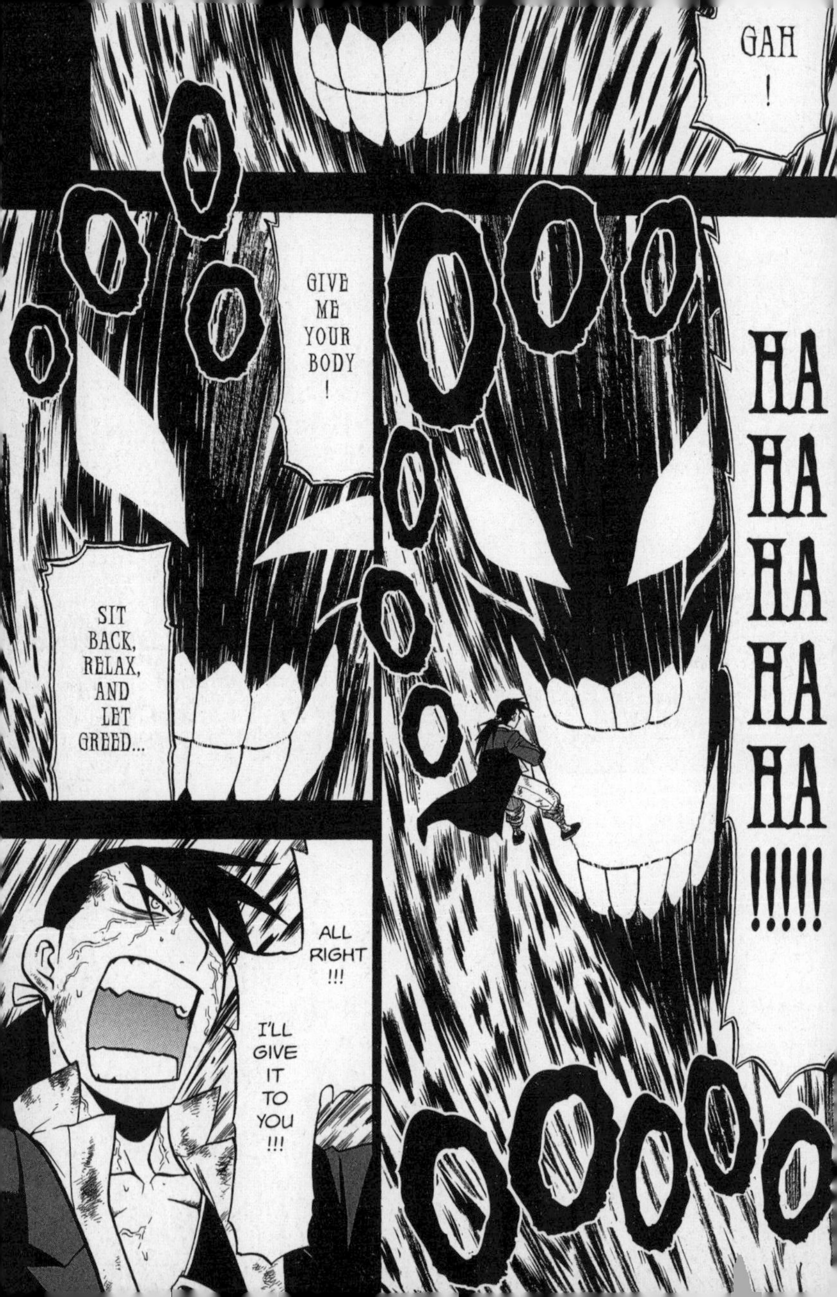
GAH!
HAHAHAHAHAHAHAHAHAHAHAHA!!!!!
GIVE ME YOUR BODY!
SIT BACK, RELAX, AND LET GREED...
ALL RIGHT!!!
I'LL GIVE IT TO YOU!!!

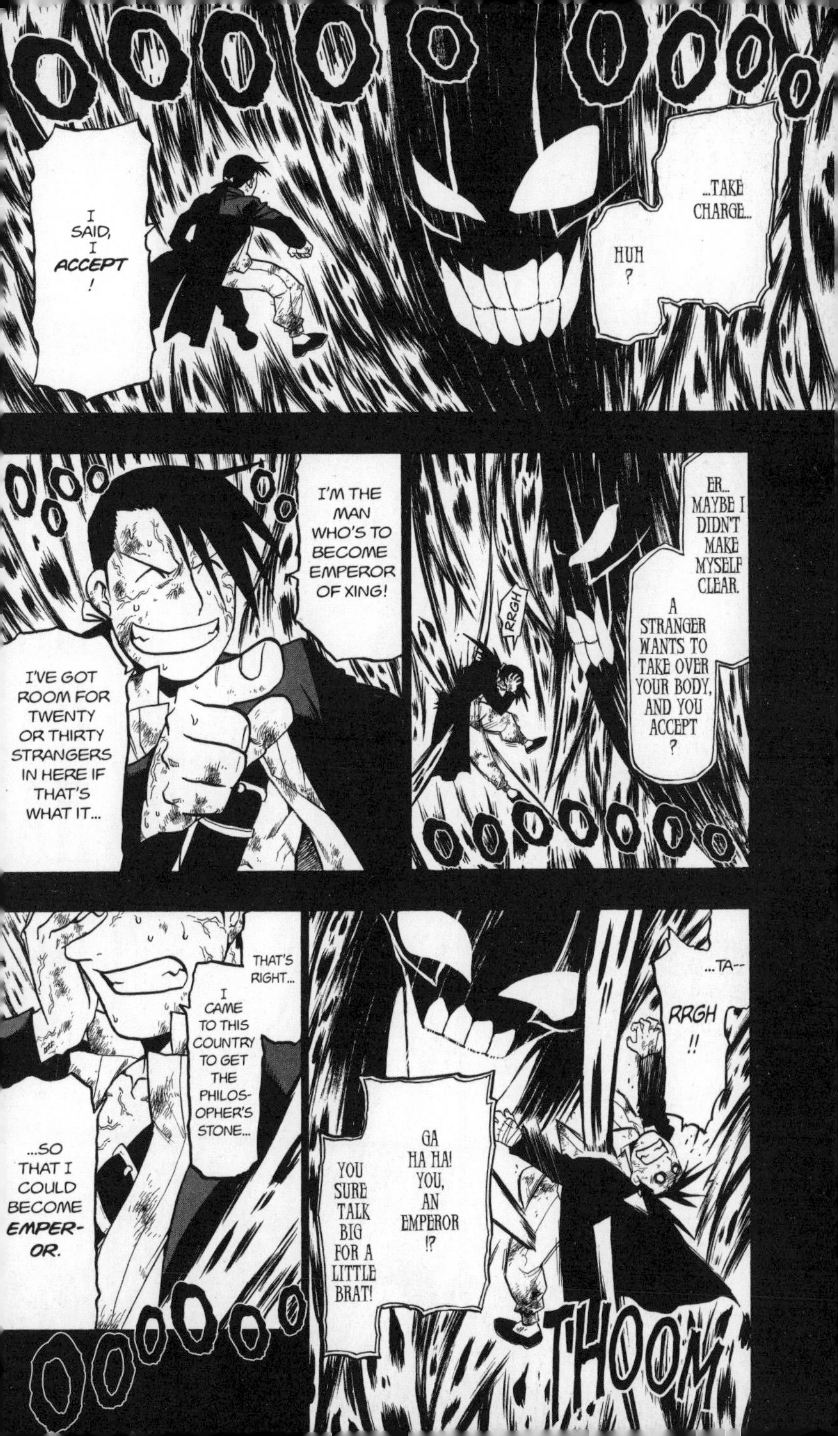
...TAKE CHARGE...
HUH?
I SAID, I ACCEPT!
ER... MAYBE I DIDN'T MAKE MYSELF CLEAR.
A STRANGER WANTS TO TAKE OVER YOUR BODY, AND YOU ACCEPT?
RRGH
I'M THE MAN WHO'S TO BECOME EMPEROR OF XING!
I'VE GOT ROOM FOR TWENTY OR THIRTY STRANGERS IN HERE IF THAT'S WHAT IT...
...TA--
RRGH!!
GA HA HA! YOU, AN EMPEROR!?
YOU SURE TALK BIG FOR A LITTLE BRAT!
THOOM
THAT'S RIGHT...
I CAME TO THIS COUNTRY TO GET THE PHILOSOPHER'S STONE...
...SO THAT I COULD BECOME EMPEROR.

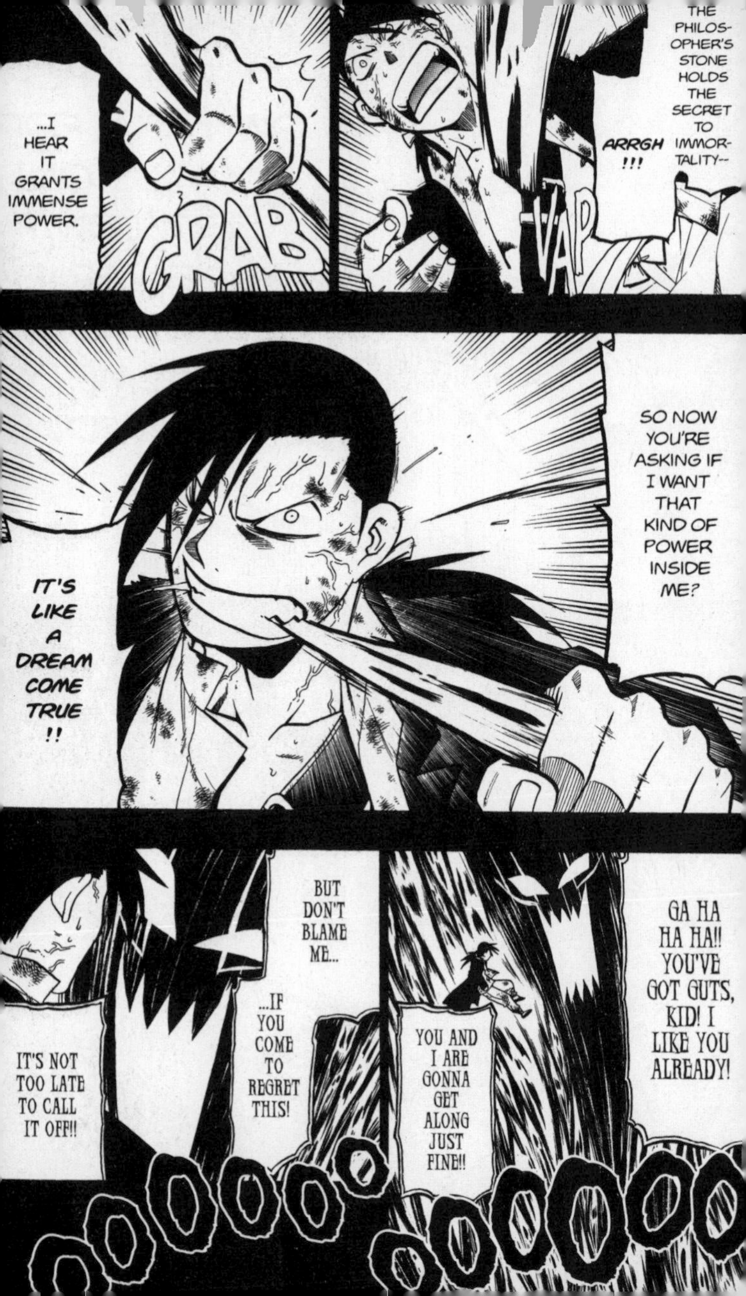
THE PHILOSOPHER'S STONE HOLDS THE SECRET TO IMMORTALITY--
ARRGH !!!
VAP
...I HEAR IT GRANTS IMMENSE POWER.
GRAB
SO NOW YOU'RE ASKING IF I WANT THAT KIND OF POWER INSIDE ME?
IT'S LIKE A DREAM COME TRUE !!
GA HA HA HA!! YOU'VE GOT GUTS, KID! I LIKE YOU ALREADY!
YOU AND I ARE GONNA GET ALONG JUST FINE!!
BUT DON'T BLAME ME...
...IF YOU COME TO REGRET THIS!
IT'S NOT TOO LATE TO CALL IT OFF!!

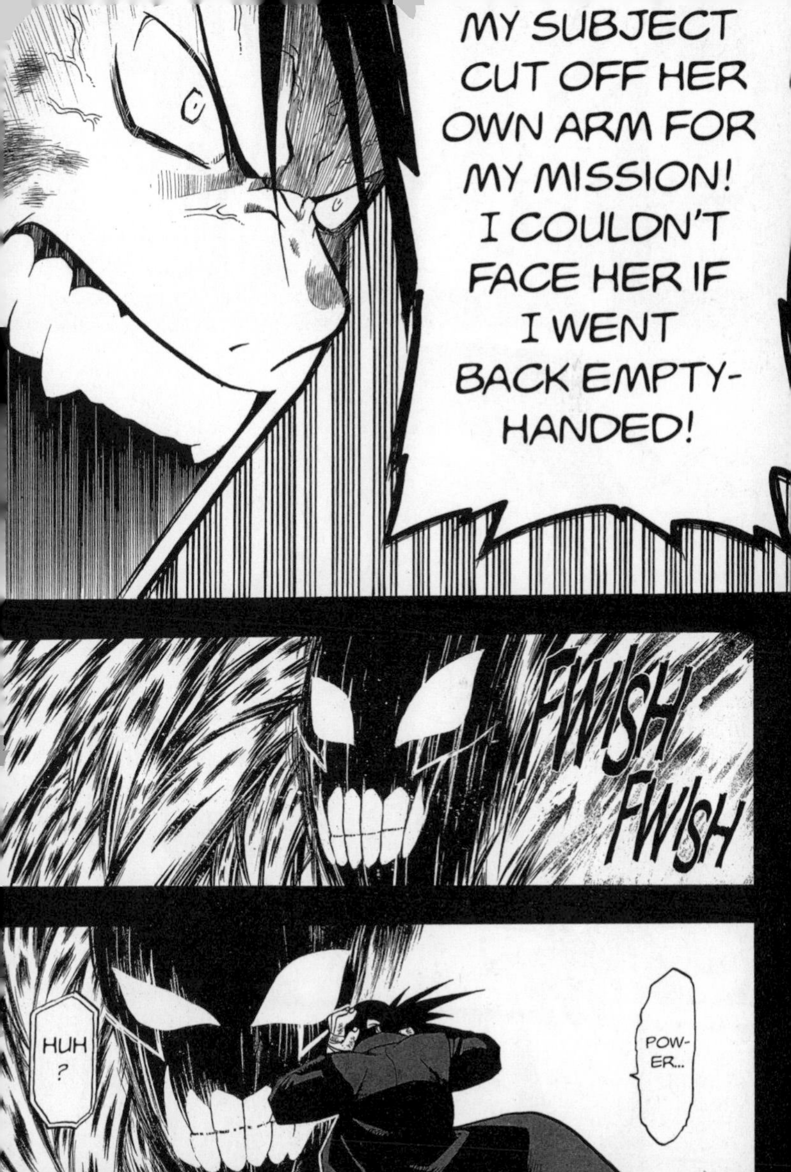
MY SUBJECT CUT OFF HER OWN ARM FOR MY MISSION! I COULDN'T FACE HER IF I WENT BACK EMPTY-HANDED!
FWISH FWISH
POW-ER...
HUH?

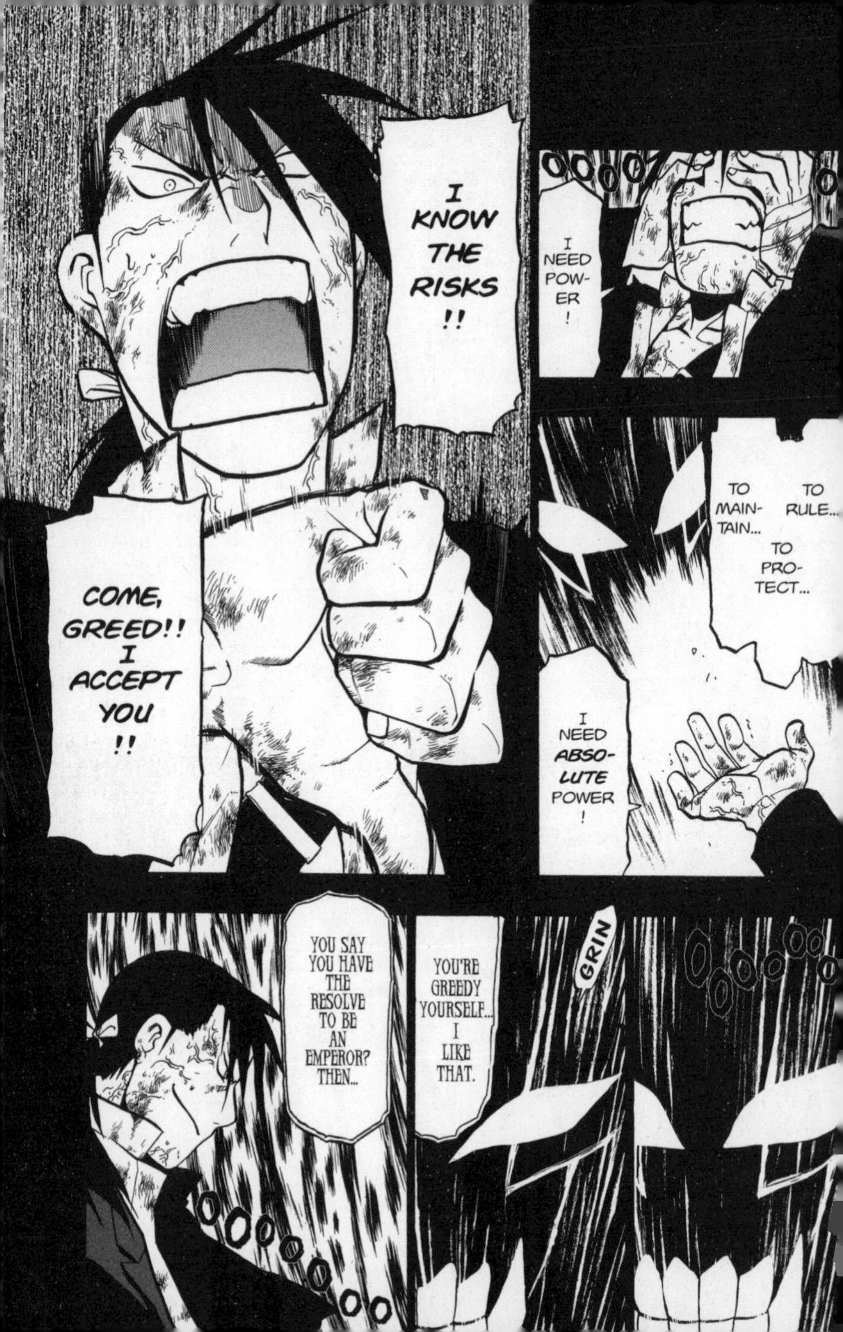
I NEED POWER!
TO RULE...
TO MAINTAIN...
TO PROTECT...
I NEED ABSOLUTE POWER!
I KNOW THE RISKS!!
COME, GREED!! I ACCEPT YOU!!
GRIN
YOU'RE GREEDY YOURSELF... I LIKE THAT.
YOU SAY YOU HAVE THE RESOLVE TO BE AN EMPEROR? THEN...

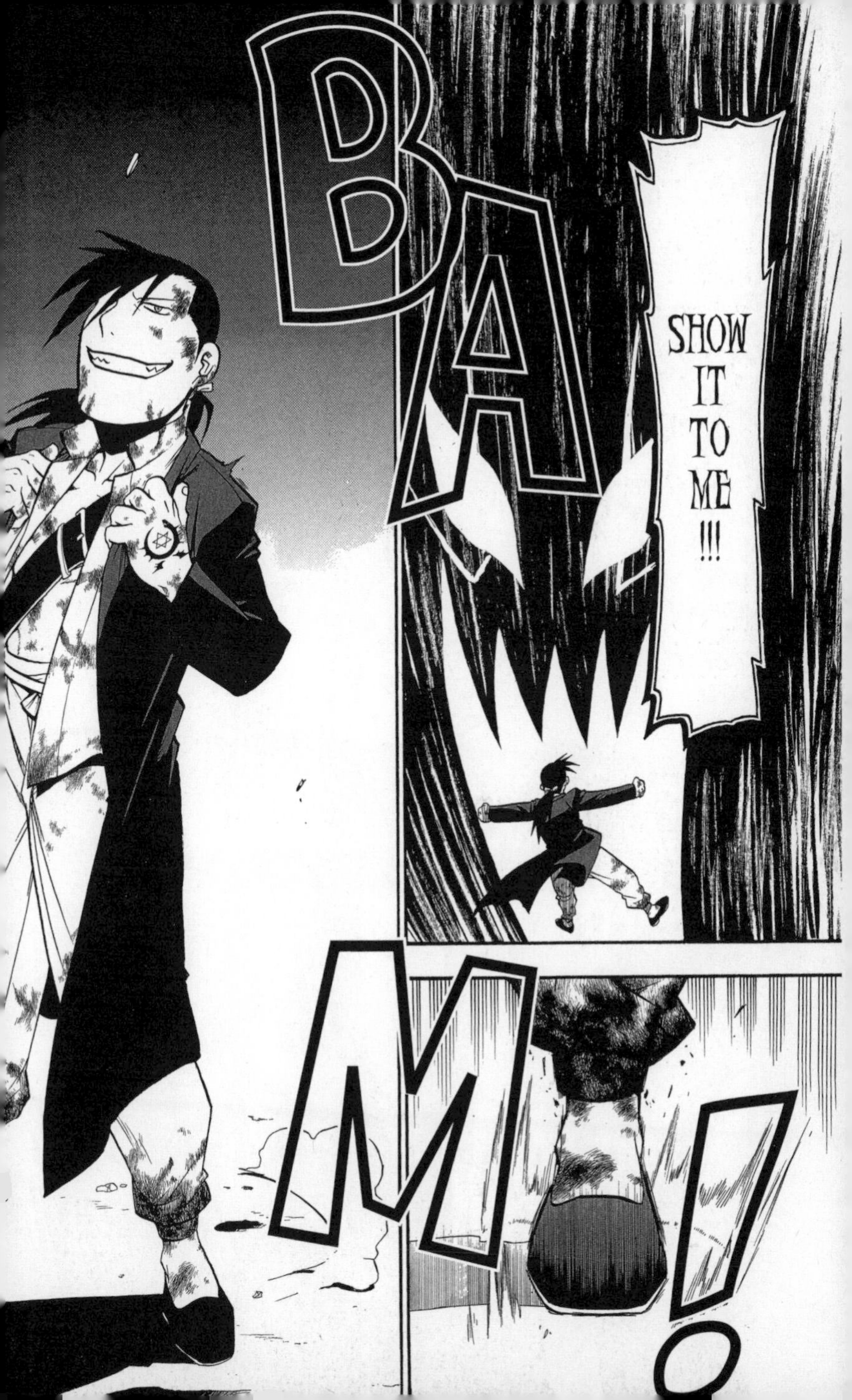
SHOW IT TO ME!!!
BAM!

Chapter 55 The Avarice of Two

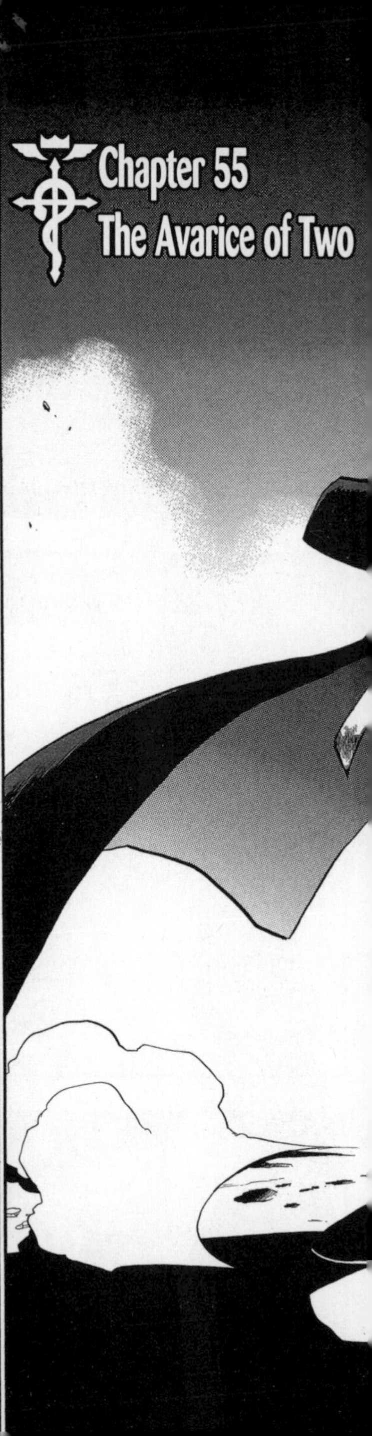

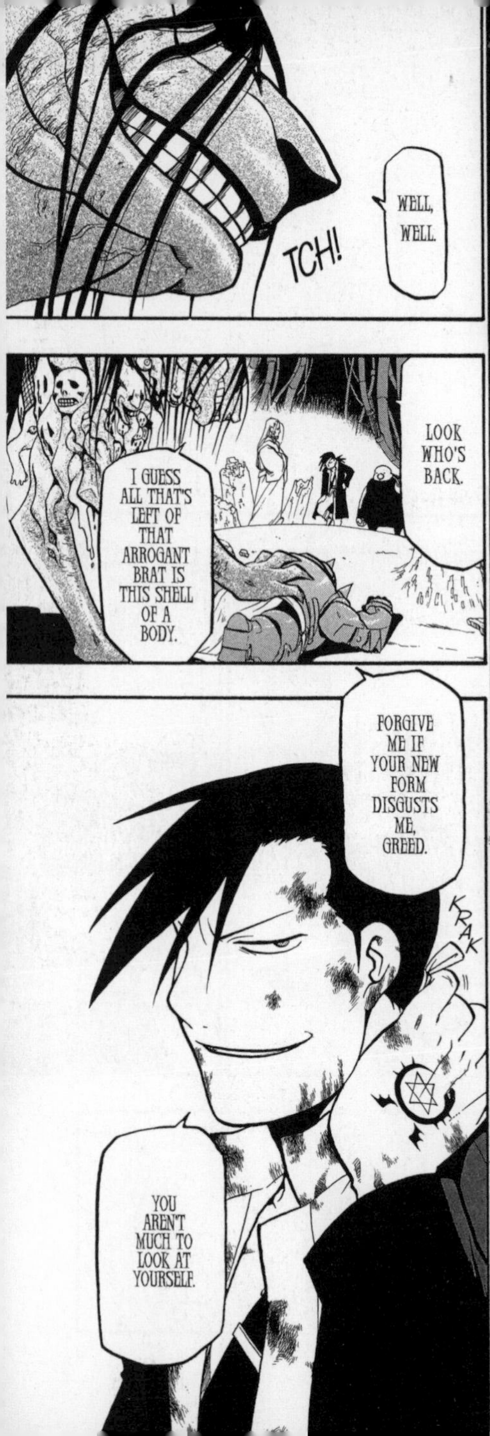
WELL, WELL.
TCH!
LOOK WHO'S BACK.
I GUESS ALL THAT'S LEFT OF THAT ARROGANT BRAT IS THIS SHELL OF A BODY.
FORGIVE ME IF YOUR NEW FORM DISGUSTS ME, GREED.
KRAK
YOU AREN'T MUCH TO LOOK AT YOURSELF.

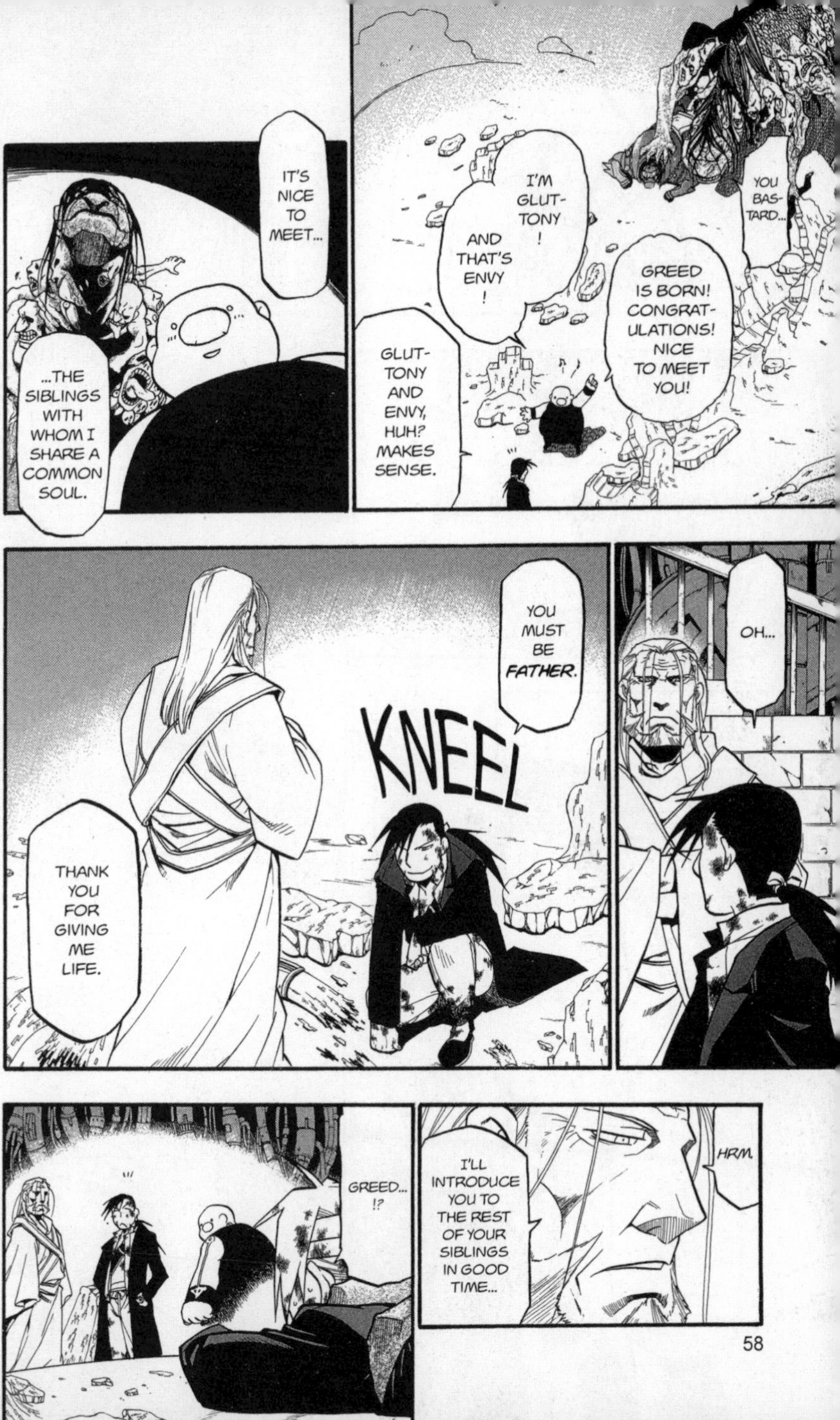
YOU BASTARD...
GREED IS BORN! CONGRATULATIONS! NICE TO MEET YOU!
I'M GLUTTONY!
AND THAT'S ENVY!
GLUTTONY AND ENVY, HUH? MAKES SENSE.
IT'S NICE TO MEET...
...THE SIBLINGS WITH WHOM I SHARE A COMMON SOUL.
OH...
YOU MUST BE *FATHER*.
KNEEL
THANK YOU FOR GIVING ME LIFE.
HRM.
I'LL INTRODUCE YOU TO THE REST OF YOUR SIBLINGS IN GOOD TIME...
GREED... !?

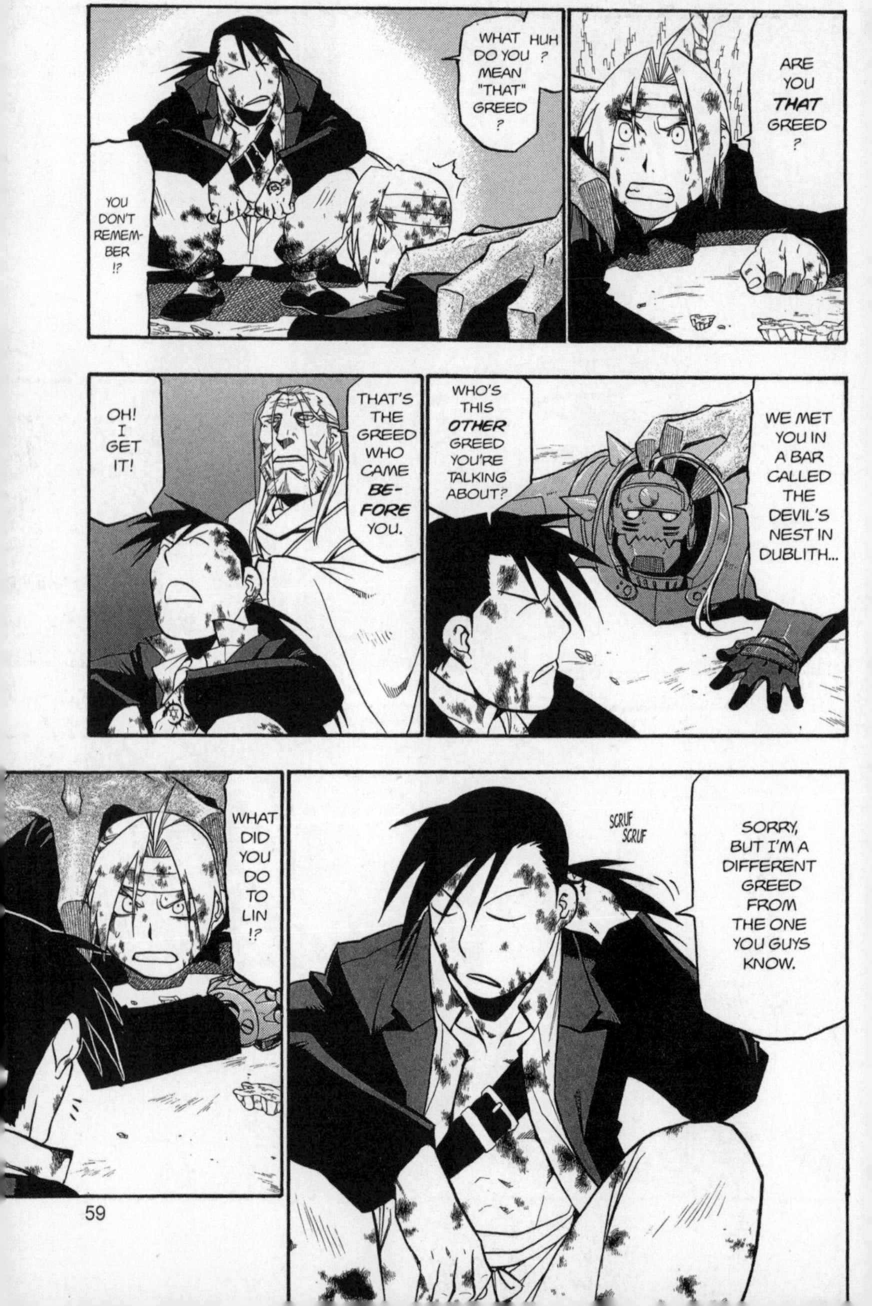
ARE YOU THAT GREED?
HUH?
WHAT DO YOU MEAN "THAT" GREED?
YOU DON'T REMEMBER!?
WE MET YOU IN A BAR CALLED THE DEVIL'S NEST IN DUBLITH...
WHO'S THIS OTHER GREED YOU'RE TALKING ABOUT?
THAT'S THE GREED WHO CAME BEFORE YOU.
OH! I GET IT!
SORRY, BUT I'M A DIFFERENT GREED FROM THE ONE YOU GUYS KNOW.
SCRUF SCRUF
WHAT DID YOU DO TO LIN!?

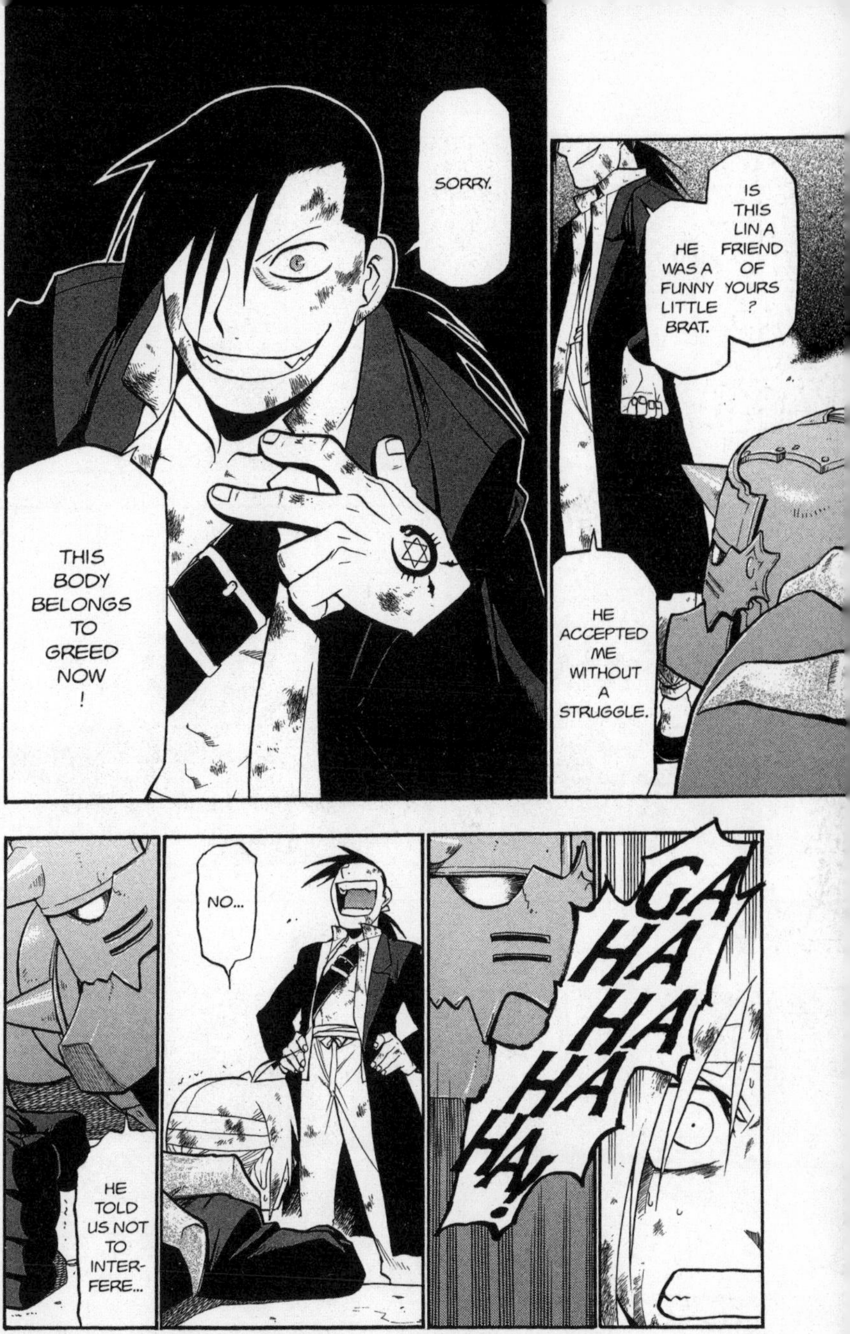
IS THIS LIN A FRIEND OF YOURS?
HE WAS A FUNNY LITTLE BRAT.
HE ACCEPTED ME WITHOUT A STRUGGLE.
SORRY.
THIS BODY BELONGS TO GREED NOW!
GAHAHAHAHAHA!
NO...
HE TOLD US NOT TO INTERFERE...

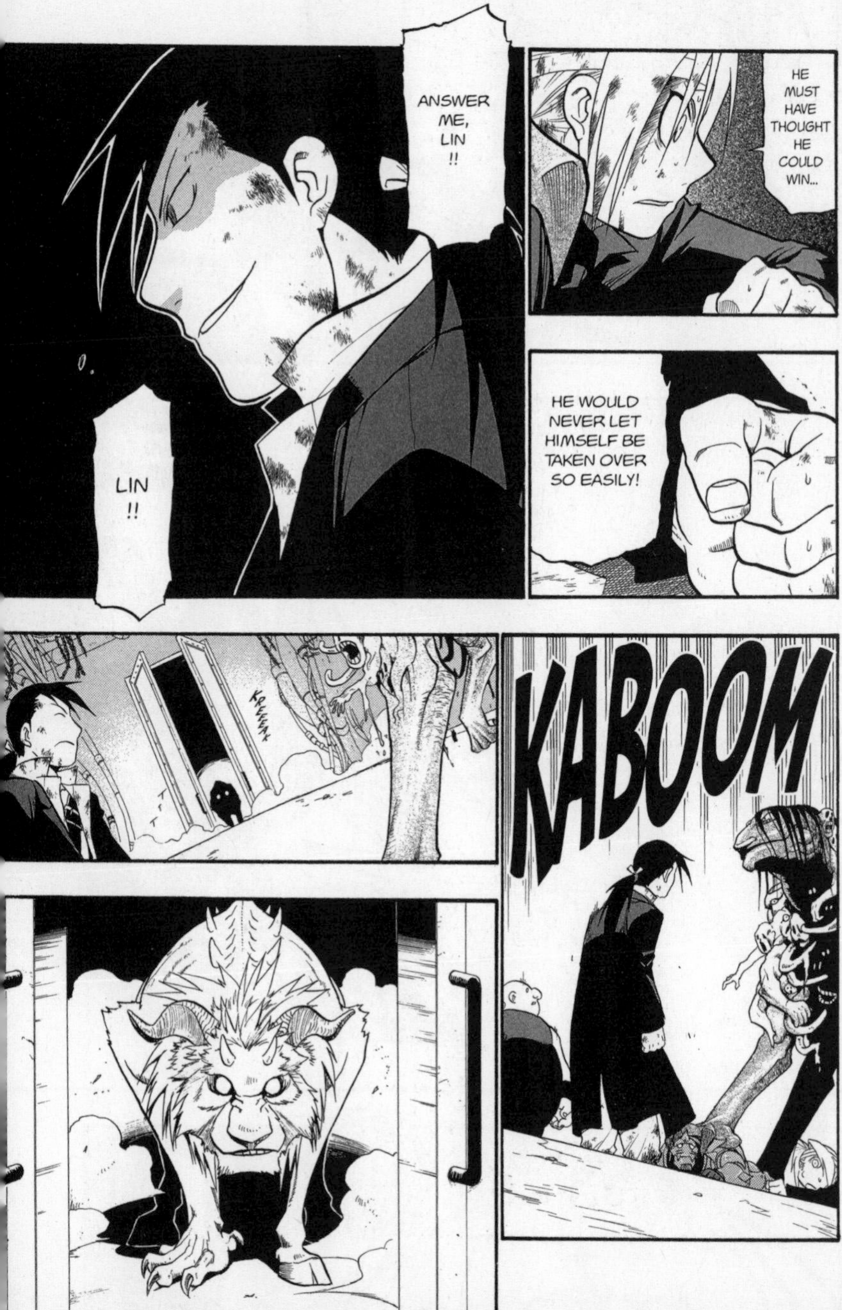
HE MUST HAVE THOUGHT HE COULD WIN...
HE WOULD NEVER LET HIMSELF BE TAKEN OVER SO EASILY!
ANSWER ME, LIN !!
LIN !!
KABOOM

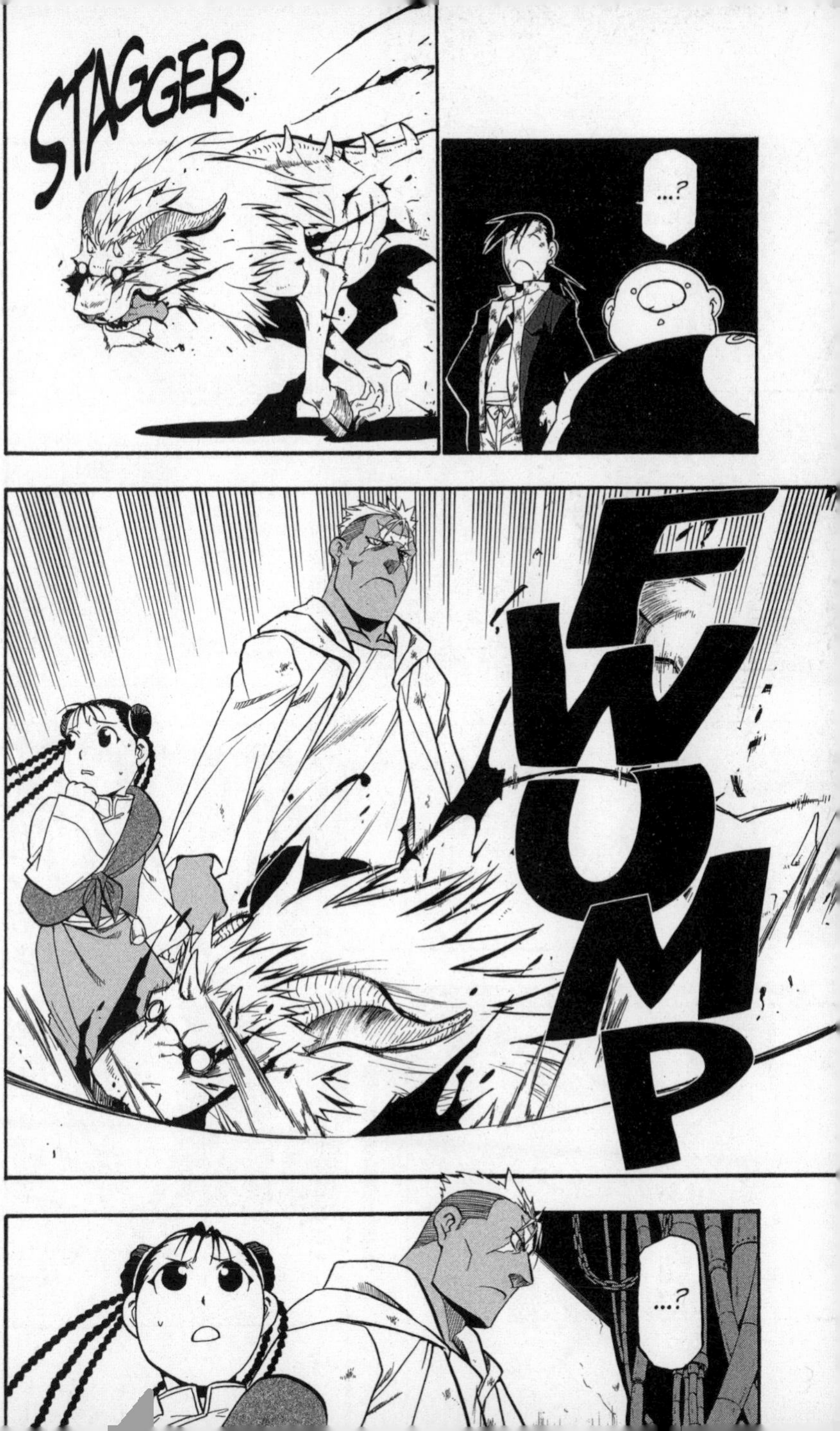
...?
STAGGER
FWUMP
...?

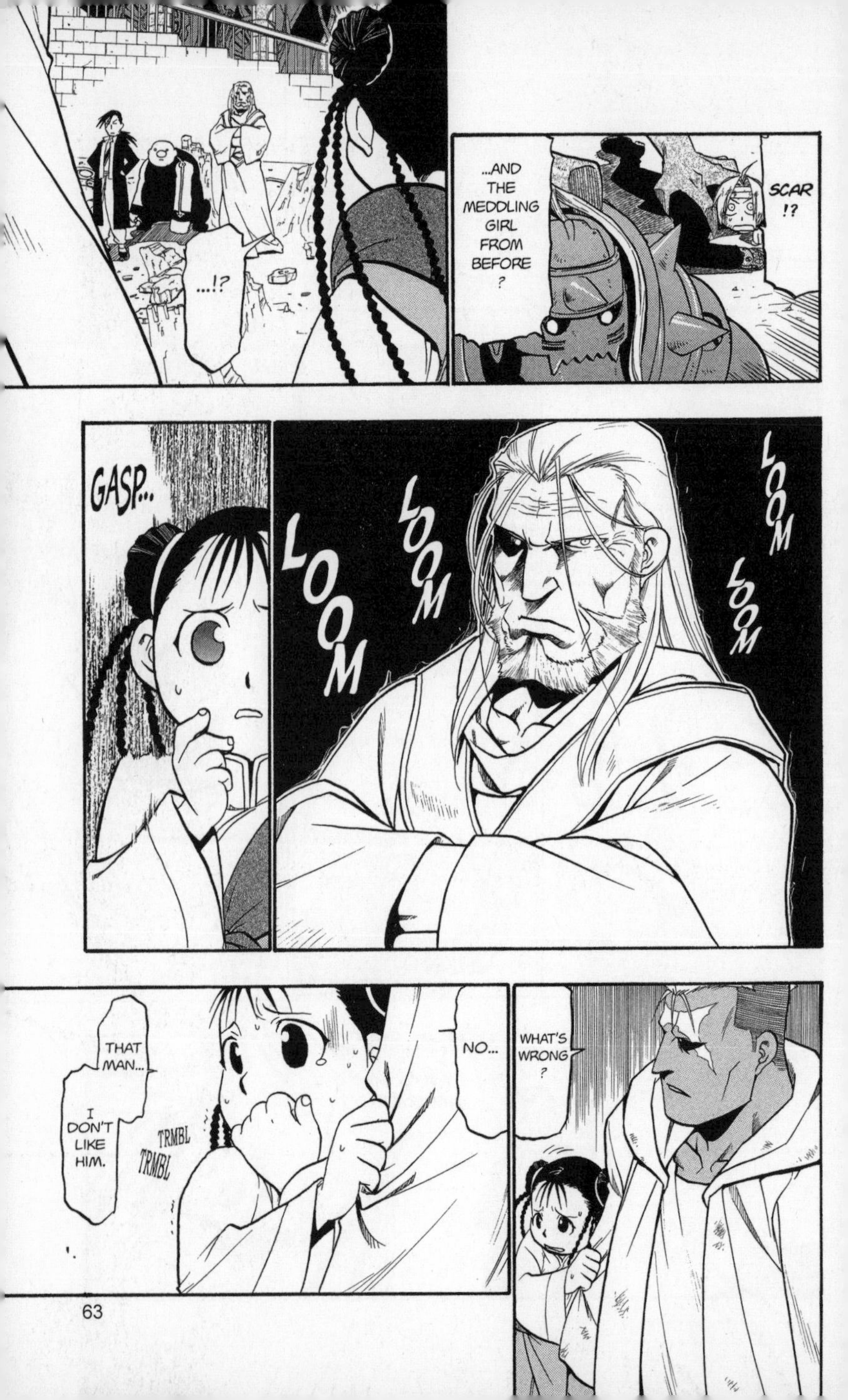

SCAR !?
...AND THE MEDDLING GIRL FROM BEFORE ?
...!?
LOOM LOOM
LOOM LOOM
GASP...
WHAT'S WRONG ?
NO...
THAT MAN...
I DON'T LIKE HIM.
TRMBL TRMBL

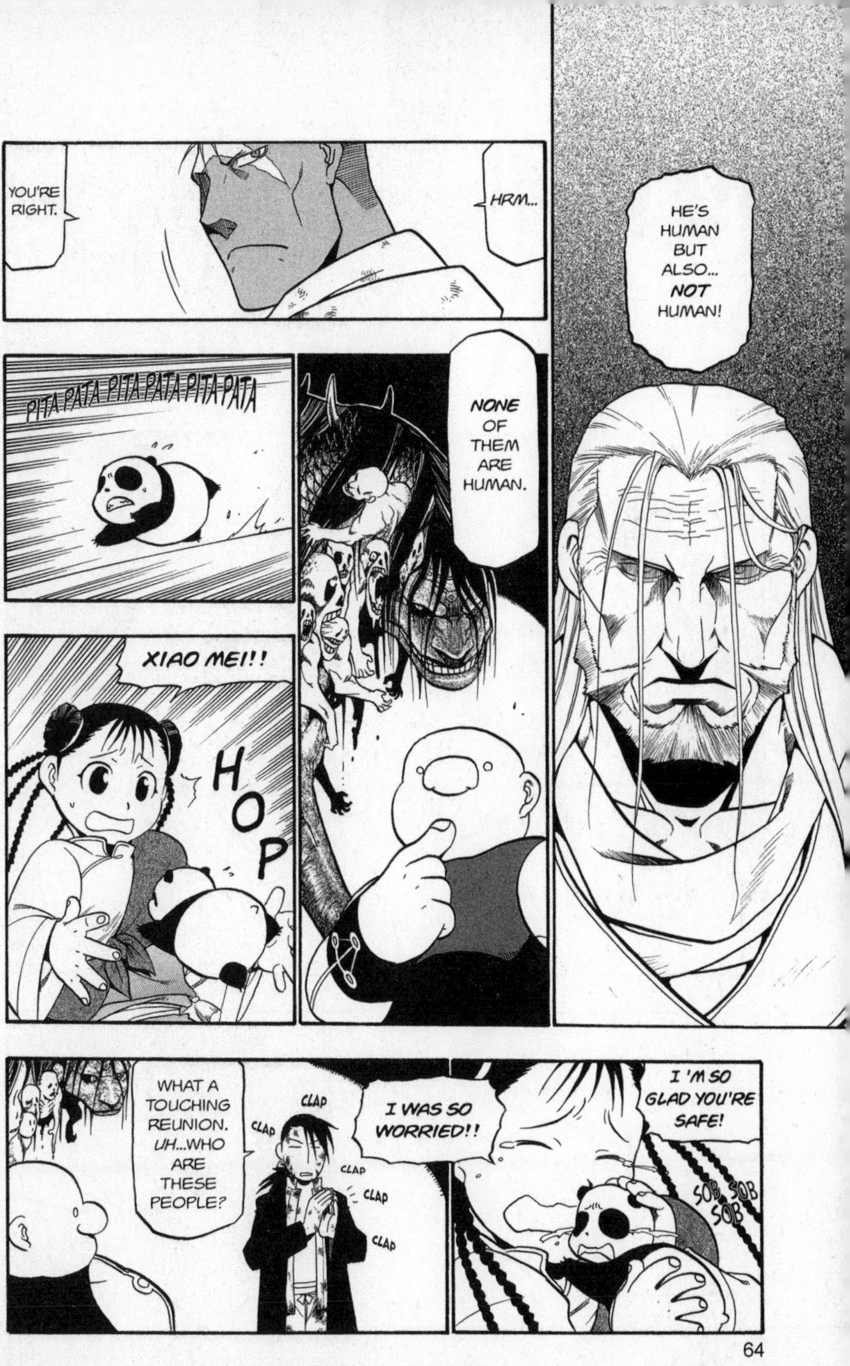
HE'S HUMAN BUT ALSO... NOT HUMAN!
HRM...
YOU'RE RIGHT.
NONE OF THEM ARE HUMAN.
PITA PATA PITA PATA PITA PATA
XIAO MEI!!
HOP
I'M SO GLAD YOU'RE SAFE!
SOB SOB SOB
I WAS SO WORRIED!!
CLAP CLAP CLAP CLAP CLAP
WHAT A TOUCHING REUNION. UH...WHO ARE THESE PEOPLE?

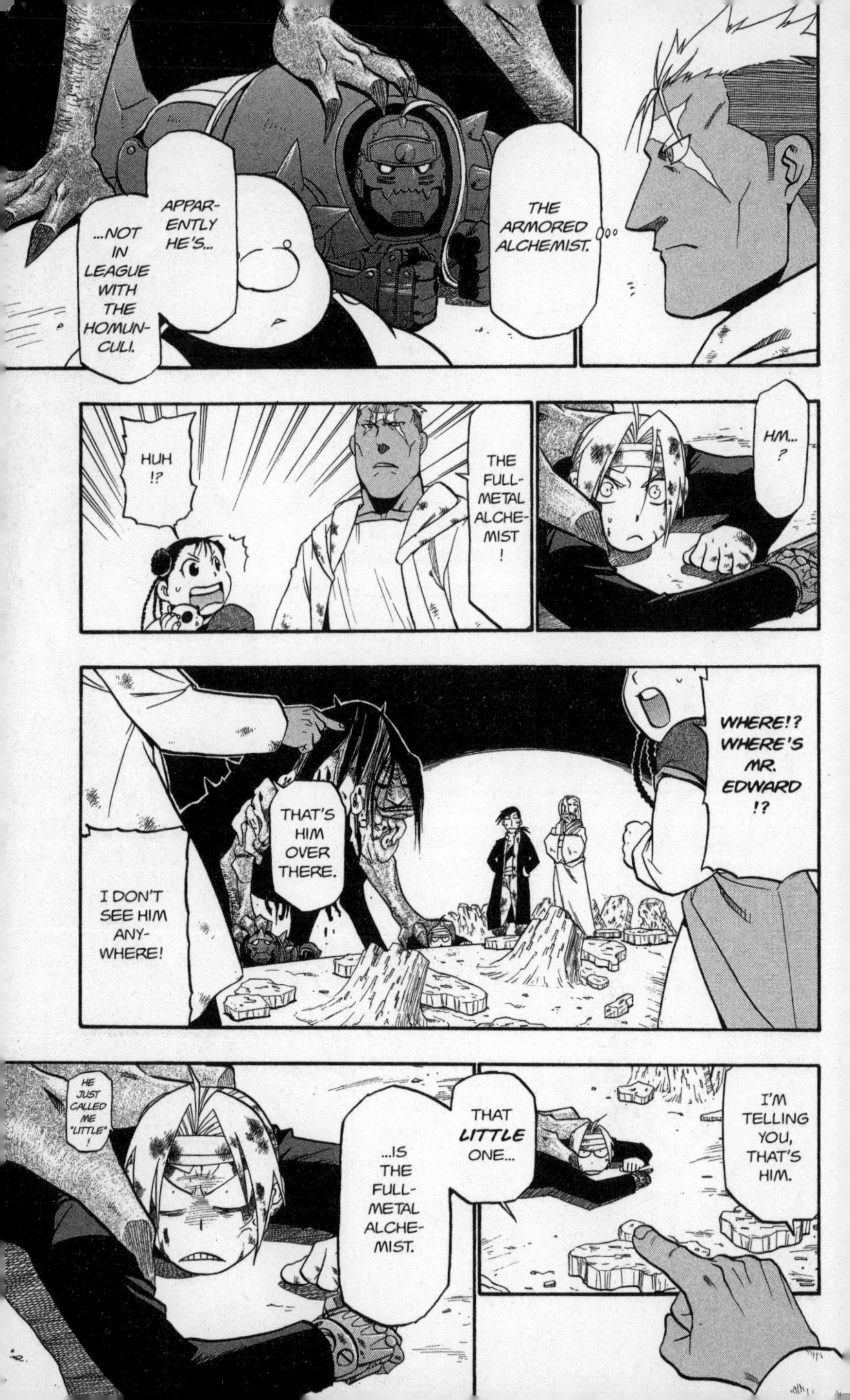
THE ARMORED ALCHEMIST.
APPARENTLY HE'S...
...NOT IN LEAGUE WITH THE HOMUNCULI.
HM...?
THE FULLMETAL ALCHEMIST!
HUH!?
WHERE!? WHERE'S MR. EDWARD!?
THAT'S HIM OVER THERE.
I DON'T SEE HIM ANYWHERE!
I'M TELLING YOU, THAT'S HIM.
THAT *LITTLE* ONE...
...IS THE FULLMETAL ALCHEMIST.
HE JUST CALLED ME "LITTLE"!

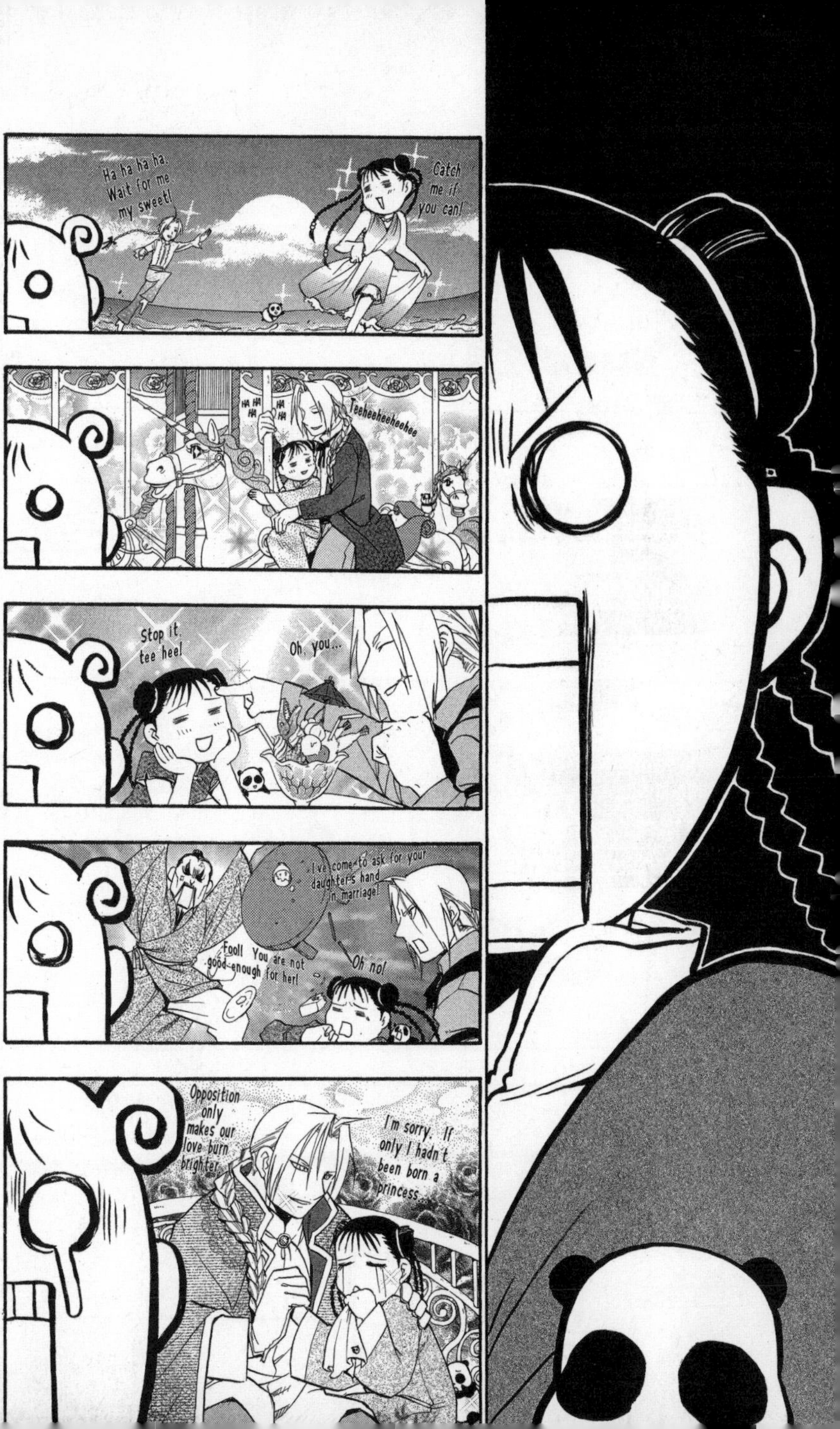
Catch me if you can!
Ha ha ha ha. Wait for me, my sweet!
Teeheeheeheehee
HA HA
HA HA HA
Oh, you...
Stop it, tee hee!
I've come to ask for your daughter's hand in marriage!
Oh no!
Fool! You are not good enough for her!
I'm sorry. If only I hadn't been born a princess...
Opposition only makes our love burn brighter.

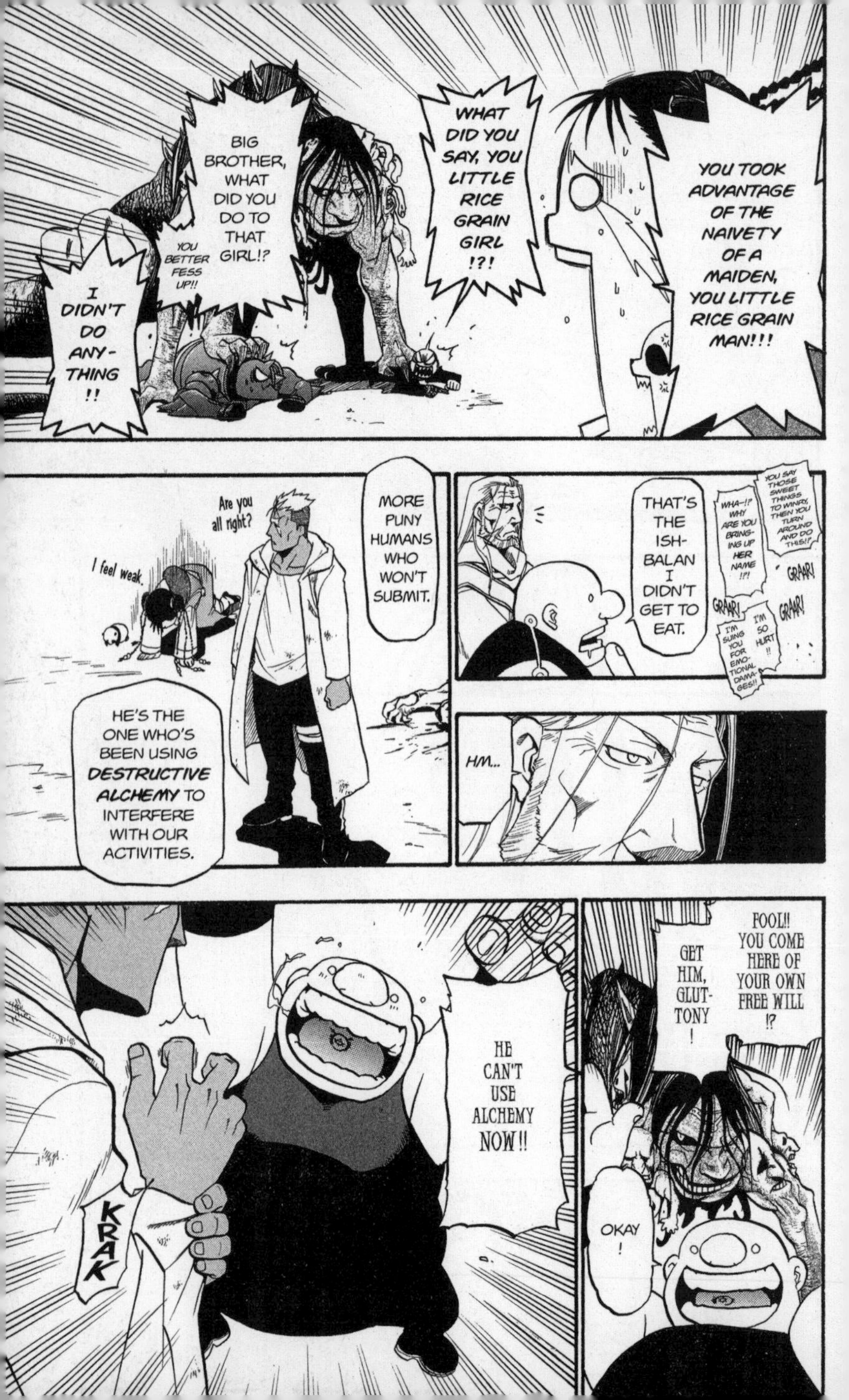
YOU TOOK ADVANTAGE OF THE NAIVETY OF A MAIDEN, YOU LITTLE RICE GRAIN MAN!!!
WHAT DID YOU SAY, YOU LITTLE RICE GRAIN GIRL !?!
BIG BROTHER, WHAT DID YOU DO TO THAT GIRL!?
YOU BETTER FESS UP!!
I DIDN'T DO ANY-THING !!
THAT'S THE ISH-BALAN I DIDN'T GET TO EAT.
YOU SAY THOSE SWEET THINGS TO WINRY, THEN YOU TURN AROUND AND DO THIS!?
WHA-!? WHY ARE YOU BRINGING UP HER NAME !?!
GRAAR!
GRAAR!
I'M SO HURT !!
GRAAR!
I'M SUING YOU FOR EMO-TIONAL DAMA-GES!!
HM...
MORE PUNY HUMANS WHO WON'T SUBMIT.
Are you all right?
I feel weak.
HE'S THE ONE WHO'S BEEN USING DESTRUCTIVE ALCHEMY TO INTERFERE WITH OUR ACTIVITIES.
FOOL!! YOU COME HERE OF YOUR OWN FREE WILL !?
GET HIM, GLUT-TONY !
OKAY !
HE CAN'T USE ALCHEMY NOW!!
KRAK

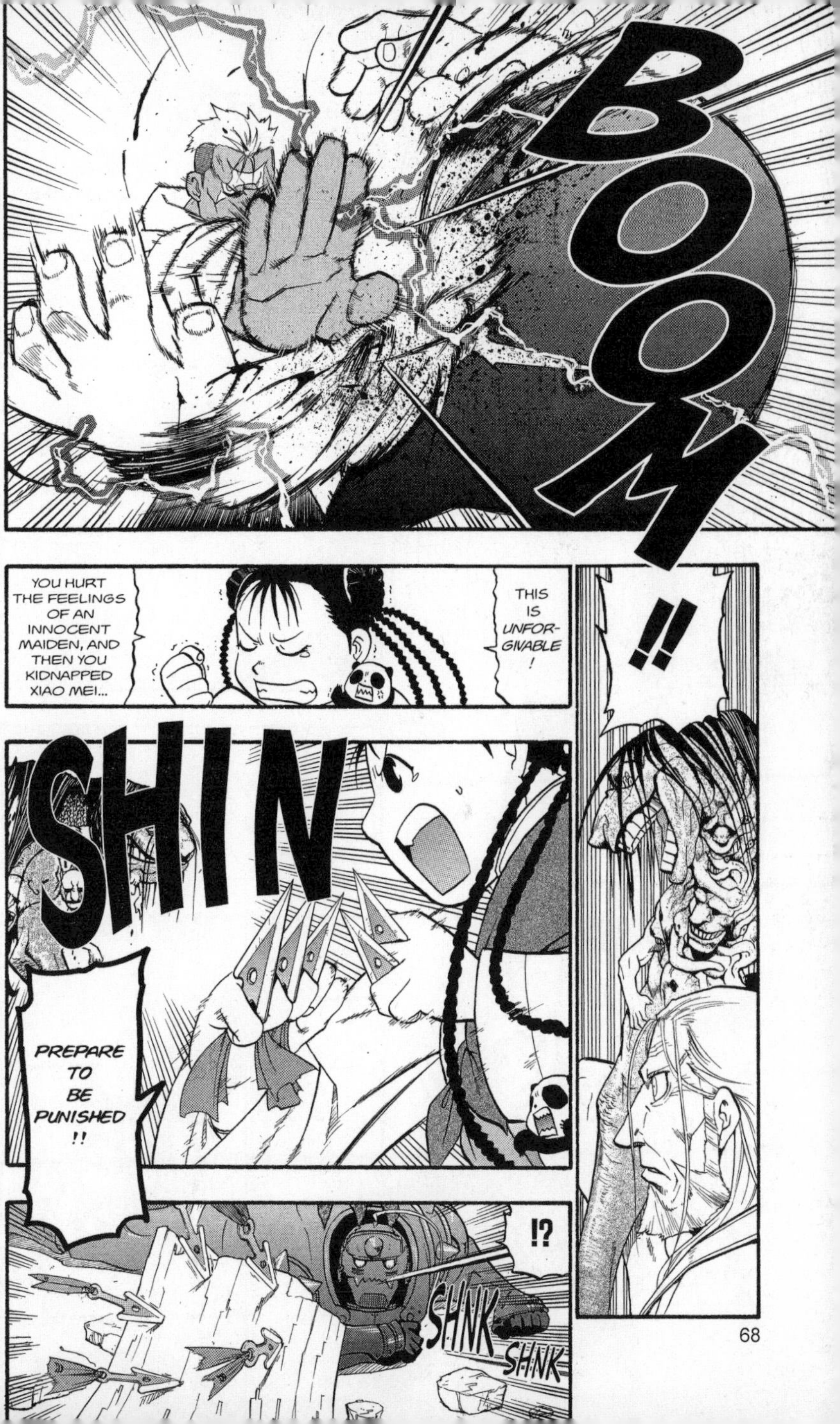
BOOM
!!
THIS IS UNFORGIVABLE!
YOU HURT THE FEELINGS OF AN INNOCENT MAIDEN, AND THEN YOU KIDNAPPED XIAO MEI...
SHIN
PREPARE TO BE PUNISHED!!
!?
SHNK
SHNK

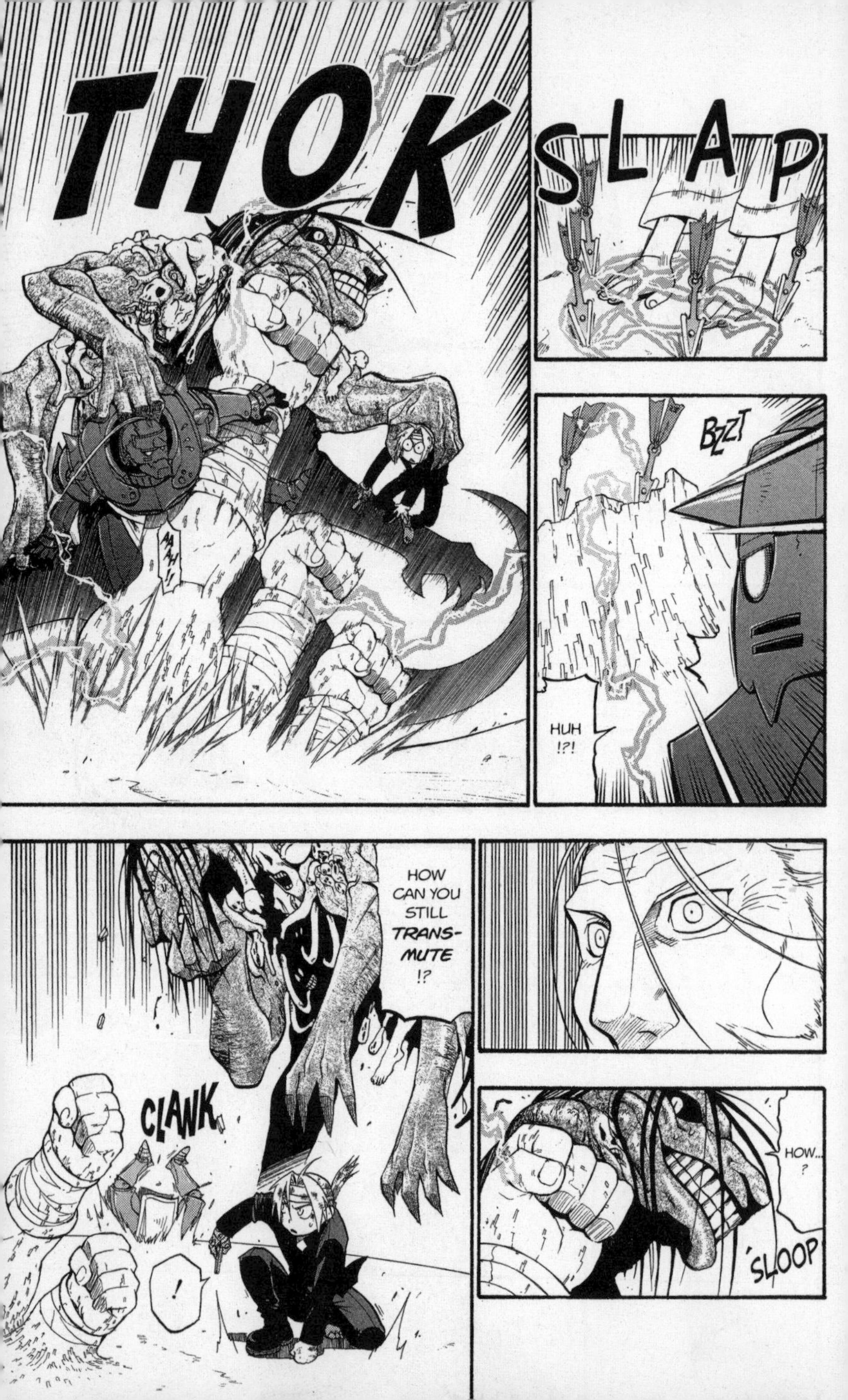

SLAP
BZZT
HUH !?!
THOK
AAAH !!
HOW...?
SLOOP
HOW CAN YOU STILL TRANSMUTE !?
CLANK
!

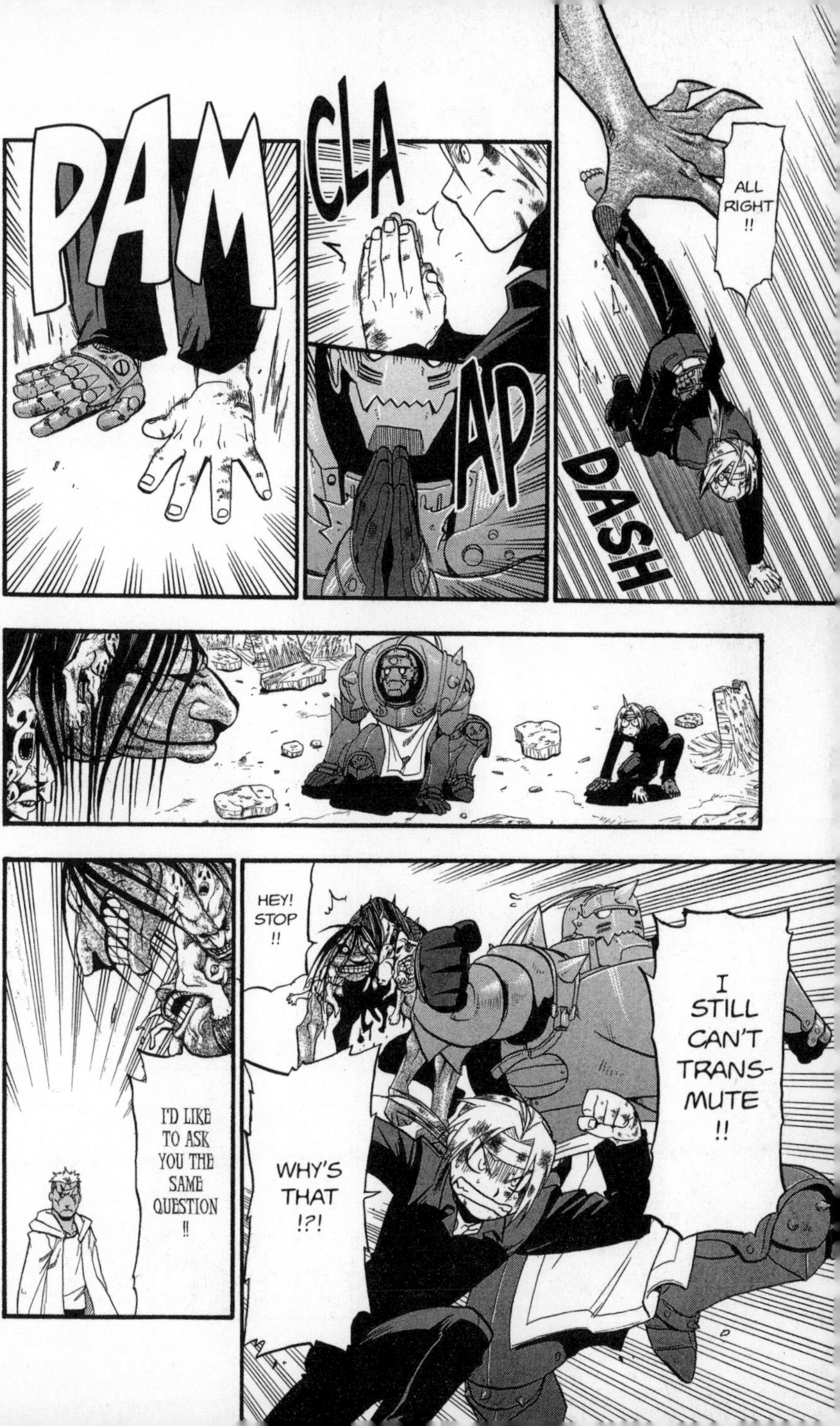
ALL RIGHT!!
DASH
CLA
AP
PAM
I STILL CAN'T TRANS-MUTE!!
HEY! STOP!!
WHY'S THAT!?!
I'D LIKE TO ASK YOU THE SAME QUESTION!!

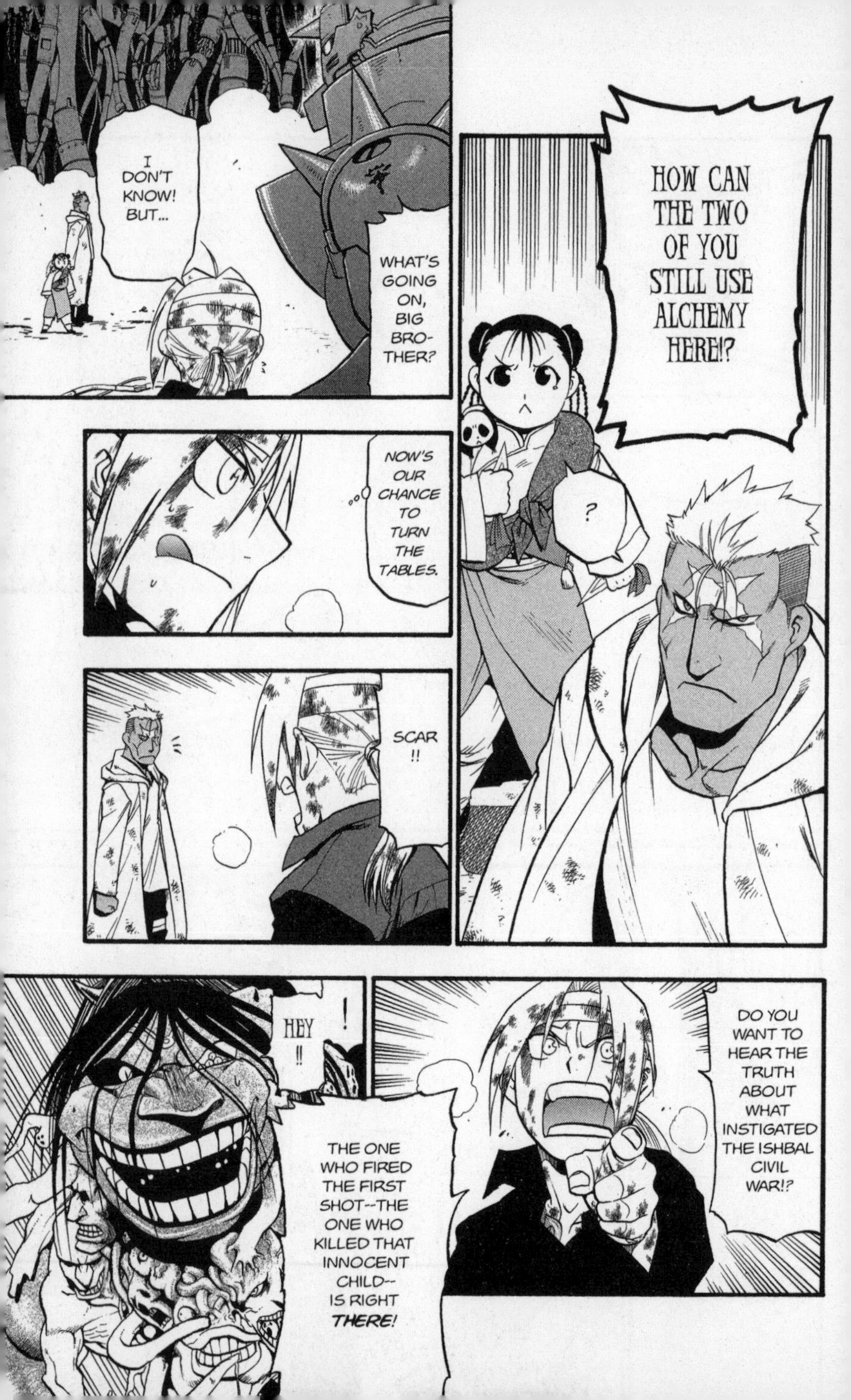
HOW CAN THE TWO OF YOU STILL USE ALCHEMY HERE!?
?
WHAT'S GOING ON, BIG BRO-THER?
I DON'T KNOW! BUT...
NOW'S OUR CHANCE TO TURN THE TABLES.
SCAR !!
DO YOU WANT TO HEAR THE TRUTH ABOUT WHAT INSTIGATED THE ISHBAL CIVIL WAR!?
THE ONE WHO FIRED THE FIRST SHOT--THE ONE WHO KILLED THAT INNOCENT CHILD-- IS RIGHT *THERE!*
!
HEY !!

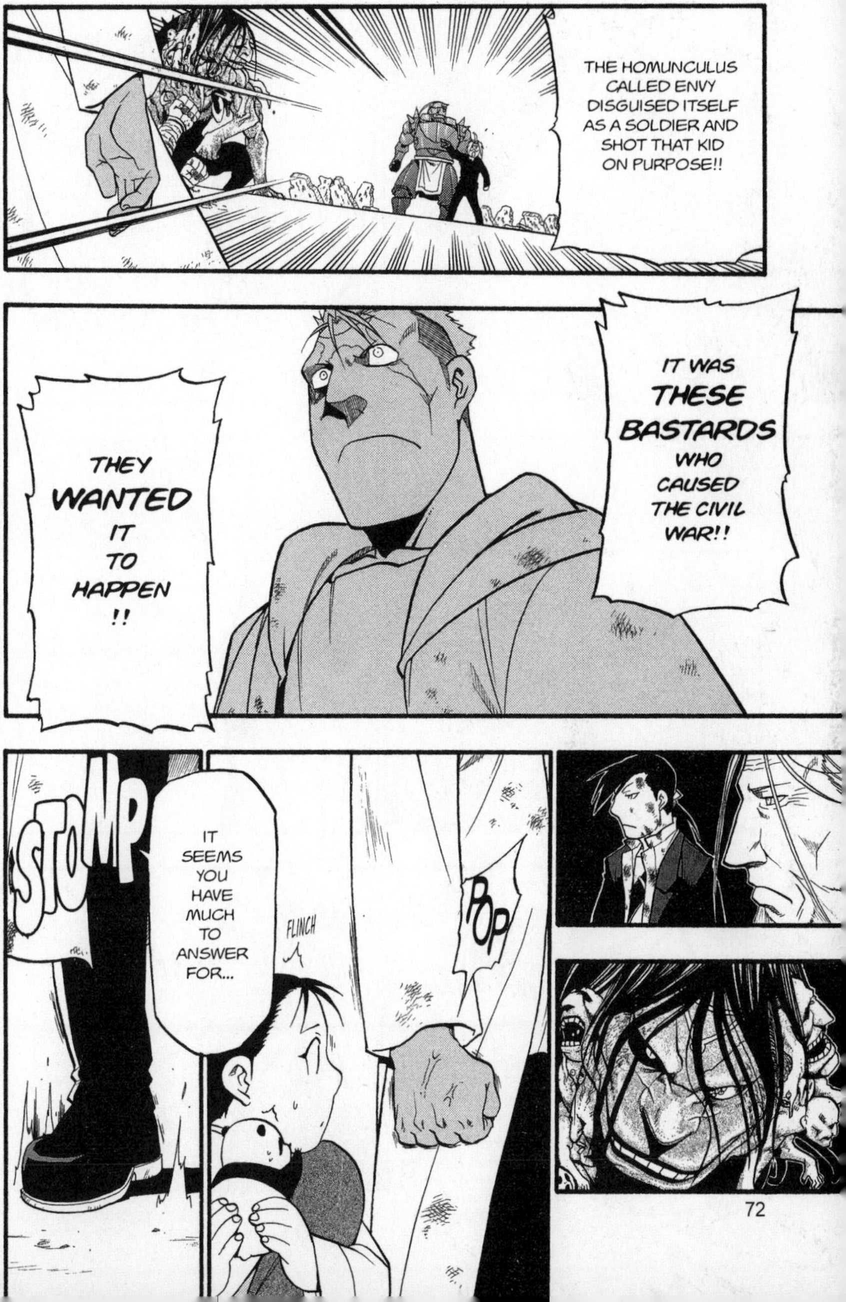
THE HOMUNCULUS CALLED ENVY DISGUISED ITSELF AS A SOLDIER AND SHOT THAT KID ON PURPOSE!!
IT WAS THESE BASTARDS WHO CAUSED THE CIVIL WAR!!
THEY WANTED IT TO HAPPEN!!
POP
FLINCH
IT SEEMS YOU HAVE MUCH TO ANSWER FOR...
STOMP

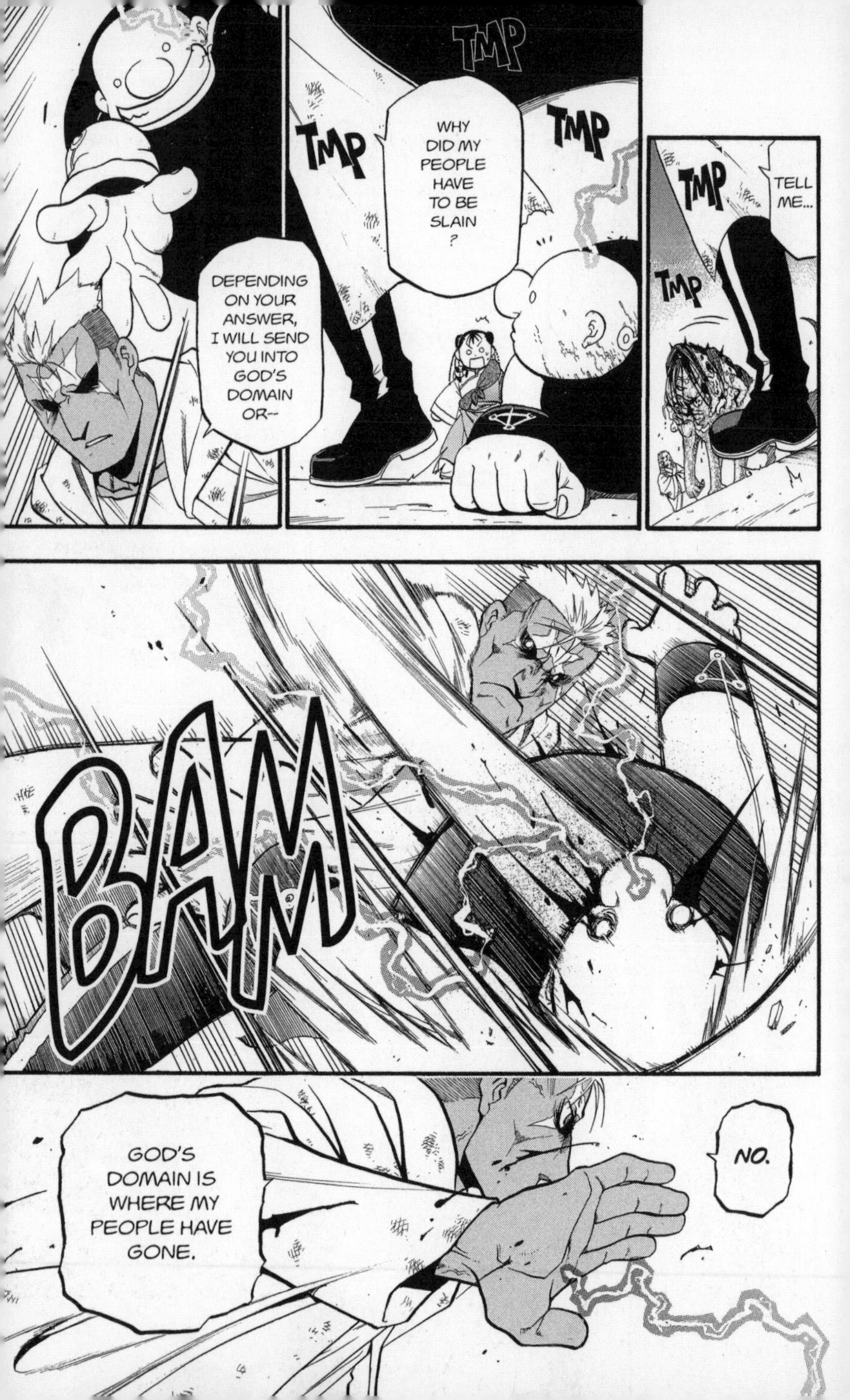
TMP
TELL ME...
TMP
TMP
TMP
WHY DID MY PEOPLE HAVE TO BE SLAIN?
TMP
DEPENDING ON YOUR ANSWER, I WILL SEND YOU INTO GOD'S DOMAIN OR--
BAM
NO.
GOD'S DOMAIN IS WHERE MY PEOPLE HAVE GONE.

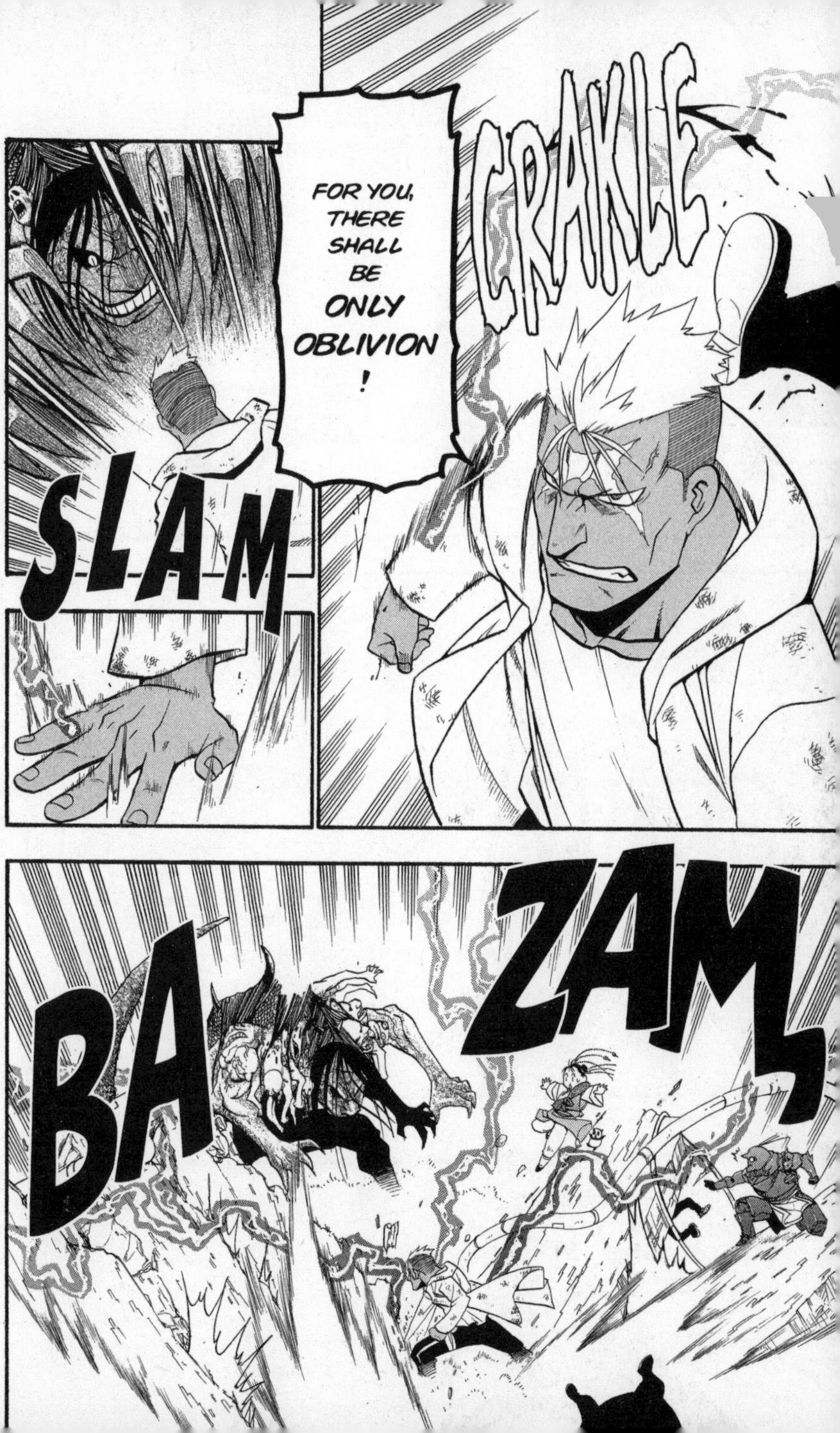
CRAKLE
FOR YOU, THERE SHALL BE ONLY OBLIVION!
SLAM
BA ZAM

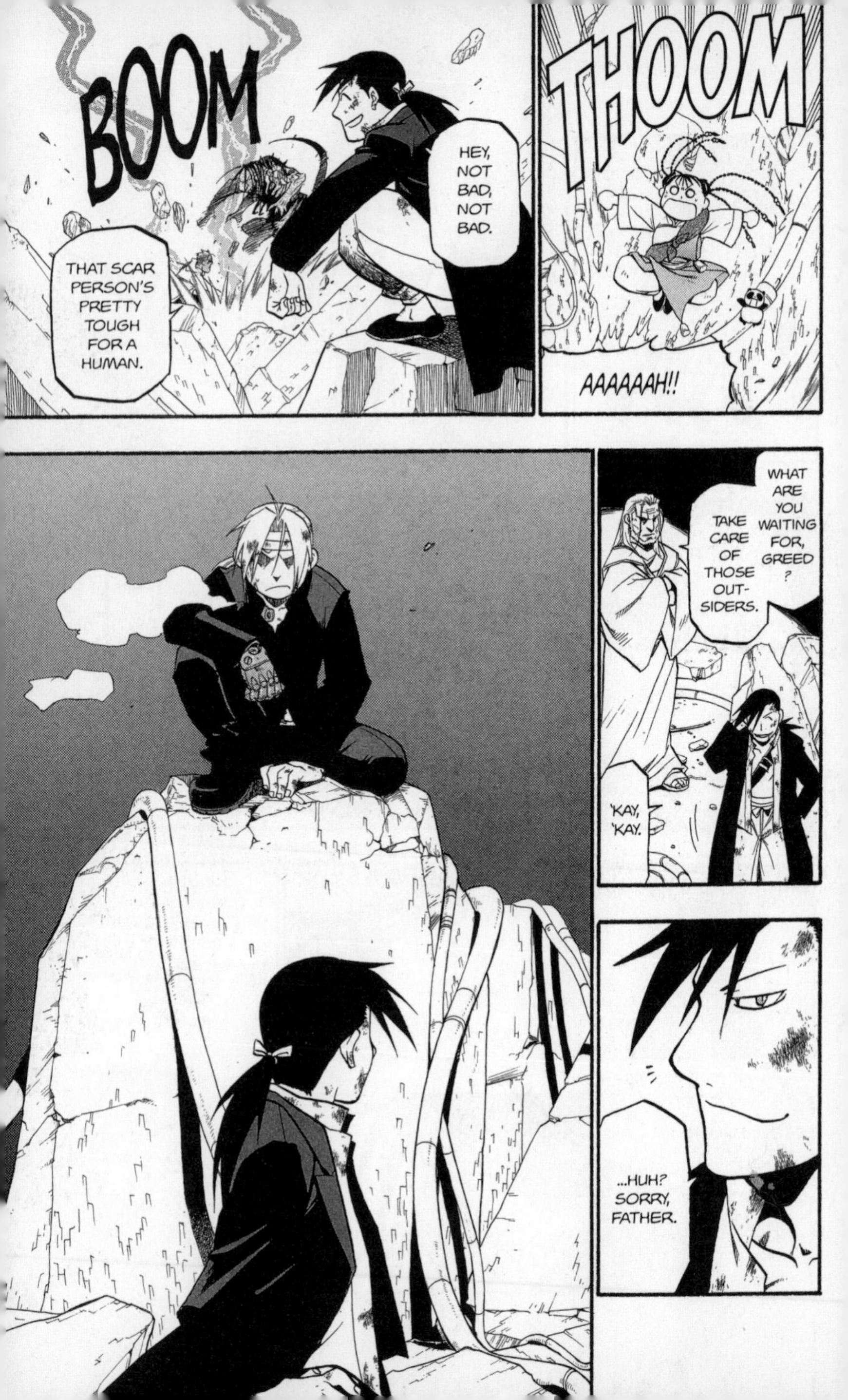
THOOM
AAAAAAH!!
BOOM
HEY, NOT BAD, NOT BAD.
THAT SCAR PERSON'S PRETTY TOUGH FOR A HUMAN.
WHAT ARE YOU WAITING FOR, GREED?
TAKE CARE OF THOSE OUT-SIDERS.
'KAY, 'KAY.
...HUH? SORRY, FATHER.

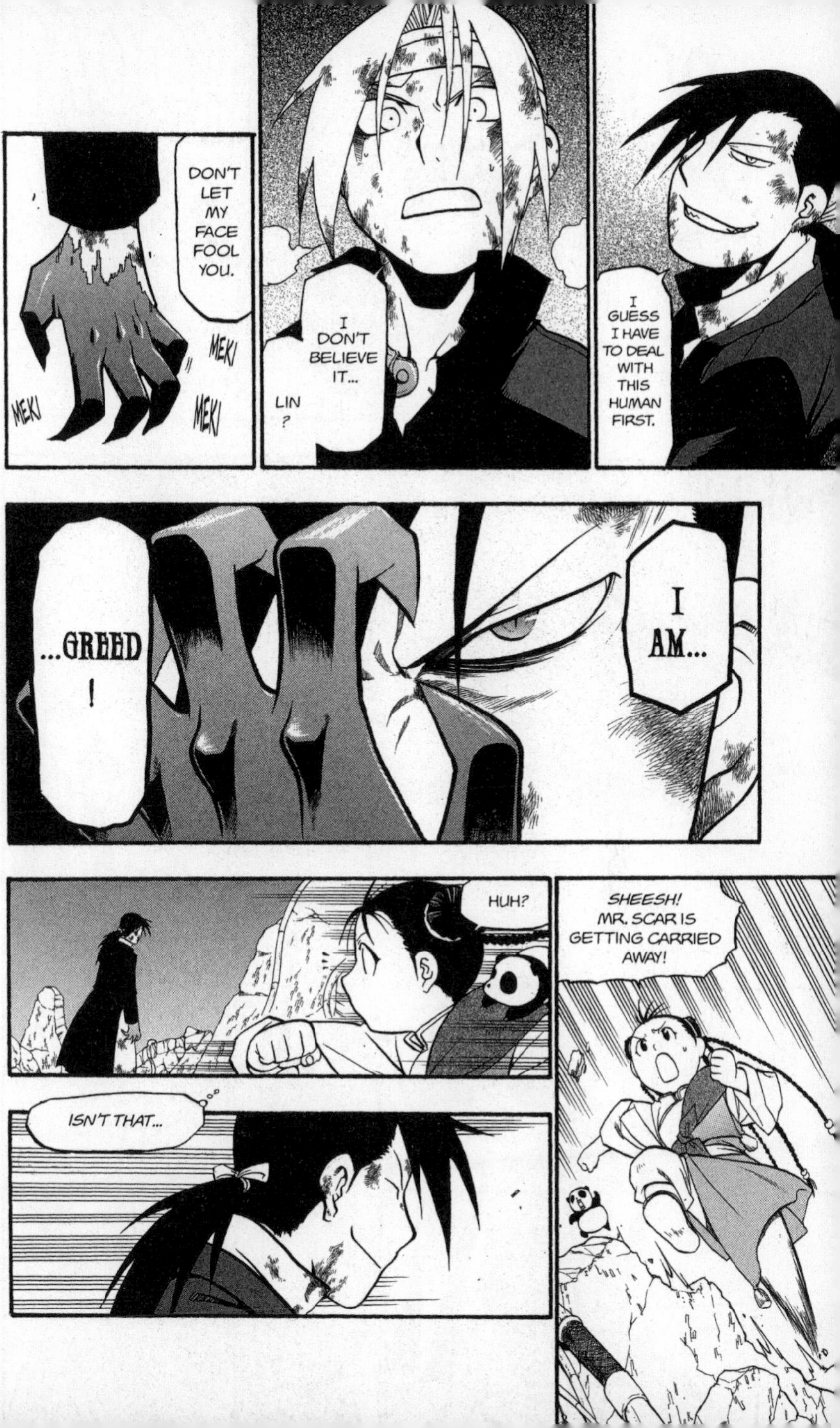
I GUESS I HAVE TO DEAL WITH THIS HUMAN FIRST.
I DON'T BELIEVE IT...
LIN?
DON'T LET MY FACE FOOL YOU.
MEKI
MEKI
MEKI
I AM...
...GREED!
SHEESH! MR. SCAR IS GETTING CARRIED AWAY!
HUH?
ISN'T THAT...

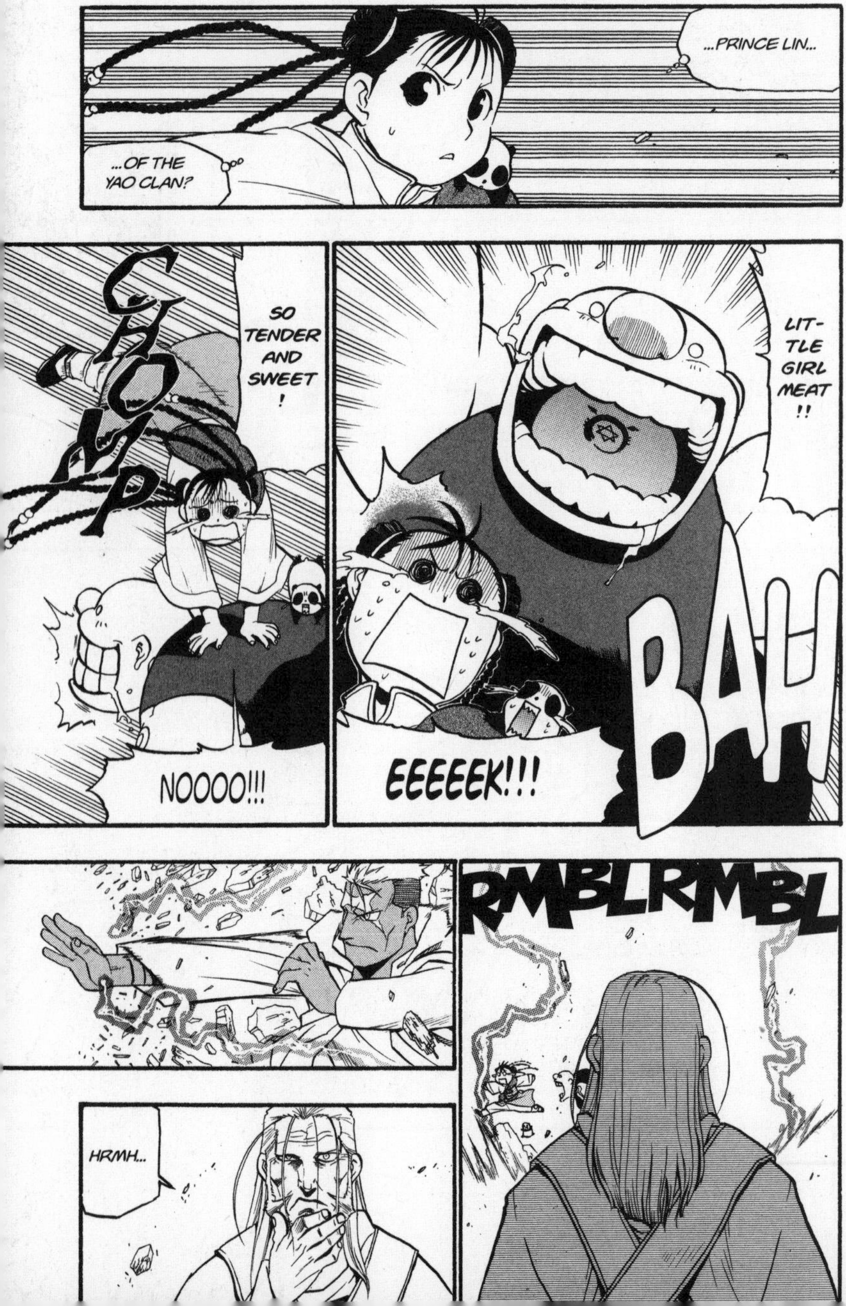
...PRINCE LIN...
...OF THE YAO CLAN?
LITTLE GIRL MEAT!!
BAH
EEEEEK!!!
CHOMP
SO TENDER AND SWEET!
NOOOO!!!
RMBLRMBL
HRMH...

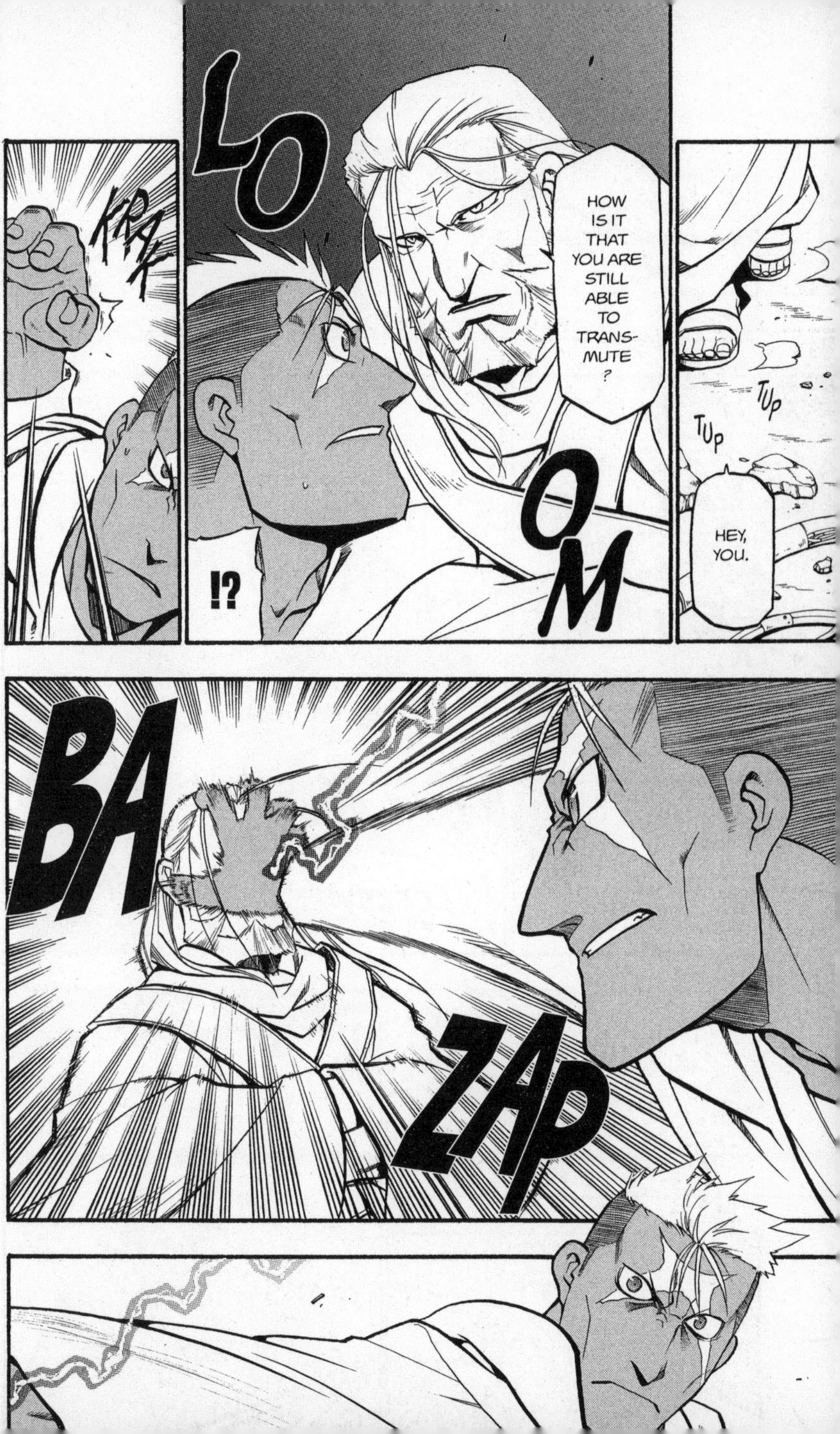
TUP
TUP
HEY, YOU.
HOW IS IT THAT YOU ARE STILL ABLE TO TRANSMUTE?
LO
OM
!?
KRAK
BA
ZAP

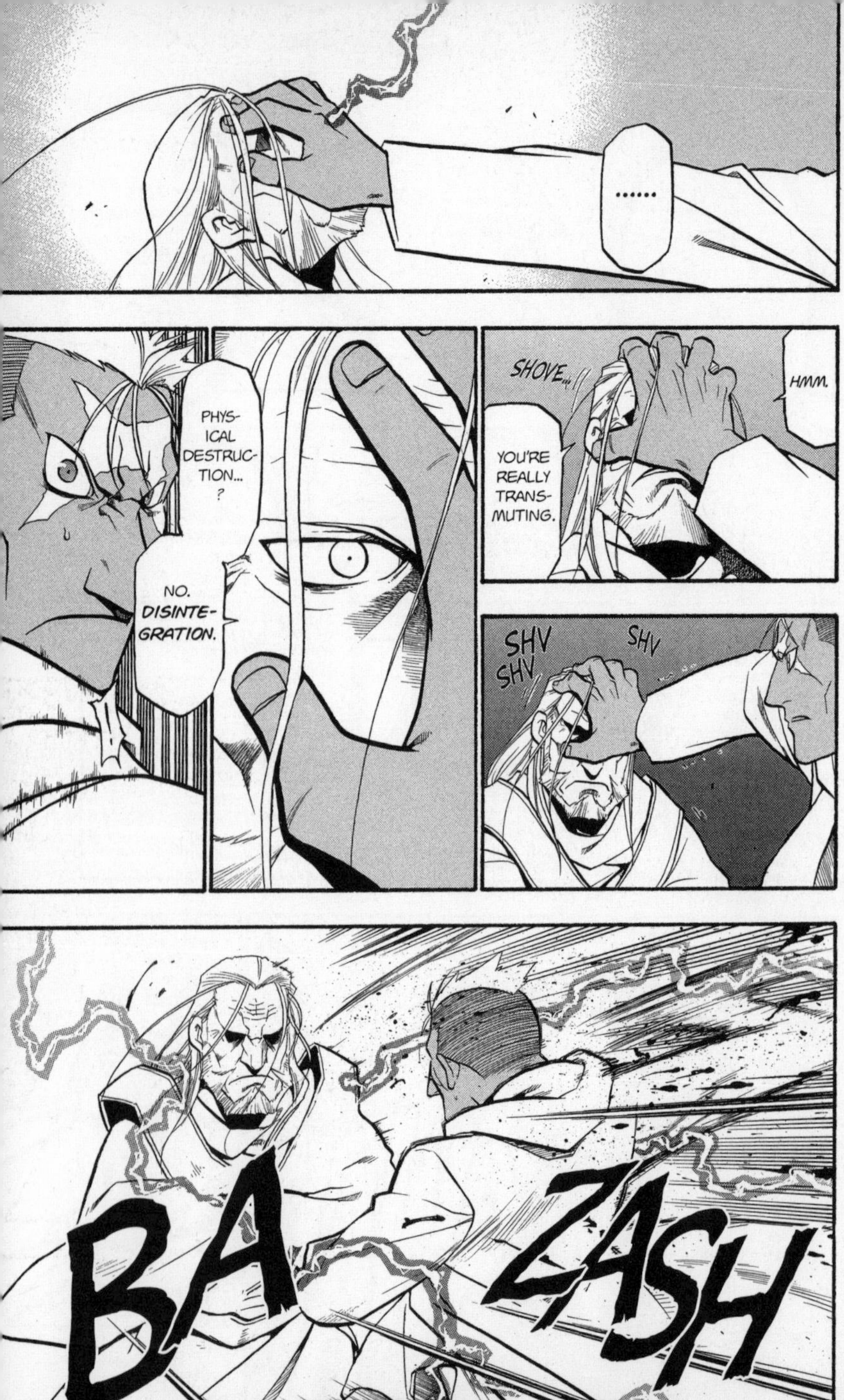
......
HMM.
SHOVE...
YOU'RE REALLY TRANSMUTING.
SHV
SHV
SHV
PHYSICAL DESTRUCTION...?
NO. DISINTEGRATION.
BA
ZASH

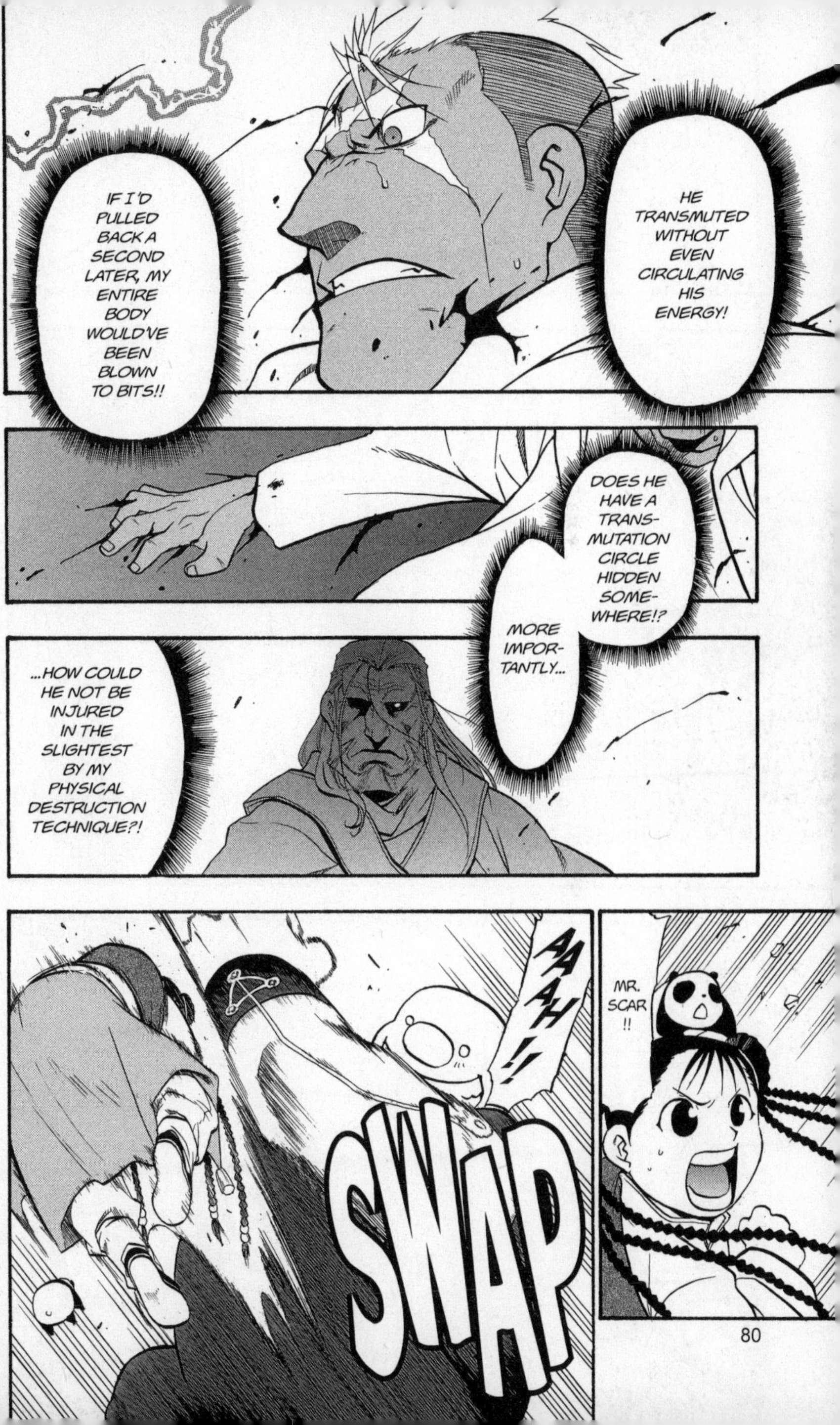

HE TRANSMUTED WITHOUT EVEN CIRCULATING HIS ENERGY!
IF I'D PULLED BACK A SECOND LATER, MY ENTIRE BODY WOULD'VE BEEN BLOWN TO BITS!!
DOES HE HAVE A TRANS-MUTATION CIRCLE HIDDEN SOME-WHERE!?
MORE IMPOR-TANTLY...
...HOW COULD HE NOT BE INJURED IN THE SLIGHTEST BY MY PHYSICAL DESTRUCTION TECHNIQUE?!
MR. SCAR !!
AAAH!!
SNAP

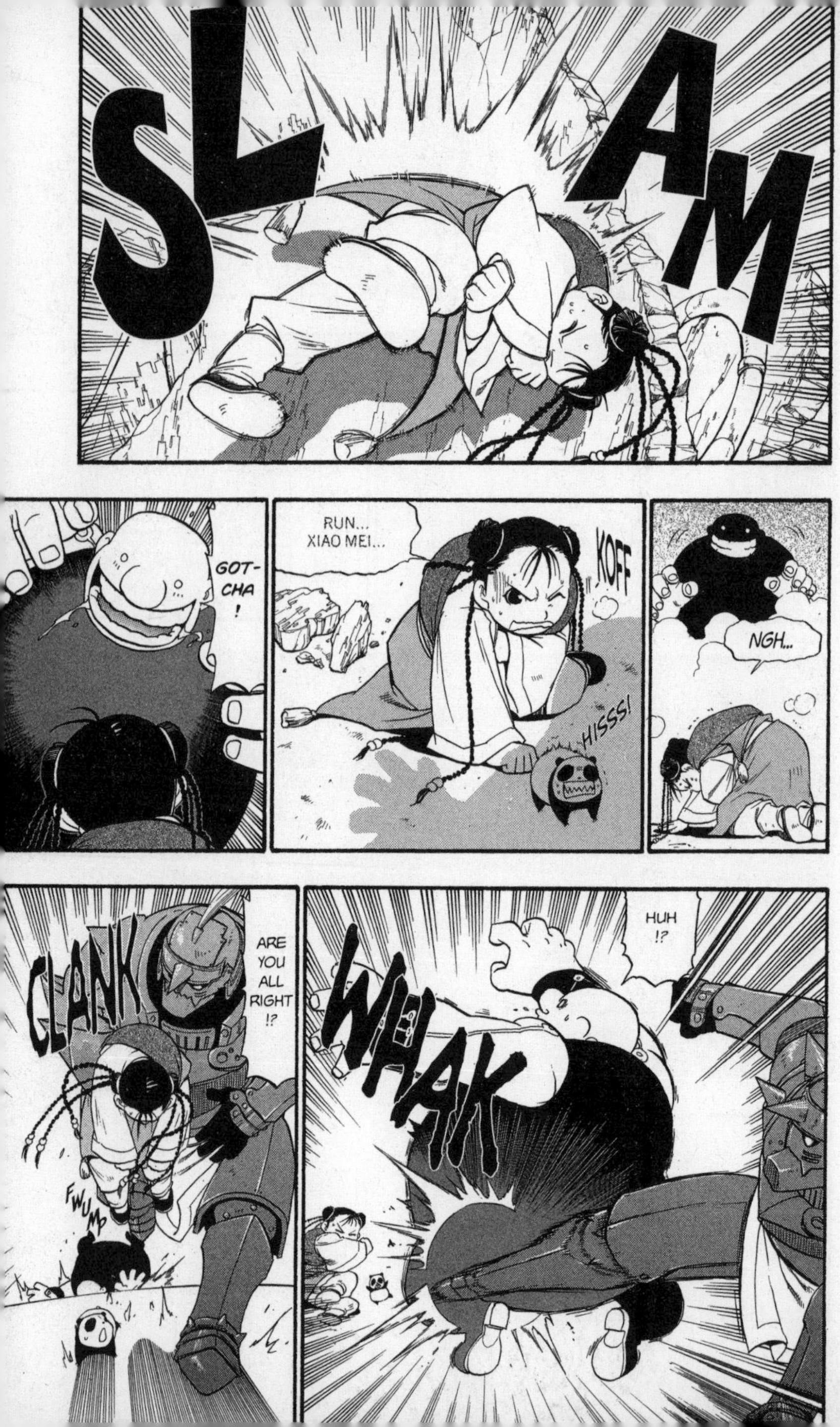
SLAM
NGH...
RUN... XIAO MEI...
KOFF
HISSS!
GOT-CHA!
HUH!?
WHAK
ARE YOU ALL RIGHT!?
CLANK
FWUMP

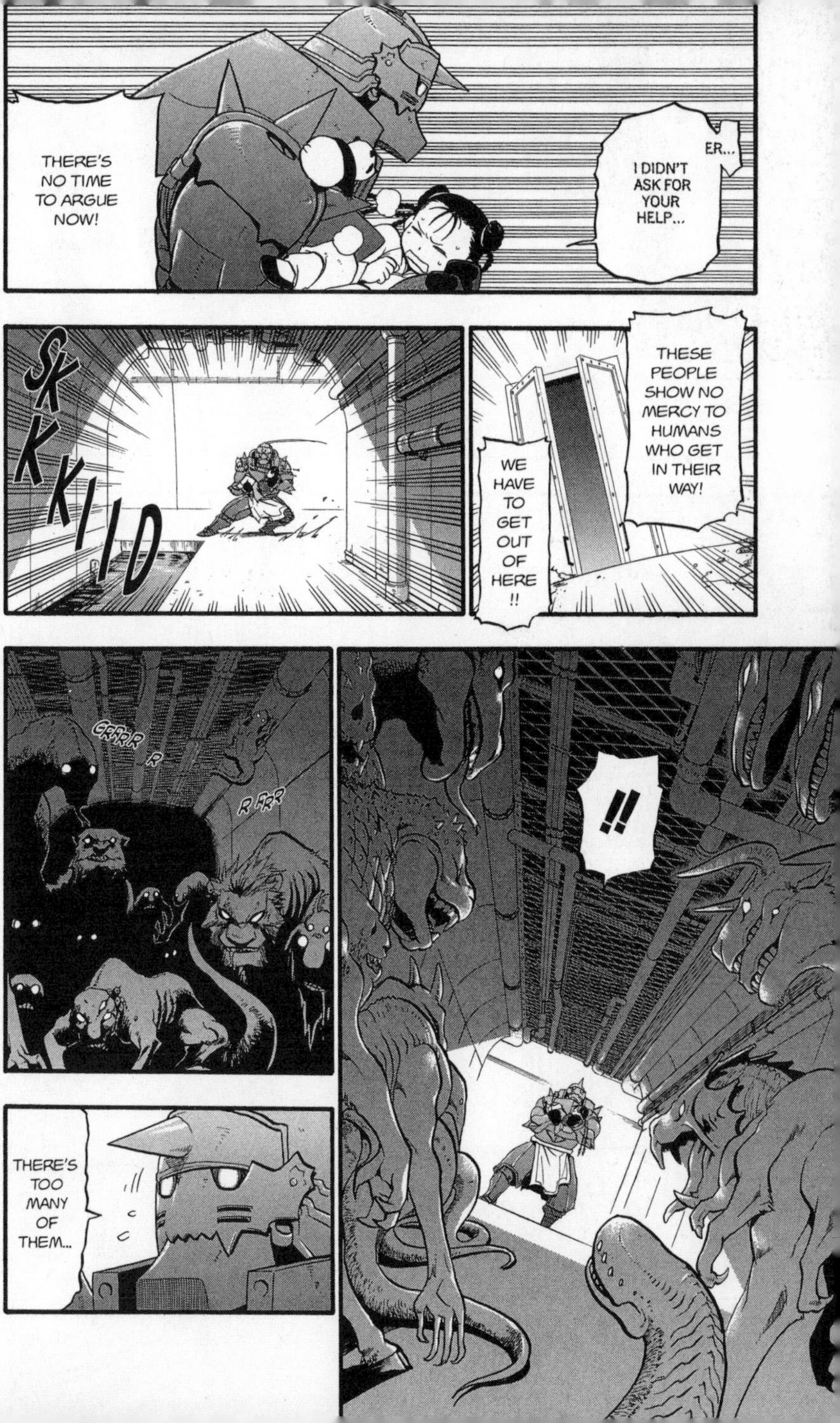
ER...
I DIDN'T ASK FOR YOUR HELP...
THERE'S NO TIME TO ARGUE NOW!
THESE PEOPLE SHOW NO MERCY TO HUMANS WHO GET IN THEIR WAY!
WE HAVE TO GET OUT OF HERE !!
SKKKIID
!!
GRRRR R
R RRR
THERE'S TOO MANY OF THEM...

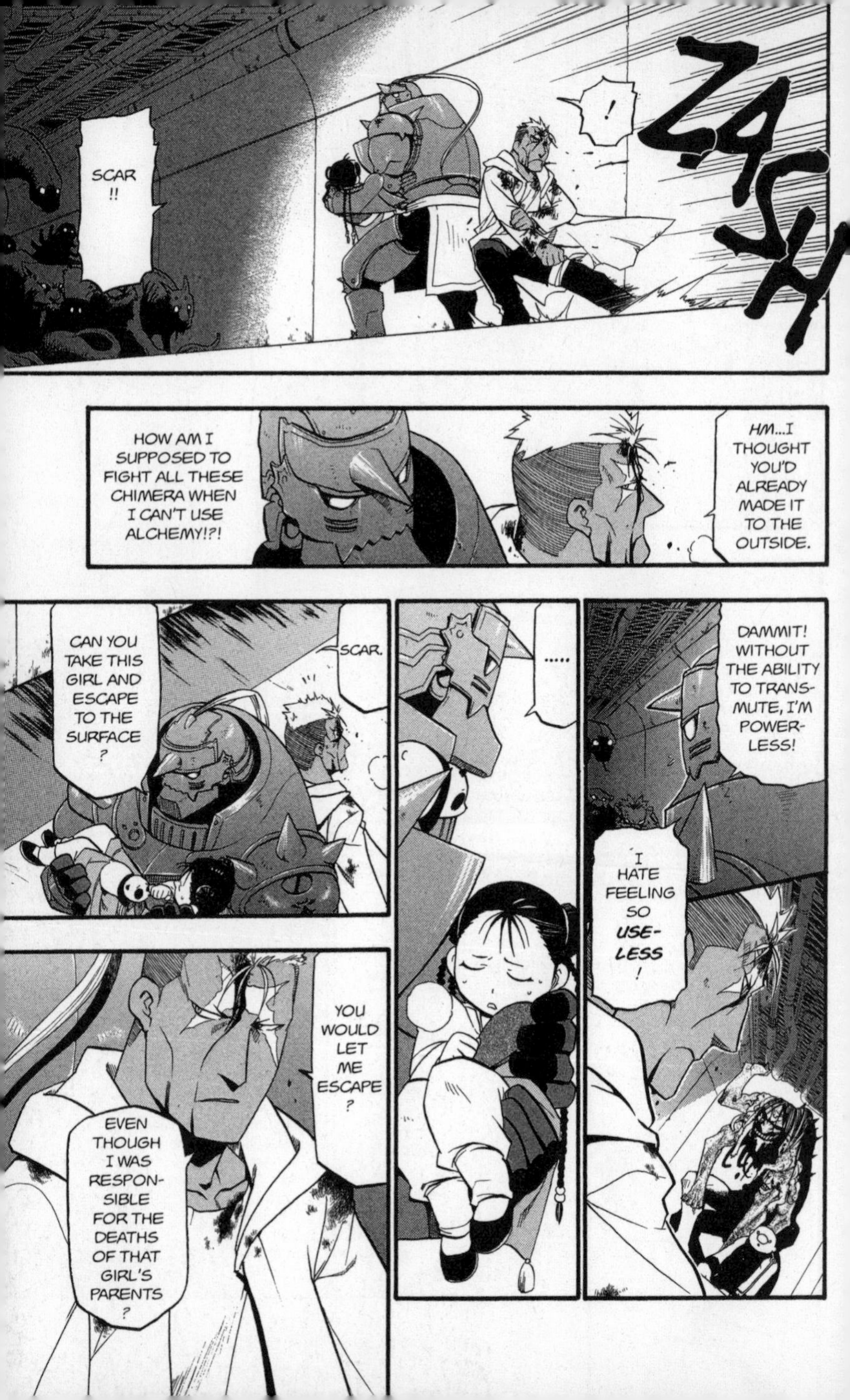
ZASH
!
SCAR !!
HM...I THOUGHT YOU'D ALREADY MADE IT TO THE OUTSIDE.
HOW AM I SUPPOSED TO FIGHT ALL THESE CHIMERA WHEN I CAN'T USE ALCHEMY!?!
DAMMIT! WITHOUT THE ABILITY TO TRANSMUTE, I'M POWERLESS!
I HATE FEELING SO *USELESS*!
.....
SCAR.
CAN YOU TAKE THIS GIRL AND ESCAPE TO THE SURFACE?
YOU WOULD LET ME ESCAPE?
EVEN THOUGH I WAS RESPONSIBLE FOR THE DEATHS OF THAT GIRL'S PARENTS?

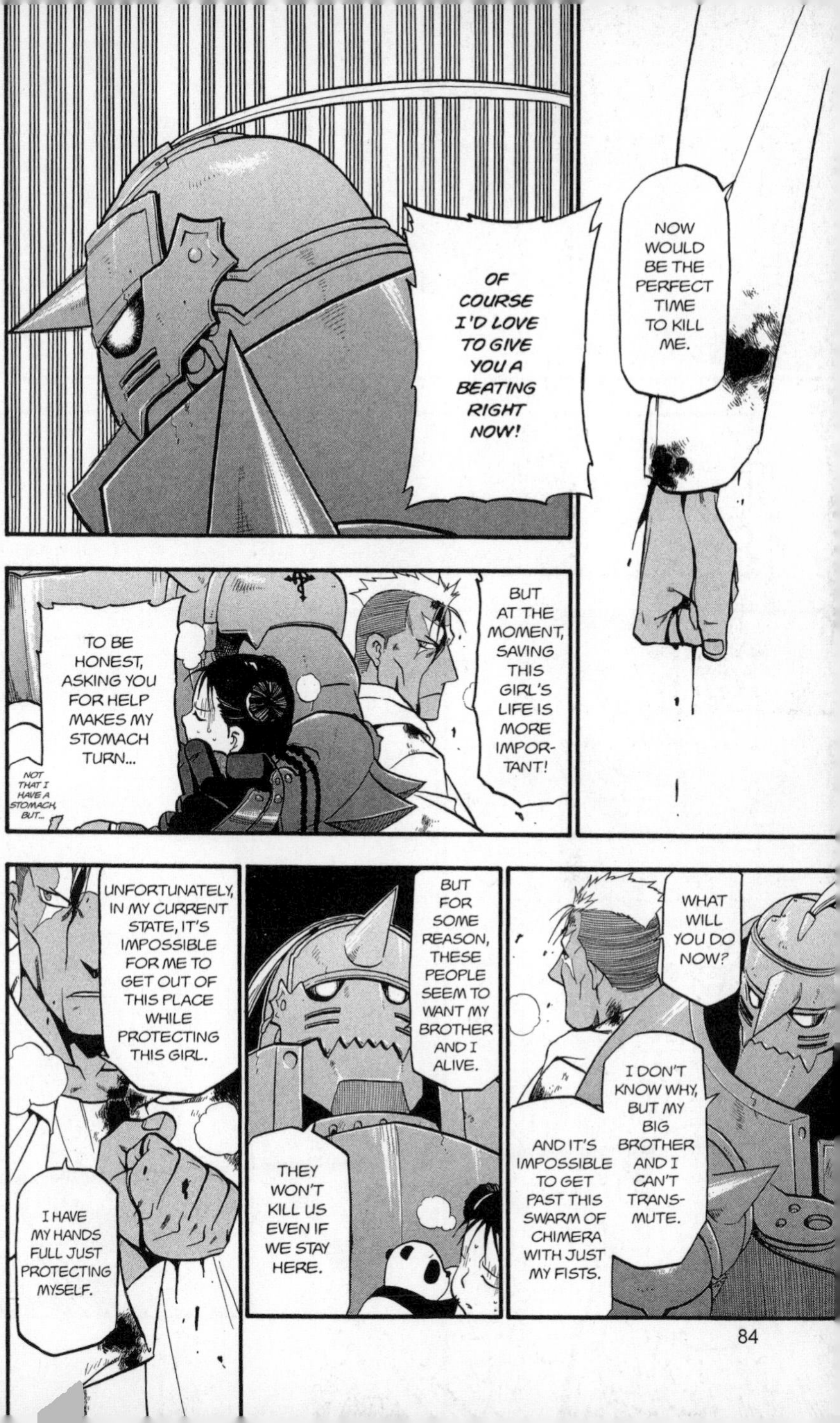
NOW WOULD BE THE PERFECT TIME TO KILL ME.
OF COURSE I'D LOVE TO GIVE YOU A BEATING RIGHT NOW!
BUT AT THE MOMENT, SAVING THIS GIRL'S LIFE IS MORE IMPOR-TANT!
TO BE HONEST, ASKING YOU FOR HELP MAKES MY STOMACH TURN...
NOT THAT I HAVE A STOMACH, BUT...
WHAT WILL YOU DO NOW?
I DON'T KNOW WHY, BUT MY BIG BROTHER AND I CAN'T TRANS-MUTE.
AND IT'S IMPOSSIBLE TO GET PAST THIS SWARM OF CHIMERA WITH JUST MY FISTS.
BUT FOR SOME REASON, THESE PEOPLE SEEM TO WANT MY BROTHER AND I ALIVE.
THEY WON'T KILL US EVEN IF WE STAY HERE.
UNFORTUNATELY, IN MY CURRENT STATE, IT'S IMPOSSIBLE FOR ME TO GET OUT OF THIS PLACE WHILE PROTECTING THIS GIRL.
I HAVE MY HANDS FULL JUST PROTECTING MYSELF.

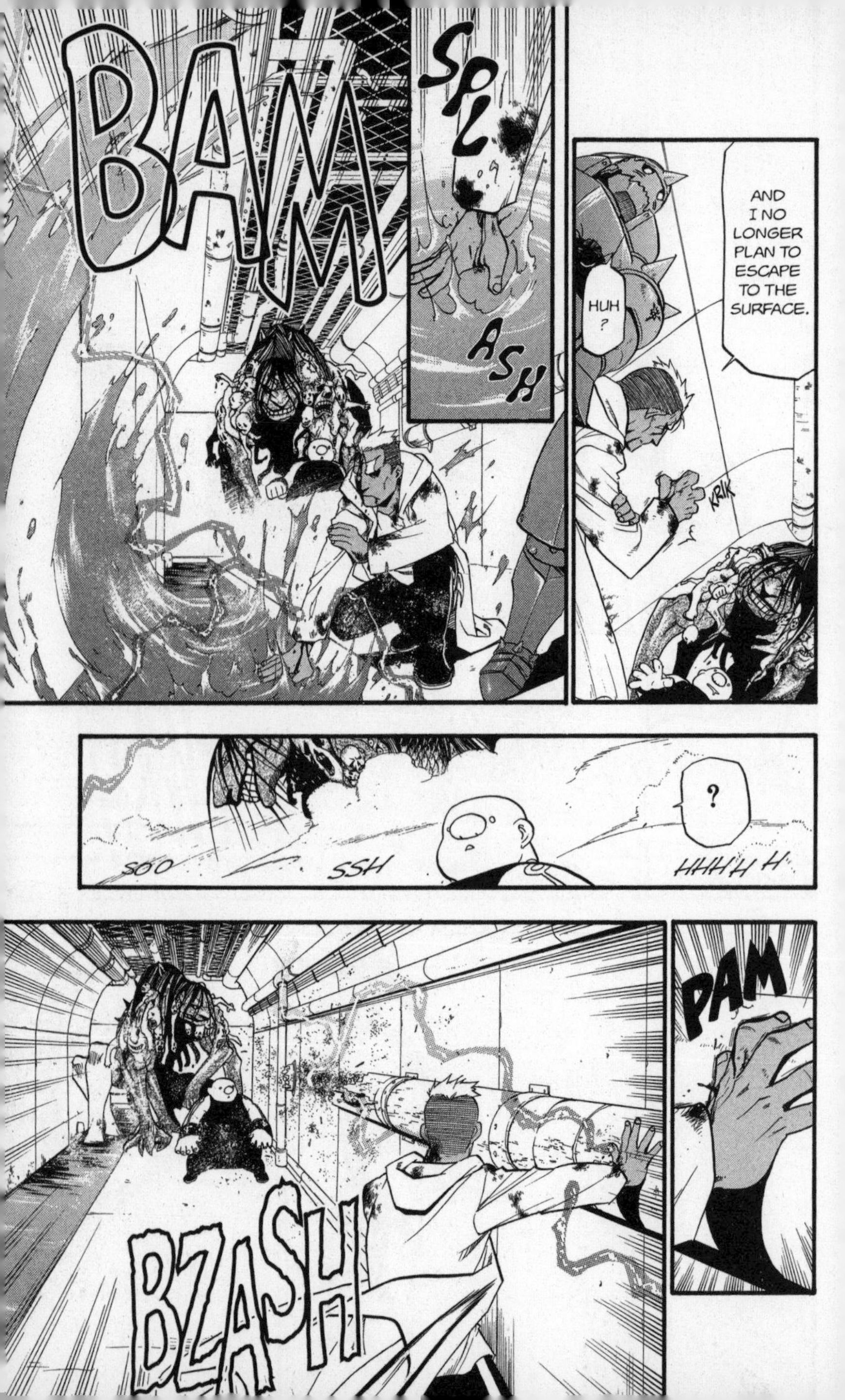
AND I NO LONGER PLAN TO ESCAPE TO THE SURFACE.
HUH?
KRIK
SPLASH
BAM
?
SOO
SSH
HHHH
PAM
BZASH

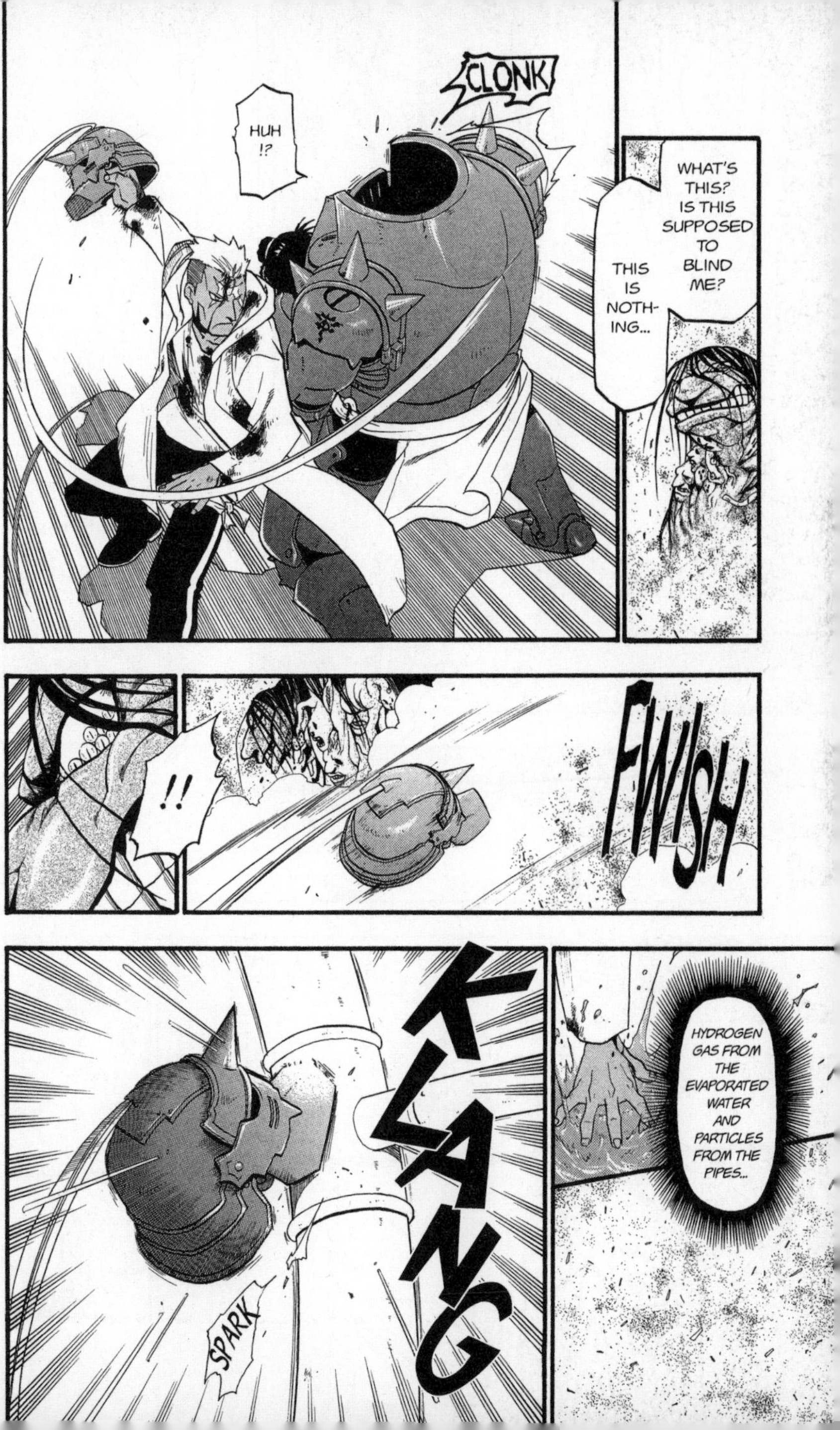
WHAT'S THIS? IS THIS SUPPOSED TO BLIND ME?
THIS IS NOTHING...
CLONK
HUH !?
FWISH
!!
HYDROGEN GAS FROM THE EVAPORATED WATER AND PARTICLES FROM THE PIPES...
KLANG
SPARK

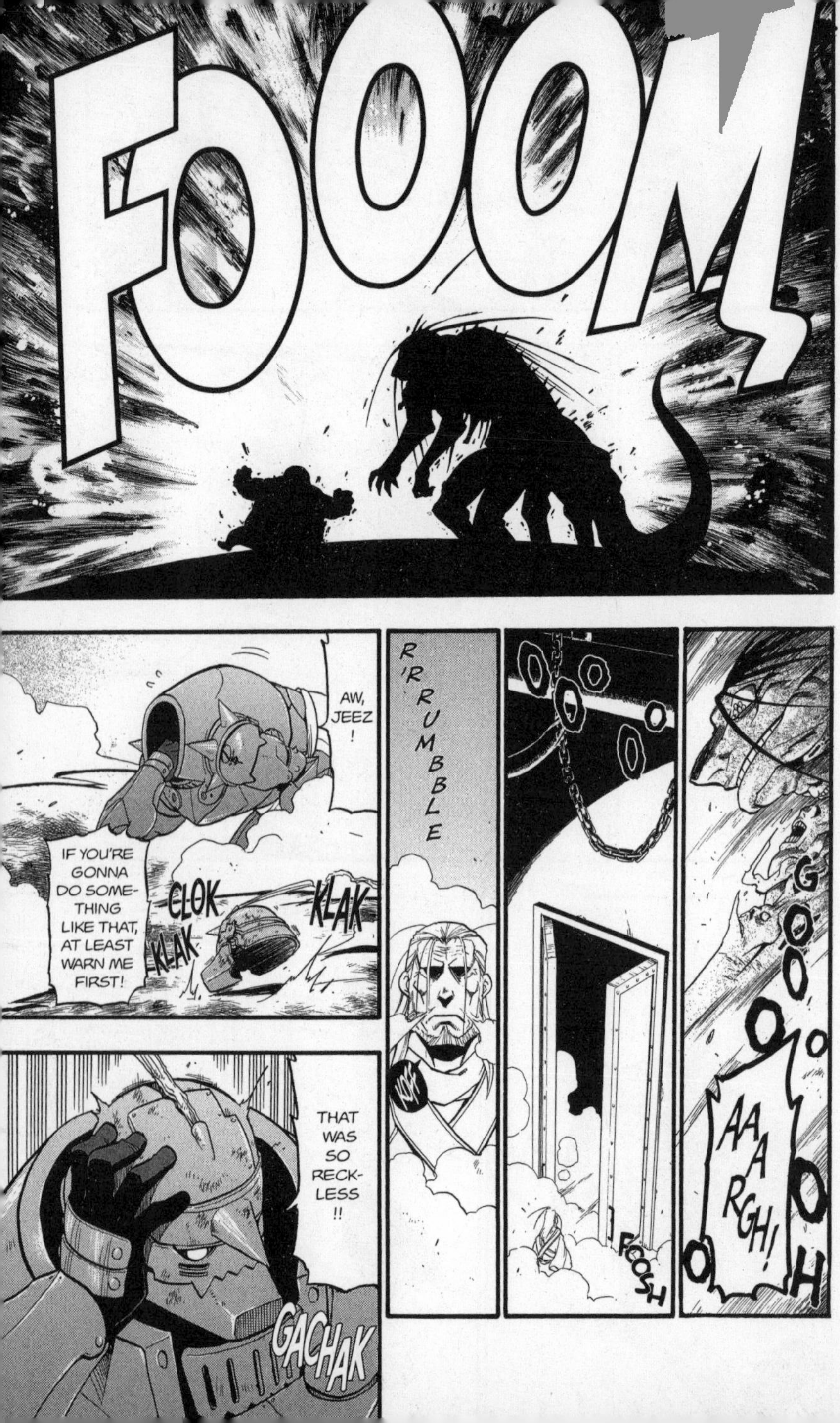
FOOOM!
GOOOOOOOH
AAARGH!
FOOSH
R'R'RUMBLE
AW, JEEZ!
IF YOU'RE GONNA DO SOME-THING LIKE THAT, AT LEAST WARN ME FIRST!
KLAK
CLOK
KLAK
THAT WAS SO RECK-LESS!!
GACHAK

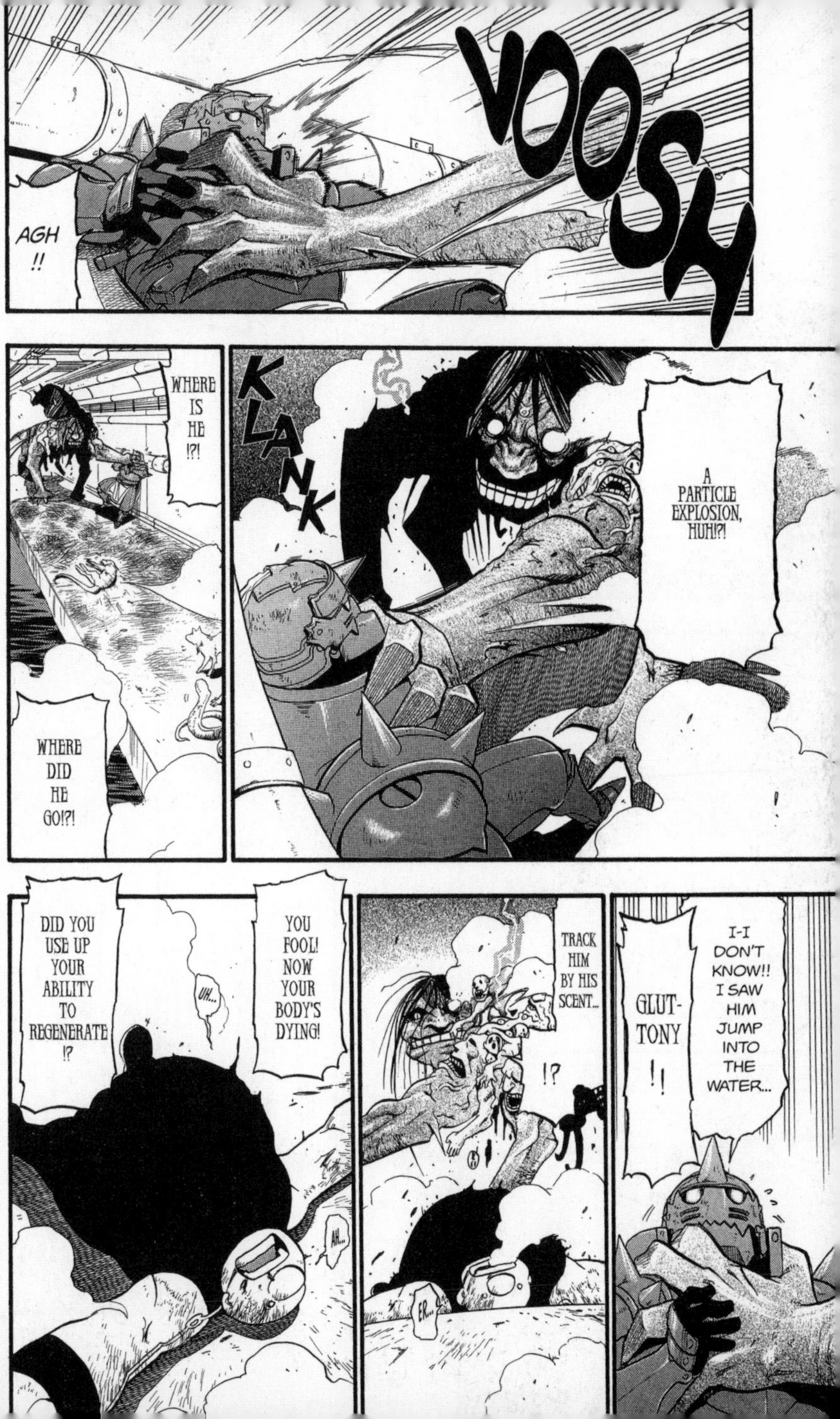
VOOSH
AGH!!
KLANK
A PARTICLE EXPLOSION, HUH!?!
WHERE IS HE !?!
WHERE DID HE GO!?!
I-I DON'T KNOW!! I SAW HIM JUMP INTO THE WATER...
GLUT-TONY!!
TRACK HIM BY HIS SCENT...
!?
ER...
YOU FOOL! NOW YOUR BODY'S DYING!
DID YOU USE UP YOUR ABILITY TO REGENERATE!?
UH...
AH...

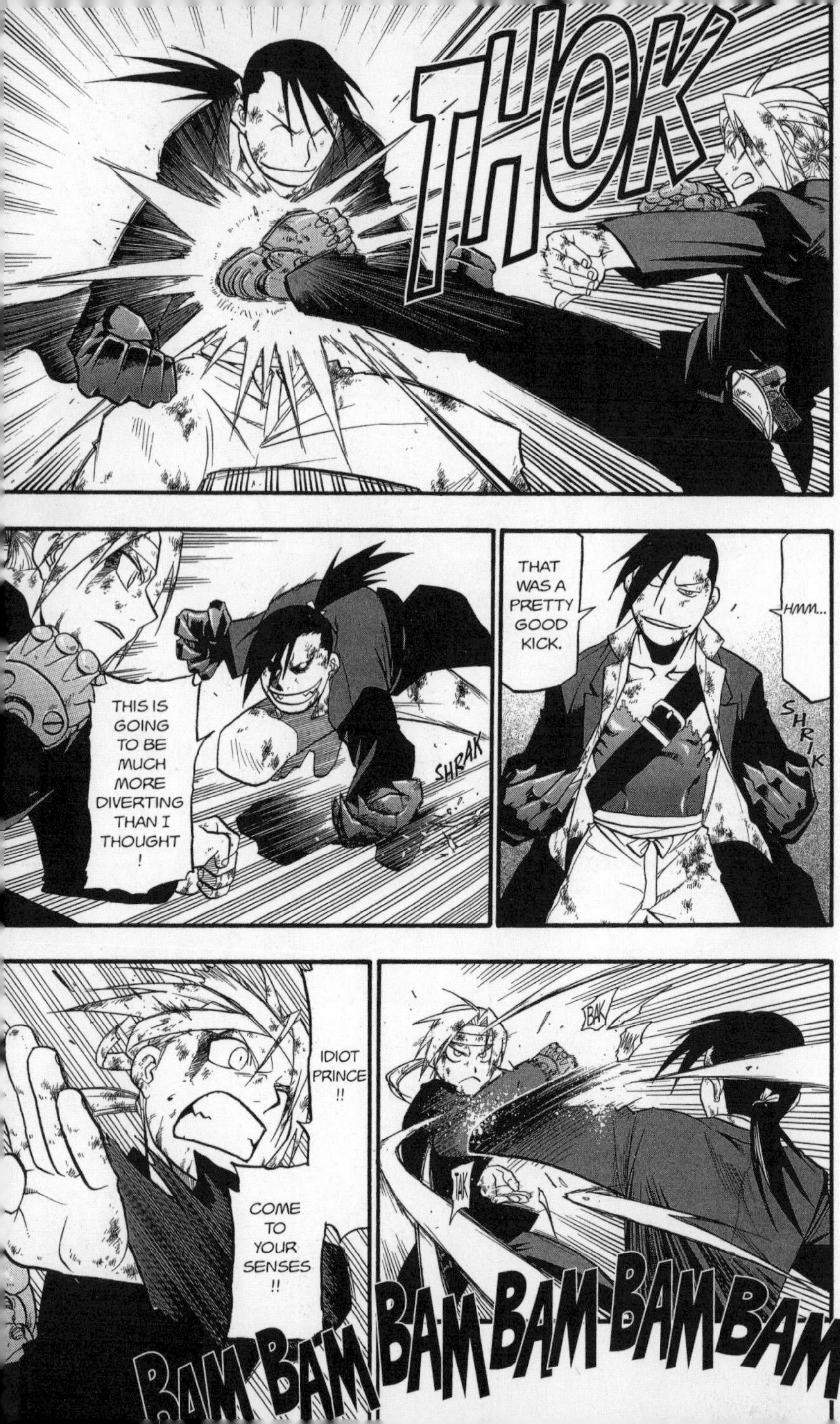
THOK
HMM...
SHRIK
THAT WAS A PRETTY GOOD KICK.
SHRAK
THIS IS GOING TO BE MUCH MORE DIVERTING THAN I THOUGHT!
BAK
TAK
IDIOT PRINCE!!
COME TO YOUR SENSES!!
BAM BAM BAM BAM BAM BAM

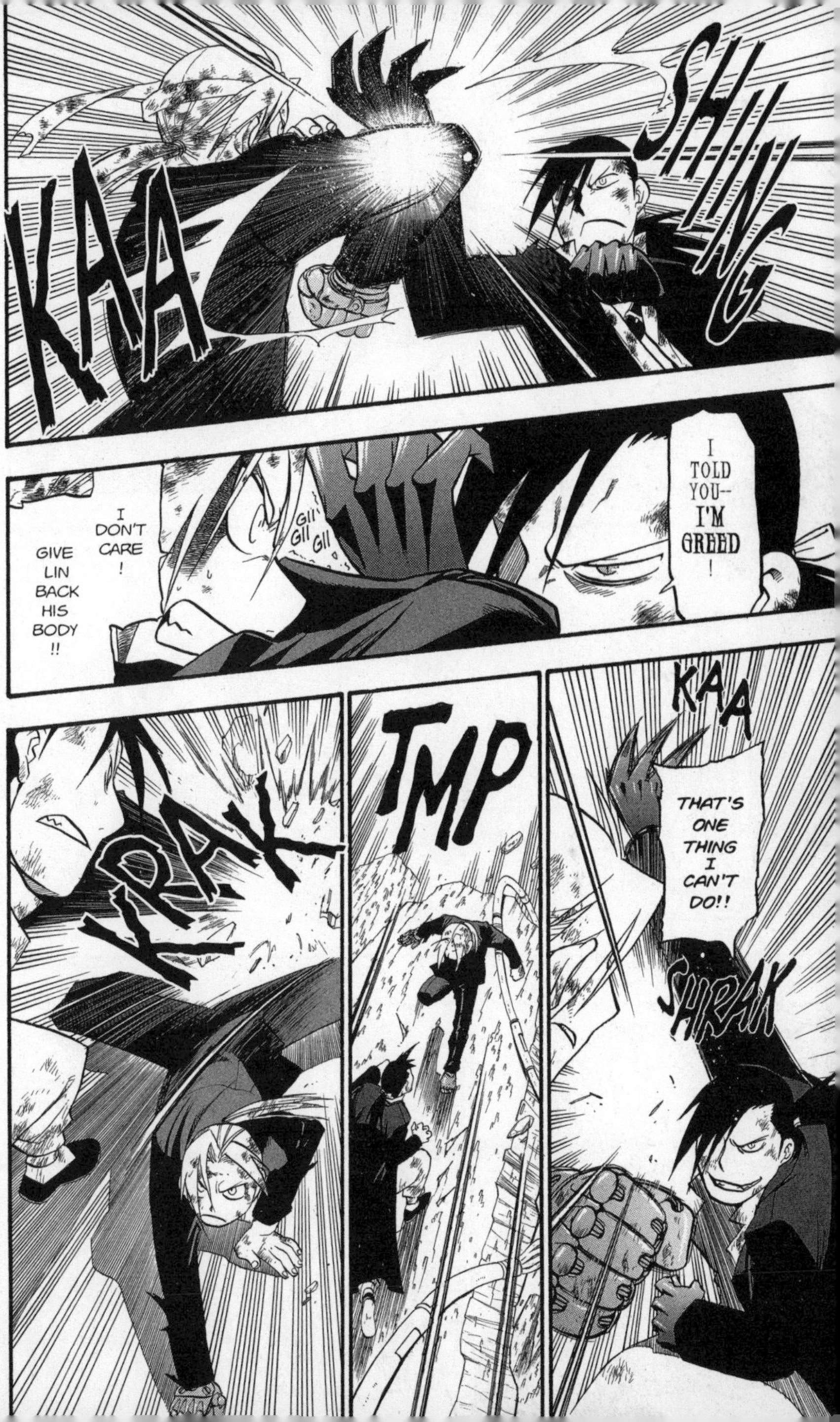
SHING
KAA
I TOLD YOU-- I'M GREED!
GII GII GII
I DON'T CARE!
GIVE LIN BACK HIS BODY!!
KAA
THAT'S ONE THING I CAN'T DO!!
SHRAK
TMP
KRAK

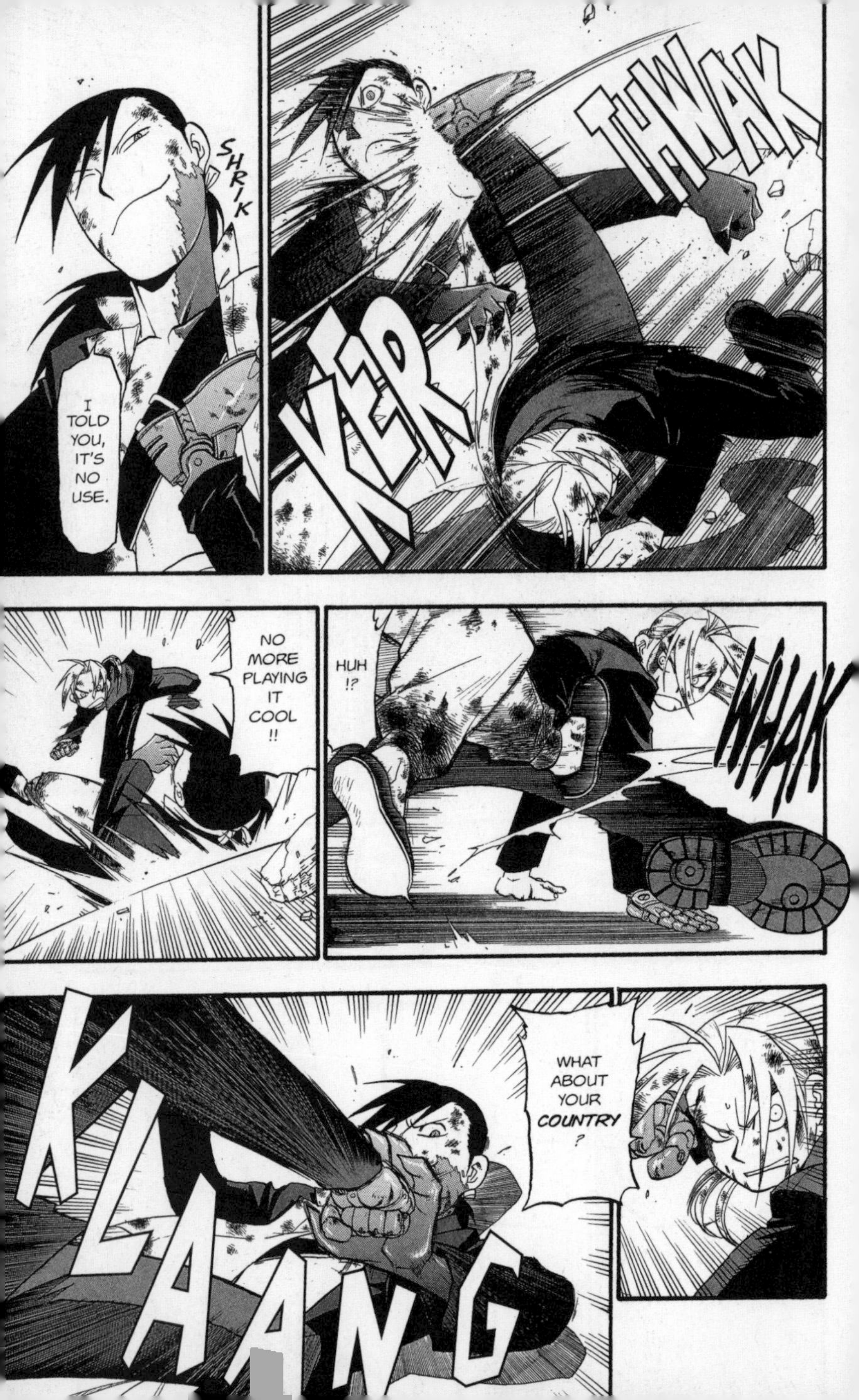
THWAK
KZR
SHRIK
I TOLD YOU, IT'S NO USE.
HUH !?
WHAK
NO MORE PLAYING IT COOL !!
WHAT ABOUT YOUR COUNTRY ?
KLAANG

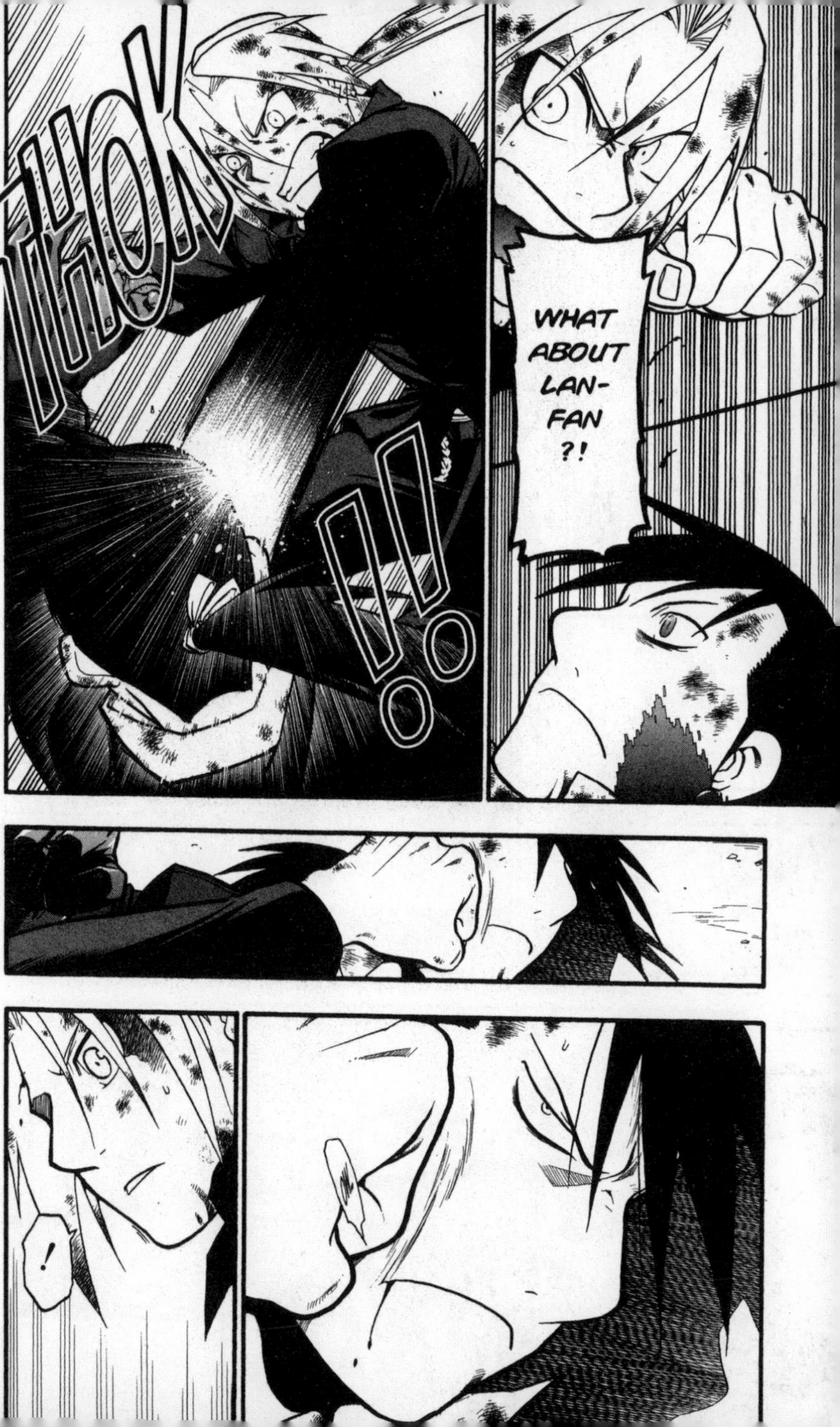
WHAT ABOUT LAN-FAN?!
THOK
!!
!

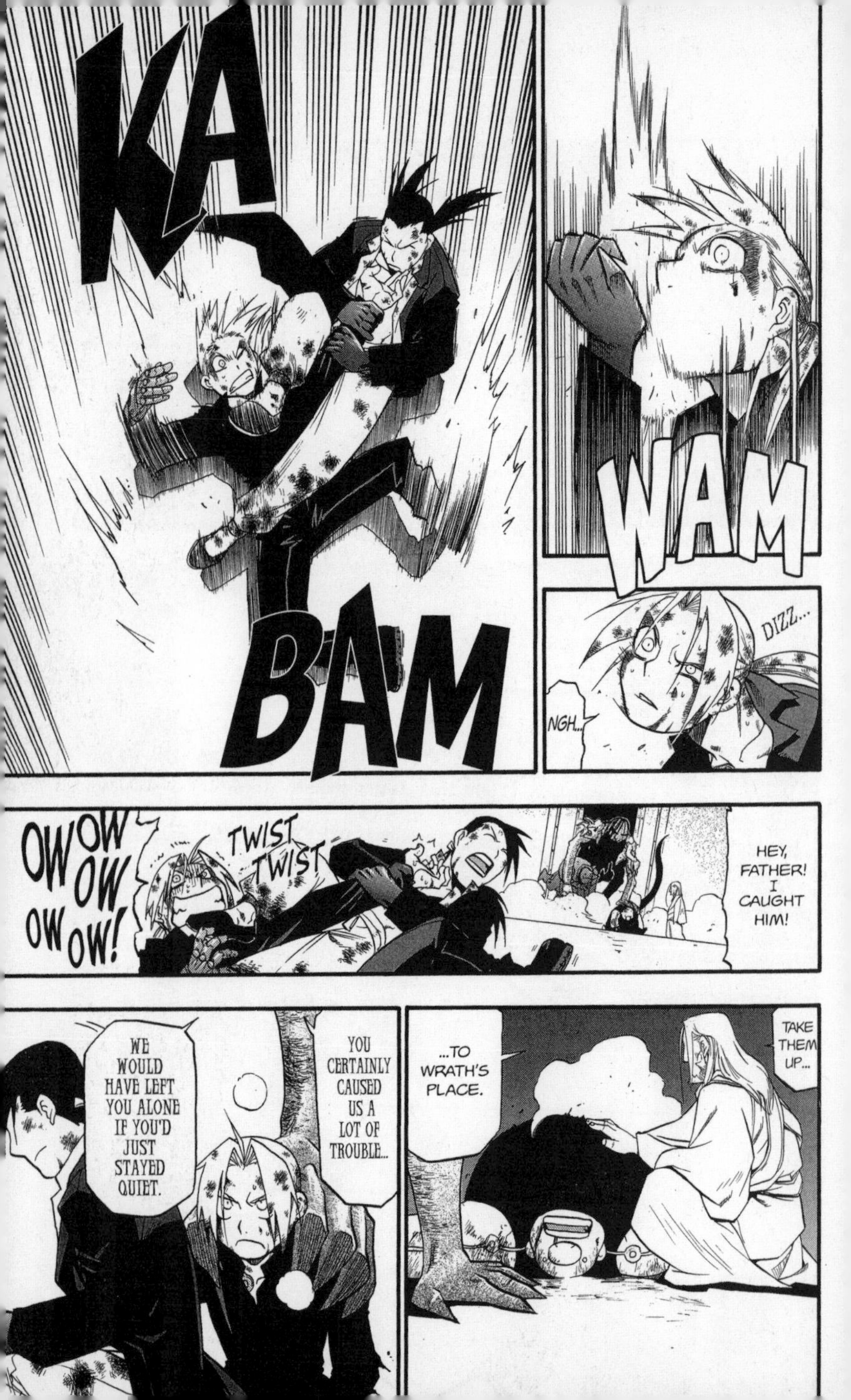
WAM
DIZZ...
NGH...
KA
BAM
HEY, FATHER! I CAUGHT HIM!
TWIST TWIST
OW OW OW OW OW OW!
TAKE THEM UP...
...TO WRATH'S PLACE.
YOU CERTAINLY CAUSED US A LOT OF TROUBLE...
WE WOULD HAVE LEFT YOU ALONE IF YOU'D JUST STAYED QUIET.

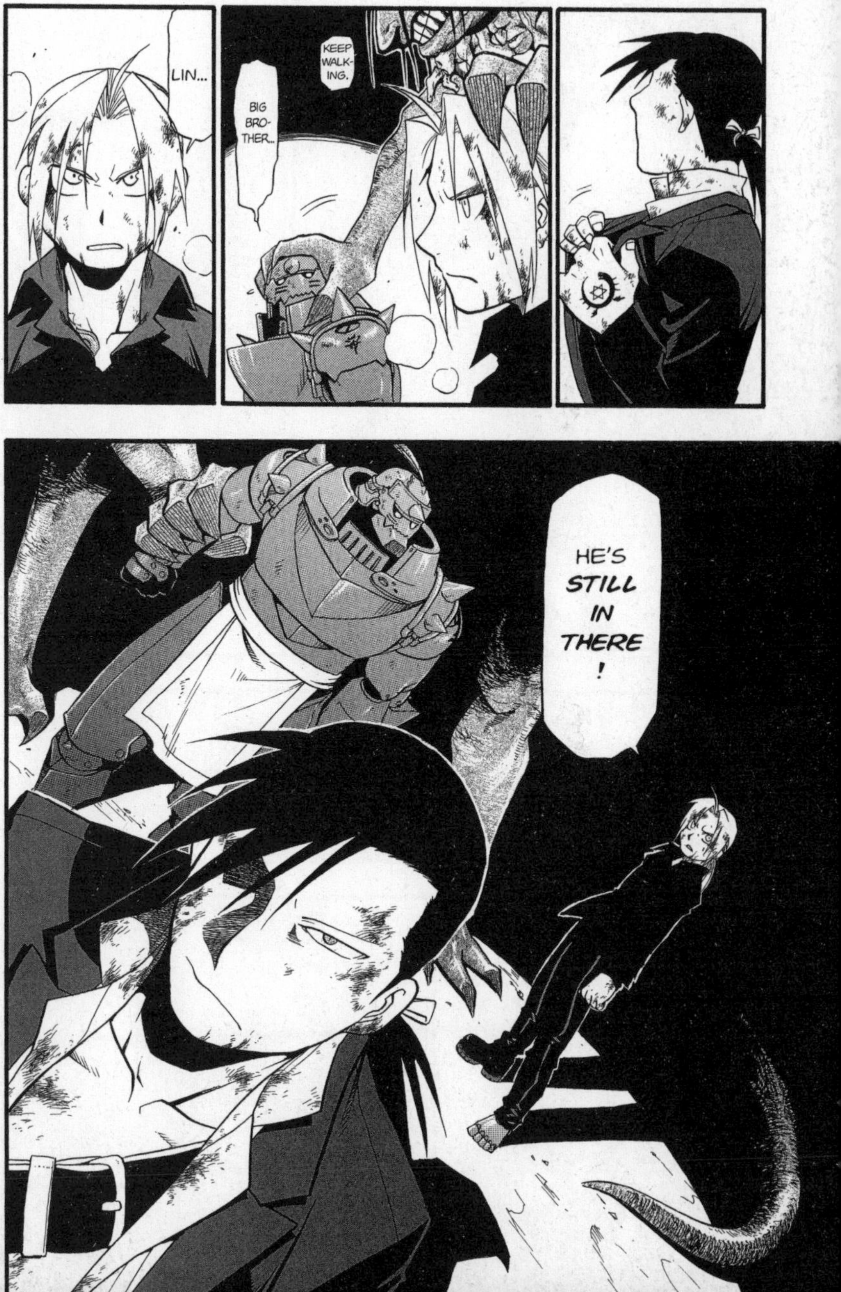
KEEP WALKING.
BIG BROTHER...
LIN...
HE'S STILL IN THERE!

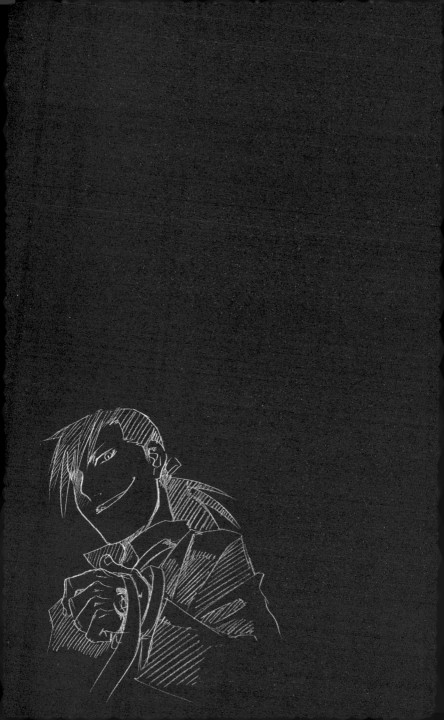

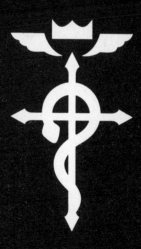

FULLMETAL
ALCHEMIST

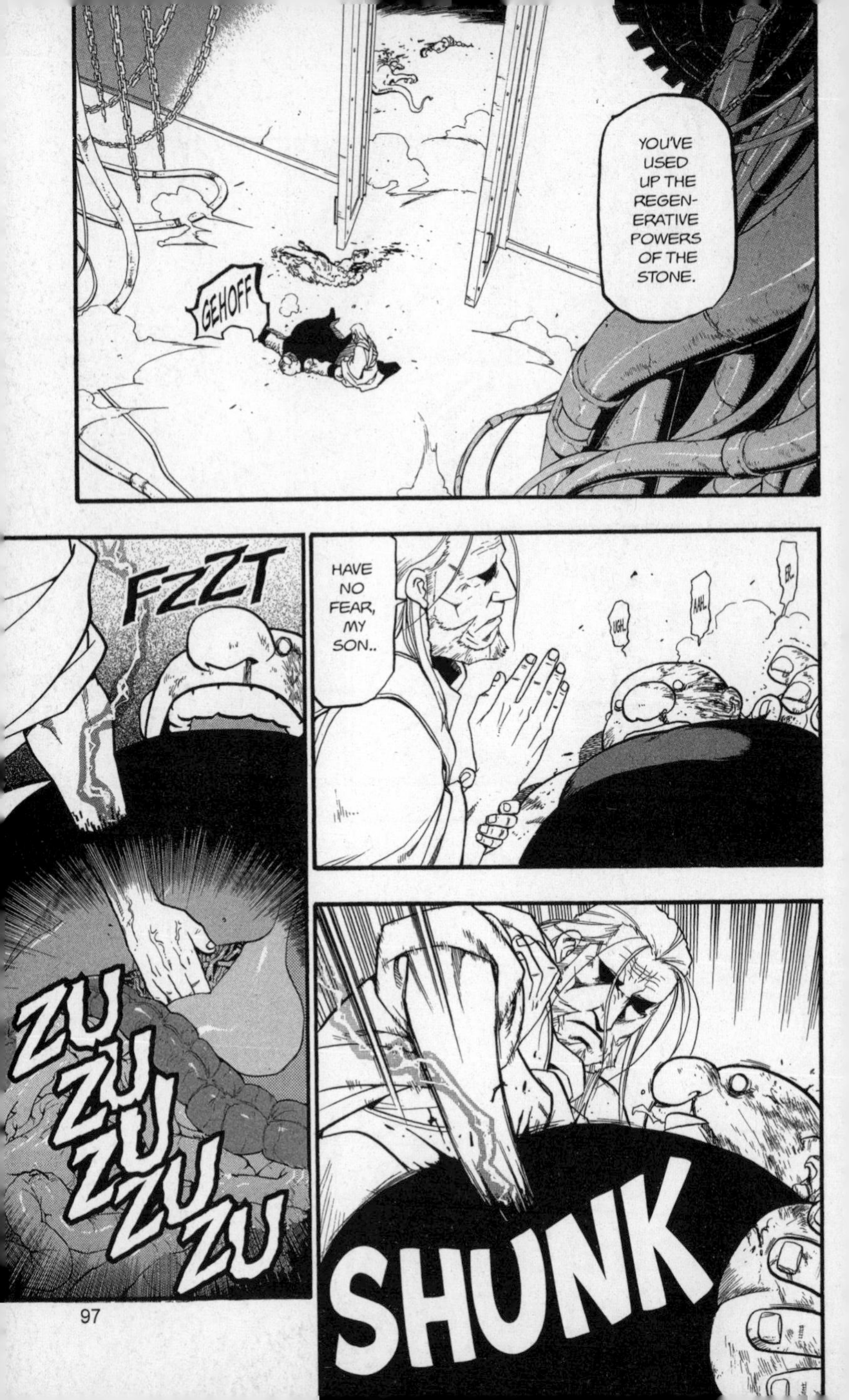
YOU'VE USED UP THE REGEN-ERATIVE POWERS OF THE STONE.
GEHOFF
ER..
AAH..
UGH..
HAVE NO FEAR, MY SON..
SHUNK
FZZT
ZUZUZUZUZUZUZU

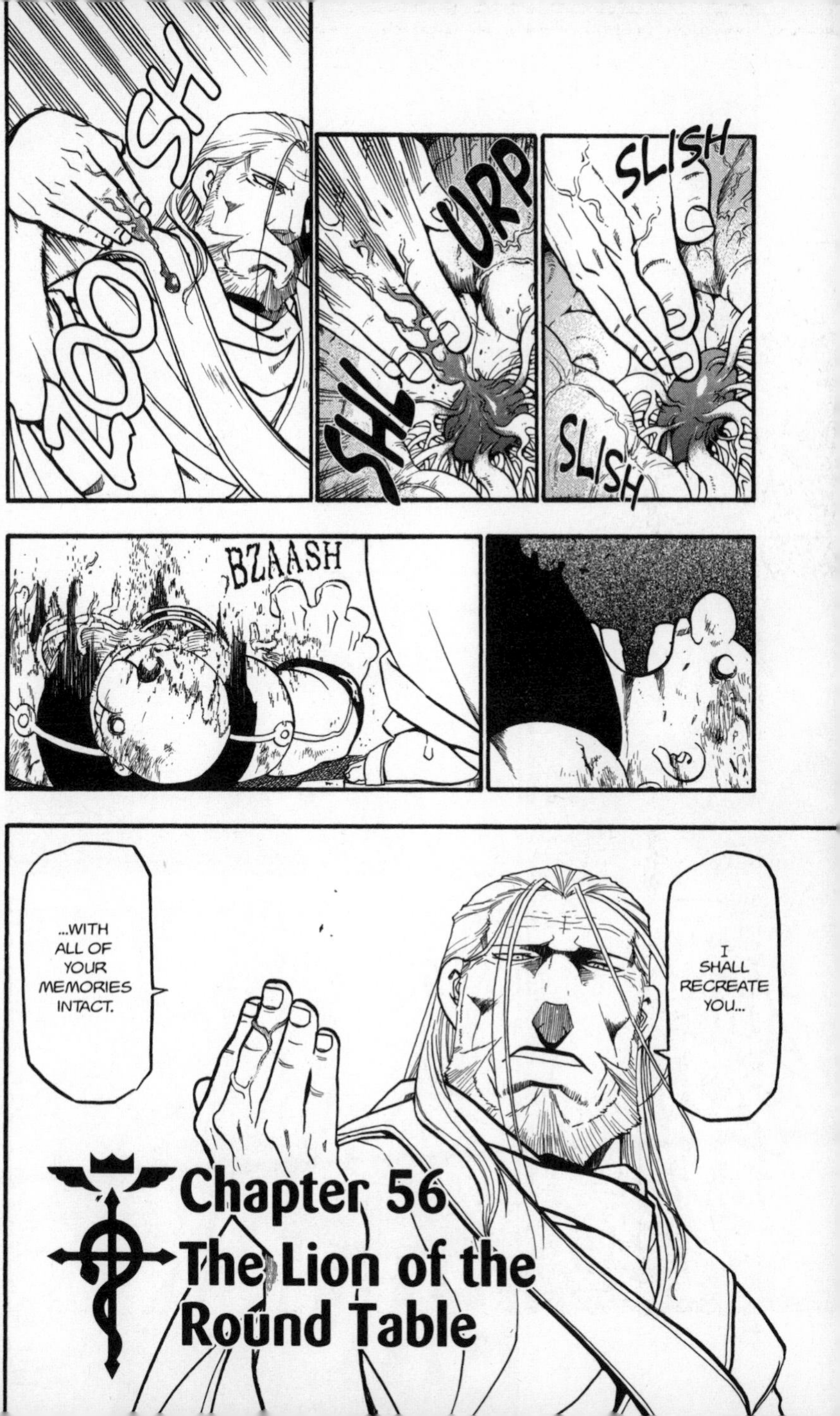
SLISH
SLISH
SHL
URP
ZOOSH
BZAASH
I SHALL RECREATE YOU...
...WITH ALL OF YOUR MEMORIES INTACT.
Chapter 56
The Lion of the Round Table

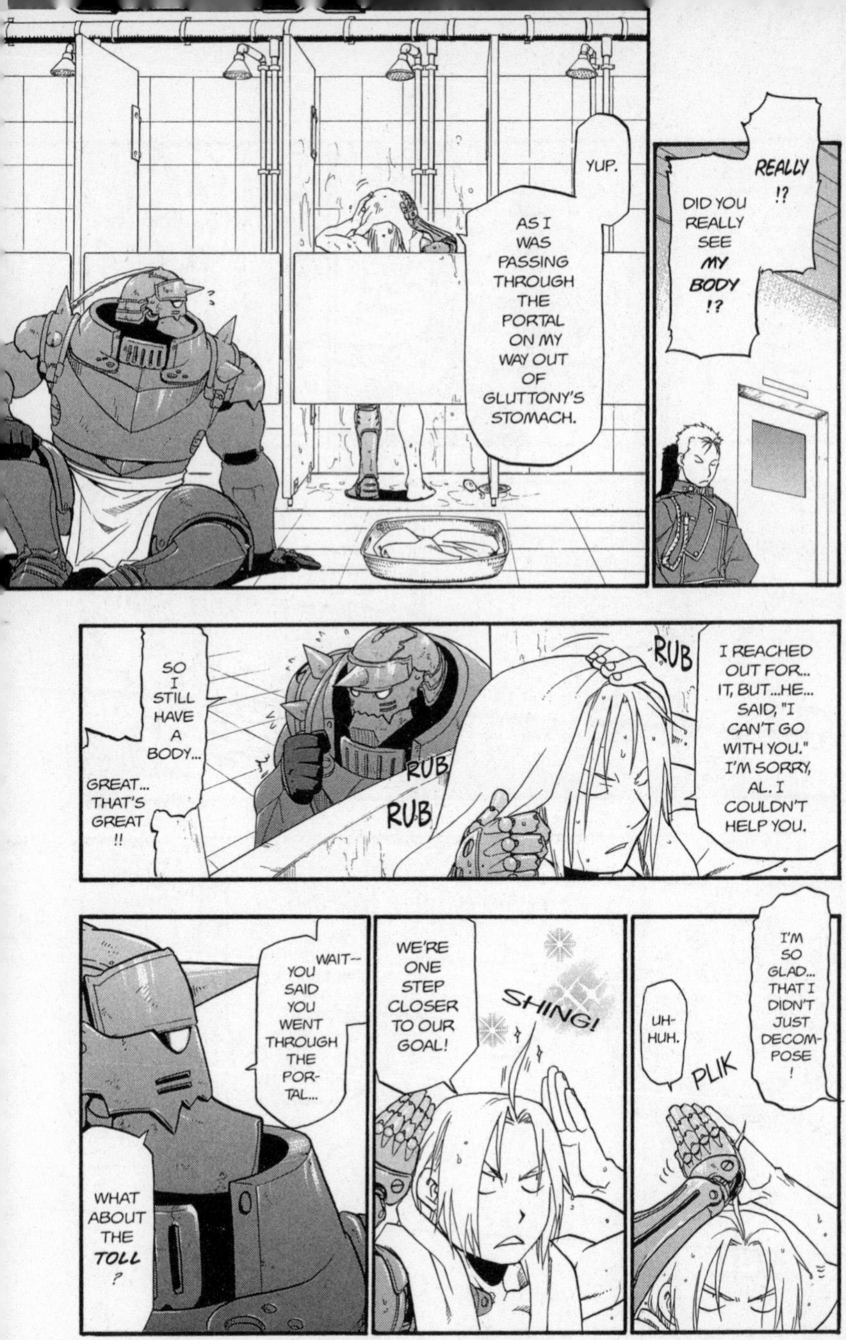

REALLY!? DID YOU REALLY SEE *MY BODY*!?
YUP.
AS I WAS PASSING THROUGH THE PORTAL ON MY WAY OUT OF GLUTTONY'S STOMACH.
RUB
I REACHED OUT FOR... IT, BUT...HE... SAID, "I CAN'T GO WITH YOU." I'M SORRY, AL. I COULDN'T HELP YOU.
RUB
RUB
SO I STILL HAVE A BODY...
GREAT... THAT'S GREAT!!
I'M SO GLAD... THAT I DIDN'T JUST DECOMPOSE!
UH-HUH.
PLIK
SHING!
WE'RE ONE STEP CLOSER TO OUR GOAL!
WAIT-- YOU SAID YOU WENT THROUGH THE PORTAL...
WHAT ABOUT THE *TOLL*?

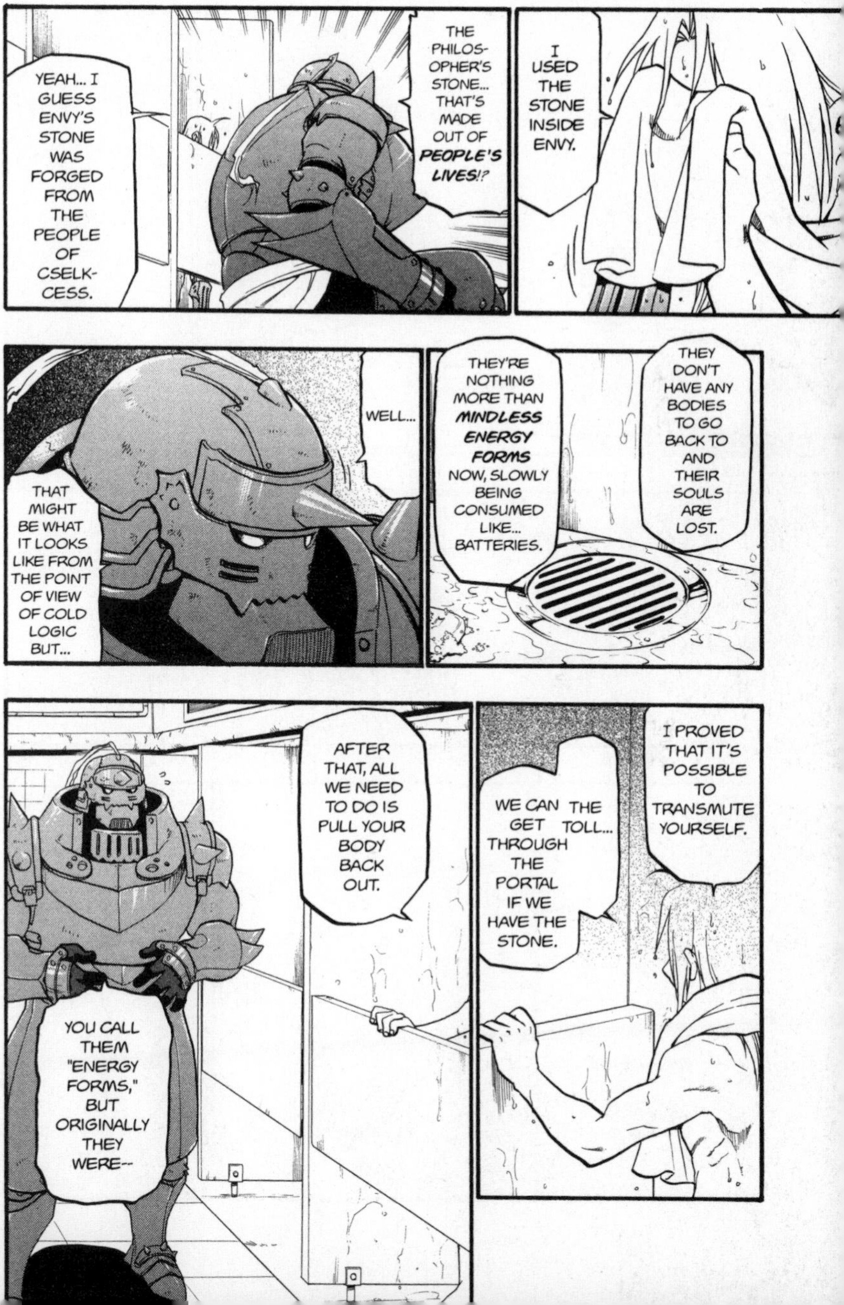
I USED THE STONE INSIDE ENVY.
THE PHILOSOPHER'S STONE... THAT'S MADE OUT OF **PEOPLE'S LIVES!?**
YEAH... I GUESS ENVY'S STONE WAS FORGED FROM THE PEOPLE OF CSELKCESS.
THEY DON'T HAVE ANY BODIES TO GO BACK TO AND THEIR SOULS ARE LOST.
THEY'RE NOTHING MORE THAN **MINDLESS ENERGY FORMS** NOW, SLOWLY BEING CONSUMED LIKE... BATTERIES.
WELL...
THAT MIGHT BE WHAT IT LOOKS LIKE FROM THE POINT OF VIEW OF COLD LOGIC BUT...
I PROVED THAT IT'S POSSIBLE TO TRANSMUTE YOURSELF.
THE TOLL... WE CAN GET THROUGH THE PORTAL IF WE HAVE THE STONE.
AFTER THAT, ALL WE NEED TO DO IS PULL YOUR BODY BACK OUT.
YOU CALL THEM "ENERGY FORMS," BUT ORIGINALLY THEY WERE--

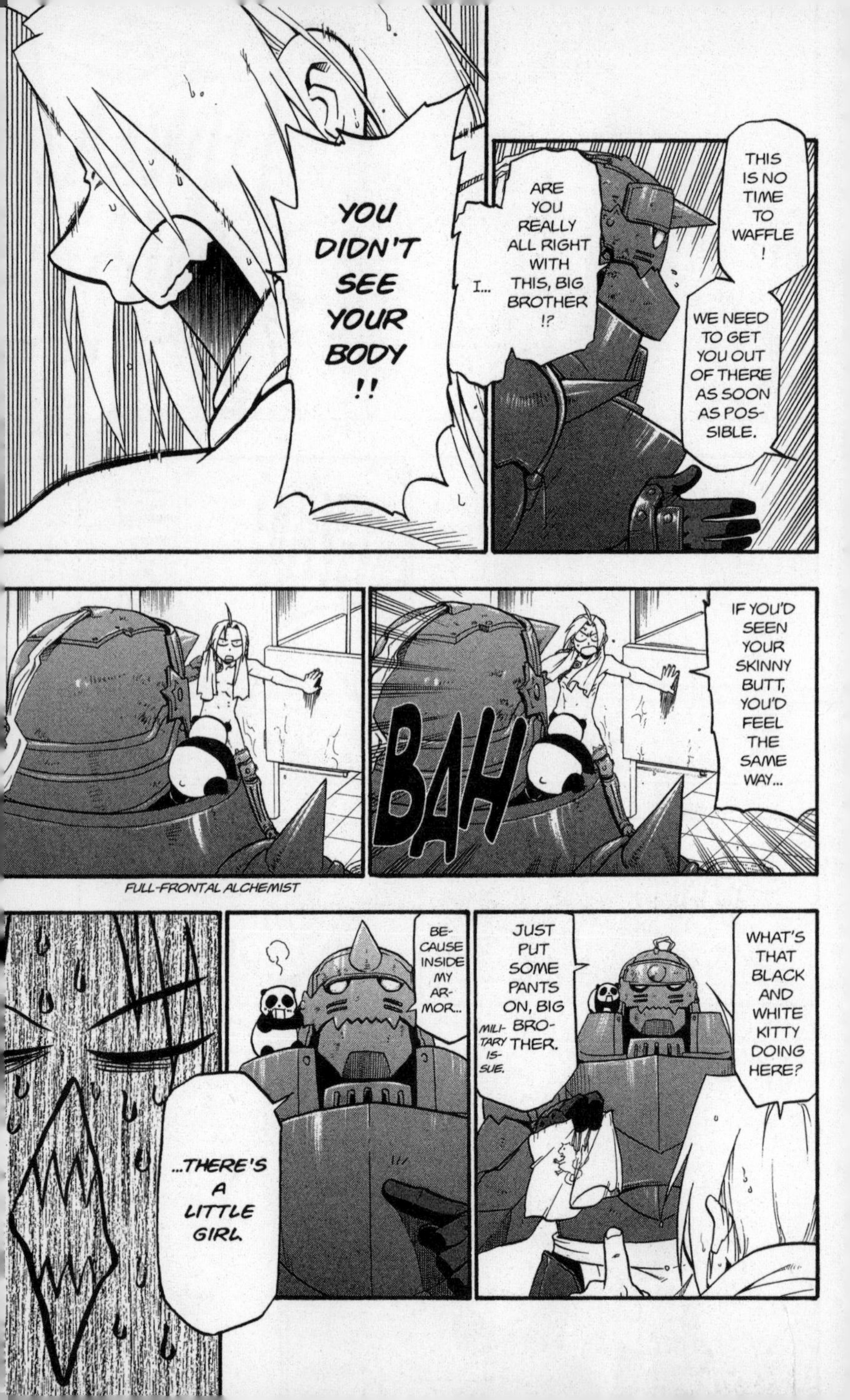
THIS IS NO TIME TO WAFFLE!
WE NEED TO GET YOU OUT OF THERE AS SOON AS POSSIBLE.
ARE YOU REALLY ALL RIGHT WITH THIS, BIG BROTHER!?
I...
YOU DIDN'T SEE YOUR BODY!!
IF YOU'D SEEN YOUR SKINNY BUTT, YOU'D FEEL THE SAME WAY...
BAH
FULL-FRONTAL ALCHEMIST
WHAT'S THAT BLACK AND WHITE KITTY DOING HERE?
JUST PUT SOME PANTS ON, BIG BROTHER.
MILITARY ISSUE.
BECAUSE INSIDE MY ARMOR...
...THERE'S A LITTLE GIRL.

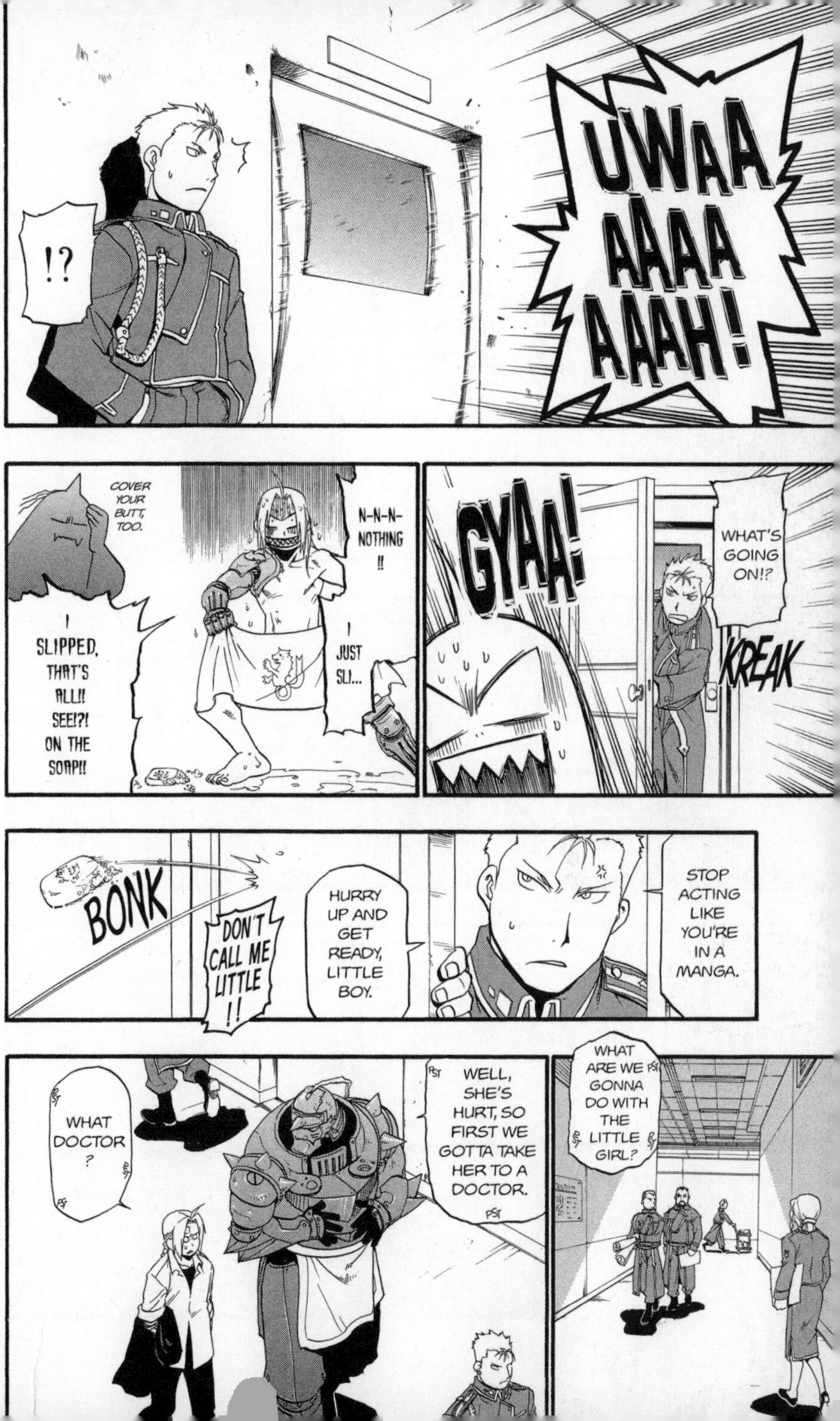
UWAAAAAAAAAH!
!?
WHAT'S GOING ON!?
KREAK
GYAA!
N-N-N-NOTHING!!
COVER YOUR BUTT, TOO.
I JUST SLI...
I SLIPPED, THAT'S ALL!! SEE!?! ON THE SOAP!!
STOP ACTING LIKE YOU'RE IN A MANGA.
HURRY UP AND GET READY, LITTLE BOY.
DON'T CALL ME LITTLE!!
BONK
WHAT ARE WE GONNA DO WITH THE LITTLE GIRL?
WELL, SHE'S HURT, SO FIRST WE GOTTA TAKE HER TO A DOCTOR.
WHAT DOCTOR?

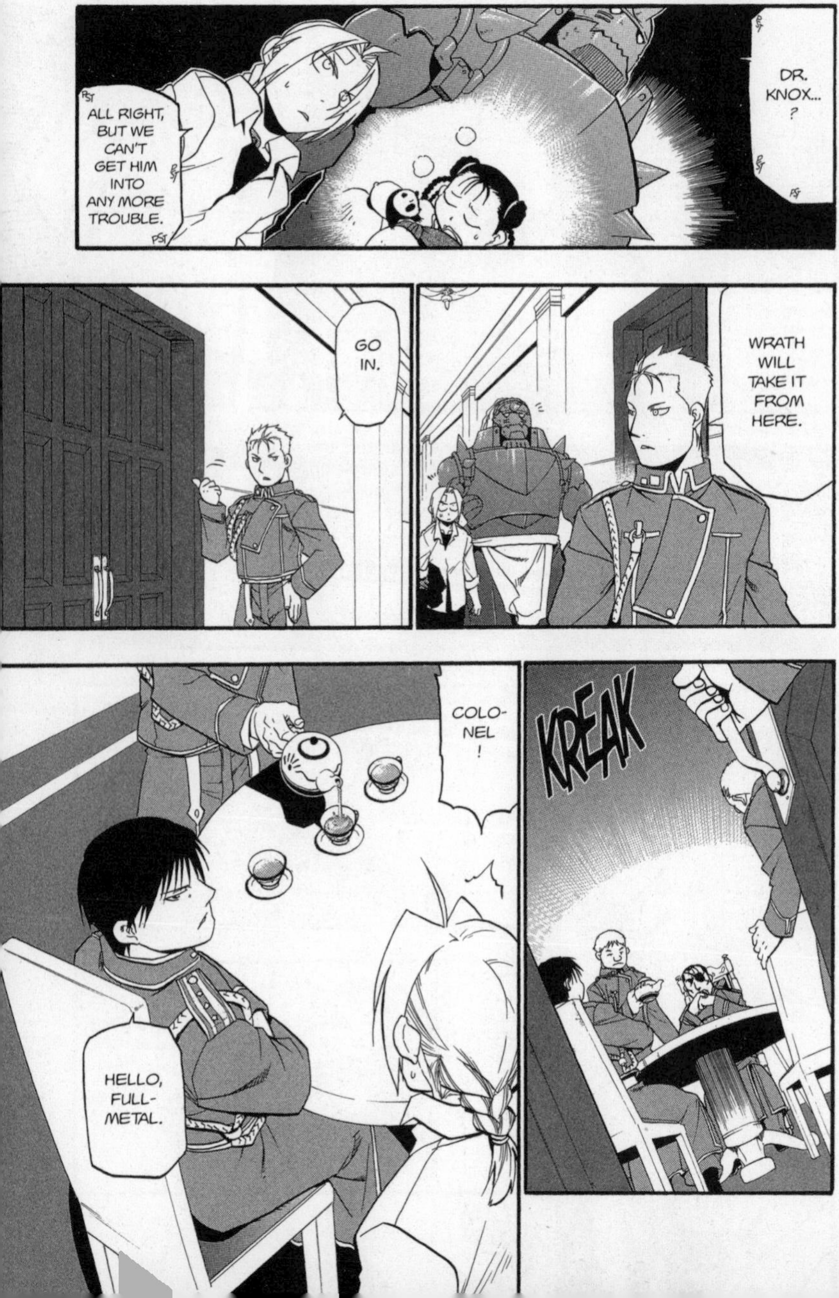
PST
DR. KNOX...?
PST
PST
PST
ALL RIGHT, BUT WE CAN'T GET HIM INTO ANY MORE TROUBLE.
PST
PST
WRATH WILL TAKE IT FROM HERE.
GO IN.
KREAK
COLO-NEL!
HELLO, FULL-METAL.

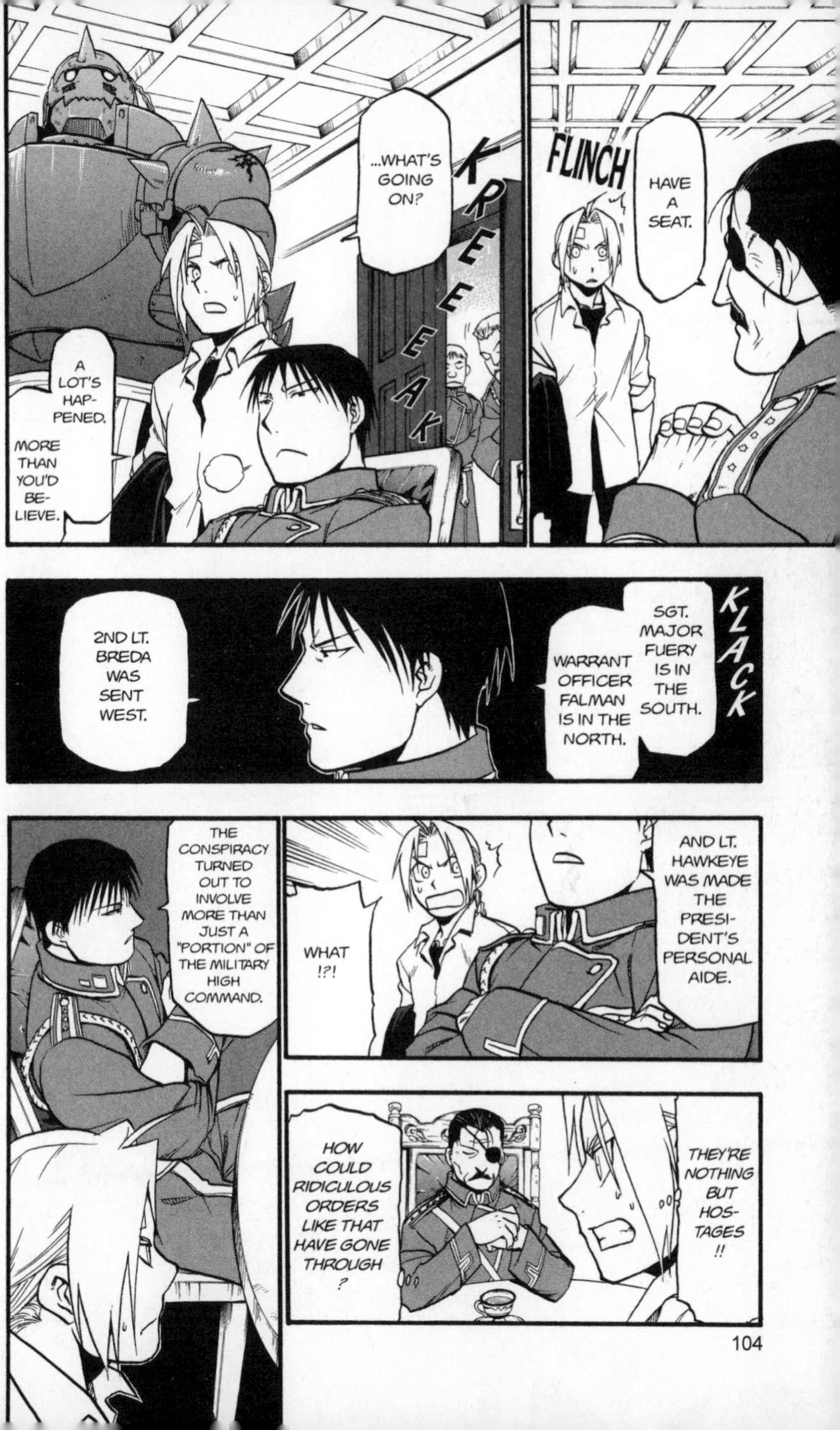
FLINCH
HAVE A SEAT.
KREEEEAK
...WHAT'S GOING ON?
A LOT'S HAPPENED.
MORE THAN YOU'D BELIEVE.
KLACK
SGT. MAJOR FUERY IS IN THE SOUTH.
WARRANT OFFICER FALMAN IS IN THE NORTH.
2ND LT. BREDA WAS SENT WEST.
AND LT. HAWKEYE WAS MADE THE PRESIDENT'S PERSONAL AIDE.
WHAT !?!
THEY'RE NOTHING BUT HOSTAGES !!
HOW COULD RIDICULOUS ORDERS LIKE THAT HAVE GONE THROUGH ?
THE CONSPIRACY TURNED OUT TO INVOLVE MORE THAN JUST A "PORTION" OF THE MILITARY HIGH COMMAND.

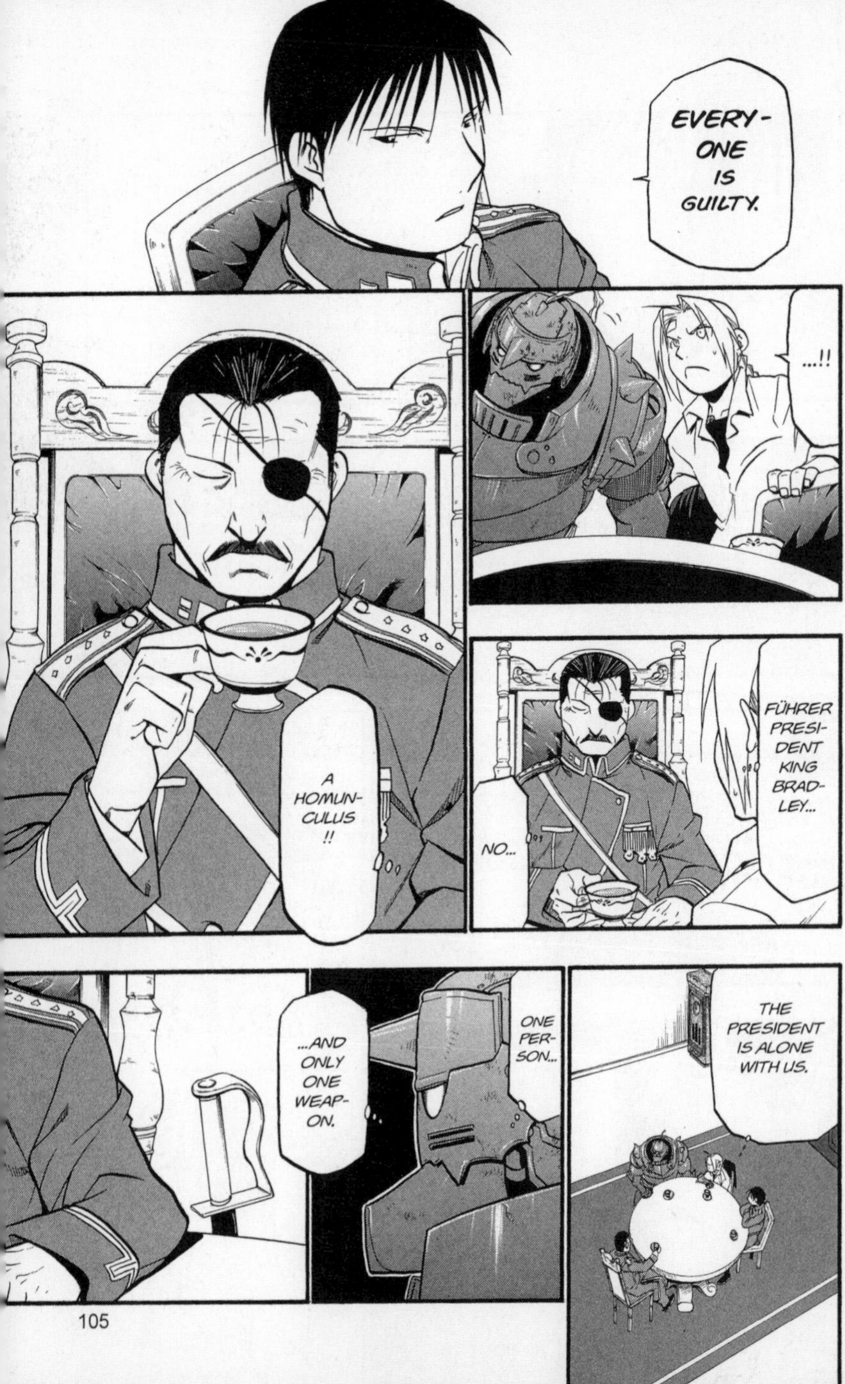
EVERYONE IS GUILTY.
...!!
FÜHRER PRESIDENT KING BRADLEY...
NO...
A HOMUNCULUS !!
THE PRESIDENT IS ALONE WITH US.
ONE PERSON...
...AND ONLY ONE WEAPON.

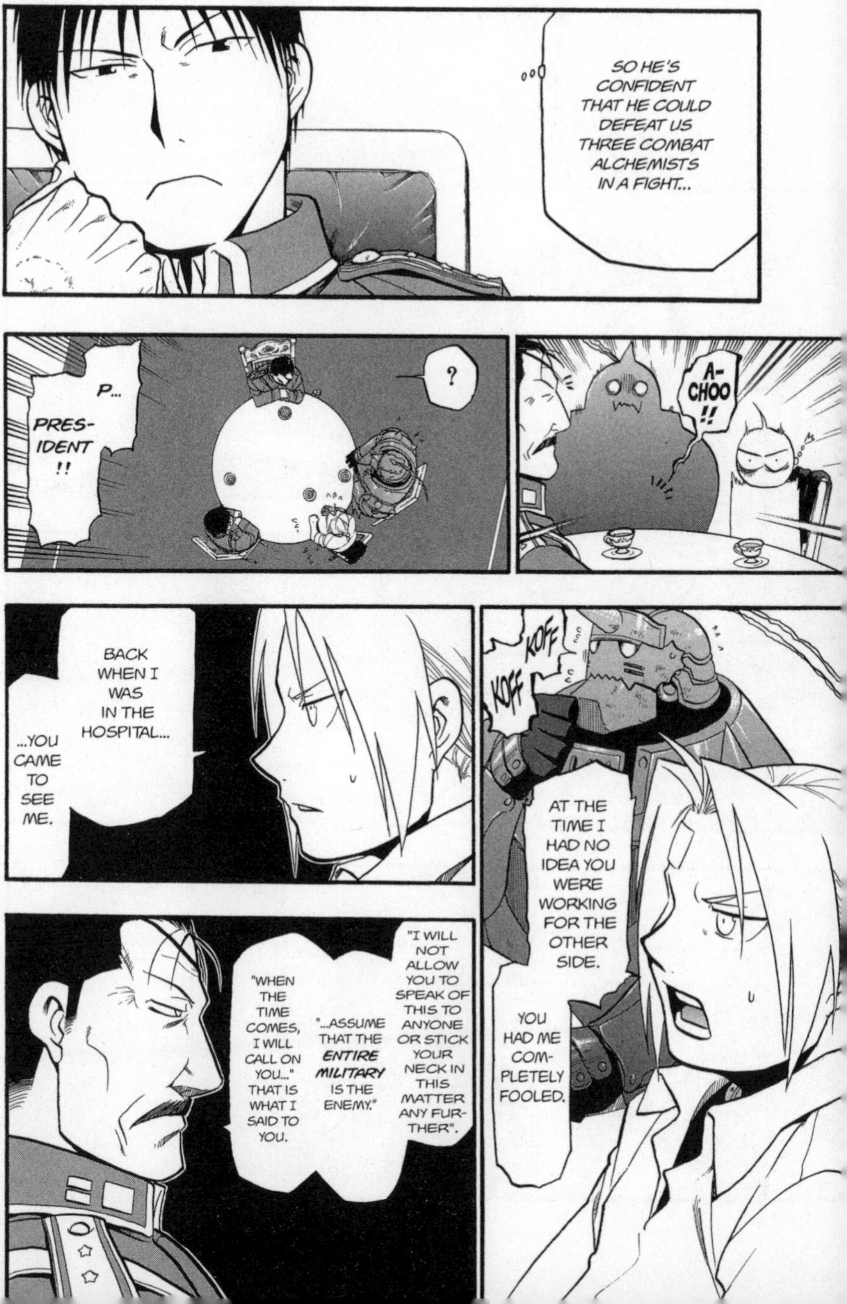
SO HE'S CONFIDENT THAT HE COULD DEFEAT US THREE COMBAT ALCHEMISTS IN A FIGHT...
A-CHOO!!
?
P... PRES-IDENT!!
KOFF KOFF
AT THE TIME I HAD NO IDEA YOU WERE WORKING FOR THE OTHER SIDE.
YOU HAD ME COM-PLETELY FOOLED.
BACK WHEN I WAS IN THE HOSPITAL...
...YOU CAME TO SEE ME.
"I WILL NOT ALLOW YOU TO SPEAK OF THIS TO ANYONE OR STICK YOUR NECK IN THIS MATTER ANY FUR-THER".
"...ASSUME THAT THE *ENTIRE MILITARY* IS THE ENEMY."
"WHEN THE TIME COMES, I WILL CALL ON YOU..." THAT IS WHAT I SAID TO YOU.

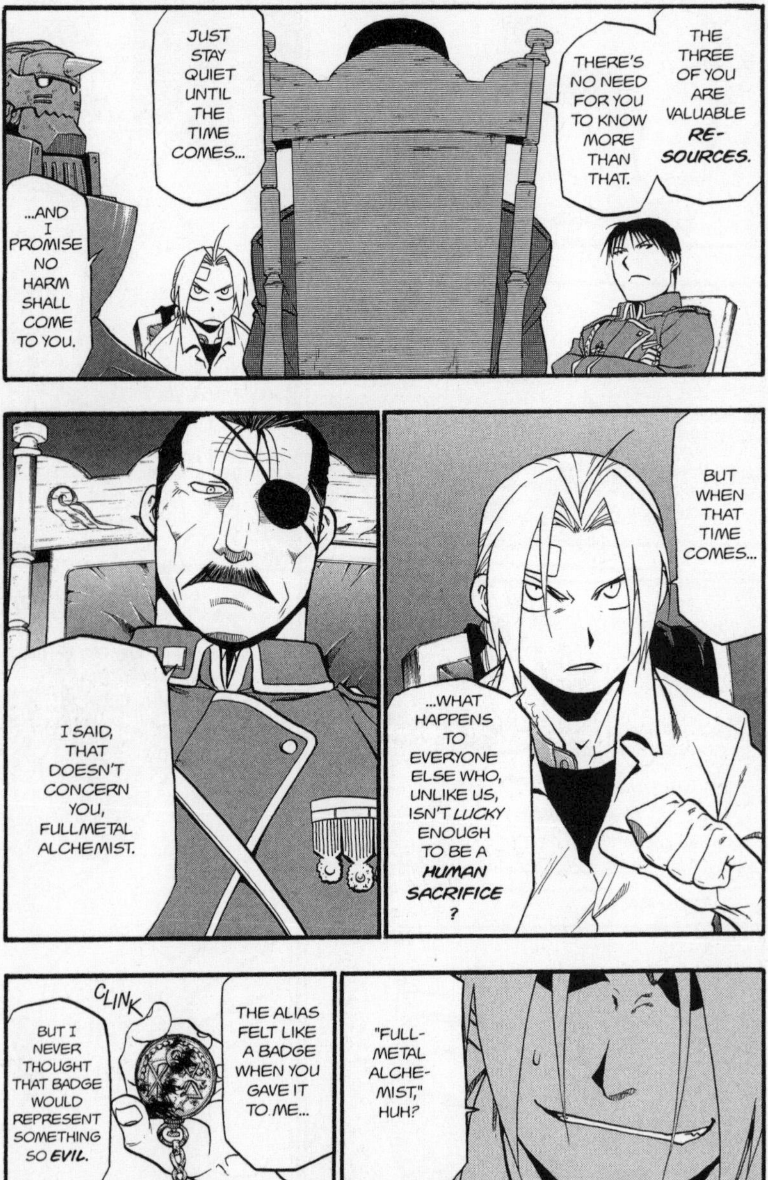
THE THREE OF YOU ARE VALUABLE ***RE-SOURCES.***
THERE'S NO NEED FOR YOU TO KNOW MORE THAN THAT.
JUST STAY QUIET UNTIL THE TIME COMES...
...AND I PROMISE NO HARM SHALL COME TO YOU.
BUT WHEN THAT TIME COMES...
...WHAT HAPPENS TO EVERYONE ELSE WHO, UNLIKE US, ISN'T *LUCKY* ENOUGH TO BE A ***HUMAN SACRIFICE*** ?
I SAID, THAT DOESN'T CONCERN YOU, FULLMETAL ALCHEMIST.
"FULL-METAL ALCHE-MIST," HUH?
THE ALIAS FELT LIKE A BADGE WHEN YOU GAVE IT TO ME...
CLINK
BUT I NEVER THOUGHT THAT BADGE WOULD REPRESENT SOMETHING SO ***EVIL.***

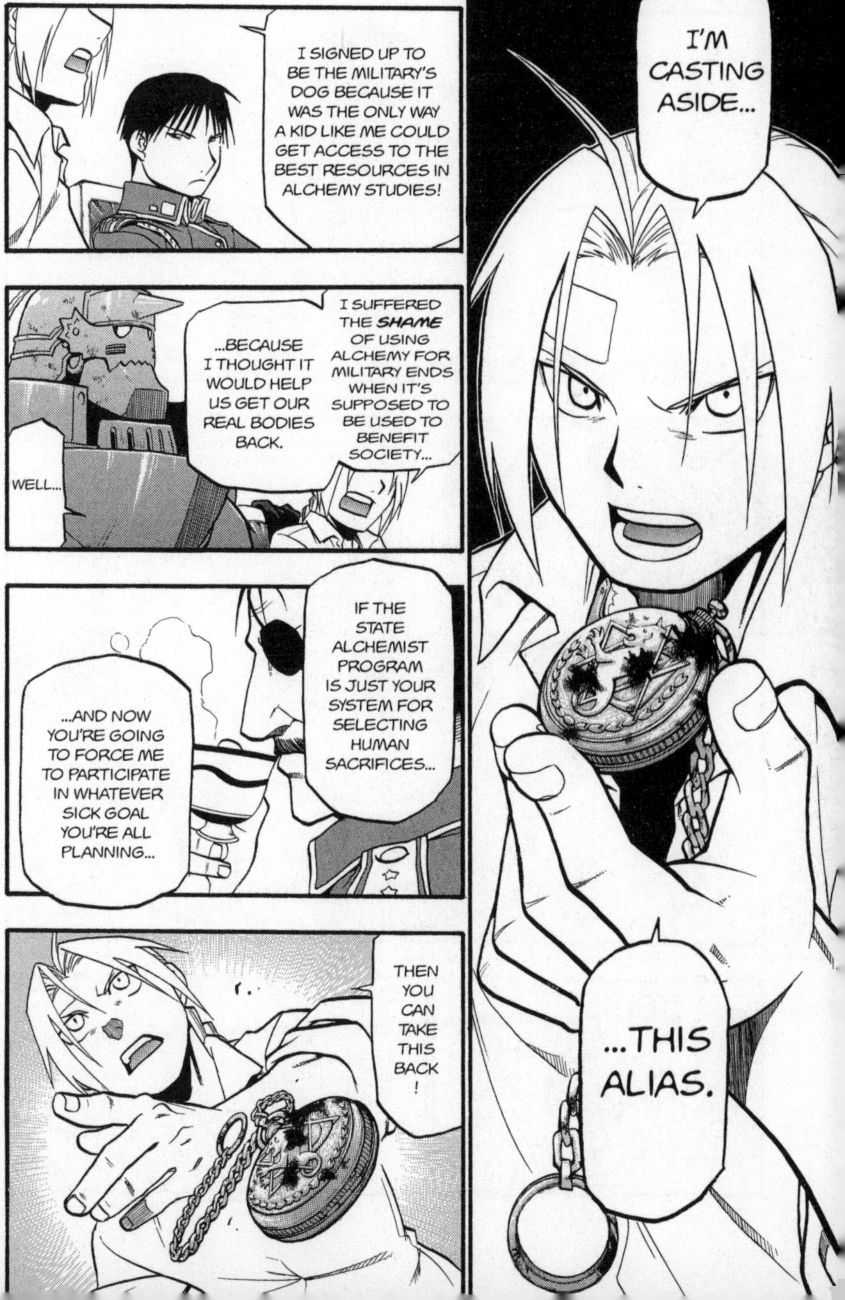
I'M CASTING ASIDE...
...THIS ALIAS.
I SIGNED UP TO BE THE MILITARY'S DOG BECAUSE IT WAS THE ONLY WAY A KID LIKE ME COULD GET ACCESS TO THE BEST RESOURCES IN ALCHEMY STUDIES!
I SUFFERED THE ***SHAME*** OF USING ALCHEMY FOR MILITARY ENDS WHEN IT'S SUPPOSED TO BE USED TO BENEFIT SOCIETY...
...BECAUSE I THOUGHT IT WOULD HELP US GET OUR REAL BODIES BACK.
WELL...
IF THE STATE ALCHEMIST PROGRAM IS JUST YOUR SYSTEM FOR SELECTING HUMAN SACRIFICES...
...AND NOW YOU'RE GOING TO FORCE ME TO PARTICIPATE IN WHATEVER SICK GOAL YOU'RE ALL PLANNING...
THEN YOU CAN TAKE THIS BACK!

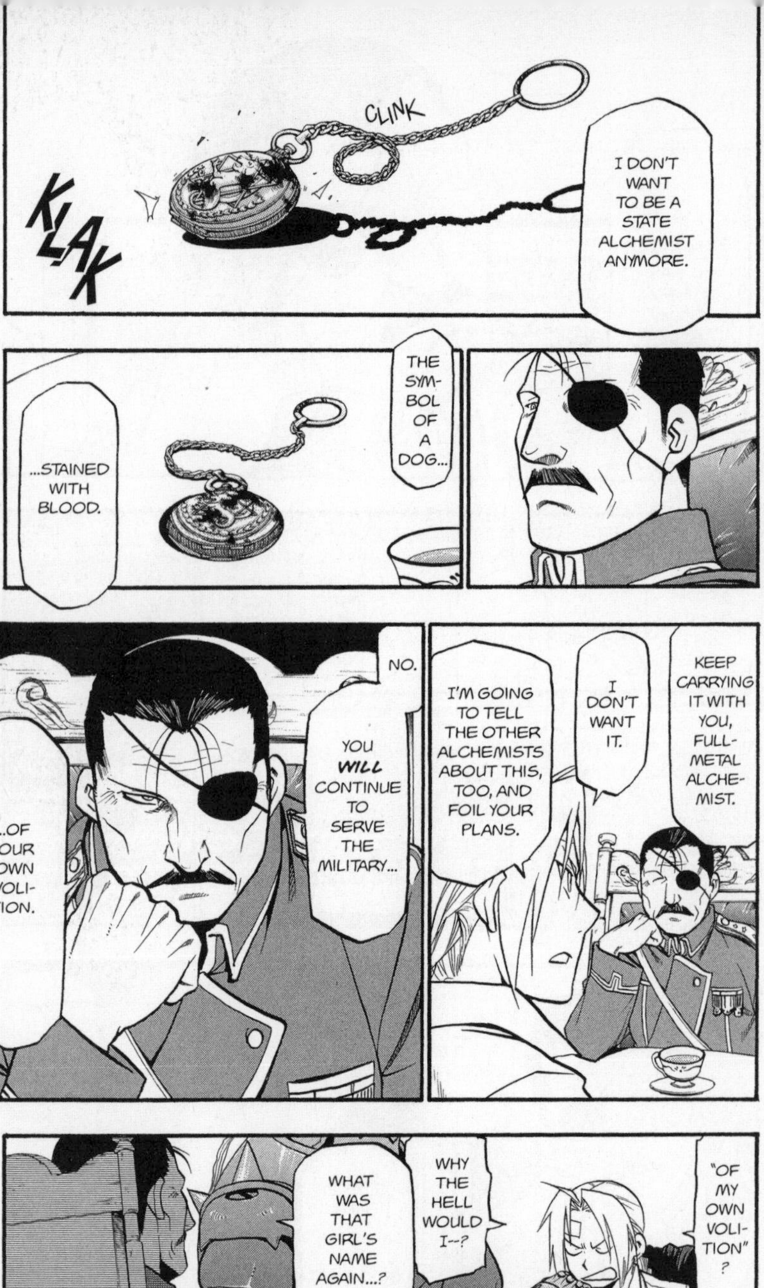
I DON'T WANT TO BE A STATE ALCHEMIST ANYMORE.
CLINK
KLAK
THE SYMBOL OF A DOG...
...STAINED WITH BLOOD.
KEEP CARRYING IT WITH YOU, FULLMETAL ALCHEMIST.
I DON'T WANT IT.
I'M GOING TO TELL THE OTHER ALCHEMISTS ABOUT THIS, TOO, AND FOIL YOUR PLANS.
NO.
YOU **WILL** CONTINUE TO SERVE THE MILITARY...
...OF YOUR OWN VOLITION.
"OF MY OWN VOLITION"?
WHY THE HELL WOULD I--?
WHAT WAS THAT GIRL'S NAME AGAIN...?

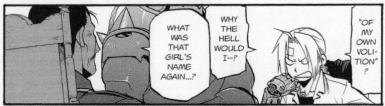

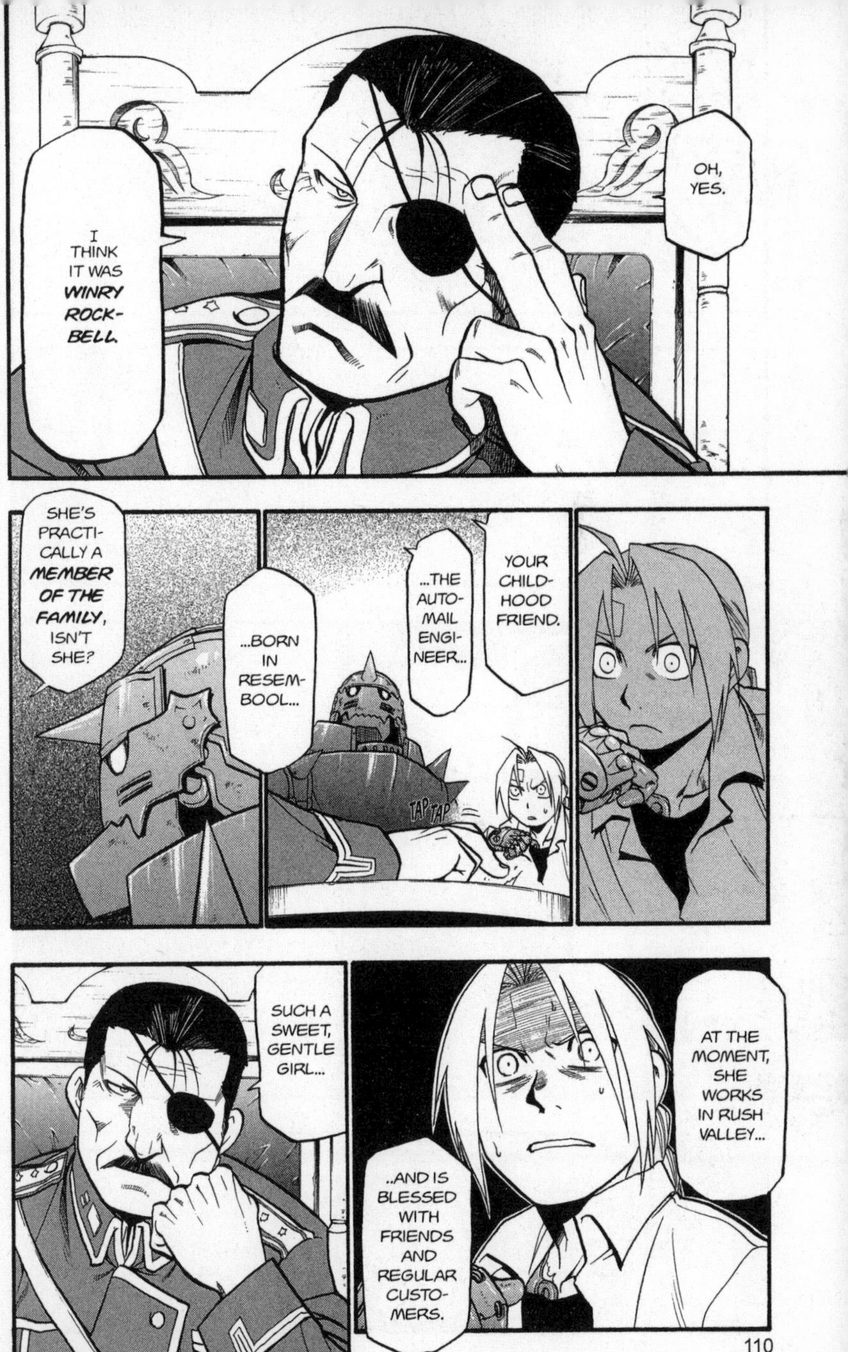
OH, YES.
I THINK IT WAS WINRY ROCKBELL.
YOUR CHILDHOOD FRIEND.
...THE AUTOMAIL ENGINEER...
...BORN IN RESEMBOOL...
TAP TAP
SHE'S PRACTICALLY A MEMBER OF THE FAMILY, ISN'T SHE?
AT THE MOMENT, SHE WORKS IN RUSH VALLEY...
..AND IS BLESSED WITH FRIENDS AND REGULAR CUSTOMERS.
SUCH A SWEET, GENTLE GIRL...

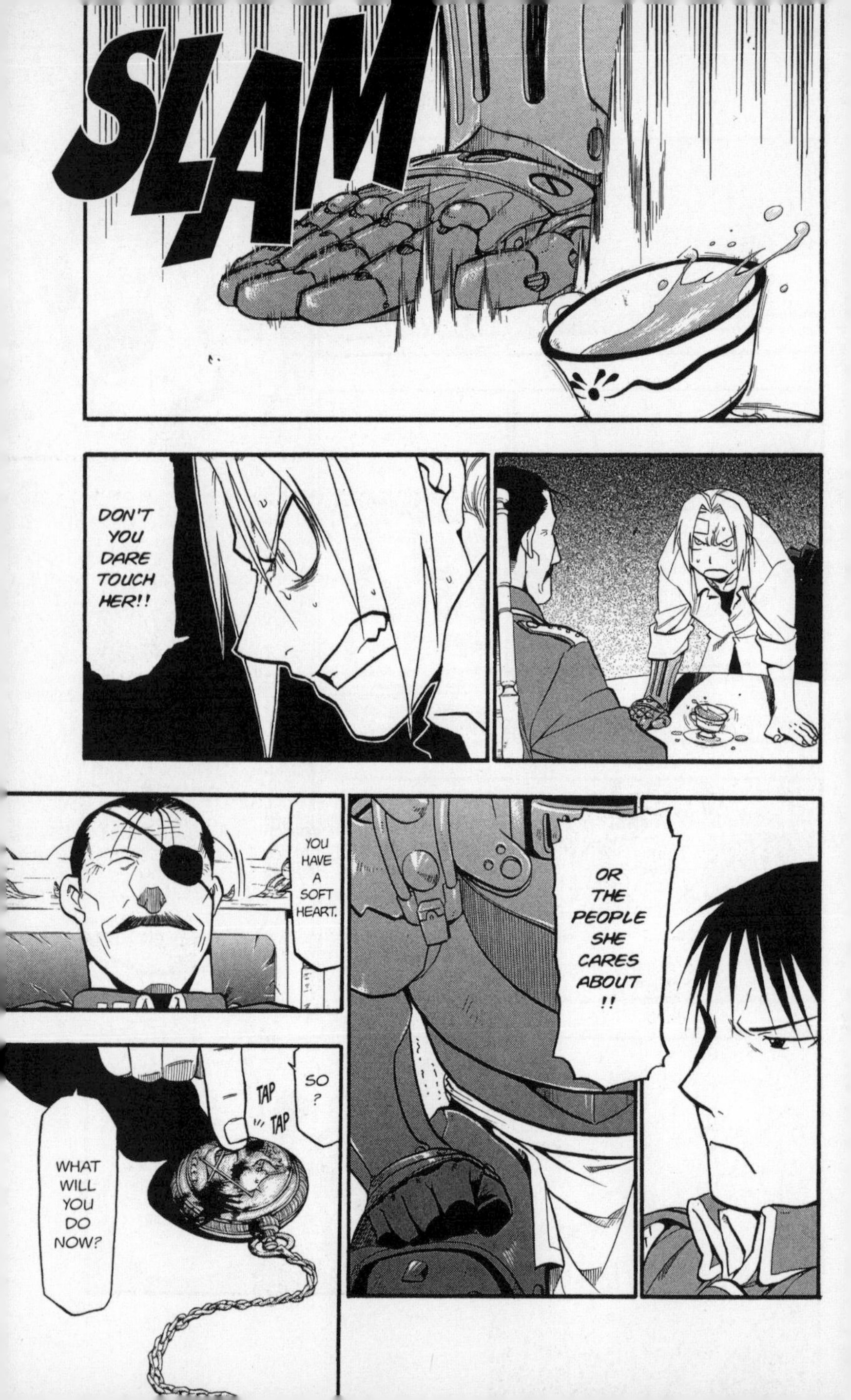
SLAM
DON'T YOU DARE TOUCH HER!!
OR THE PEOPLE SHE CARES ABOUT!!
YOU HAVE A SOFT HEART.
SO?
TAP TAP
WHAT WILL YOU DO NOW?

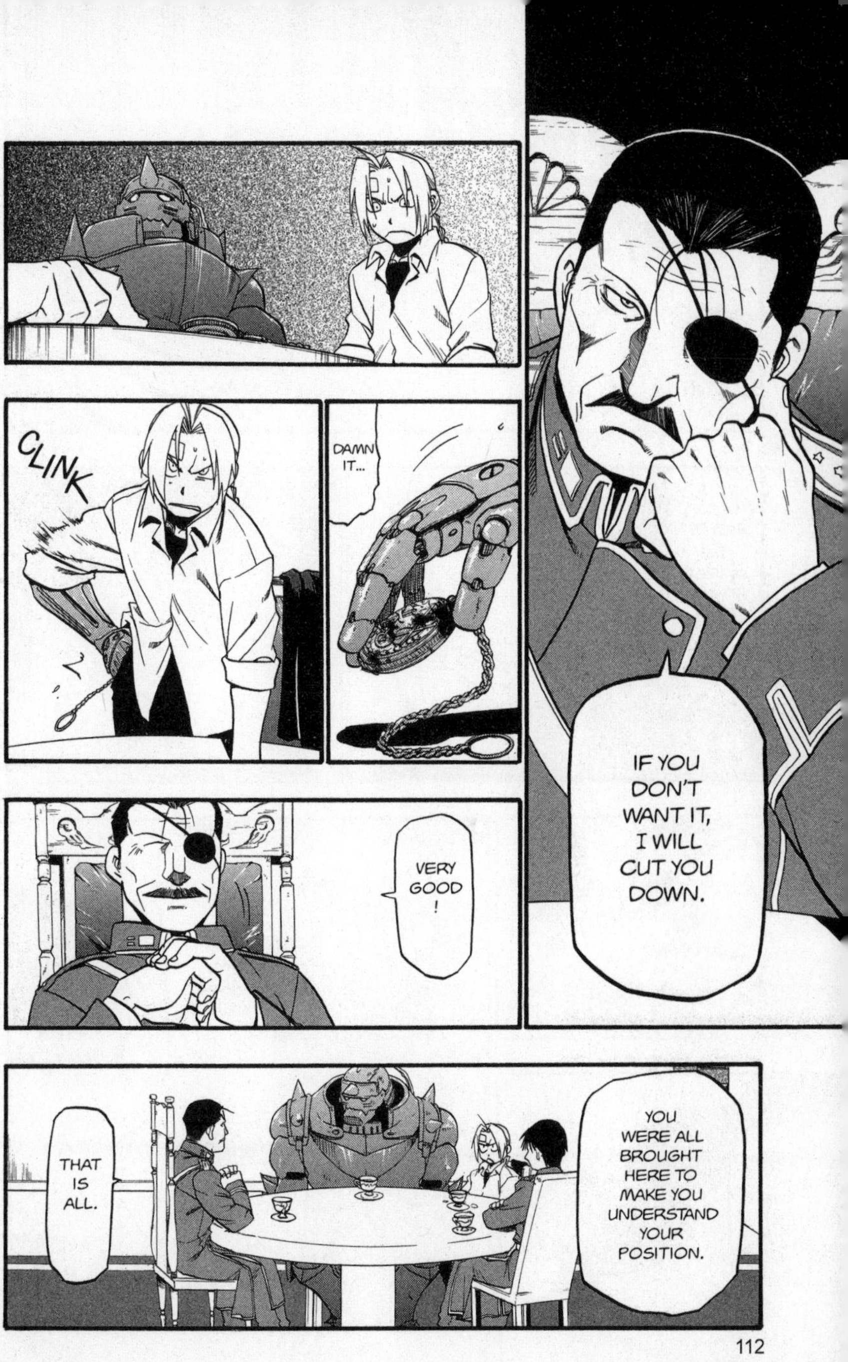
IF YOU DON'T WANT IT, I WILL CUT YOU DOWN.
DAMN IT...
CLINK
VERY GOOD!
YOU WERE ALL BROUGHT HERE TO MAKE YOU UNDERSTAND YOUR POSITION.
THAT IS ALL.

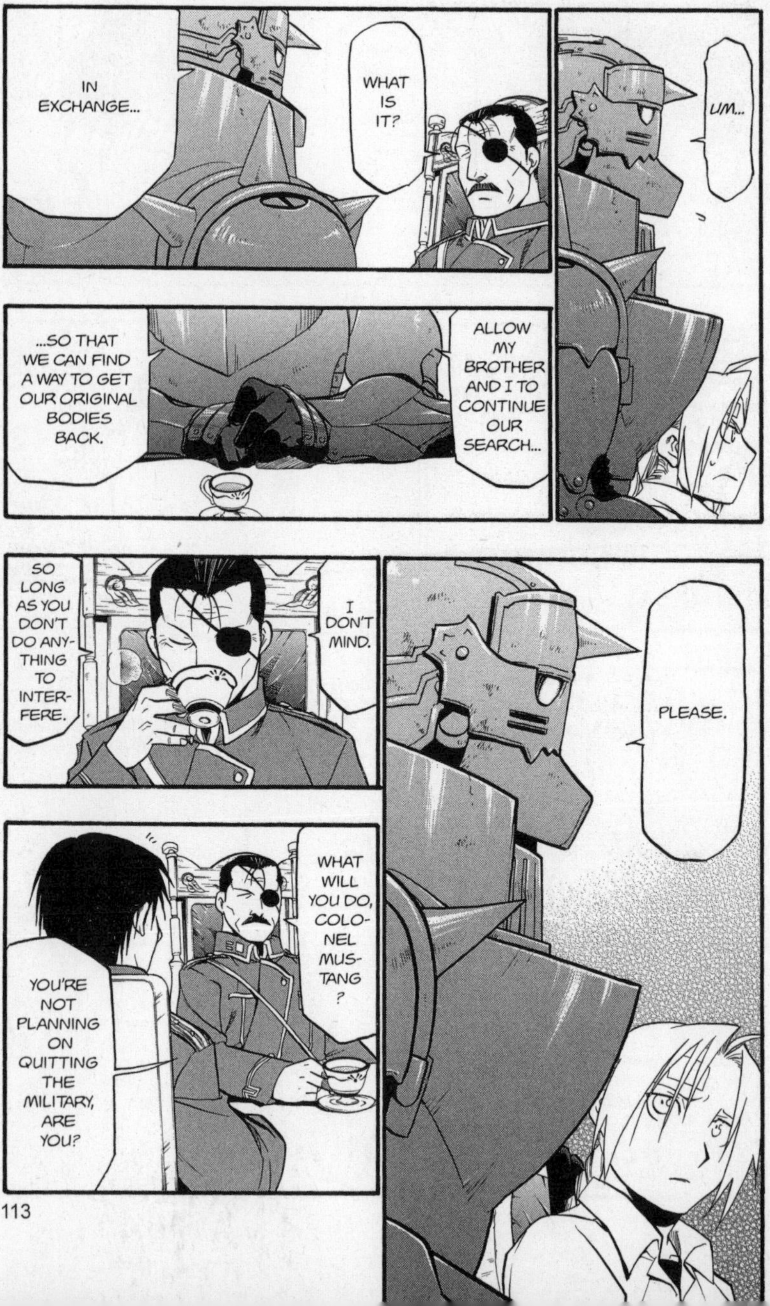
UM...
WHAT IS IT?
IN EXCHANGE...
ALLOW MY BROTHER AND I TO CONTINUE OUR SEARCH...
...SO THAT WE CAN FIND A WAY TO GET OUR ORIGINAL BODIES BACK.
PLEASE.
I DON'T MIND.
SO LONG AS YOU DON'T DO ANY-THING TO INTER-FERE.
WHAT WILL YOU DO, COLO-NEL MUS-TANG?
YOU'RE NOT PLANNING ON QUITTING THE MILITARY, ARE YOU?

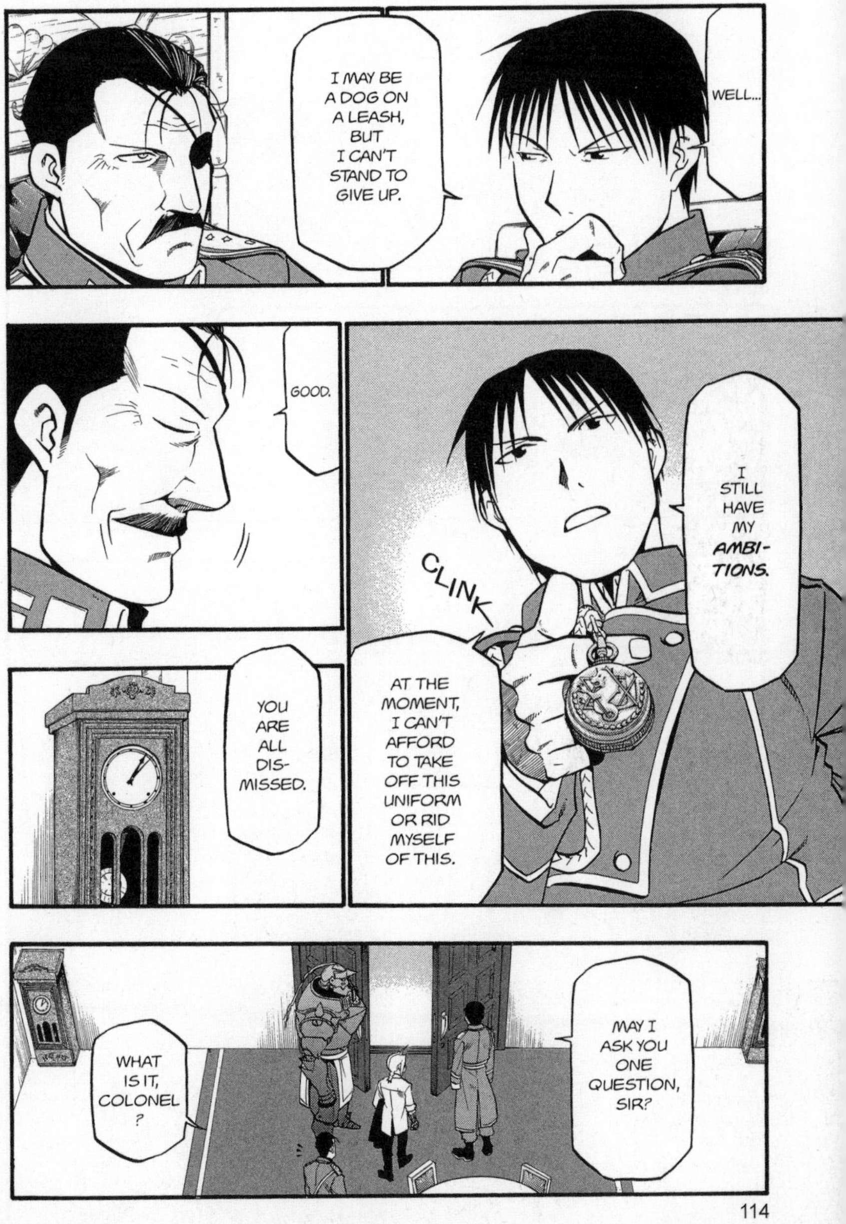
WELL...
I MAY BE A DOG ON A LEASH, BUT I CAN'T STAND TO GIVE UP.
I STILL HAVE MY **AMBITIONS.**
CLINK
AT THE MOMENT, I CAN'T AFFORD TO TAKE OFF THIS UNIFORM OR RID MYSELF OF THIS.
GOOD.
YOU ARE ALL DIS-MISSED.
MAY I ASK YOU ONE QUESTION, SIR?
WHAT IS IT, COLONEL?

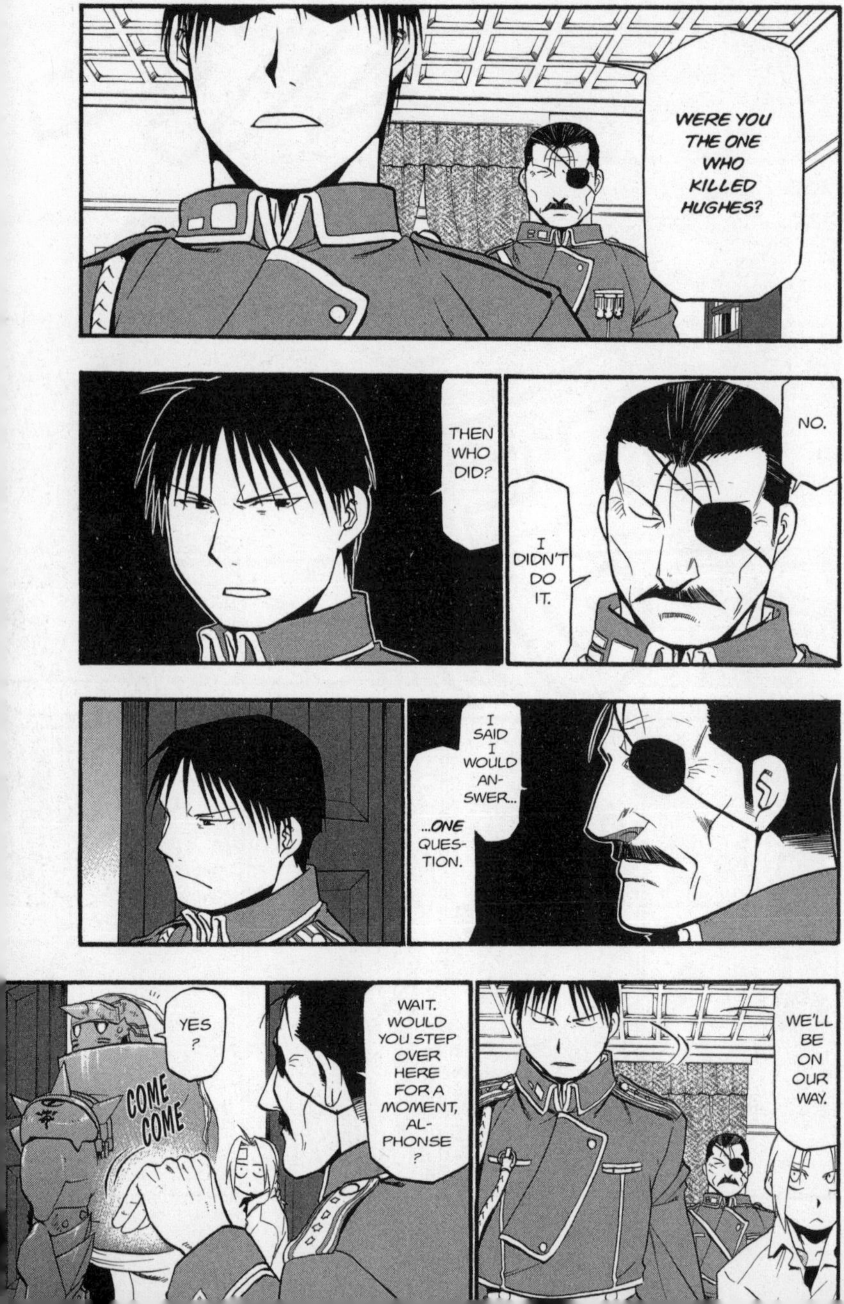
WERE YOU THE ONE WHO KILLED HUGHES?
NO.
I DIDN'T DO IT.
THEN WHO DID?
I SAID I WOULD ANSWER...
...ONE QUESTION.
WE'LL BE ON OUR WAY.
WAIT. WOULD YOU STEP OVER HERE FOR A MOMENT, ALPHONSE?
YES?
COME COME

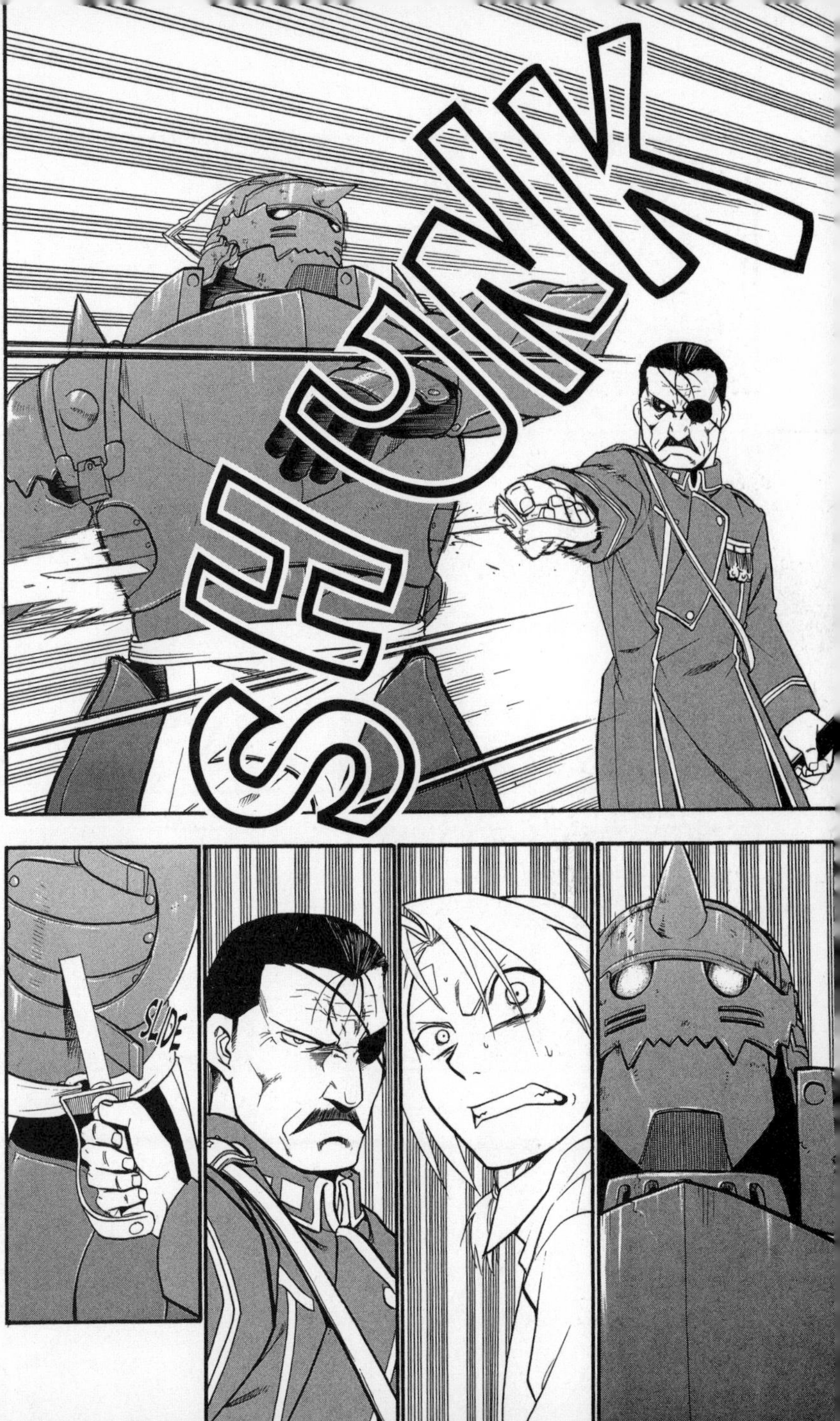
SHUNK
SLIDE

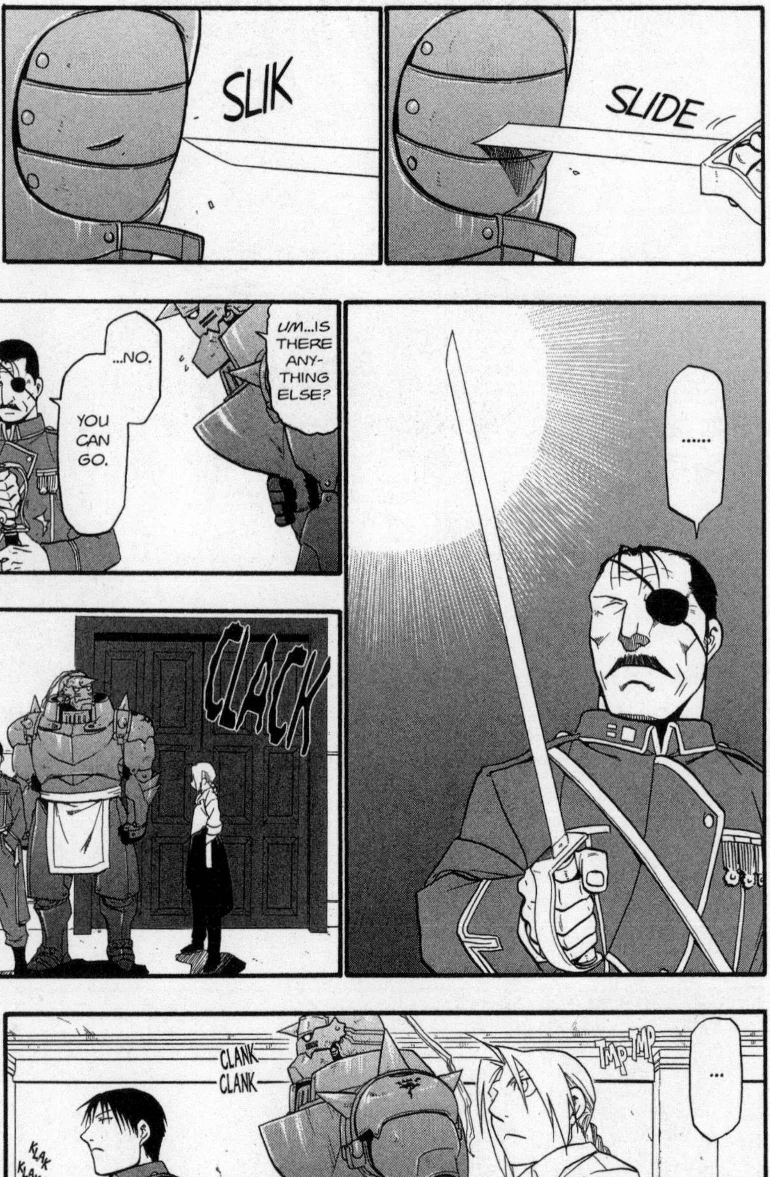
SLIDE
SLIK
......
UM...IS THERE ANYTHING ELSE?
...NO.
YOU CAN GO.
SNAP
CLACK
...
TMP TMP
CLANK CLANK
KLAK KLAK

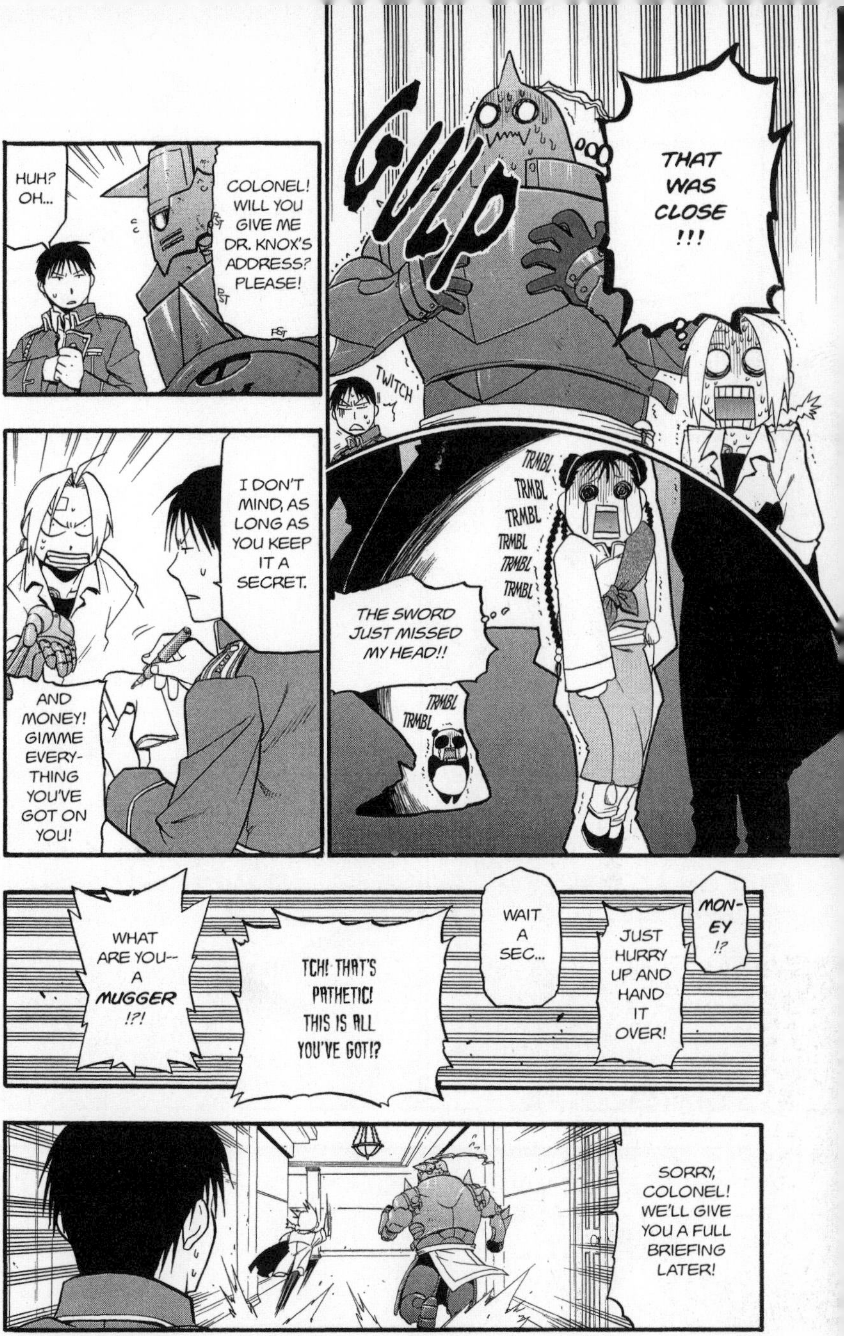
THAT WAS CLOSE !!!
GULP
TWITCH
TRMBL TRMBL TRMBL TRMBL TRMBL TRMBL
THE SWORD JUST MISSED MY HEAD!!
TRMBL TRMBL
COLONEL! WILL YOU GIVE ME DR. KNOX'S ADDRESS? PLEASE!
PST PST PST
HUH? OH...
I DON'T MIND, AS LONG AS YOU KEEP IT A SECRET.
AND MONEY! GIMME EVERY-THING YOU'VE GOT ON YOU!
MON-EY !?
JUST HURRY UP AND HAND IT OVER!
WAIT A SEC...
TCH! THAT'S PATHETIC! THIS IS ALL YOU'VE GOT!?
WHAT ARE YOU-- A MUGGER !?!
SORRY, COLONEL! WE'LL GIVE YOU A FULL BRIEFING LATER!

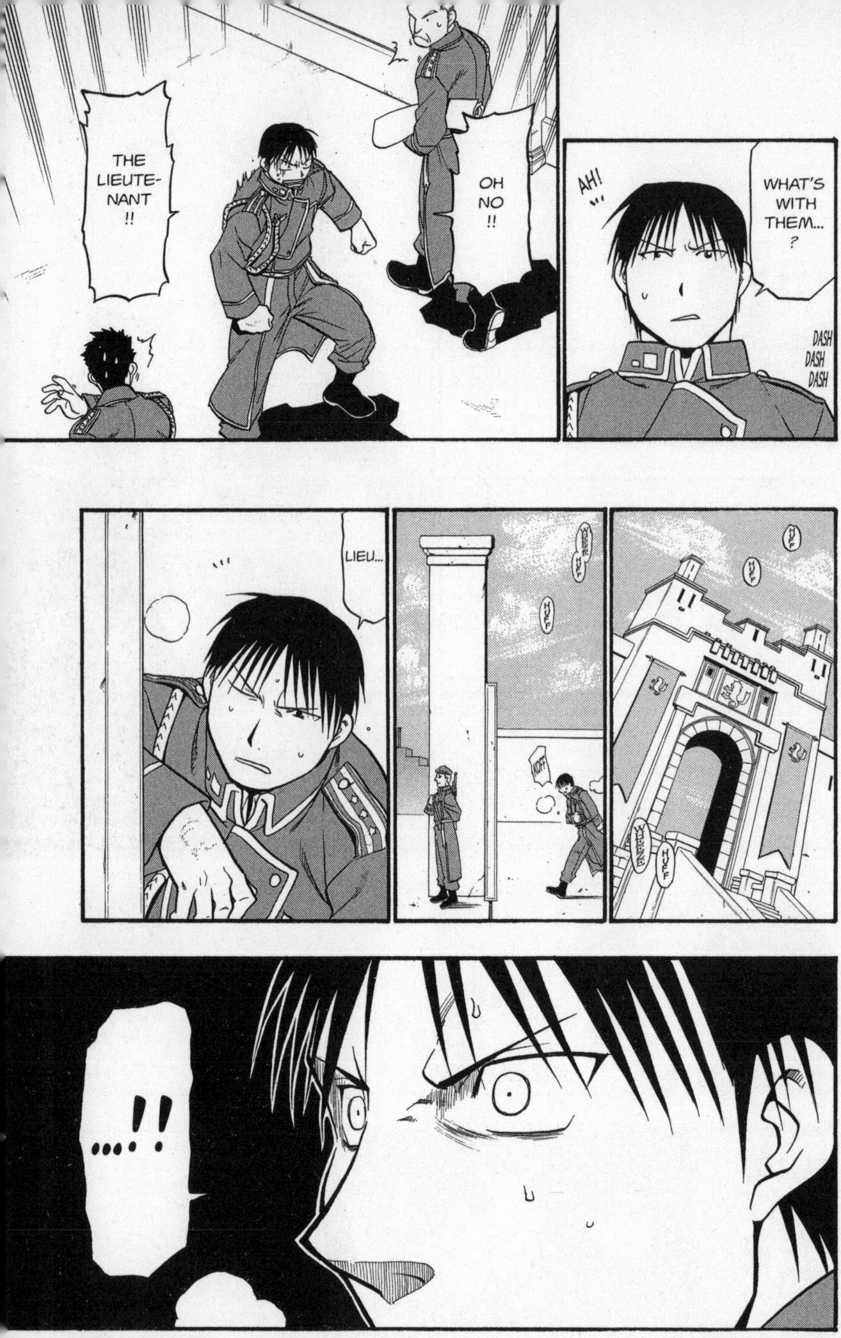
WHAT'S WITH THEM...?
AH!
DASH DASH DASH
OH NO!!
THE LIEUTENANT!!
HUFF
HUFF
HUFF
HUFF
KOFF
LIEU...
...!!

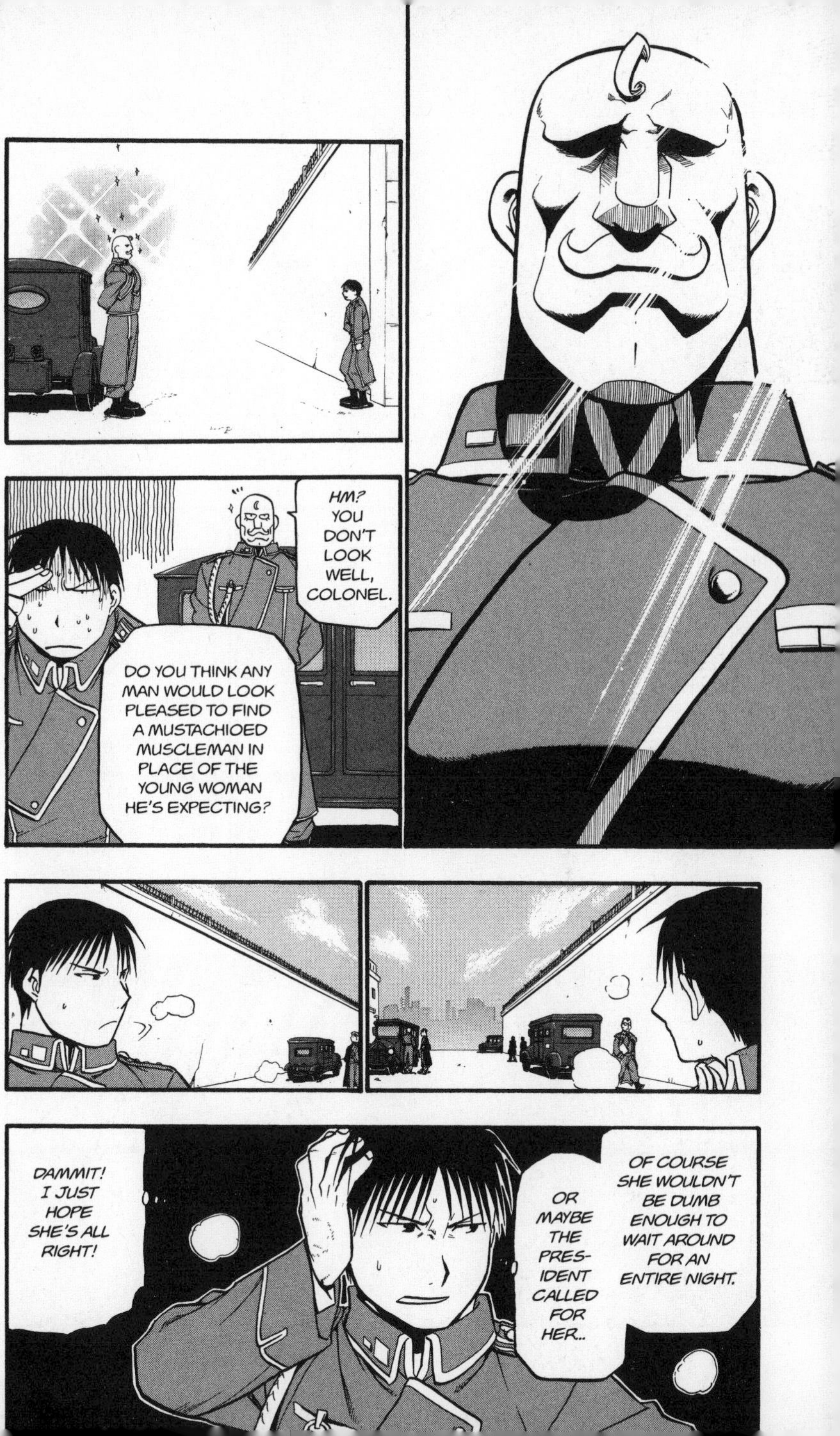
HM? YOU DON'T LOOK WELL, COLONEL.
DO YOU THINK ANY MAN WOULD LOOK PLEASED TO FIND A MUSTACHIOED MUSCLEMAN IN PLACE OF THE YOUNG WOMAN HE'S EXPECTING?
OF COURSE SHE WOULDN'T BE DUMB ENOUGH TO WAIT AROUND FOR AN ENTIRE NIGHT.
OR MAYBE THE PRES-IDENT CALLED FOR HER...
DAMMIT! I JUST HOPE SHE'S ALL RIGHT!

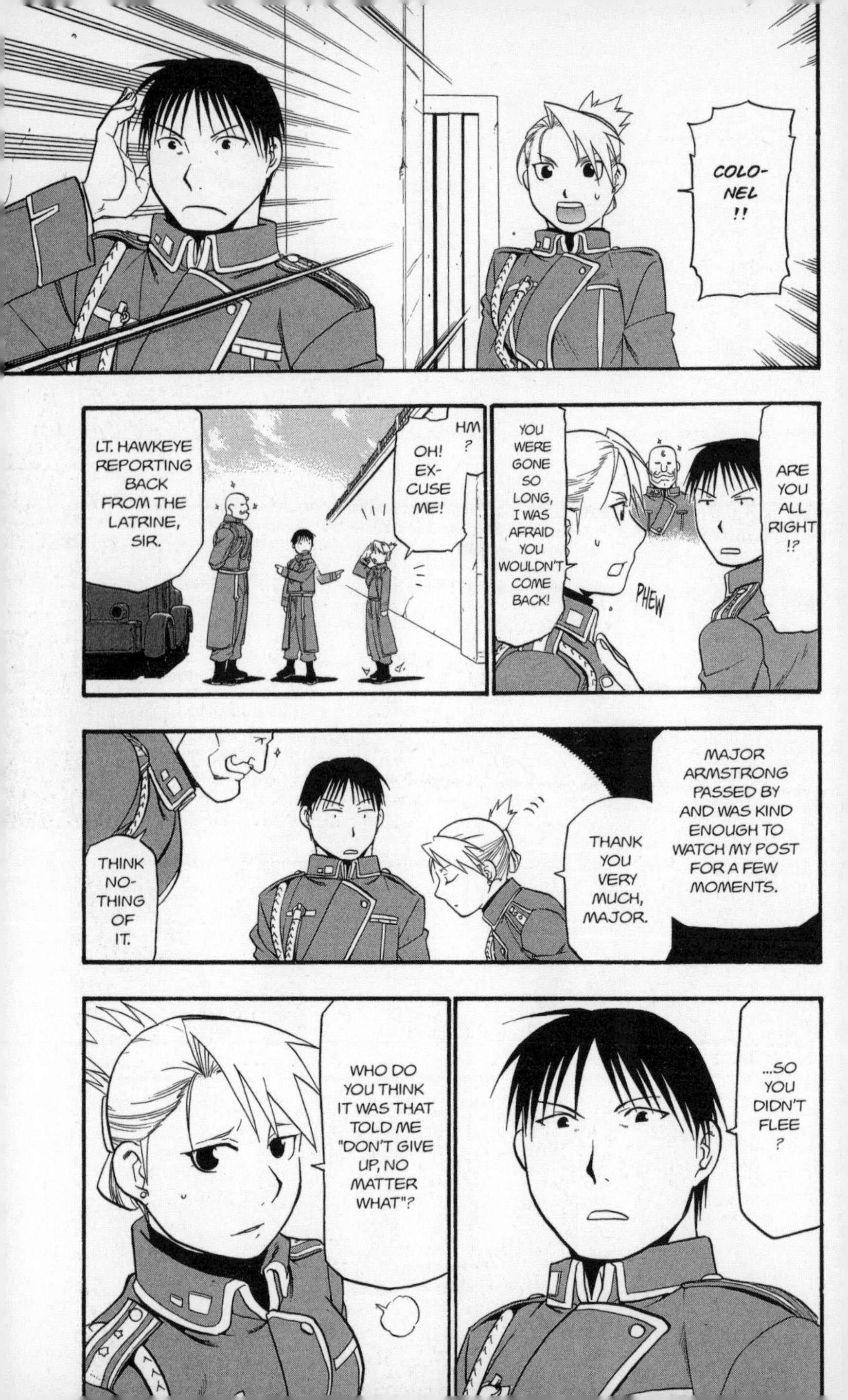
COLO-NEL !!
ARE YOU ALL RIGHT !?
YOU WERE GONE SO LONG, I WAS AFRAID YOU WOULDN'T COME BACK!
PHEW
HM ?
OH! EX-CUSE ME!
LT. HAWKEYE REPORTING BACK FROM THE LATRINE, SIR.
MAJOR ARMSTRONG PASSED BY AND WAS KIND ENOUGH TO WATCH MY POST FOR A FEW MOMENTS.
THANK YOU VERY MUCH, MAJOR.
THINK NO-THING OF IT.
...SO YOU DIDN'T FLEE ?
WHO DO YOU THINK IT WAS THAT TOLD ME "DON'T GIVE UP, NO MATTER WHAT"?

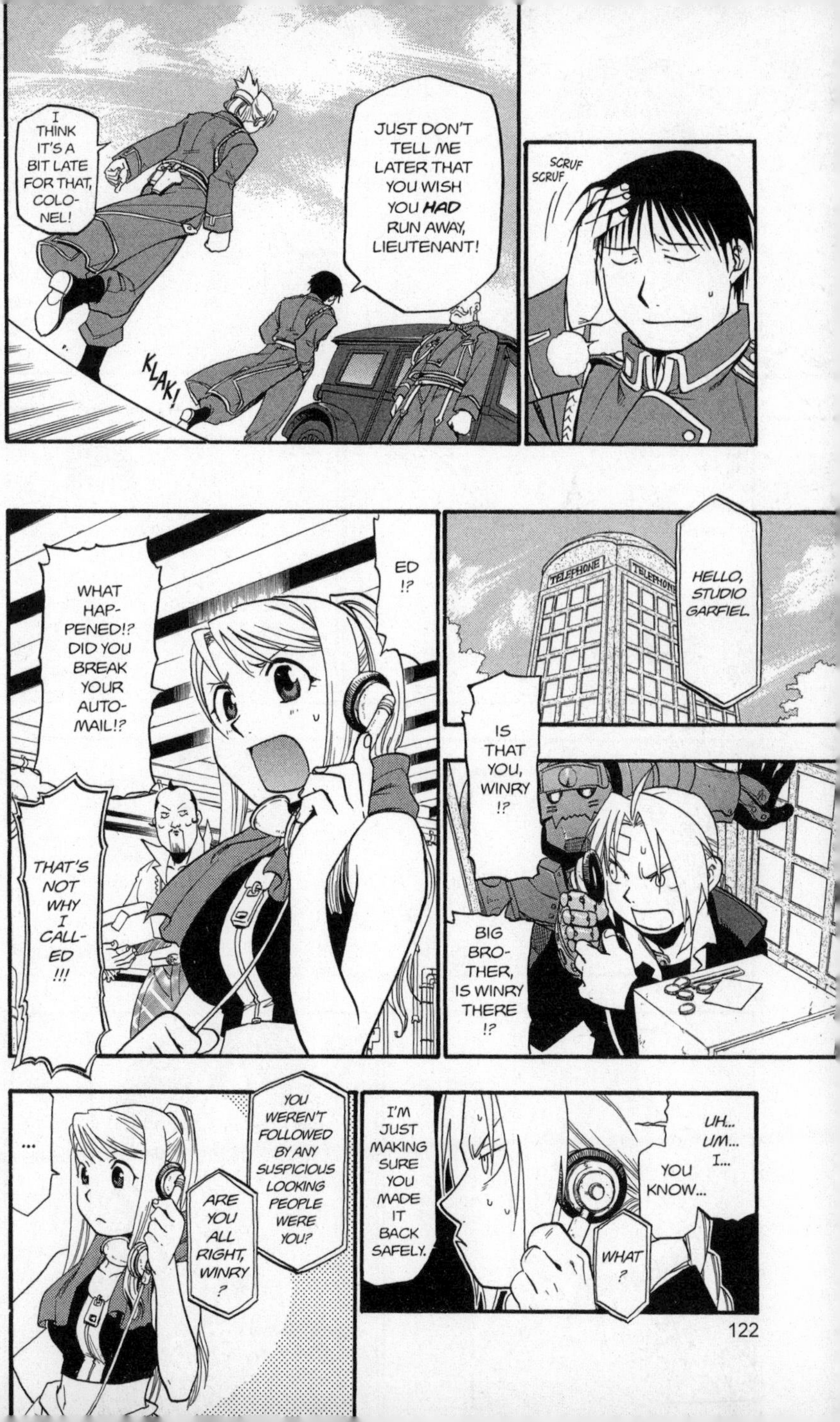
SCRUF SCRUF
JUST DON'T TELL ME LATER THAT YOU WISH YOU **HAD** RUN AWAY, LIEUTENANT!
I THINK IT'S A BIT LATE FOR THAT, COLONEL!
KLAK!
HELLO, STUDIO GARFIEL.
TELEPHONE
IS THAT YOU, WINRY!?
BIG BROTHER, IS WINRY THERE!?
ED!?
WHAT HAPPENED!? DID YOU BREAK YOUR AUTOMAIL!?
THAT'S NOT WHY I CALLED!!!
UH... UM... I...
YOU KNOW...
WHAT?
I'M JUST MAKING SURE YOU MADE IT BACK SAFELY.
YOU WEREN'T FOLLOWED BY ANY SUSPICIOUS LOOKING PEOPLE WERE YOU?
ARE YOU ALL RIGHT, WINRY?
...

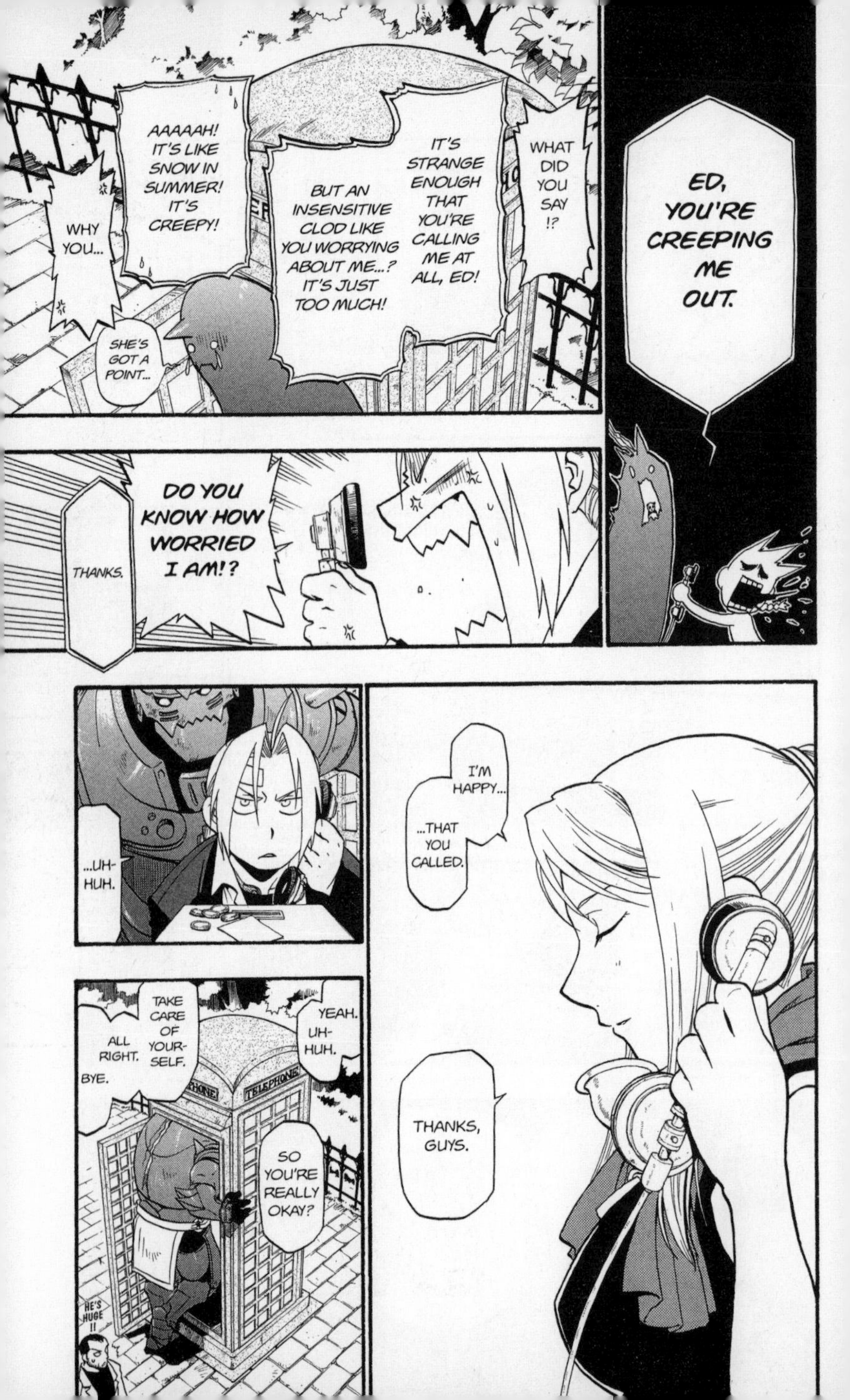
ED, YOU'RE CREEPING ME OUT.
WHAT DID YOU SAY !?
IT'S STRANGE ENOUGH THAT YOU'RE CALLING ME AT ALL, ED!
BUT AN INSENSITIVE CLOD LIKE YOU WORRYING ABOUT ME...? IT'S JUST TOO MUCH!
AAAAAH! IT'S LIKE SNOW IN SUMMER! IT'S CREEPY!
SHE'S GOT A POINT...
WHY YOU...
DO YOU KNOW HOW WORRIED I AM!?
THANKS.
I'M HAPPY...
...THAT YOU CALLED.
THANKS, GUYS.
...UH-HUH.
YEAH. UH-HUH.
TAKE CARE OF YOURSELF.
ALL RIGHT. BYE.
TELEPHONE
SO YOU'RE REALLY OKAY?
HE'S HUGE !!

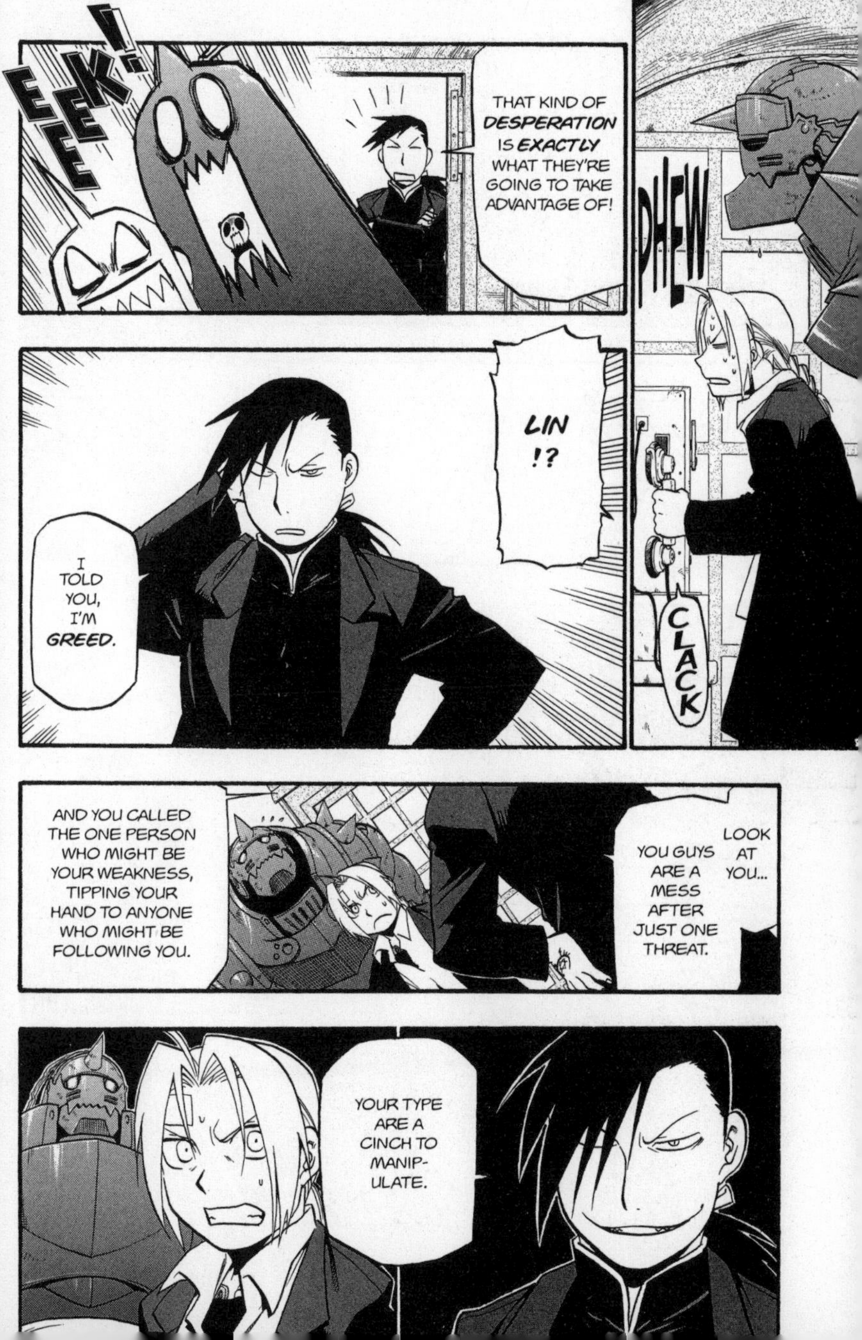
PHEW
CLACK
THAT KIND OF DESPERATION IS EXACTLY WHAT THEY'RE GOING TO TAKE ADVANTAGE OF!
EEEK!!
LIN !?
I TOLD YOU, I'M GREED.
LOOK AT YOU...
YOU GUYS ARE A MESS AFTER JUST ONE THREAT.
AND YOU CALLED THE ONE PERSON WHO MIGHT BE YOUR WEAKNESS, TIPPING YOUR HAND TO ANYONE WHO MIGHT BE FOLLOWING YOU.
YOUR TYPE ARE A CINCH TO MANIP-ULATE.

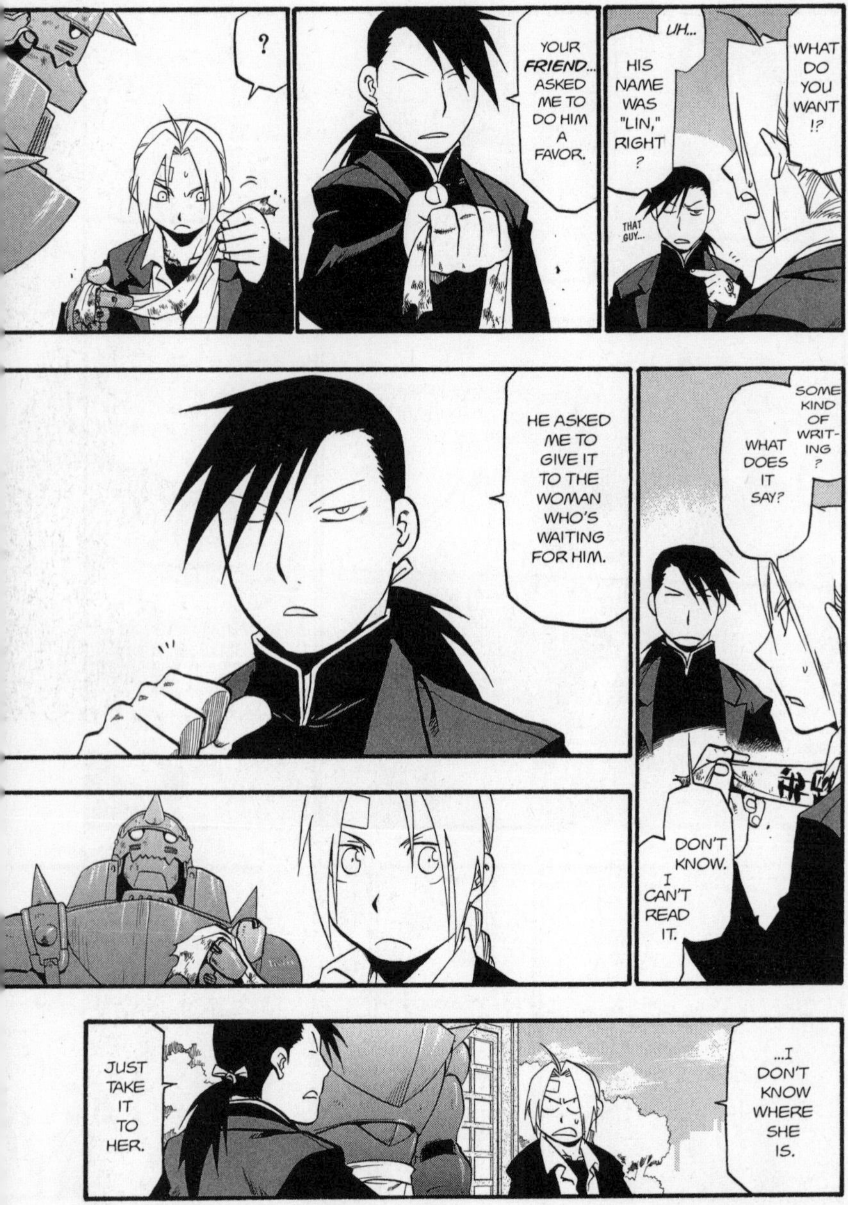
WHAT DO YOU WANT !?
UH...
HIS NAME WAS "LIN," RIGHT ?
THAT GUY...
YOUR FRIEND... ASKED ME TO DO HIM A FAVOR.
?
SOME KIND OF WRIT-ING ?
WHAT DOES IT SAY?
DON'T KNOW. I CAN'T READ IT.
HE ASKED ME TO GIVE IT TO THE WOMAN WHO'S WAITING FOR HIM.
...I DON'T KNOW WHERE SHE IS.
JUST TAKE IT TO HER.

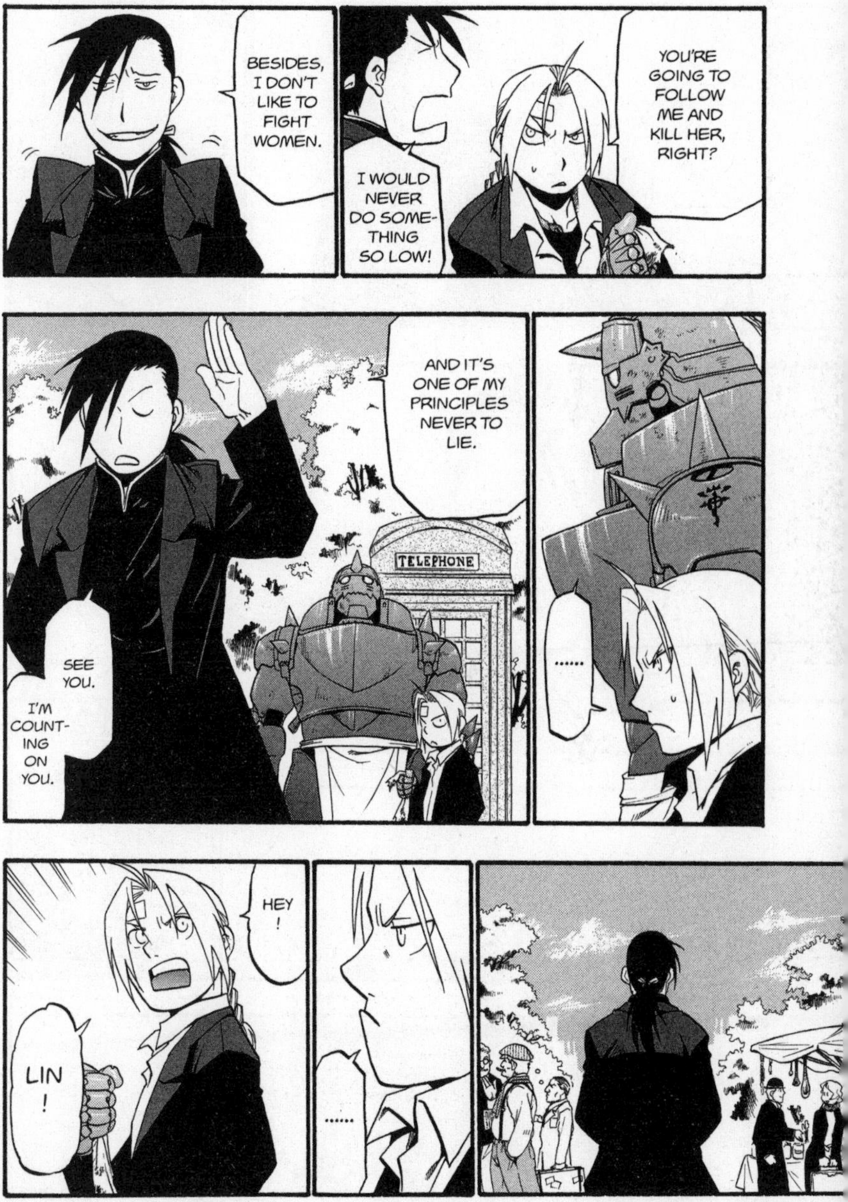
YOU'RE GOING TO FOLLOW ME AND KILL HER, RIGHT?
I WOULD NEVER DO SOME-THING SO LOW!
BESIDES, I DON'T LIKE TO FIGHT WOMEN.
......
AND IT'S ONE OF MY PRINCIPLES NEVER TO LIE.
TELEPHONE
SEE YOU.
I'M COUNT-ING ON YOU.
......
HEY!
LIN!

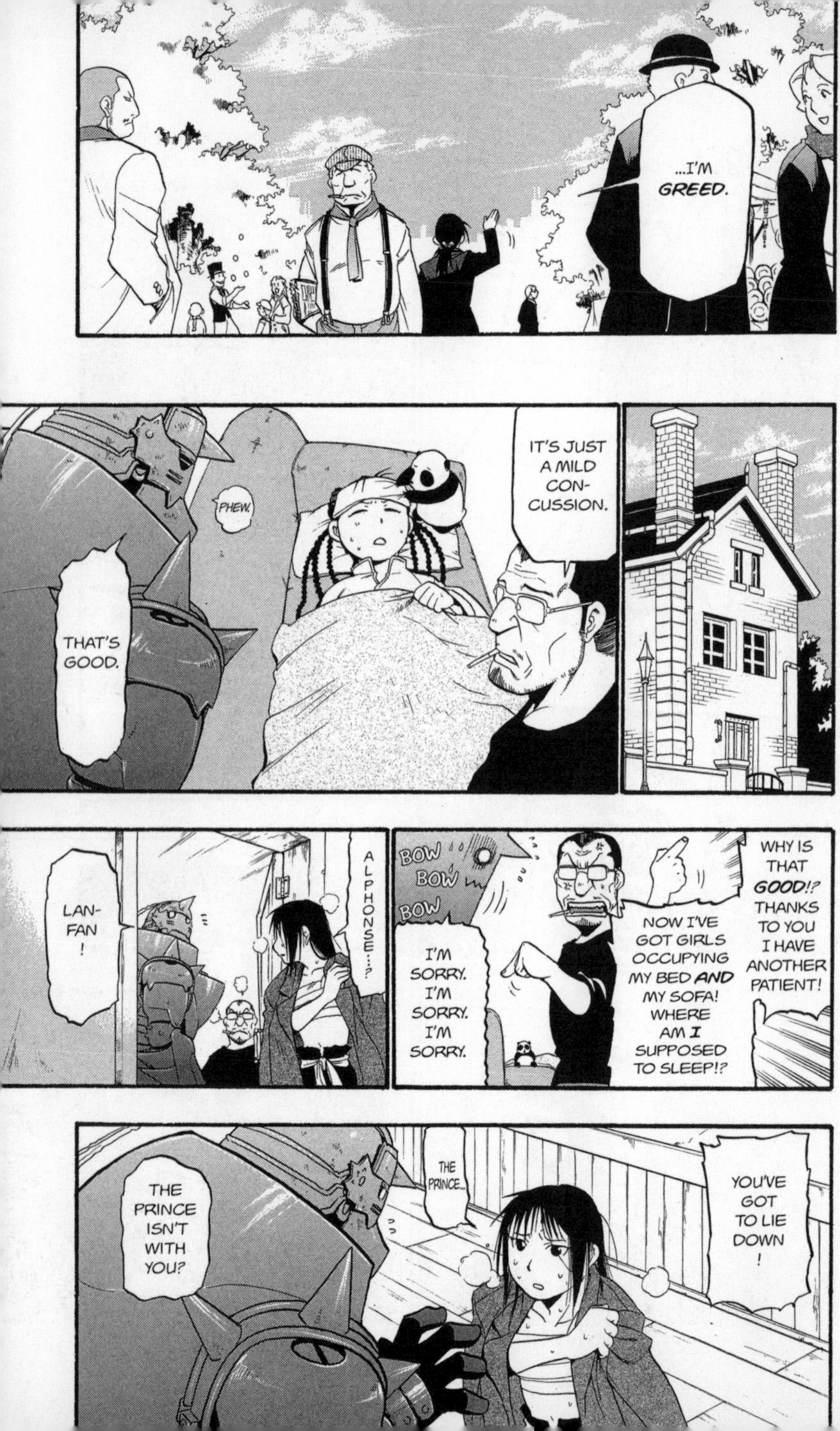
...I'M GREED.
IT'S JUST A MILD CONCUSSION.
PHEW.
THAT'S GOOD.
WHY IS THAT GOOD!? THANKS TO YOU I HAVE ANOTHER PATIENT!
NOW I'VE GOT GIRLS OCCUPYING MY BED AND MY SOFA! WHERE AM I SUPPOSED TO SLEEP!?
BOW BOW BOW
I'M SORRY. I'M SORRY. I'M SORRY.
ALPHONSE...?
LAN-FAN!
YOU'VE GOT TO LIE DOWN!
THE PRINCE...
THE PRINCE ISN'T WITH YOU?

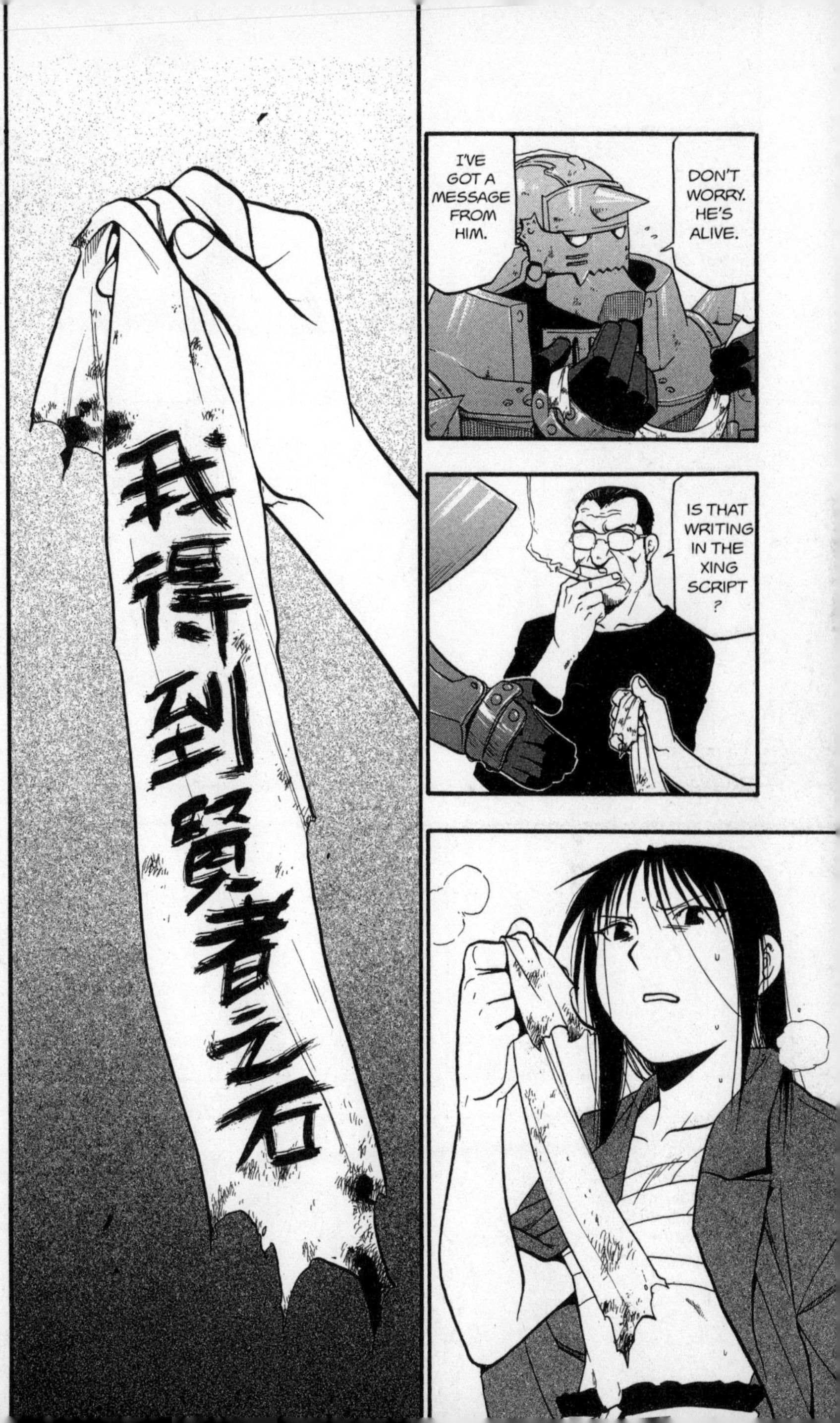
DON'T WORRY. HE'S ALIVE.
I'VE GOT A MESSAGE FROM HIM.
IS THAT WRITING IN THE XING SCRIPT?
我得到賢者之石

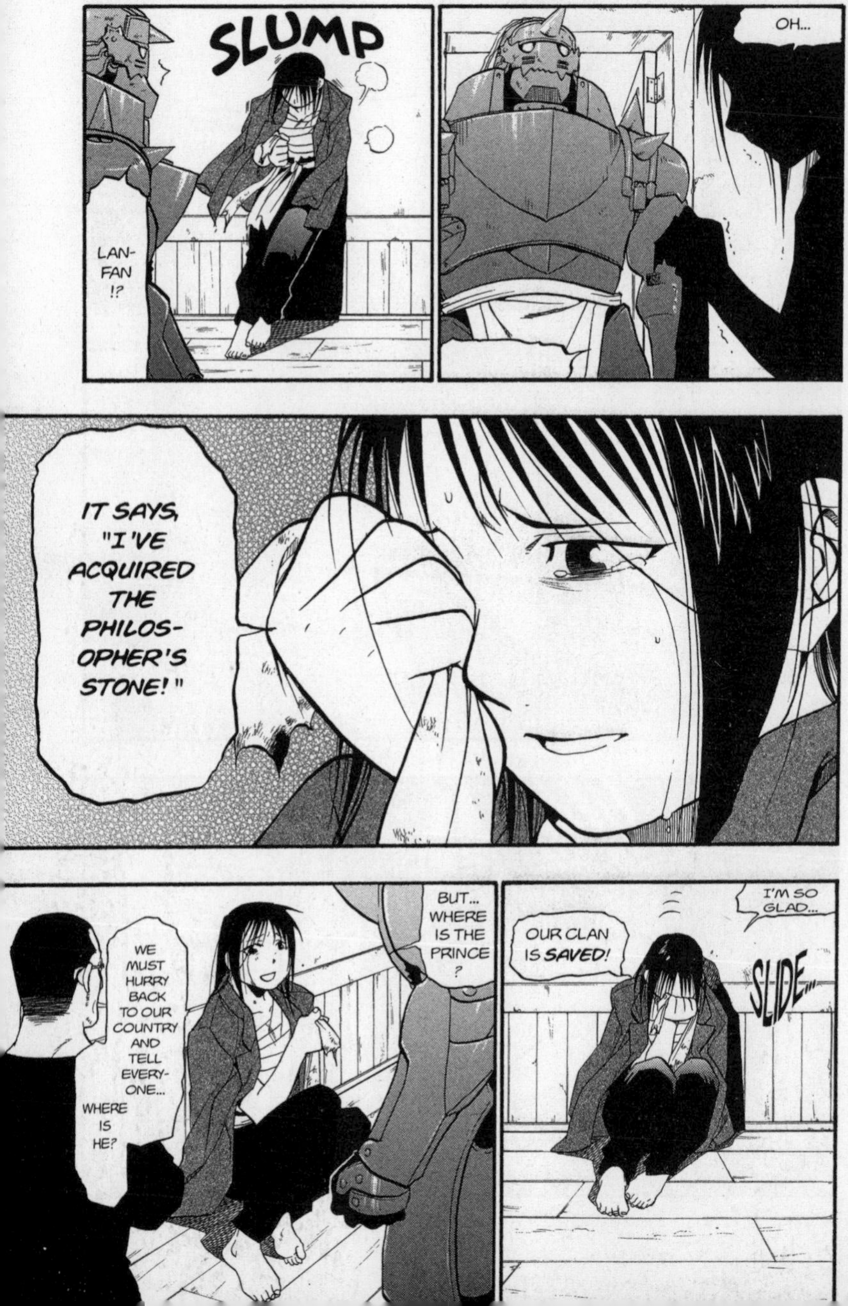
OH...
SLUMP
LAN-FAN!?
IT SAYS, "I'VE ACQUIRED THE PHILOSOPHER'S STONE!"
I'M SO GLAD...
OUR CLAN IS *SAVED!*
SLIDE...
BUT... WHERE IS THE PRINCE?
WE MUST HURRY BACK TO OUR COUNTRY AND TELL EVERYONE...
WHERE IS HE?

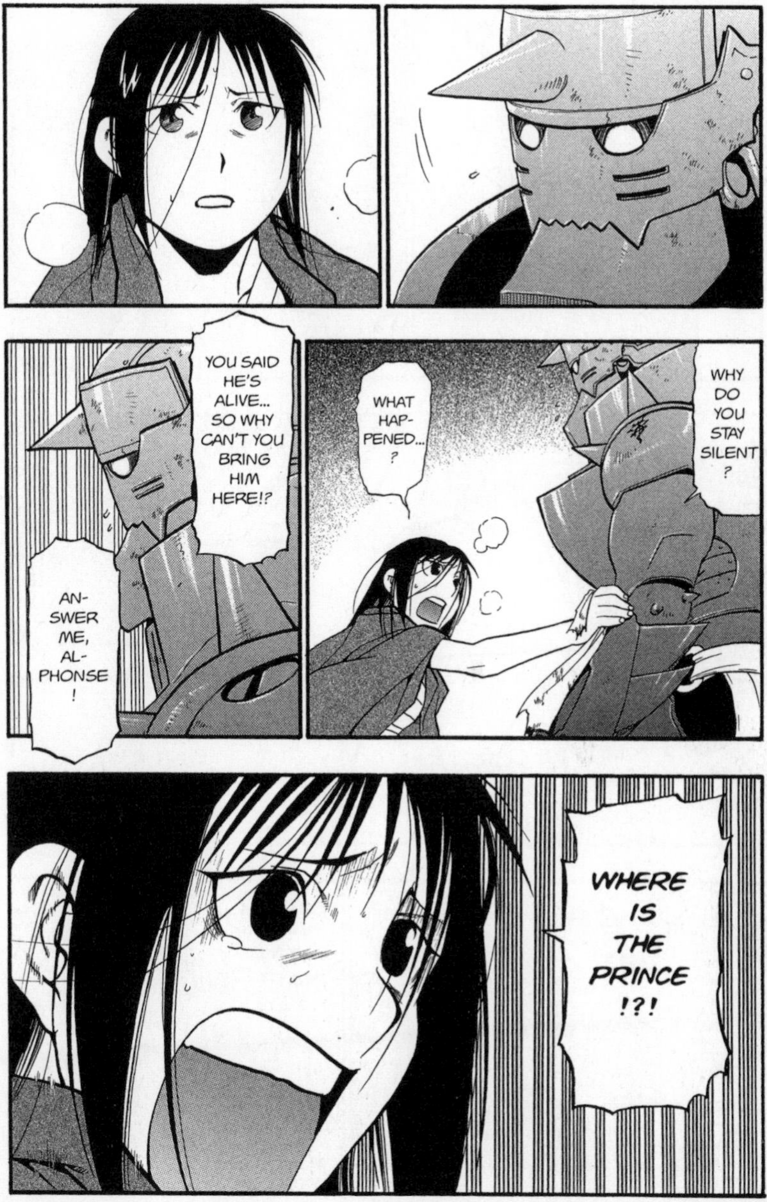
WHY DO YOU STAY SILENT?
WHAT HAPPENED...?
YOU SAID HE'S ALIVE... SO WHY CAN'T YOU BRING HIM HERE!?
ANSWER ME, ALPHONSE!
WHERE IS THE PRINCE!?!

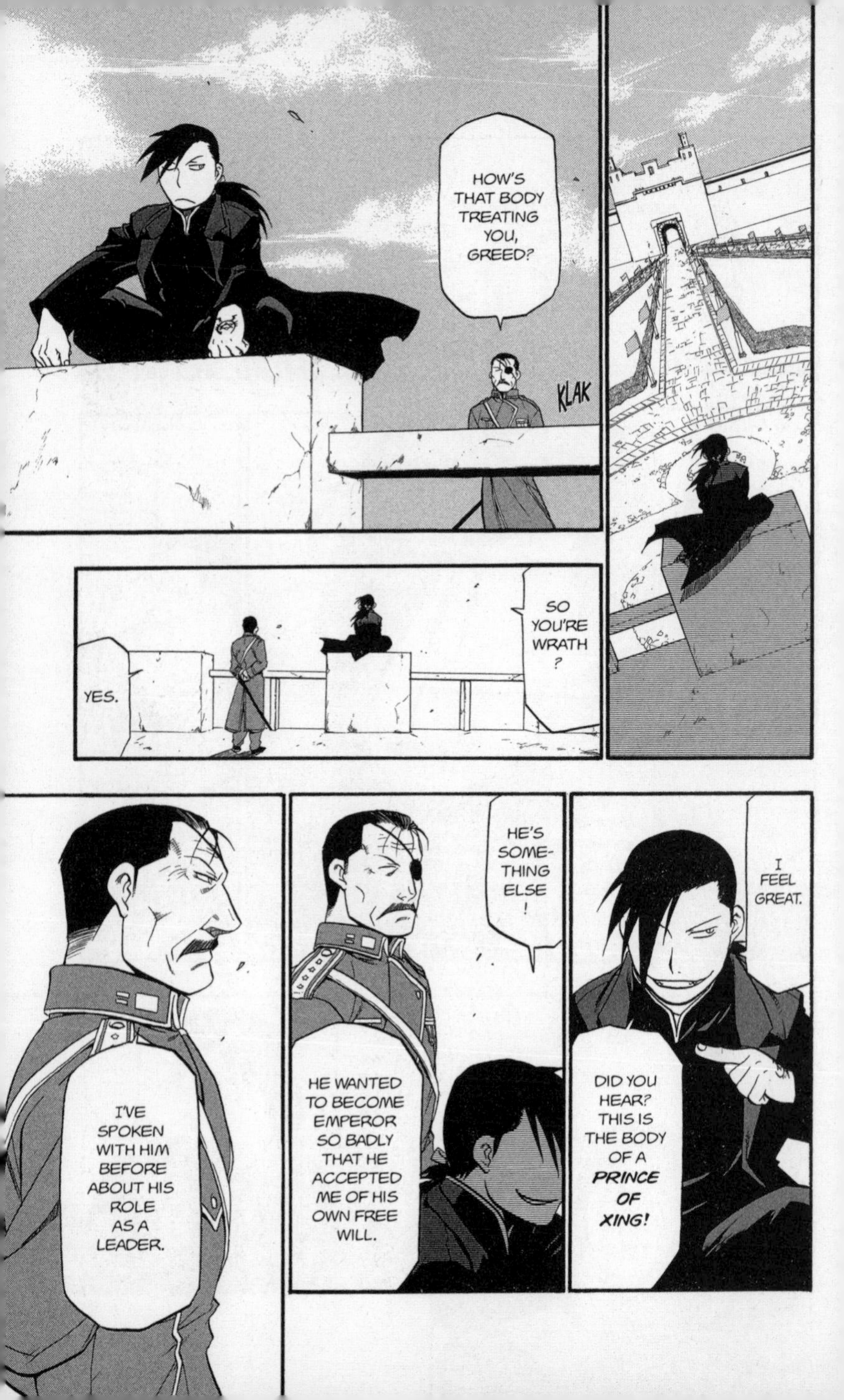
HOW'S THAT BODY TREATING YOU, GREED?
KLAK
SO YOU'RE WRATH?
YES.
I FEEL GREAT.
DID YOU HEAR? THIS IS THE BODY OF A *PRINCE OF XING!*
HE'S SOME-THING ELSE!
HE WANTED TO BECOME EMPEROR SO BADLY THAT HE ACCEPTED ME OF HIS OWN FREE WILL.
I'VE SPOKEN WITH HIM BEFORE ABOUT HIS ROLE AS A LEADER.

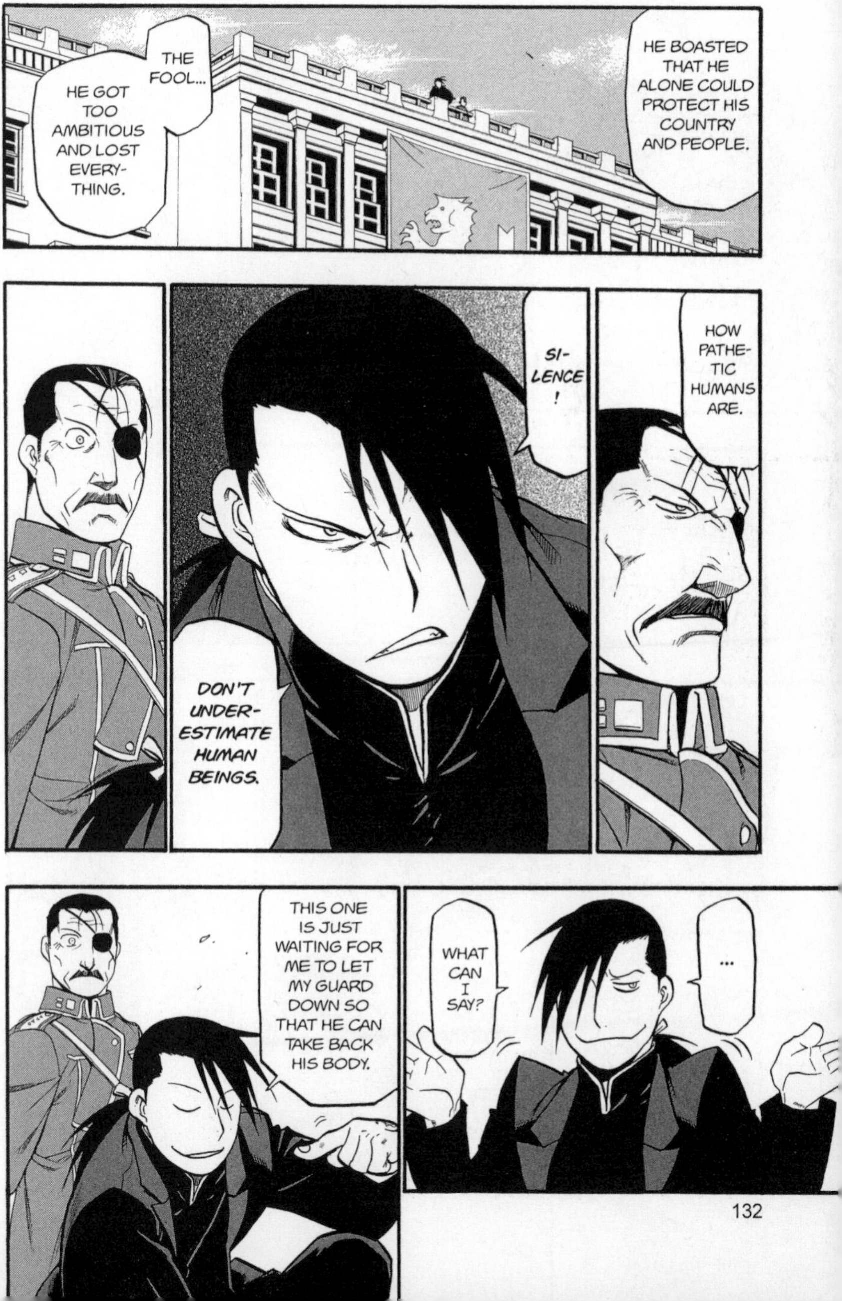
HE BOASTED THAT HE ALONE COULD PROTECT HIS COUNTRY AND PEOPLE.
THE FOOL...
HE GOT TOO AMBITIOUS AND LOST EVERYTHING.
HOW PATHETIC HUMANS ARE.
SILENCE!
DON'T UNDERESTIMATE HUMAN BEINGS.
...
WHAT CAN I SAY?
THIS ONE IS JUST WAITING FOR ME TO LET MY GUARD DOWN SO THAT HE CAN TAKE BACK HIS BODY.

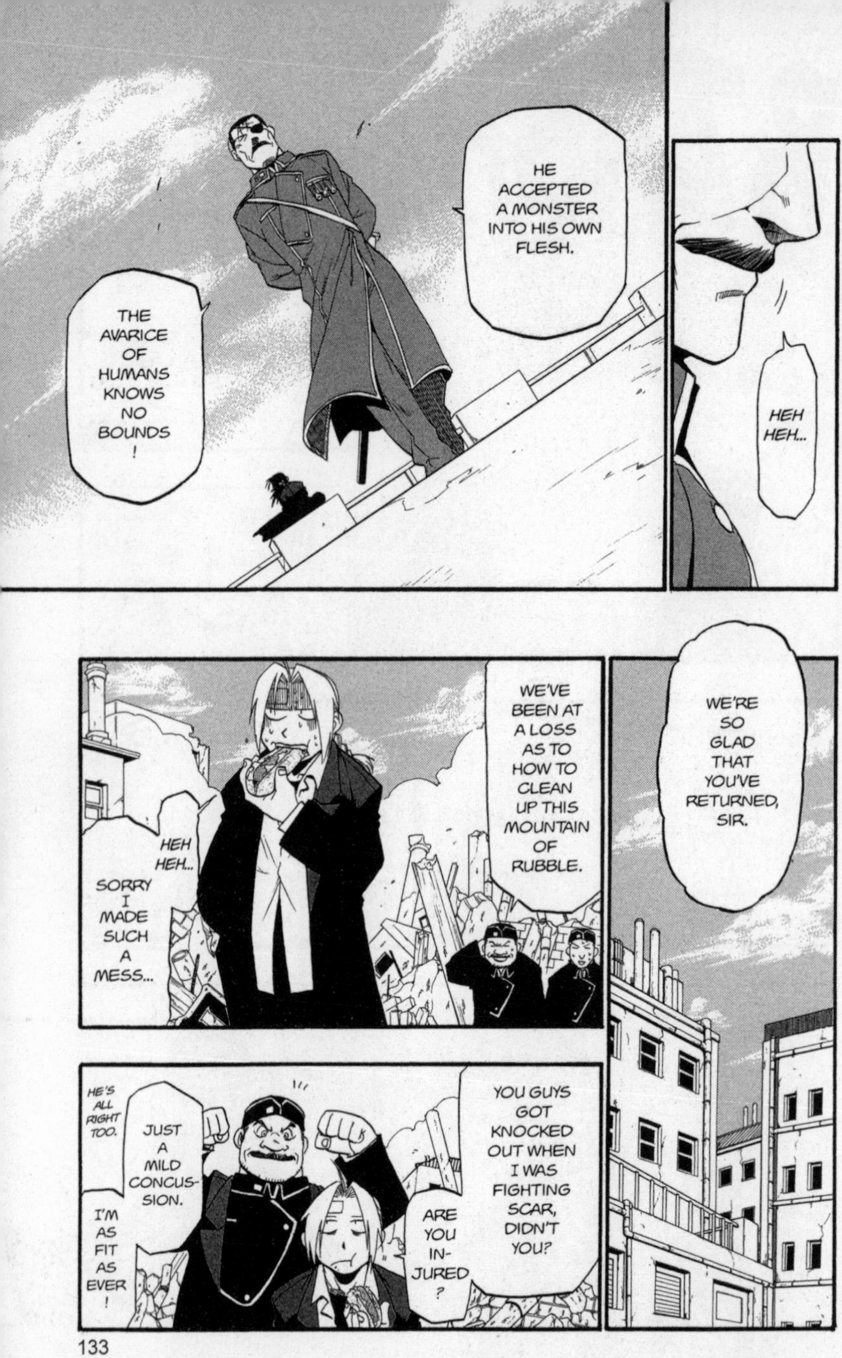
HEH HEH...
HE ACCEPTED A MONSTER INTO HIS OWN FLESH.
THE AVARICE OF HUMANS KNOWS NO BOUNDS!
WE'RE SO GLAD THAT YOU'VE RETURNED, SIR.
WE'VE BEEN AT A LOSS AS TO HOW TO CLEAN UP THIS MOUNTAIN OF RUBBLE.
HEH HEH...
SORRY I MADE SUCH A MESS...
YOU GUYS GOT KNOCKED OUT WHEN I WAS FIGHTING SCAR, DIDN'T YOU?
ARE YOU IN-JURED?
JUST A MILD CONCUS-SION.
HE'S ALL RIGHT TOO.
I'M AS FIT AS EVER!

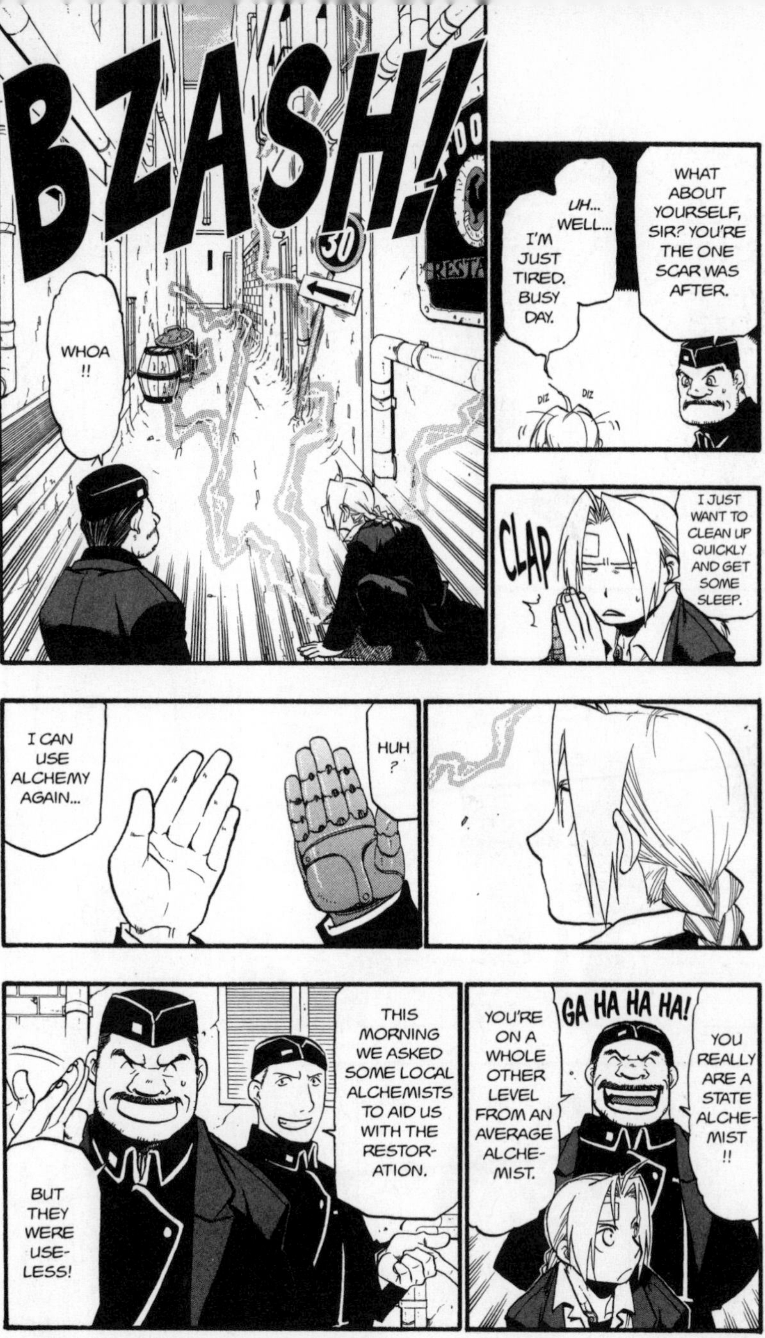
WHAT ABOUT YOURSELF, SIR? YOU'RE THE ONE SCAR WAS AFTER.
UH... WELL... I'M JUST TIRED. BUSY DAY.
DIZ
DIZ
I JUST WANT TO CLEAN UP QUICKLY AND GET SOME SLEEP.
CLAP
BZASH!
30
WHOA!!
HUH?
I CAN USE ALCHEMY AGAIN...
GA HA HA HA!
YOU REALLY ARE A STATE ALCHEMIST!!
YOU'RE ON A WHOLE OTHER LEVEL FROM AN AVERAGE ALCHEMIST.
THIS MORNING WE ASKED SOME LOCAL ALCHEMISTS TO AID US WITH THE RESTORATION.
BUT THEY WERE USELESS!

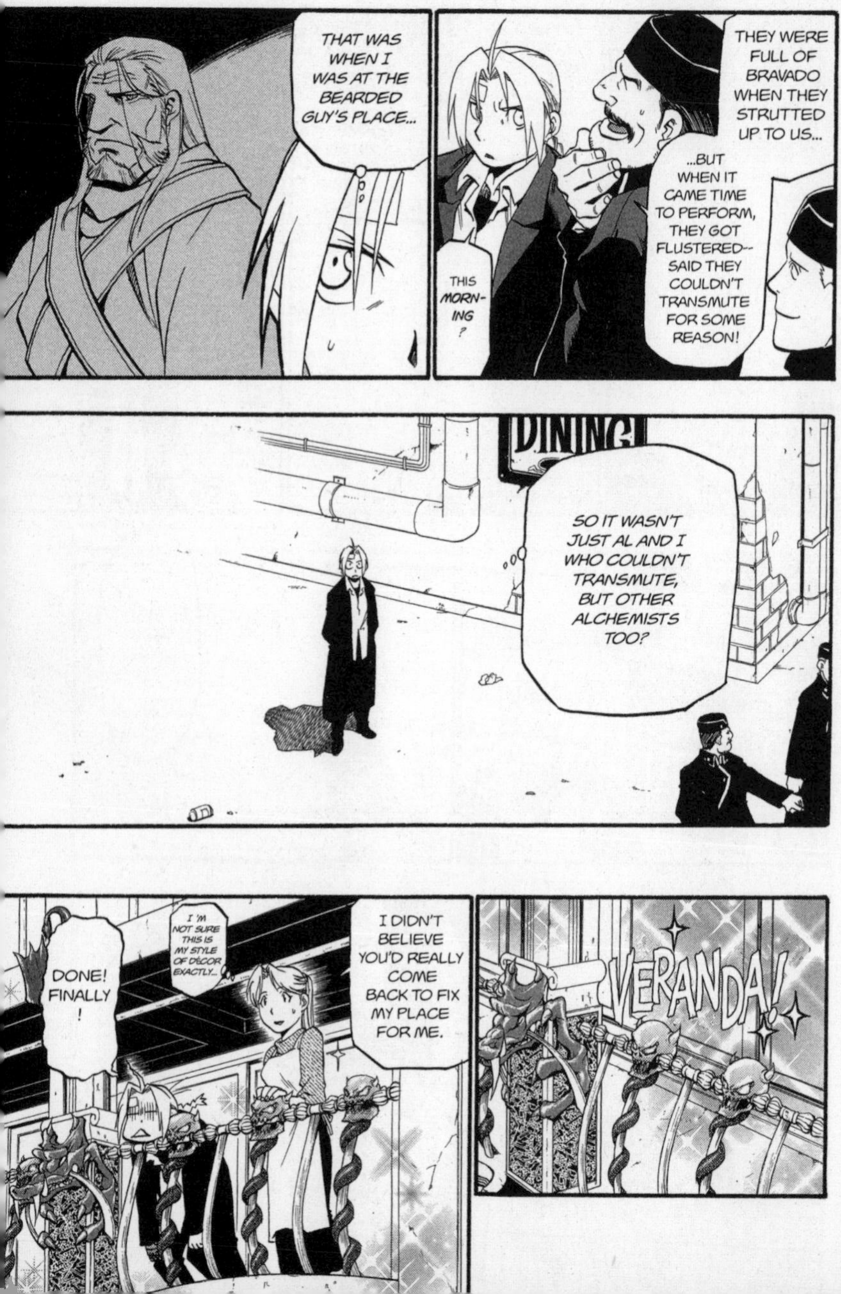
THEY WERE FULL OF BRAVADO WHEN THEY STRUTTED UP TO US...
...BUT WHEN IT CAME TIME TO PERFORM, THEY GOT FLUSTERED-- SAID THEY COULDN'T TRANSMUTE FOR SOME REASON!
THIS MORNING?
THAT WAS WHEN I WAS AT THE BEARDED GUY'S PLACE...
DINING
SO IT WASN'T JUST AL AND I WHO COULDN'T TRANSMUTE, BUT OTHER ALCHEMISTS TOO?
VERANDA!
I DIDN'T BELIEVE YOU'D REALLY COME BACK TO FIX MY PLACE FOR ME.
I'M NOT SURE THIS IS MY STYLE OF DÉCOR EXACTLY...
DONE! FINALLY!

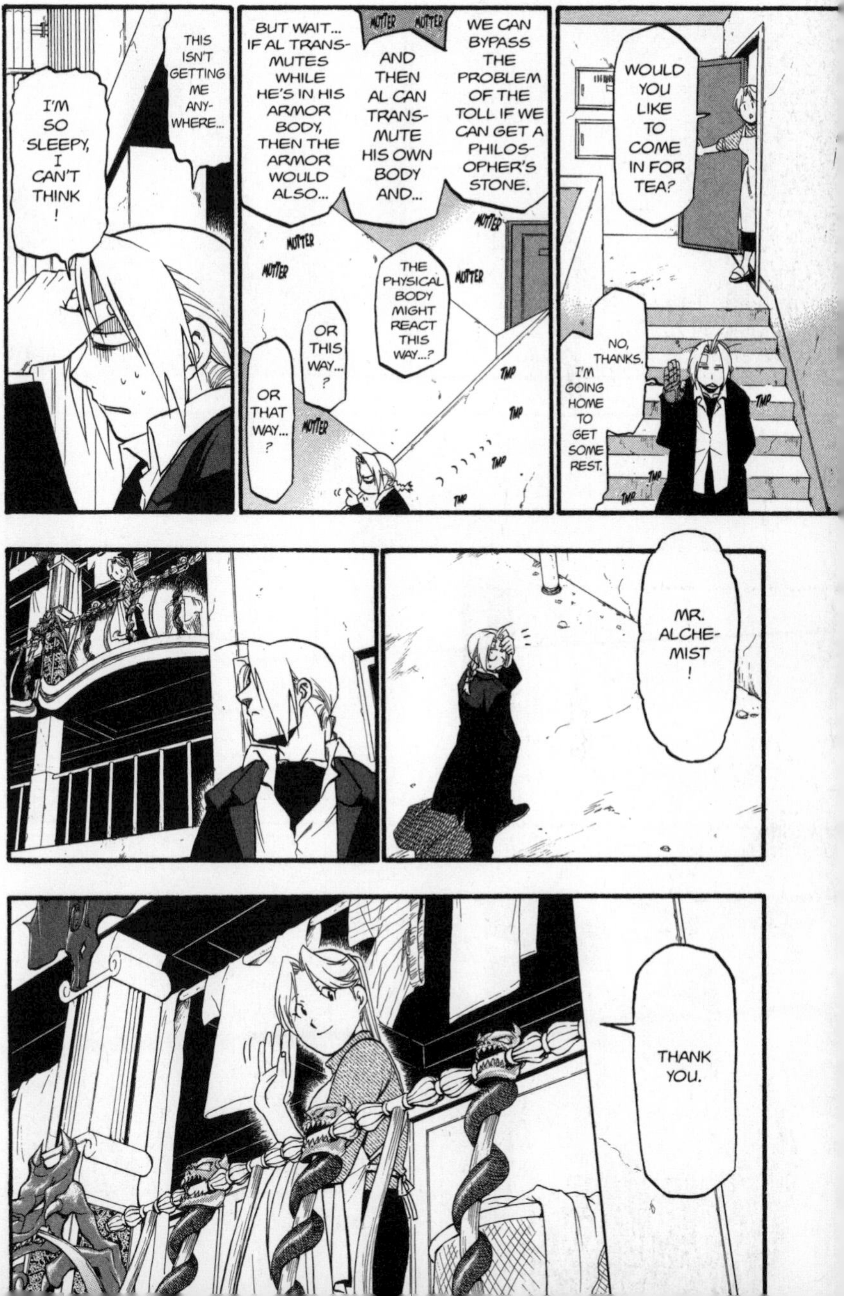
WOULD YOU LIKE TO COME IN FOR TEA?
NO, THANKS. I'M GOING HOME TO GET SOME REST.
TMP TMP TMP
WE CAN BYPASS THE PROBLEM OF THE TOLL IF WE CAN GET A PHILOSOPHER'S STONE.
MUTTER MUTTER
AND THEN AL CAN TRANSMUTE HIS OWN BODY AND...
BUT WAIT... IF AL TRANSMUTES WHILE HE'S IN HIS ARMOR BODY, THEN THE ARMOR WOULD ALSO...
MUTTER
THE PHYSICAL BODY MIGHT REACT THIS WAY...?
MUTTER MUTTER
OR THIS WAY...?
OR THAT WAY...?
MUTTER
TMP TMP TMP TMP
THIS ISN'T GETTING ME ANYWHERE...
I'M SO SLEEPY, I CAN'T THINK!
MR. ALCHEMIST!
THANK YOU.

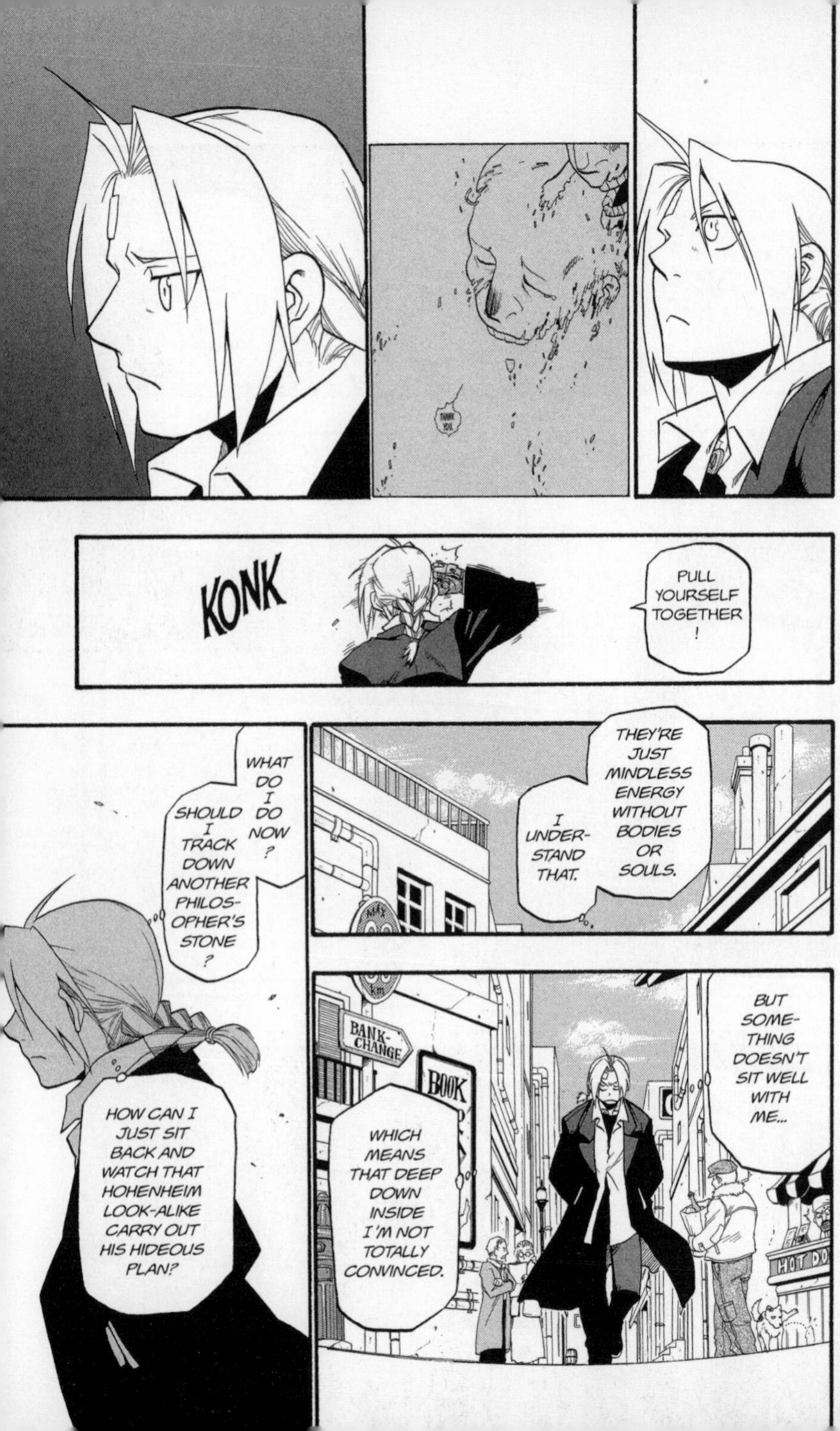
THANK YOU.
PULL YOURSELF TOGETHER!
KONK
THEY'RE JUST MINDLESS ENERGY WITHOUT BODIES OR SOULS.
I UNDERSTAND THAT.
BUT SOMETHING DOESN'T SIT WELL WITH ME...
BANK-CHANGE
BOOK
WHICH MEANS THAT DEEP DOWN INSIDE I'M NOT TOTALLY CONVINCED.
WHAT DO I DO NOW?
SHOULD I TRACK DOWN ANOTHER PHILOSOPHER'S STONE?
HOW CAN I JUST SIT BACK AND WATCH THAT HOHENHEIM LOOK-ALIKE CARRY OUT HIS HIDEOUS PLAN?

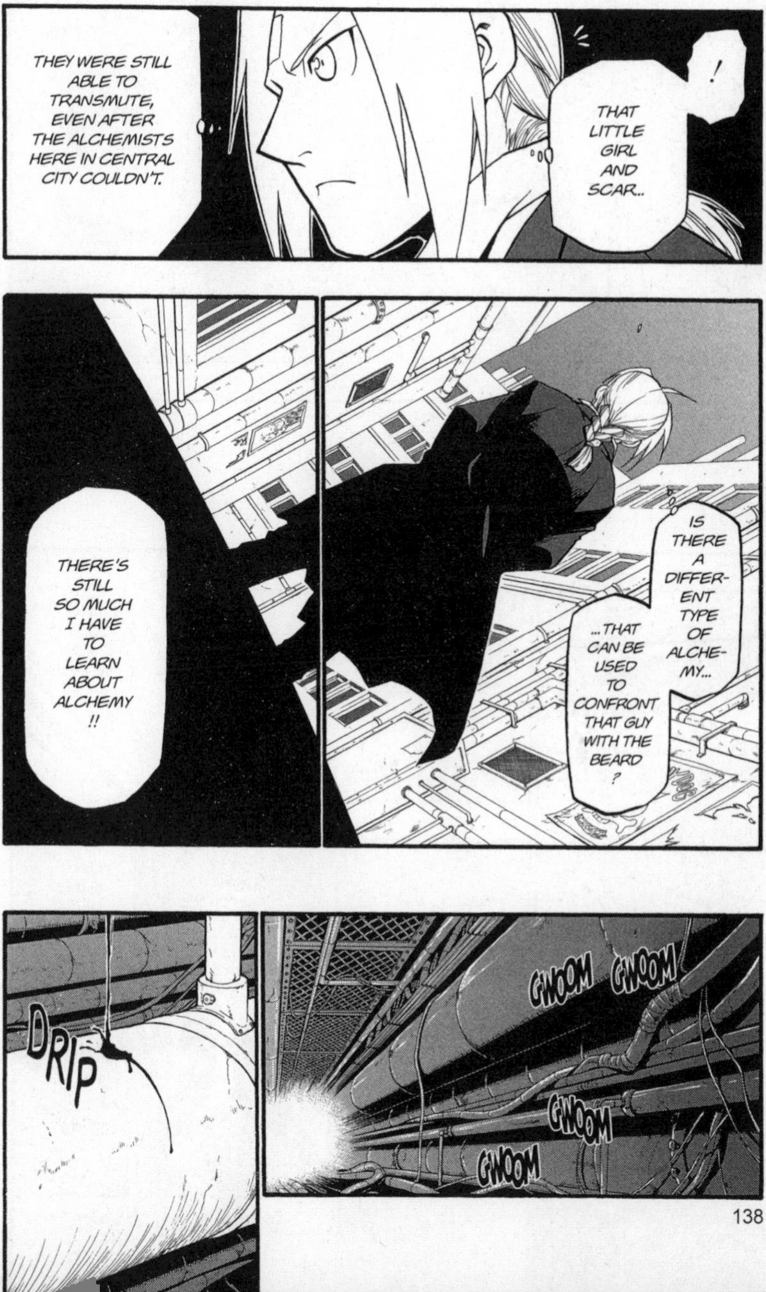
!
THAT LITTLE GIRL AND SCAR...
THEY WERE STILL ABLE TO TRANSMUTE, EVEN AFTER THE ALCHEMISTS HERE IN CENTRAL CITY COULDN'T.
IS THERE A DIFFERENT TYPE OF ALCHEMY...
...THAT CAN BE USED TO CONFRONT THAT GUY WITH THE BEARD?
THERE'S STILL SO MUCH I HAVE TO LEARN ABOUT ALCHEMY!!
GWOOM GWOOM
GWOOM
GWOOM
DRIP

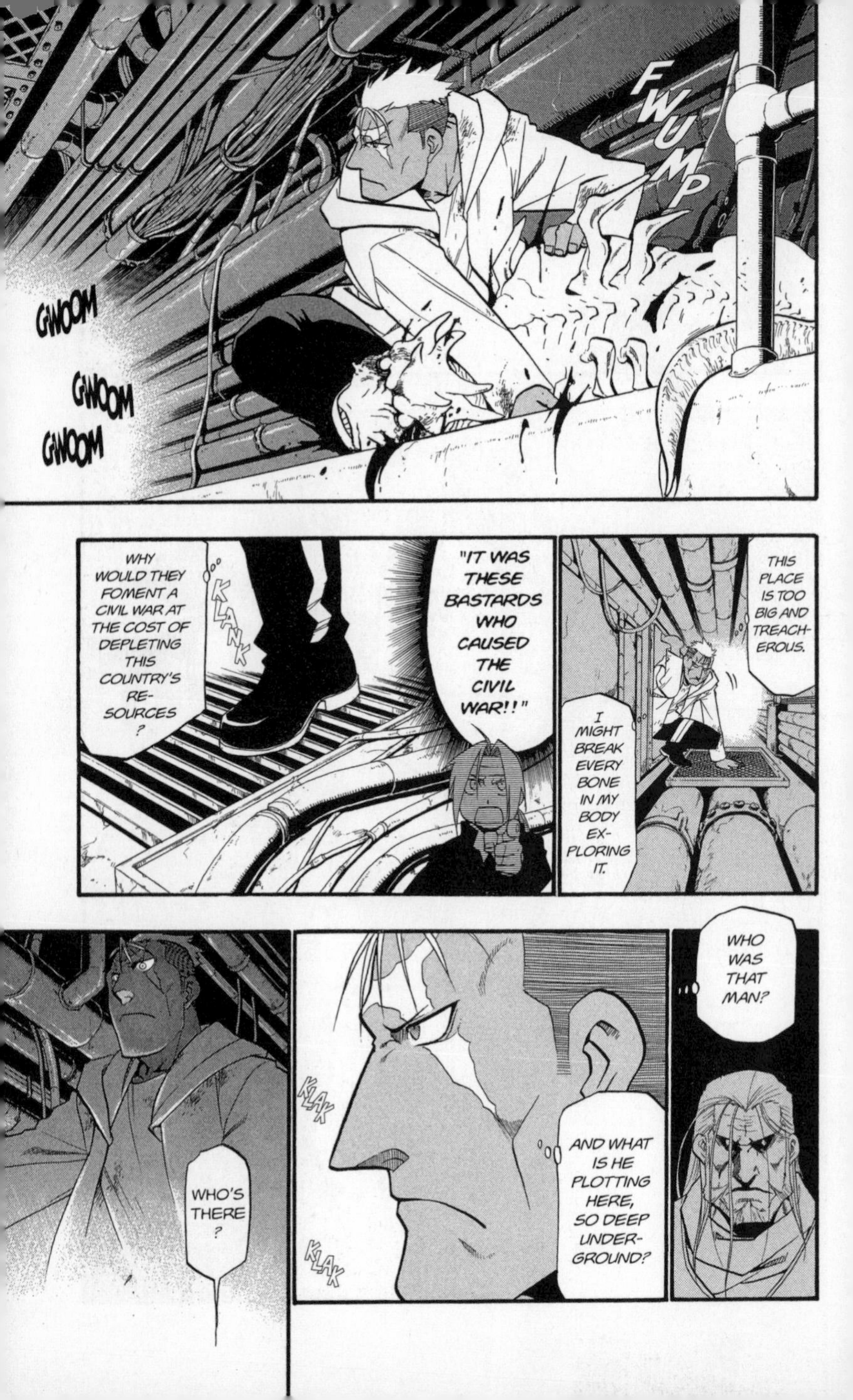
FWUMP
GWOOM
GWOOM
GWOOM
THIS PLACE IS TOO BIG AND TREACH-EROUS.
I MIGHT BREAK EVERY BONE IN MY BODY EX-PLORING IT.
"IT WAS THESE BASTARDS WHO CAUSED THE CIVIL WAR!!"
KLANK
WHY WOULD THEY FOMENT A CIVIL WAR AT THE COST OF DEPLETING THIS COUNTRY'S RE-SOURCES?
WHO WAS THAT MAN?
AND WHAT IS HE PLOTTING HERE, SO DEEP UNDER-GROUND?
KLAK
KLAK
WHO'S THERE?

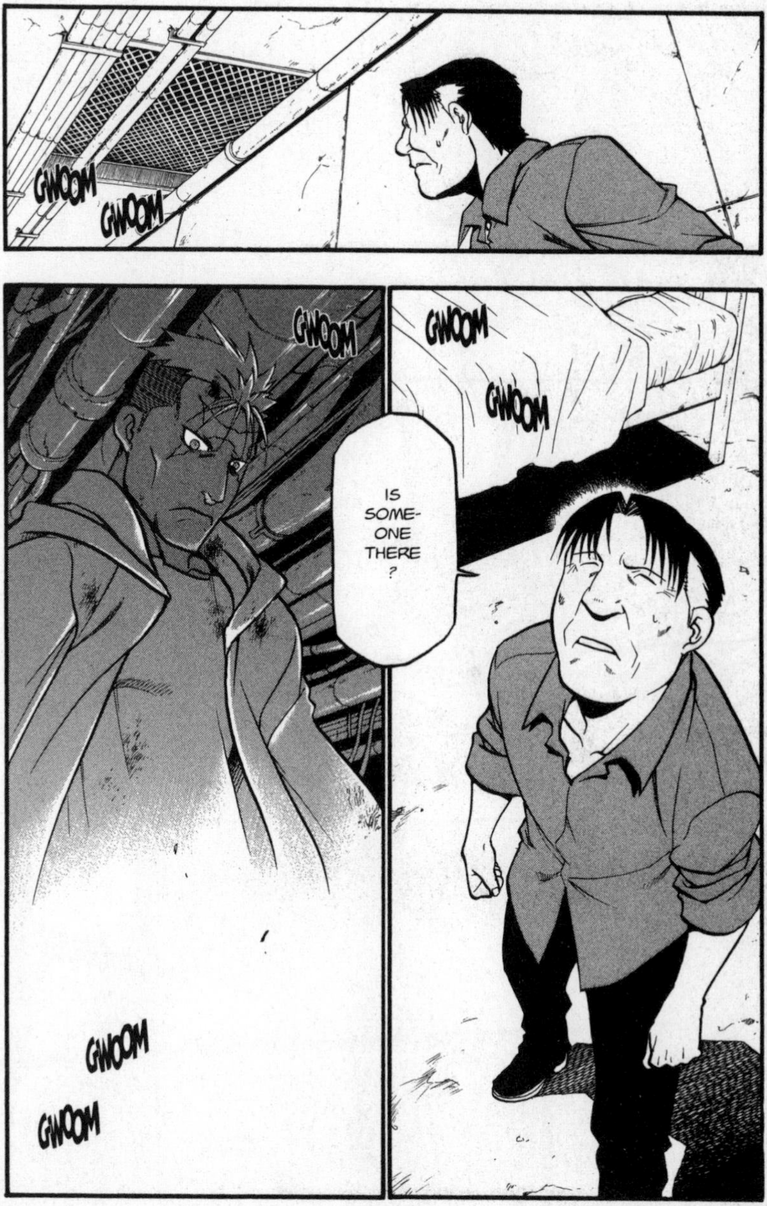
GWOOM
GWOOM
GWOOM
GWOOM
IS SOME-ONE THERE?
GWOOM
GWOOM
GWOOM

Chapter 57
Scars of Ishbal

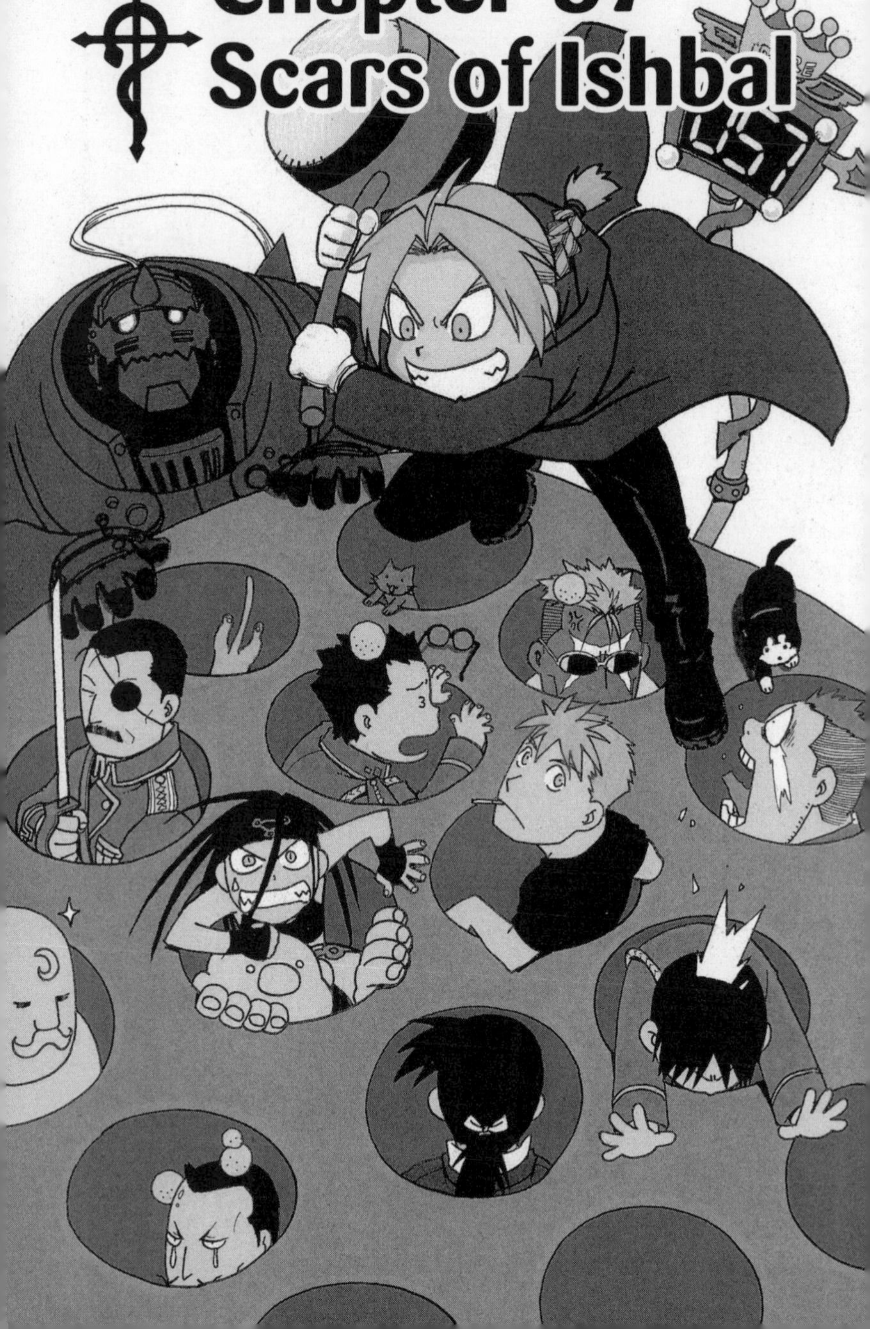

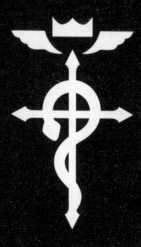

FULLMETAL
ALCHEMIST

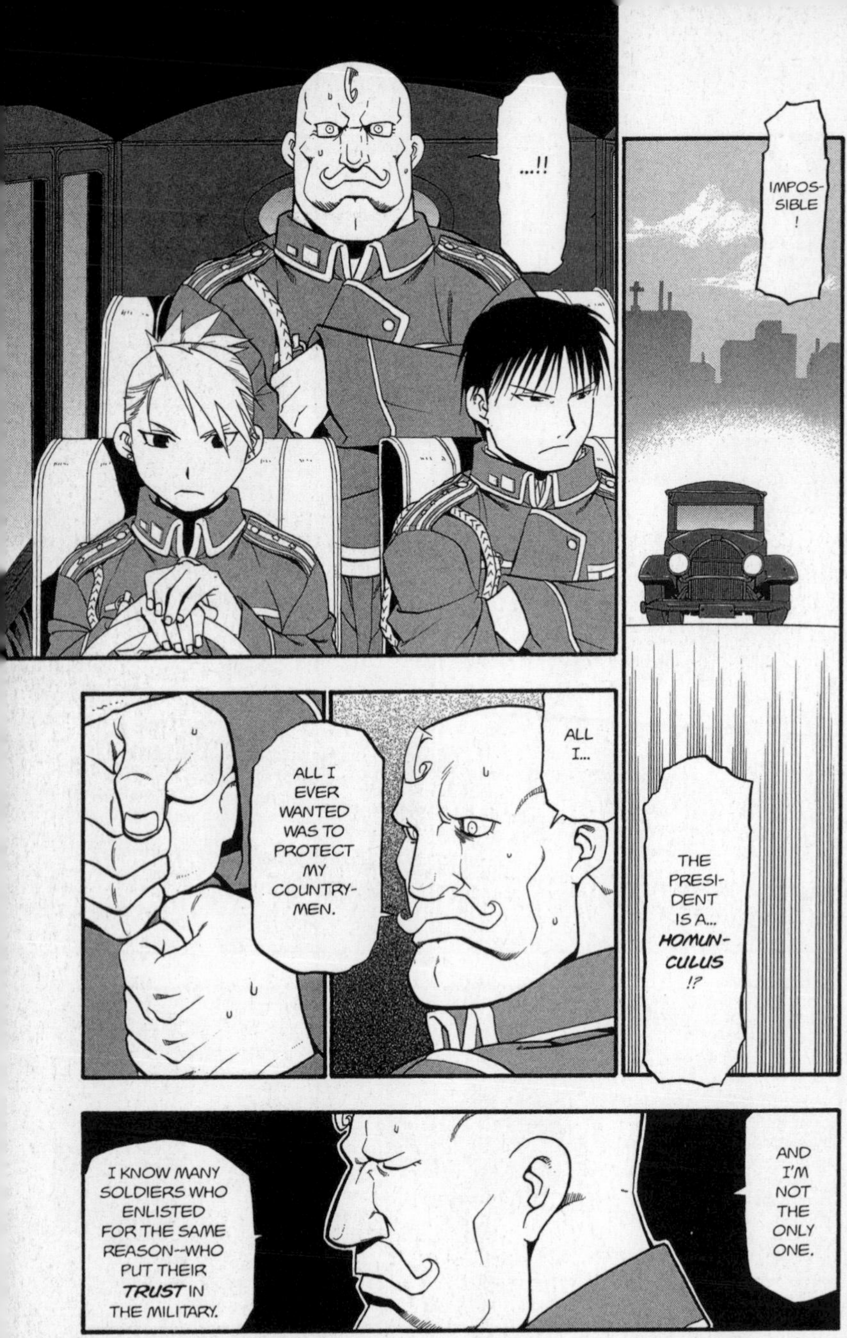
IMPOSSIBLE!
...!!
THE PRESIDENT IS A... HOMUNCULUS!?
ALL I...
ALL I EVER WANTED WAS TO PROTECT MY COUNTRYMEN.
AND I'M NOT THE ONLY ONE.
I KNOW MANY SOLDIERS WHO ENLISTED FOR THE SAME REASON--WHO PUT THEIR TRUST IN THE MILITARY.

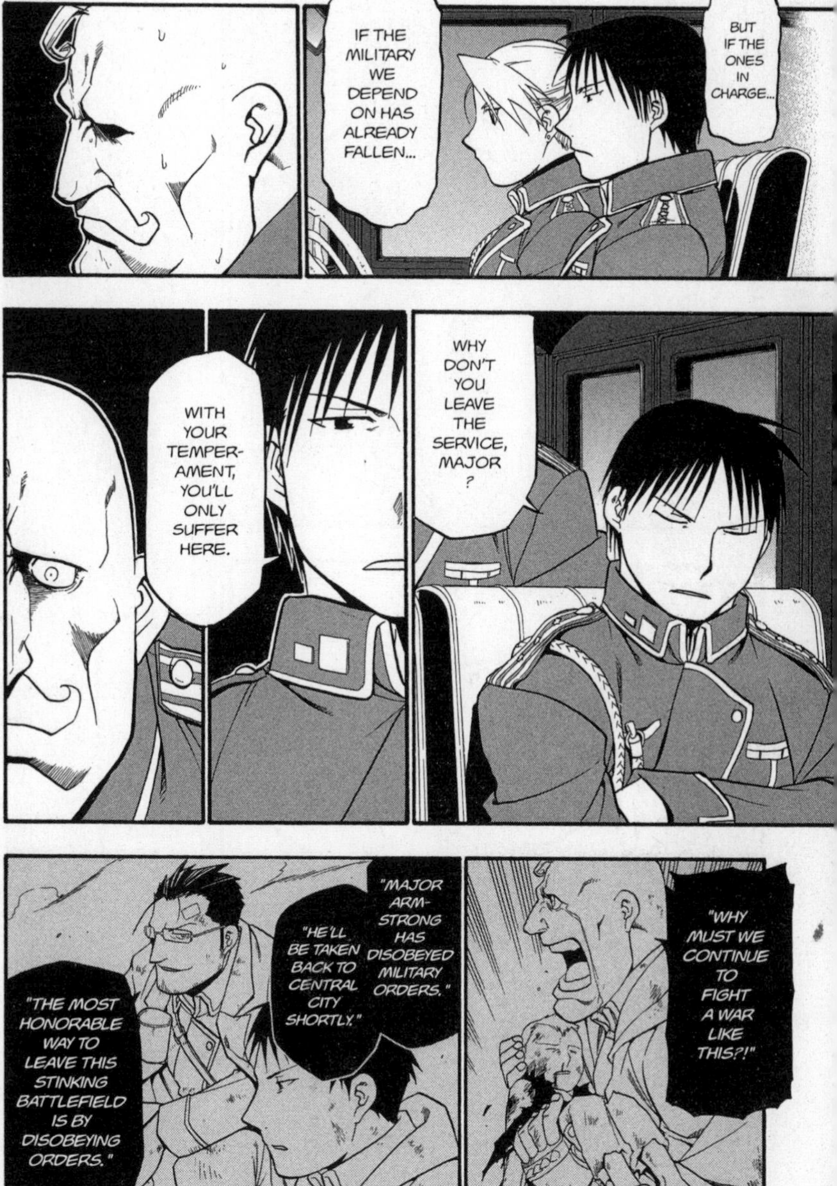
BUT IF THE ONES IN CHARGE...
IF THE MILITARY WE DEPEND ON HAS ALREADY FALLEN...
WHY DON'T YOU LEAVE THE SERVICE, MAJOR?
WITH YOUR TEMPERAMENT, YOU'LL ONLY SUFFER HERE.
"WHY MUST WE CONTINUE TO FIGHT A WAR LIKE THIS?!"
"MAJOR ARMSTRONG HAS DISOBEYED MILITARY ORDERS."
"HE'LL BE TAKEN BACK TO CENTRAL CITY SHORTLY."
"THE MOST HONORABLE WAY TO LEAVE THIS STINKING BATTLEFIELD IS BY DISOBEYING ORDERS."

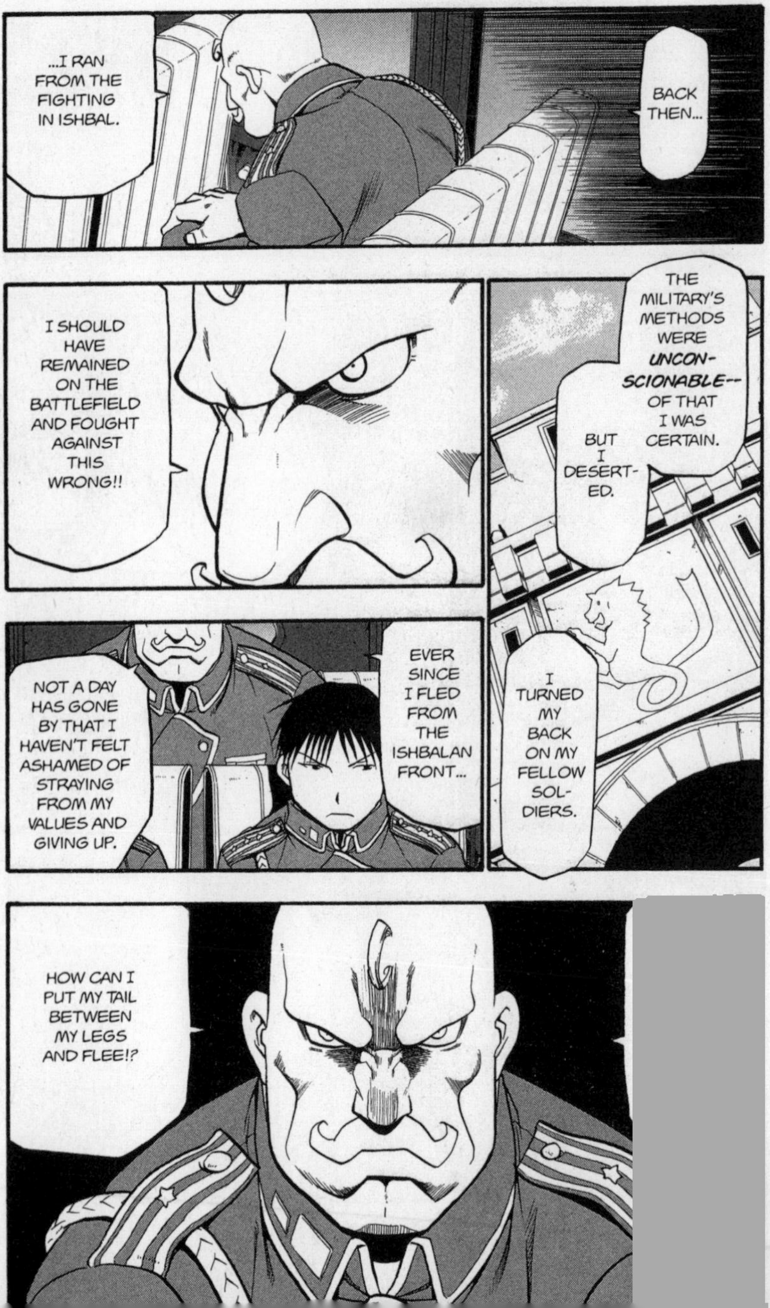
BACK THEN...
...I RAN FROM THE FIGHTING IN ISHBAL.
THE MILITARY'S METHODS WERE ***UNCONSCIONABLE***-- OF THAT I WAS CERTAIN.
BUT I DESERTED.
I TURNED MY BACK ON MY FELLOW SOLDIERS.
I SHOULD HAVE REMAINED ON THE BATTLEFIELD AND FOUGHT AGAINST THIS WRONG!!
EVER SINCE I FLED FROM THE ISHBALAN FRONT...
NOT A DAY HAS GONE BY THAT I HAVEN'T FELT ASHAMED OF STRAYING FROM MY VALUES AND GIVING UP.
HOW CAN I PUT MY TAIL BETWEEN MY LEGS AND FLEE!?

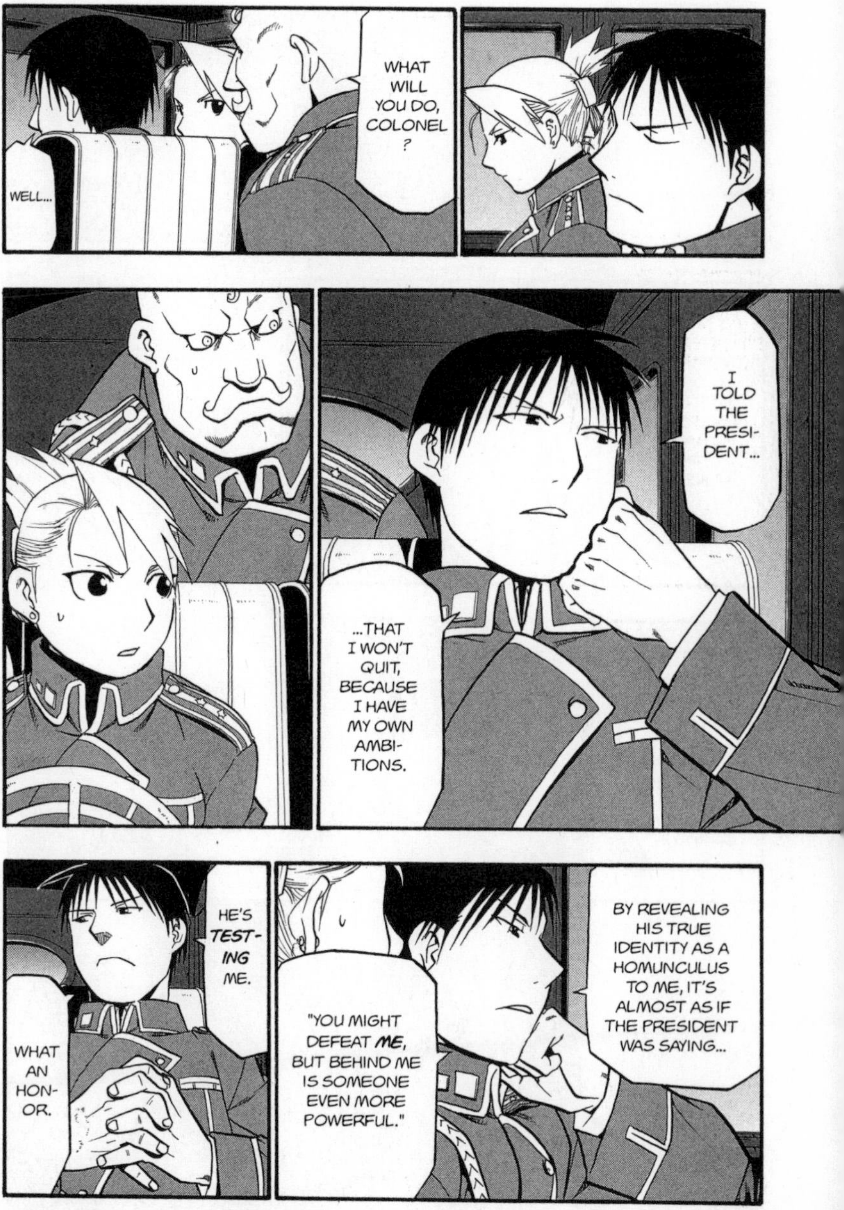
WHAT WILL YOU DO, COLONEL?
WELL...
I TOLD THE PRESIDENT...
...THAT I WON'T QUIT, BECAUSE I HAVE MY OWN AMBITIONS.
BY REVEALING HIS TRUE IDENTITY AS A HOMUNCULUS TO ME, IT'S ALMOST AS IF THE PRESIDENT WAS SAYING...
"YOU MIGHT DEFEAT *ME*, BUT BEHIND ME IS SOMEONE EVEN MORE POWERFUL."
HE'S *TESTING* ME.
WHAT AN HONOR.

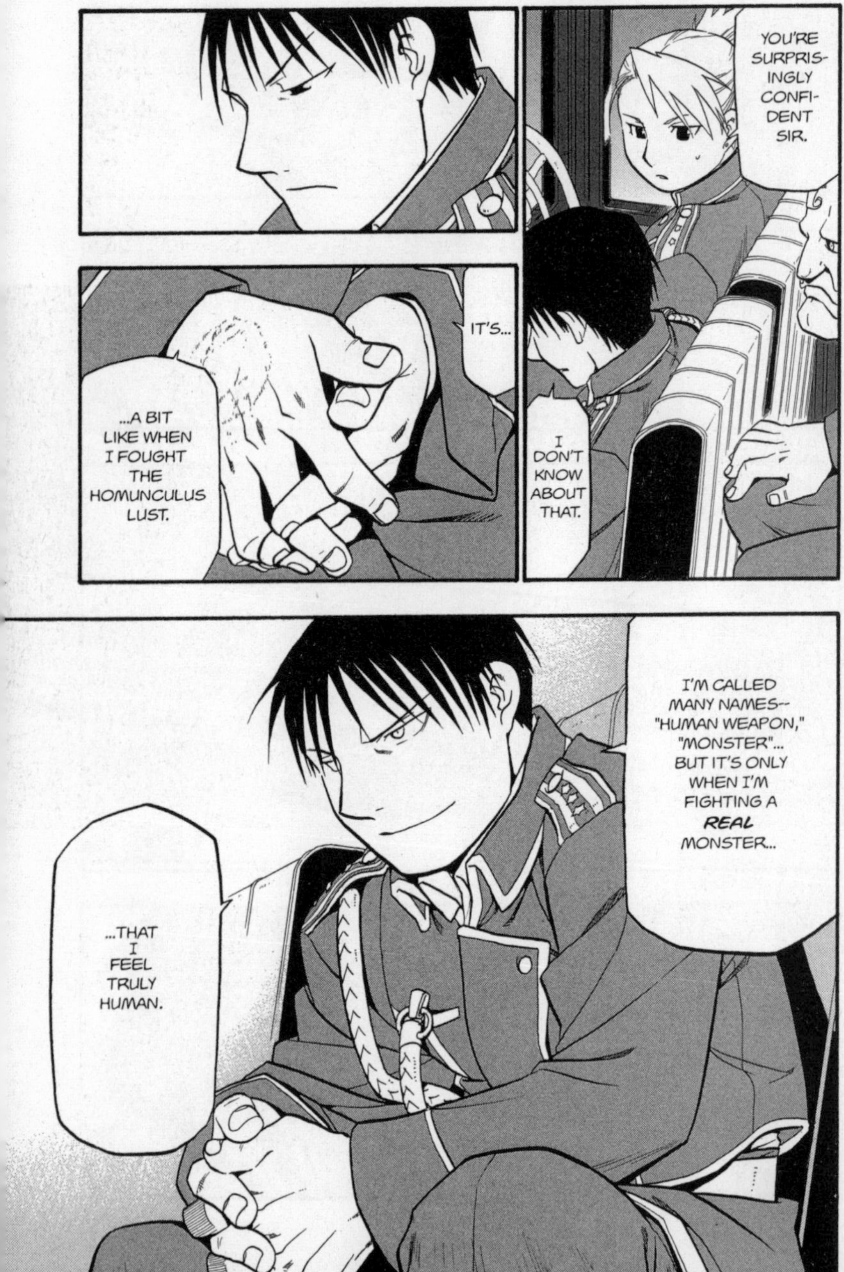
YOU'RE SURPRIS-INGLY CONFI-DENT SIR.
I DON'T KNOW ABOUT THAT.
IT'S...
...A BIT LIKE WHEN I FOUGHT THE HOMUNCULUS LUST.
I'M CALLED MANY NAMES-- "HUMAN WEAPON," "MONSTER"... BUT IT'S ONLY WHEN I'M FIGHTING A ***REAL*** MONSTER...
...THAT I FEEL TRULY HUMAN.

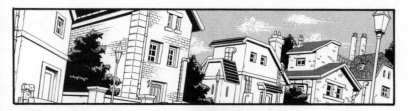

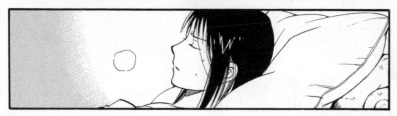

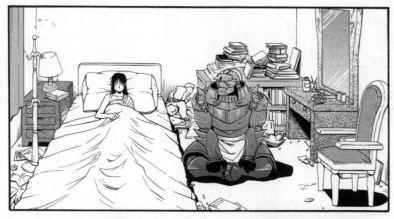

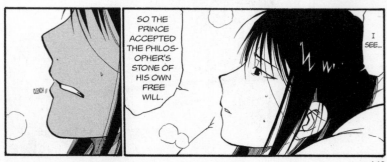

SO THE PRINCE ACCEPTED THE PHILOSOPHER'S STONE OF HIS OWN FREE WILL.

I SEE...

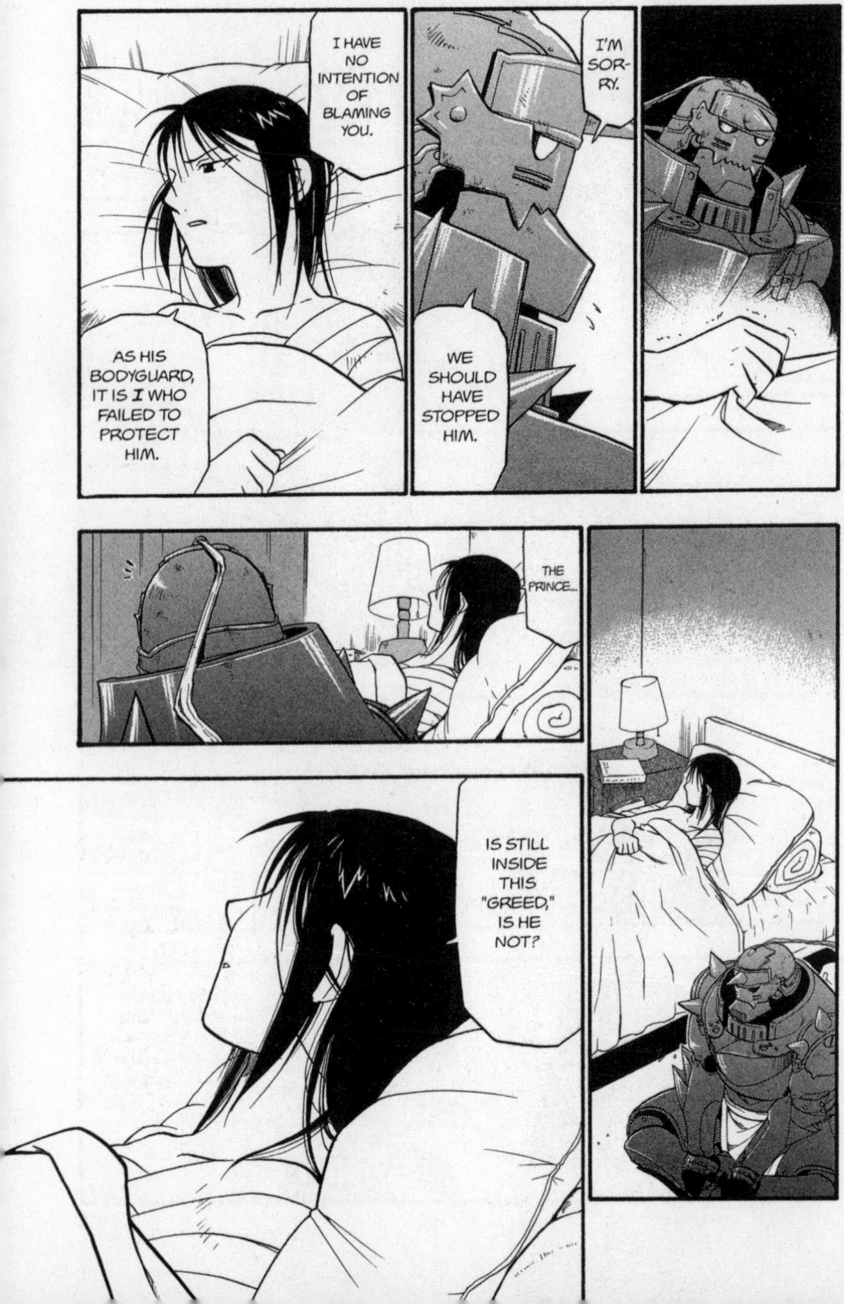
I'M SORRY.
WE SHOULD HAVE STOPPED HIM.
I HAVE NO INTENTION OF BLAMING YOU.
AS HIS BODYGUARD, IT IS I WHO FAILED TO PROTECT HIM.
THE PRINCE...
IS STILL INSIDE THIS "GREED," IS HE NOT?

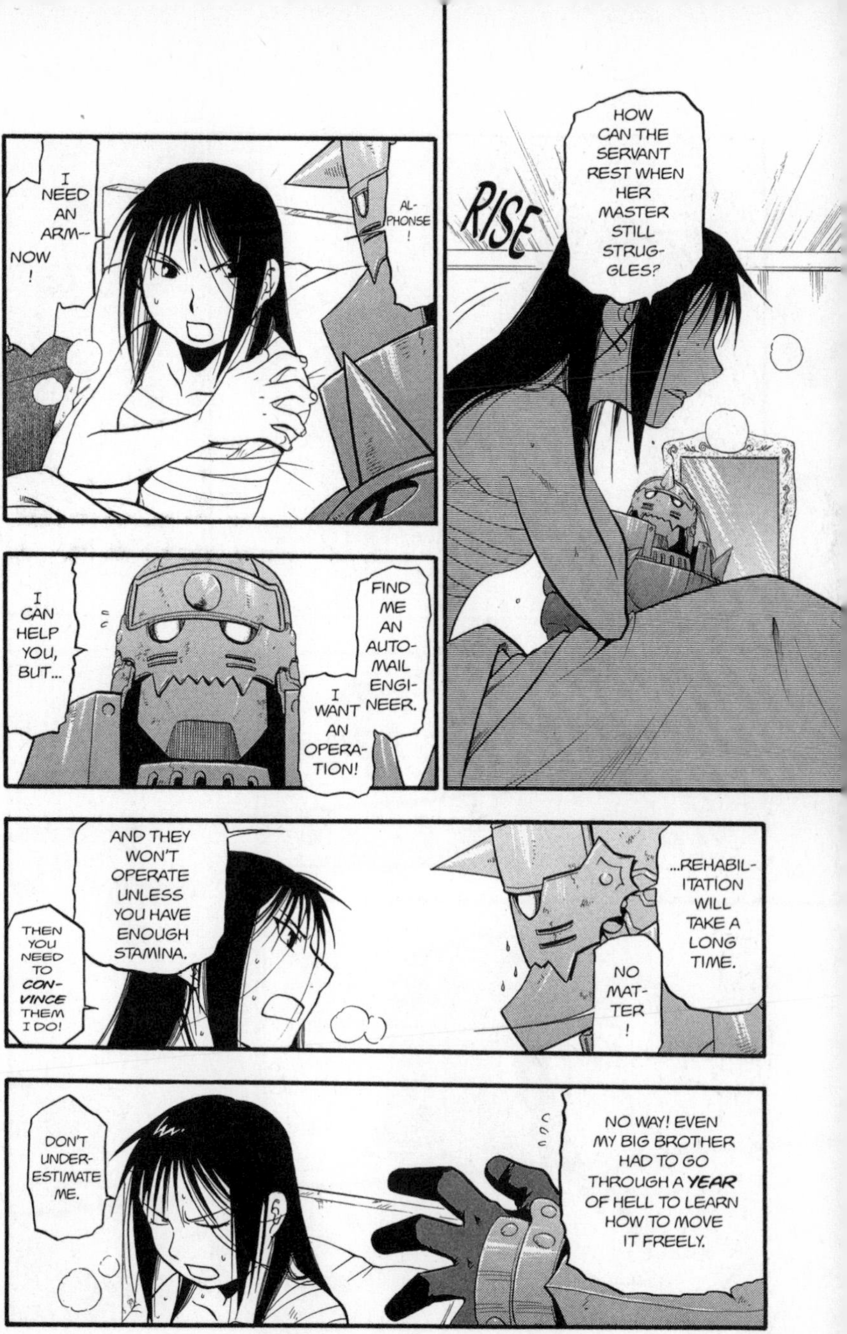
RISE
HOW CAN THE SERVANT REST WHEN HER MASTER STILL STRUGGLES?
ALPHONSE!
I NEED AN ARM-- NOW!
FIND ME AN AUTOMAIL ENGINEER.
I WANT AN OPERATION!
I CAN HELP YOU, BUT...
...REHABILITATION WILL TAKE A LONG TIME.
NO MATTER!
AND THEY WON'T OPERATE UNLESS YOU HAVE ENOUGH STAMINA.
THEN YOU NEED TO CONVINCE THEM I DO!
NO WAY! EVEN MY BIG BROTHER HAD TO GO THROUGH A YEAR OF HELL TO LEARN HOW TO MOVE IT FREELY.
DON'T UNDERESTIMATE ME.

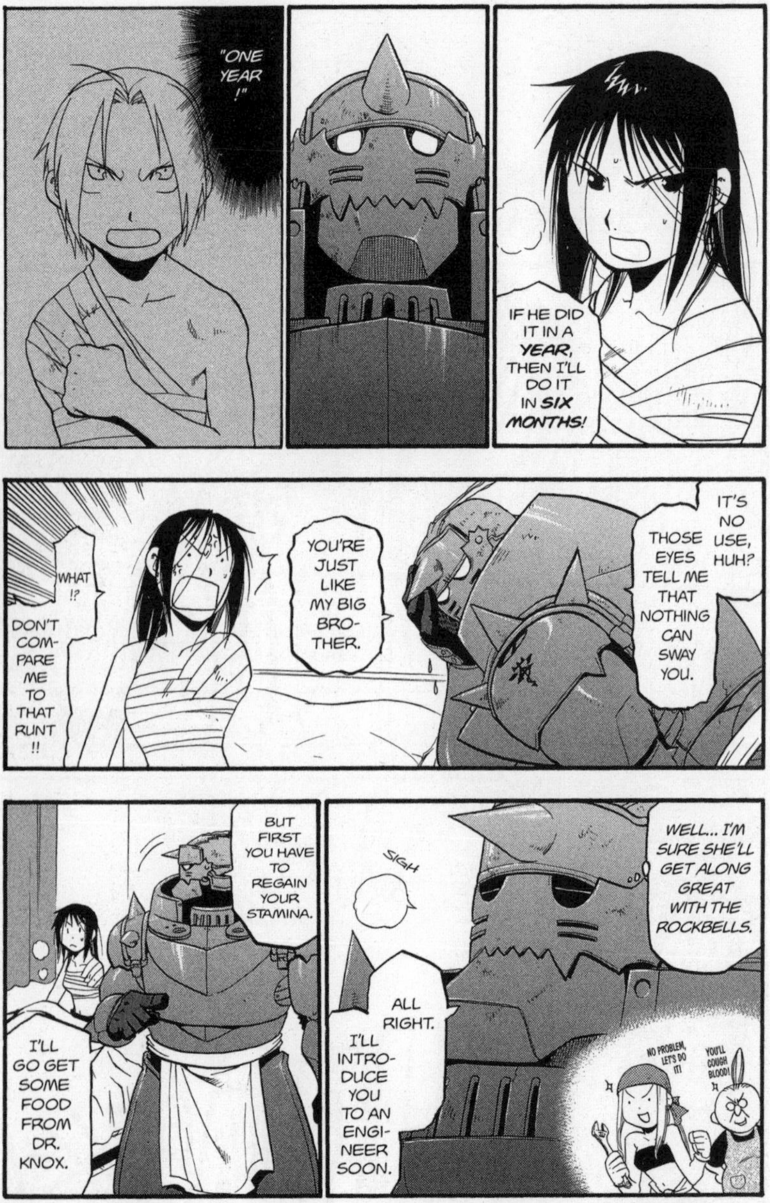
IF HE DID IT IN A YEAR, THEN I'LL DO IT IN SIX MONTHS!
"ONE YEAR!"
IT'S NO USE, HUH?
THOSE EYES TELL ME THAT NOTHING CAN SWAY YOU.
YOU'RE JUST LIKE MY BIG BRO-THER.
WHAT!?
DON'T COM-PARE ME TO THAT RUNT!!
WELL... I'M SURE SHE'LL GET ALONG GREAT WITH THE ROCKBELLS.
SIGH
ALL RIGHT.
I'LL INTRO-DUCE YOU TO AN ENGI-NEER SOON.
YOU'LL COUGH BLOOD!
NO PROBLEM, LET'S DO IT!
BUT FIRST YOU HAVE TO REGAIN YOUR STAMINA.
I'LL GO GET SOME FOOD FROM DR. KNOX.

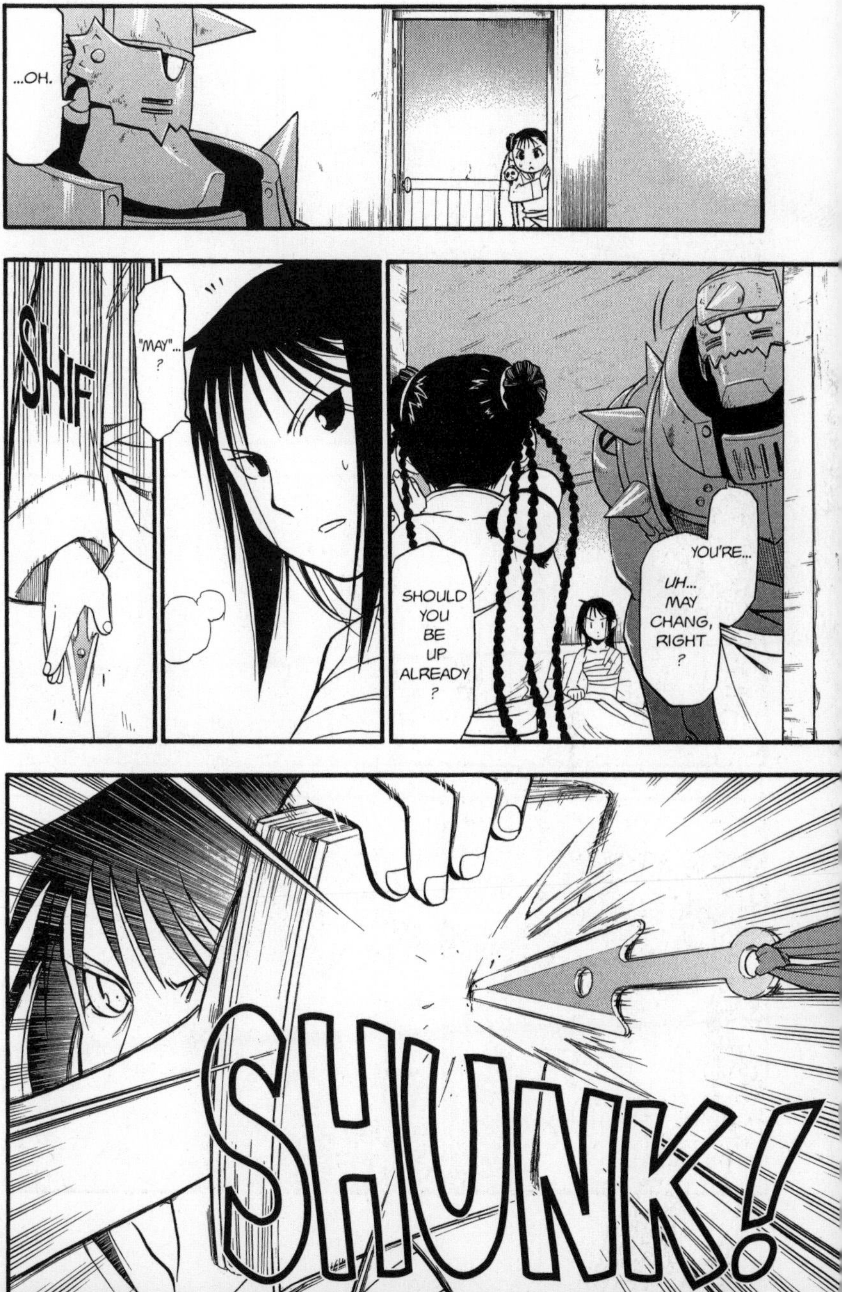
...OH.
YOU'RE... UH... MAY CHANG, RIGHT?
SHOULD YOU BE UP ALREADY?
"MAY"...?
SHIF
SHUNK!

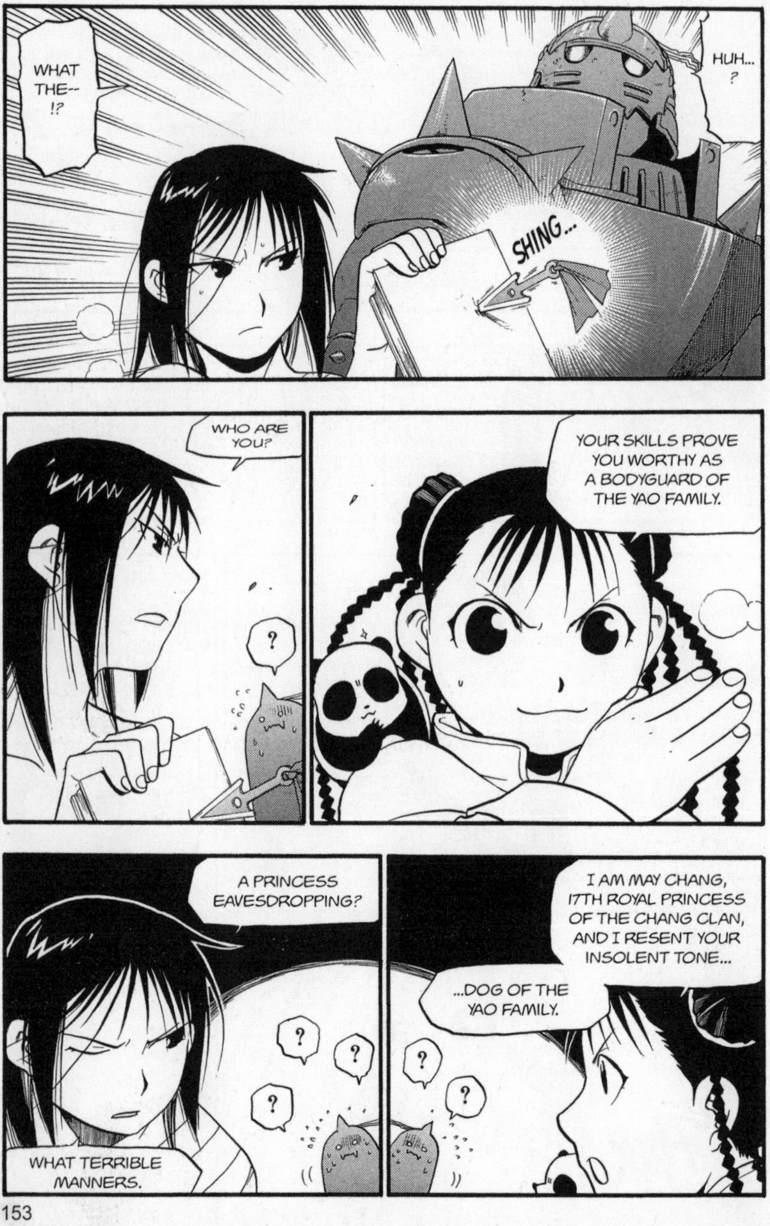
HUH... ?
SHING...
WHAT THE-- !?
YOUR SKILLS PROVE YOU WORTHY AS A BODYGUARD OF THE YAO FAMILY.
WHO ARE YOU?
?
I AM MAY CHANG, 17TH ROYAL PRINCESS OF THE CHANG CLAN, AND I RESENT YOUR INSOLENT TONE...
...DOG OF THE YAO FAMILY.
?
?
A PRINCESS EAVESDROPPING?
?
?
?
WHAT TERRIBLE MANNERS.

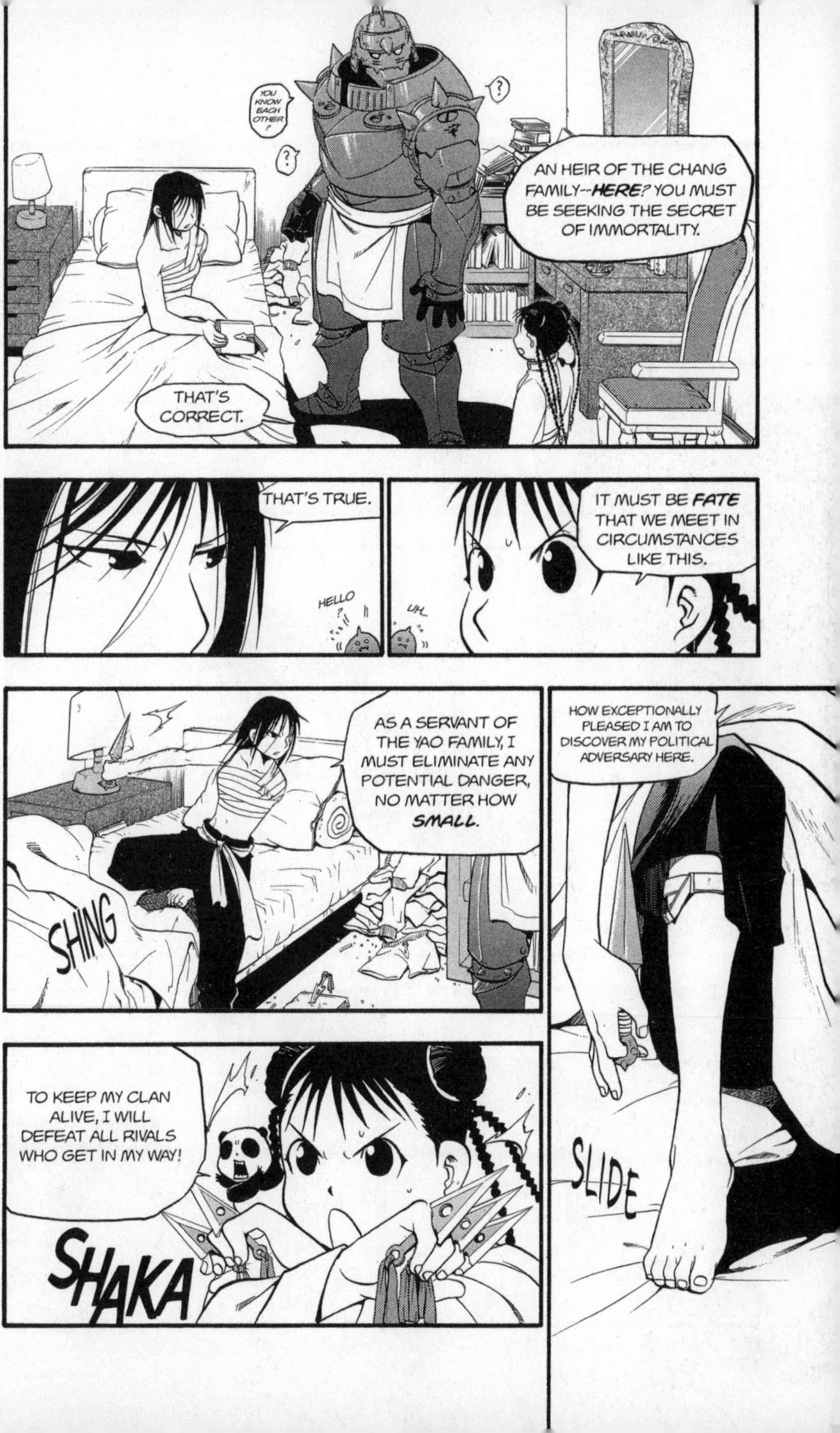

AN HEIR OF THE CHANG FAMILY--**HERE?** YOU MUST BE SEEKING THE SECRET OF IMMORTALITY.
?
YOU KNOW EACH OTHER?
?
THAT'S CORRECT.
IT MUST BE **FATE** THAT WE MEET IN CIRCUMSTANCES LIKE THIS.
UH..
THAT'S TRUE.
HELLO?
HOW EXCEPTIONALLY PLEASED I AM TO DISCOVER MY POLITICAL ADVERSARY HERE.
SLIDE
AS A SERVANT OF THE YAO FAMILY, I MUST ELIMINATE ANY POTENTIAL DANGER, NO MATTER HOW **SMALL.**
SHING
TO KEEP MY CLAN ALIVE, I WILL DEFEAT ALL RIVALS WHO GET IN MY WAY!
SHAKA

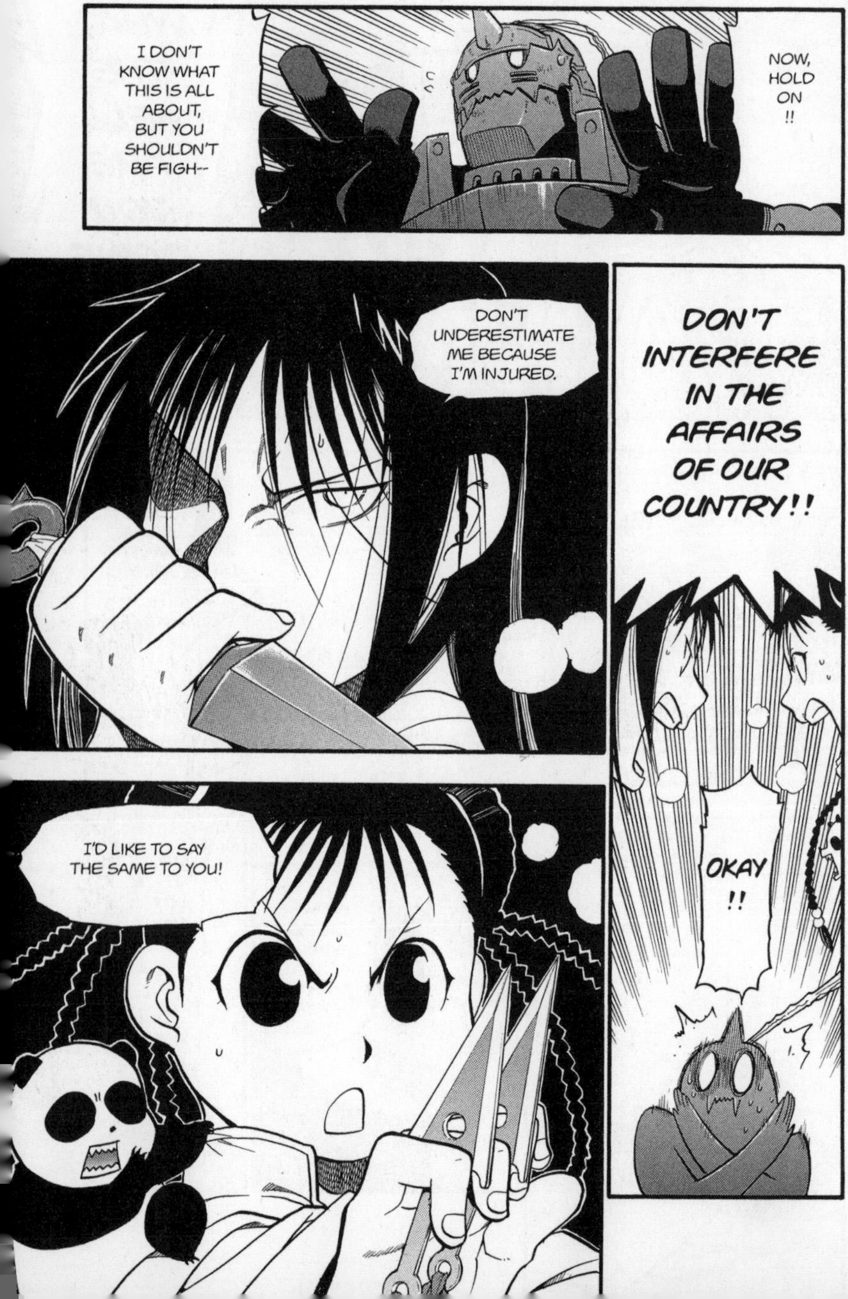
NOW, HOLD ON !!
I DON'T KNOW WHAT THIS IS ALL ABOUT, BUT YOU SHOULDN'T BE FIGH--
DON'T INTERFERE IN THE AFFAIRS OF OUR COUNTRY!!
OKAY !!
DON'T UNDERESTIMATE ME BECAUSE I'M INJURED.
I'D LIKE TO SAY THE SAME TO YOU!

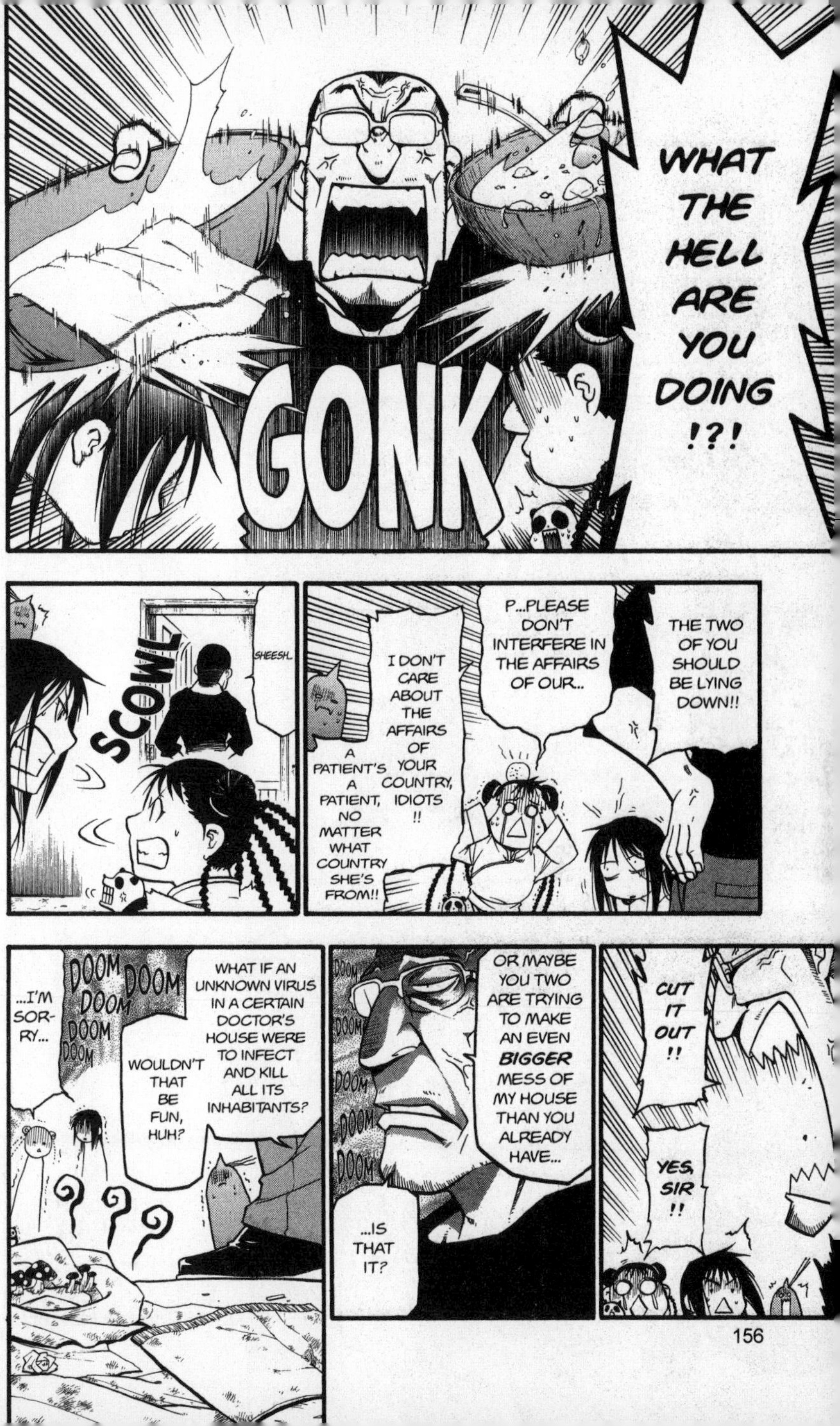
WHAT THE HELL ARE YOU DOING!?!
GONK
THE TWO OF YOU SHOULD BE LYING DOWN!!
P...PLEASE DON'T INTERFERE IN THE AFFAIRS OF OUR...
I DON'T CARE ABOUT THE AFFAIRS OF YOUR COUNTRY, IDIOTS!!
A PATIENT'S A PATIENT, NO MATTER WHAT COUNTRY SHE'S FROM!!
SHEESH.
SCOWL
CUT IT OUT!!
YES, SIR!!
OR MAYBE YOU TWO ARE TRYING TO MAKE AN EVEN **BIGGER** MESS OF MY HOUSE THAN YOU ALREADY HAVE...
DOOM DOOM DOOM DOOM
...IS THAT IT?
WHAT IF AN UNKNOWN VIRUS IN A CERTAIN DOCTOR'S HOUSE WERE TO INFECT AND KILL ALL ITS INHABITANTS?
WOULDN'T THAT BE FUN, HUH?
DOOM DOOM DOOM DOOM DOOM
...I'M SORRY...

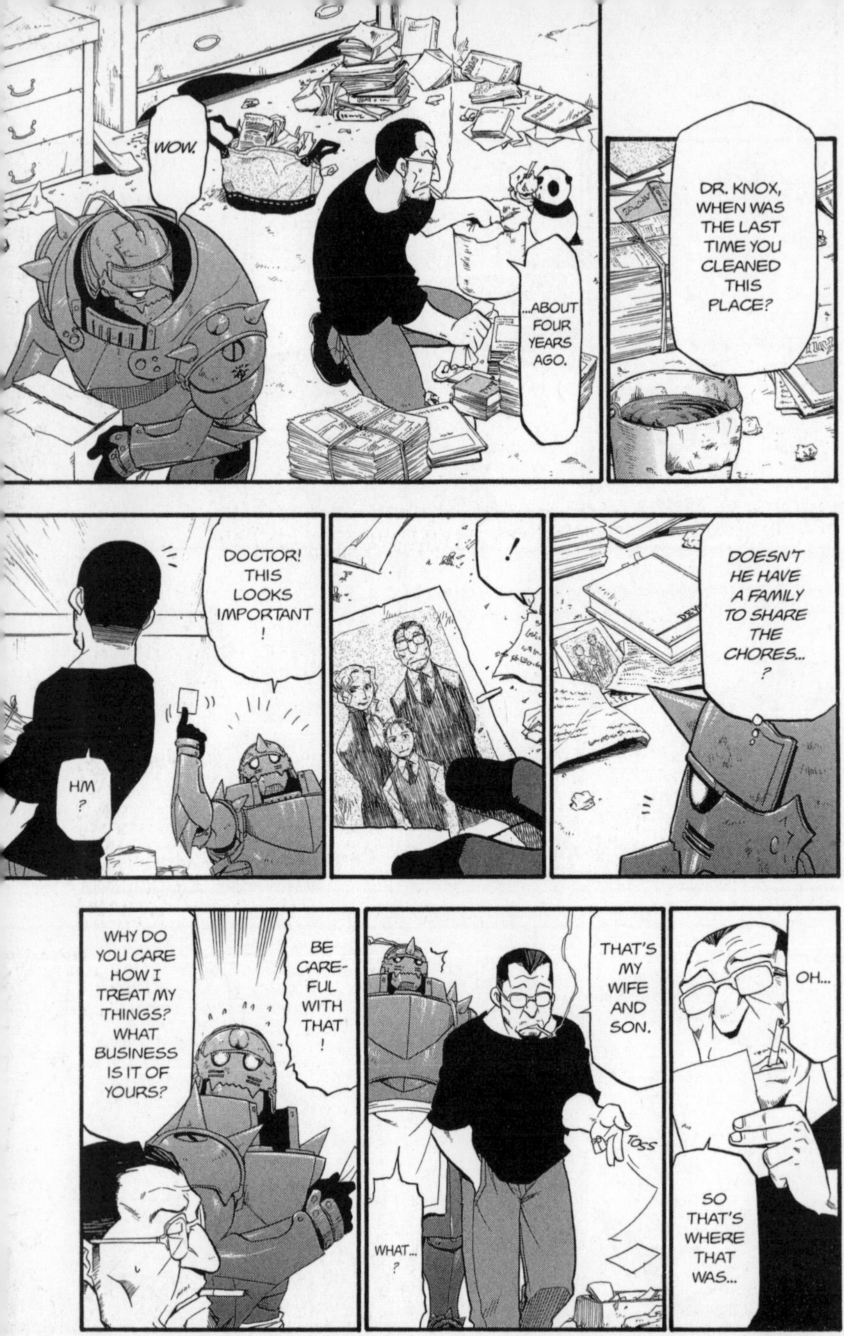
DR. KNOX, WHEN WAS THE LAST TIME YOU CLEANED THIS PLACE?
...ABOUT FOUR YEARS AGO.
WOW.
DOESN'T HE HAVE A FAMILY TO SHARE THE CHORES...?
!
DOCTOR! THIS LOOKS IMPORTANT!
HM?
OH...
SO THAT'S WHERE THAT WAS...
THAT'S MY WIFE AND SON.
TOSS
WHAT...?
BE CARE-FUL WITH THAT!
WHY DO YOU CARE HOW I TREAT MY THINGS? WHAT BUSINESS IS IT OF YOURS?

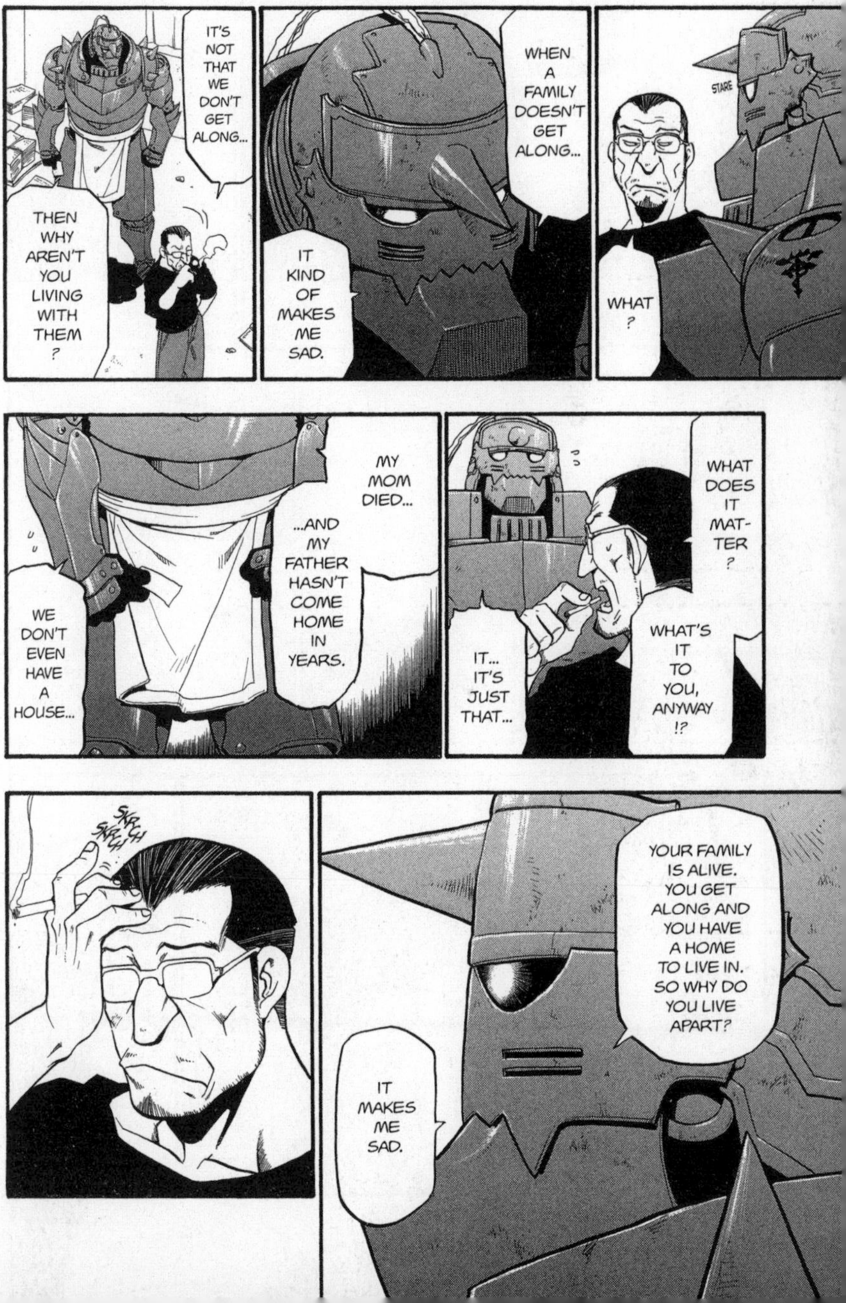
STARE
WHAT?
WHEN A FAMILY DOESN'T GET ALONG...
IT KIND OF MAKES ME SAD.
IT'S NOT THAT WE DON'T GET ALONG...
THEN WHY AREN'T YOU LIVING WITH THEM?
WHAT DOES IT MAT-TER?
WHAT'S IT TO YOU, ANYWAY!?
IT... IT'S JUST THAT...
MY MOM DIED...
...AND MY FATHER HASN'T COME HOME IN YEARS.
WE DON'T EVEN HAVE A HOUSE...
YOUR FAMILY IS ALIVE. YOU GET ALONG AND YOU HAVE A HOME TO LIVE IN. SO WHY DO YOU LIVE APART?
IT MAKES ME SAD.
SKRCH SKRCH

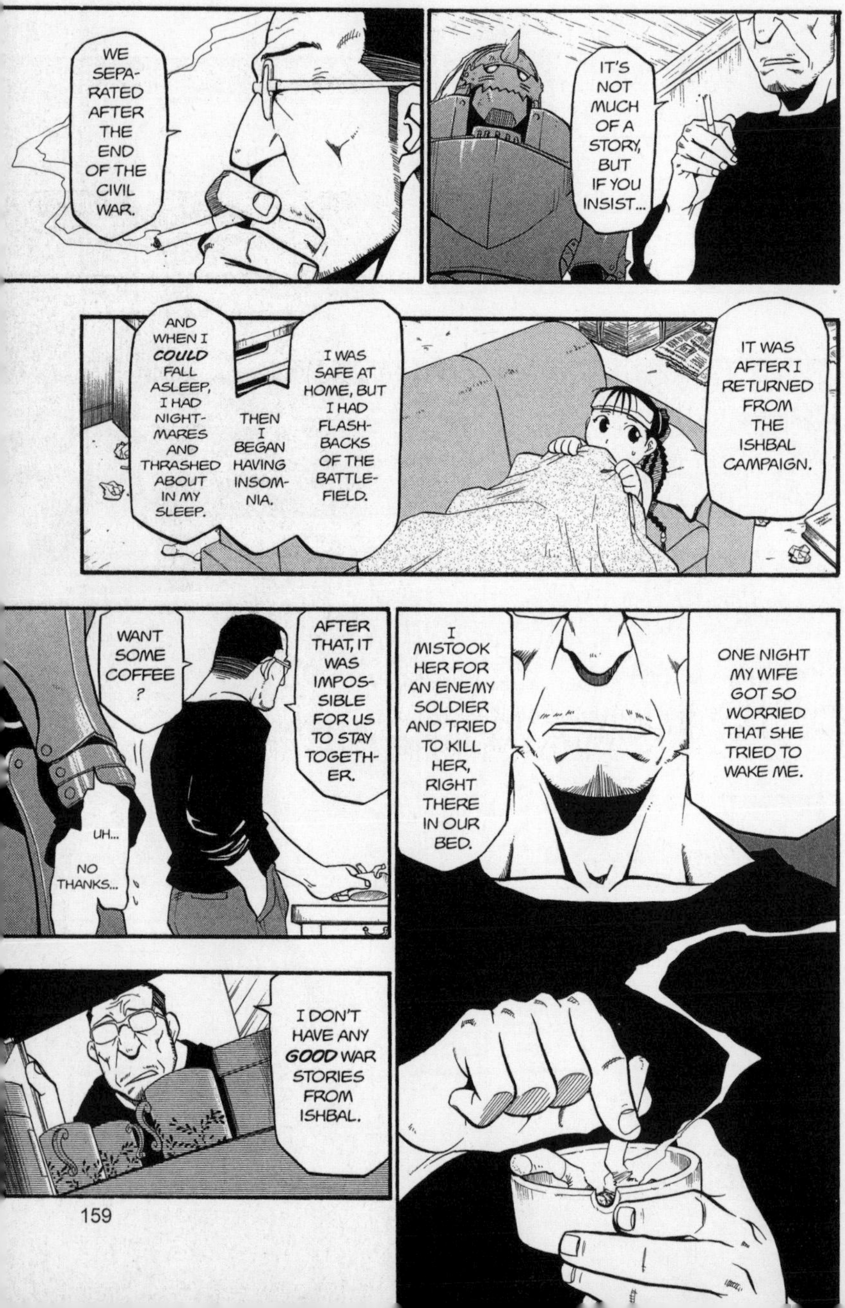
IT'S NOT MUCH OF A STORY, BUT IF YOU INSIST...
WE SEPARATED AFTER THE END OF THE CIVIL WAR.
IT WAS AFTER I RETURNED FROM THE ISHBAL CAMPAIGN.
I WAS SAFE AT HOME, BUT I HAD FLASHBACKS OF THE BATTLEFIELD.
THEN I BEGAN HAVING INSOMNIA.
AND WHEN I *COULD* FALL ASLEEP, I HAD NIGHTMARES AND THRASHED ABOUT IN MY SLEEP.
ONE NIGHT MY WIFE GOT SO WORRIED THAT SHE TRIED TO WAKE ME.
I MISTOOK HER FOR AN ENEMY SOLDIER AND TRIED TO KILL HER, RIGHT THERE IN OUR BED.
AFTER THAT, IT WAS IMPOSSIBLE FOR US TO STAY TOGETHER.
WANT SOME COFFEE?
UH...
NO THANKS...
I DON'T HAVE ANY *GOOD* WAR STORIES FROM ISHBAL.

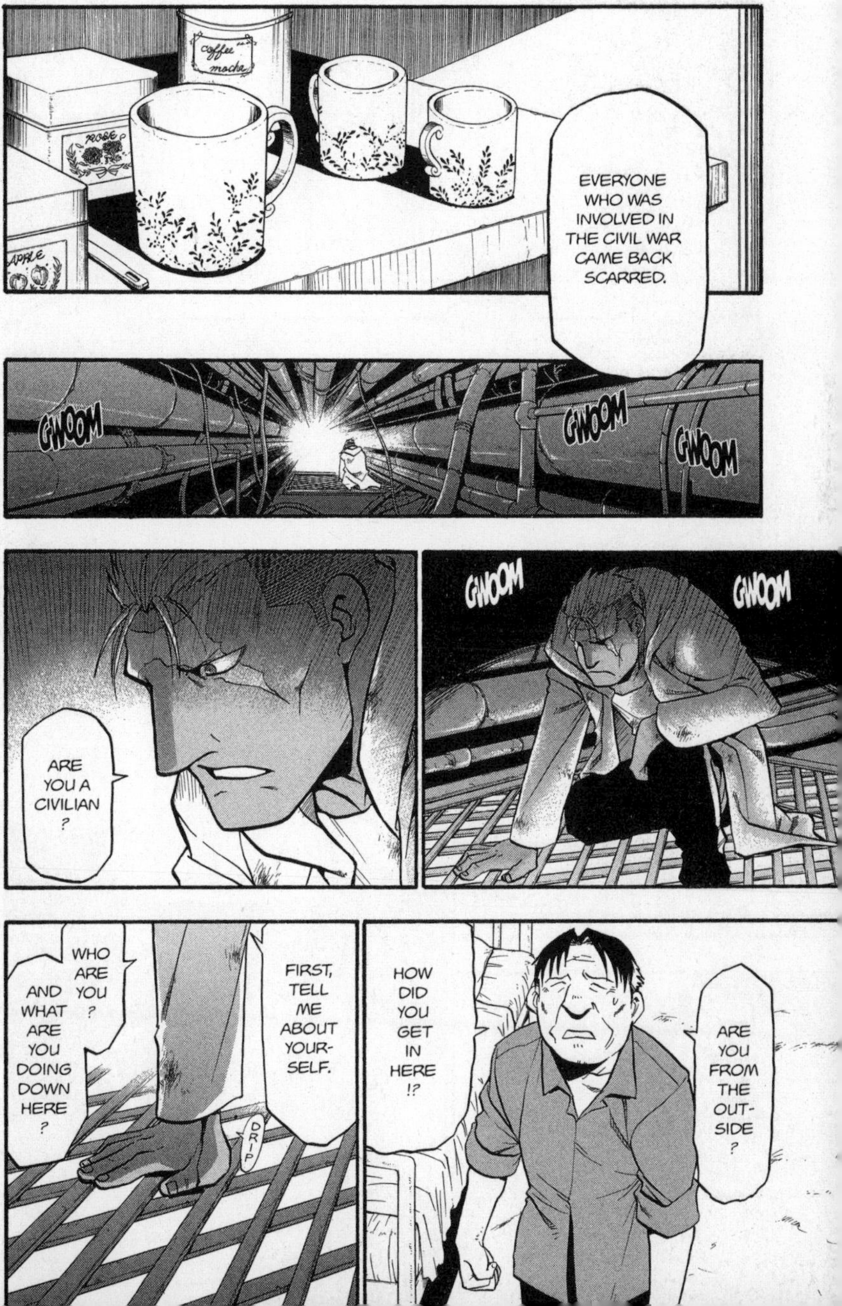
EVERYONE WHO WAS INVOLVED IN THE CIVIL WAR CAME BACK SCARRED.
GWOOM
GWOOM
GWOOM
GWOOM
GWOOM
ARE YOU A CIVILIAN?
ARE YOU FROM THE OUTSIDE?
HOW DID YOU GET IN HERE!?
FIRST, TELL ME ABOUT YOURSELF.
WHO ARE YOU?
AND WHAT ARE YOU DOING DOWN HERE?
DRIP

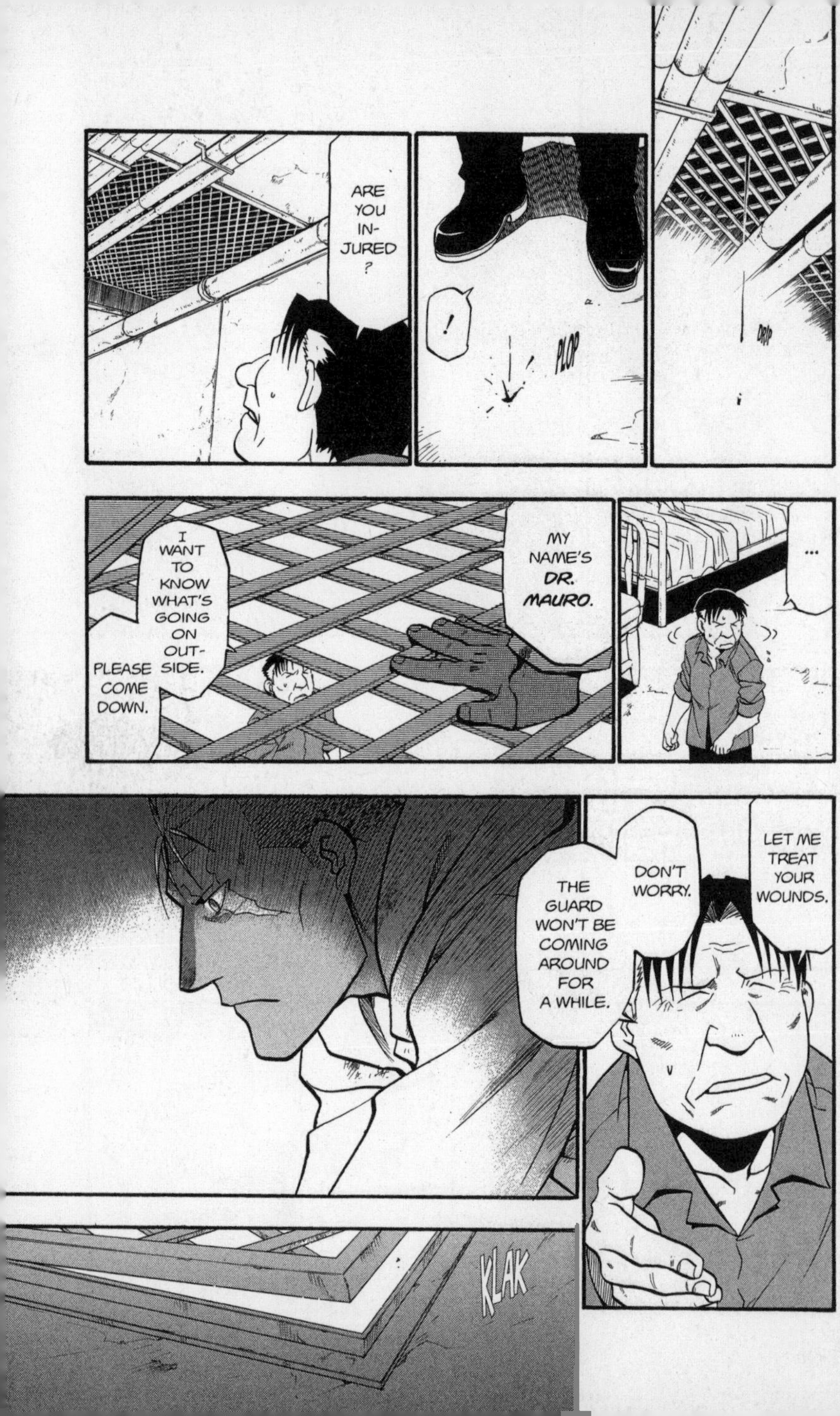
DRIP
!
PLOP
ARE YOU IN-JURED?
...
MY NAME'S DR. MAURO.
I WANT TO KNOW WHAT'S GOING ON OUT-SIDE.
PLEASE COME DOWN.
LET ME TREAT YOUR WOUNDS.
DON'T WORRY.
THE GUARD WON'T BE COMING AROUND FOR A WHILE.
KLAK

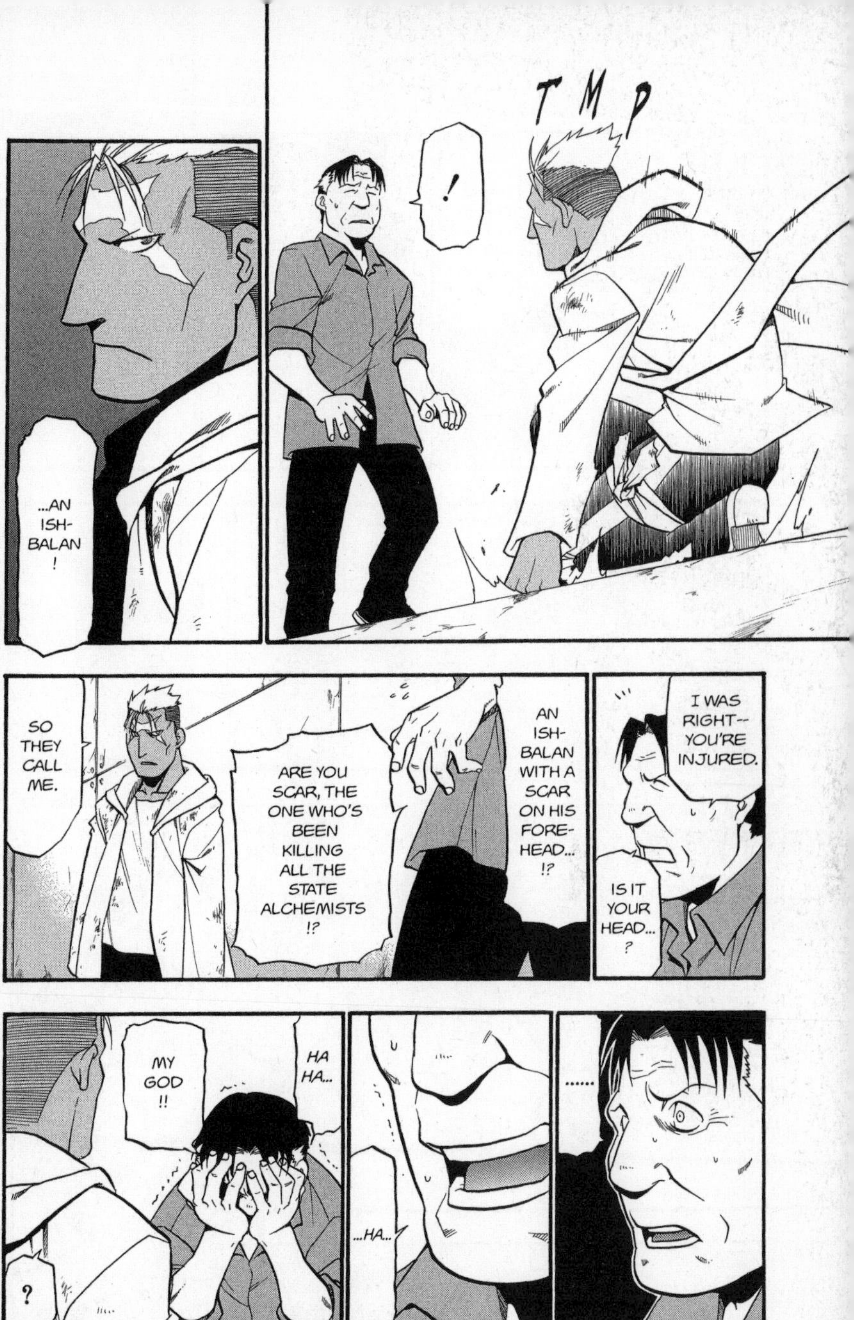
TMP
!
...AN ISH-BALAN!
I WAS RIGHT--YOU'RE INJURED.
IS IT YOUR HEAD...?
AN ISH-BALAN WITH A SCAR ON HIS FORE-HEAD...!?
ARE YOU SCAR, THE ONE WHO'S BEEN KILLING ALL THE STATE ALCHEMISTS!?
SO THEY CALL ME.
......
...HA...
HA HA...
MY GOD!!
?

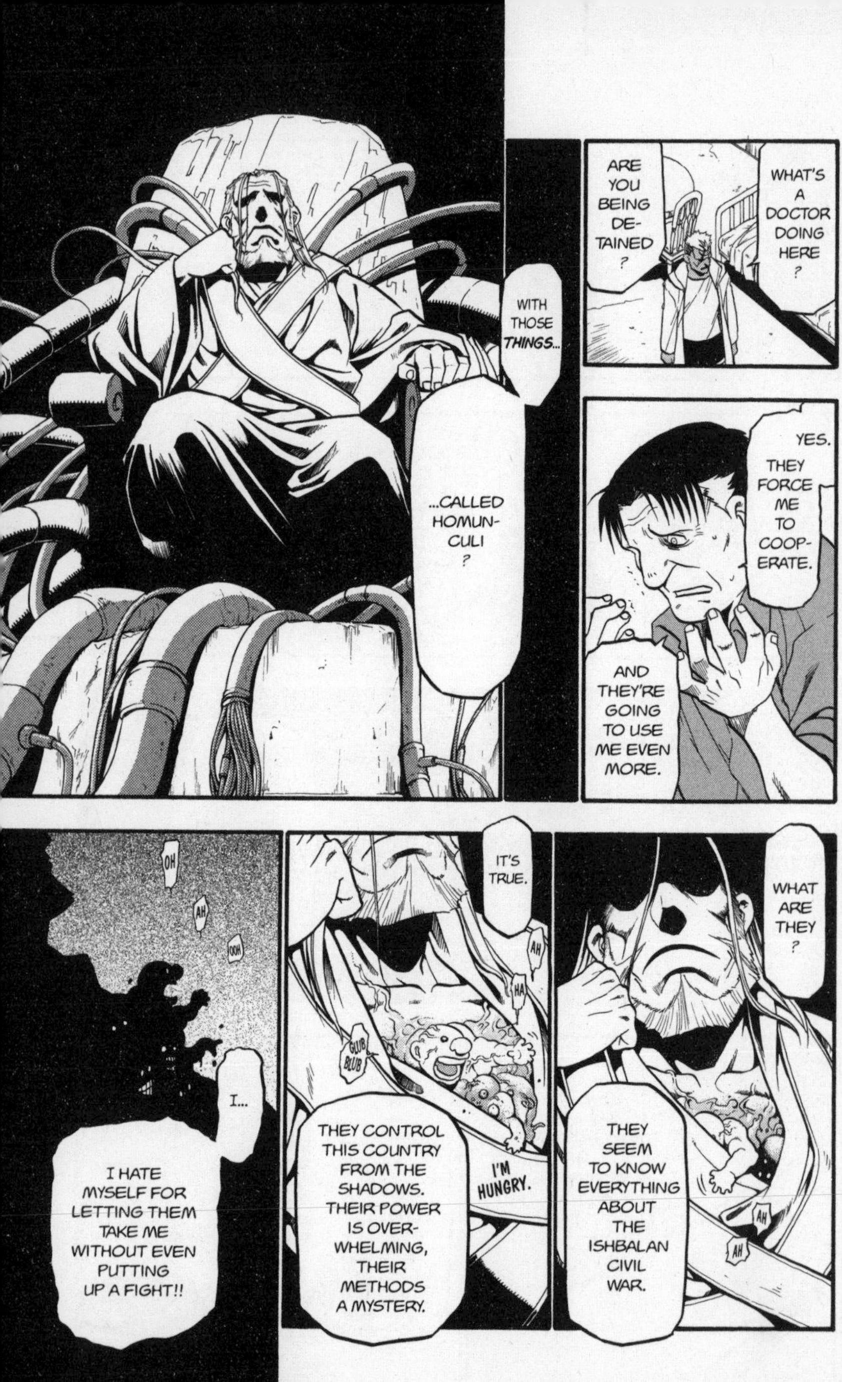
WHAT'S A DOCTOR DOING HERE?
ARE YOU BEING DE-TAINED?
YES. THEY FORCE ME TO COOP-ERATE.
AND THEY'RE GOING TO USE ME EVEN MORE.
WITH THOSE *THINGS*...
...CALLED HOMUN-CULI?
WHAT ARE THEY?
THEY SEEM TO KNOW EVERYTHING ABOUT THE ISHBALAN CIVIL WAR.
AH
AH
IT'S TRUE.
AH
HA
GLUB BLUB
THEY CONTROL THIS COUNTRY FROM THE SHADOWS. THEIR POWER IS OVER-WHELMING, THEIR METHODS A MYSTERY.
I'M HUNGRY.
OH
AH
OOH
I...
I HATE MYSELF FOR LETTING THEM TAKE ME WITHOUT EVEN PUTTING UP A FIGHT!!

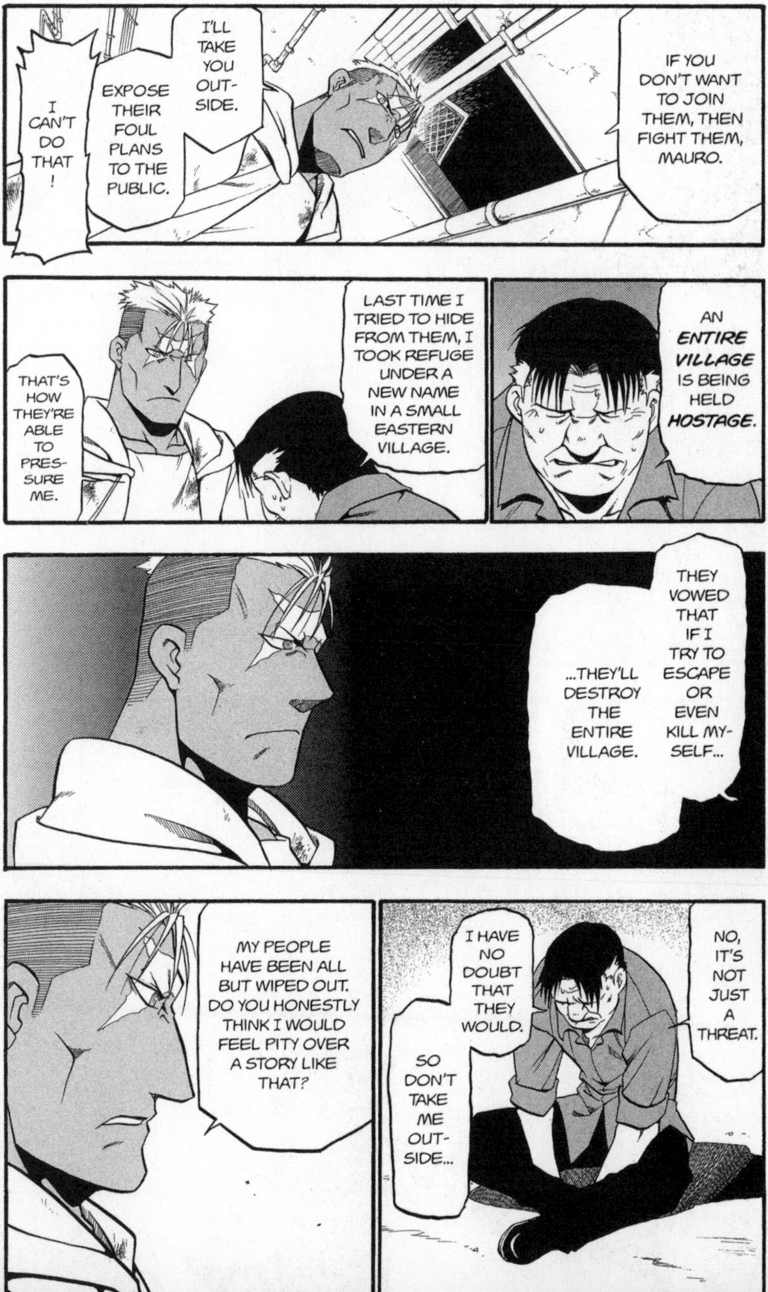
IF YOU DON'T WANT TO JOIN THEM, THEN FIGHT THEM, MAURO.
I'LL TAKE YOU OUTSIDE.
EXPOSE THEIR FOUL PLANS TO THE PUBLIC.
I CAN'T DO THAT!
AN *ENTIRE VILLAGE* IS BEING HELD *HOSTAGE*.
LAST TIME I TRIED TO HIDE FROM THEM, I TOOK REFUGE UNDER A NEW NAME IN A SMALL EASTERN VILLAGE.
THAT'S HOW THEY'RE ABLE TO PRESSURE ME.
THEY VOWED THAT IF I TRY TO ESCAPE OR EVEN KILL MYSELF...
...THEY'LL DESTROY THE ENTIRE VILLAGE.
NO, IT'S NOT JUST A THREAT.
I HAVE NO DOUBT THAT THEY WOULD.
SO DON'T TAKE ME OUTSIDE...
MY PEOPLE HAVE BEEN ALL BUT WIPED OUT. DO YOU HONESTLY THINK I WOULD FEEL PITY OVER A STORY LIKE THAT?

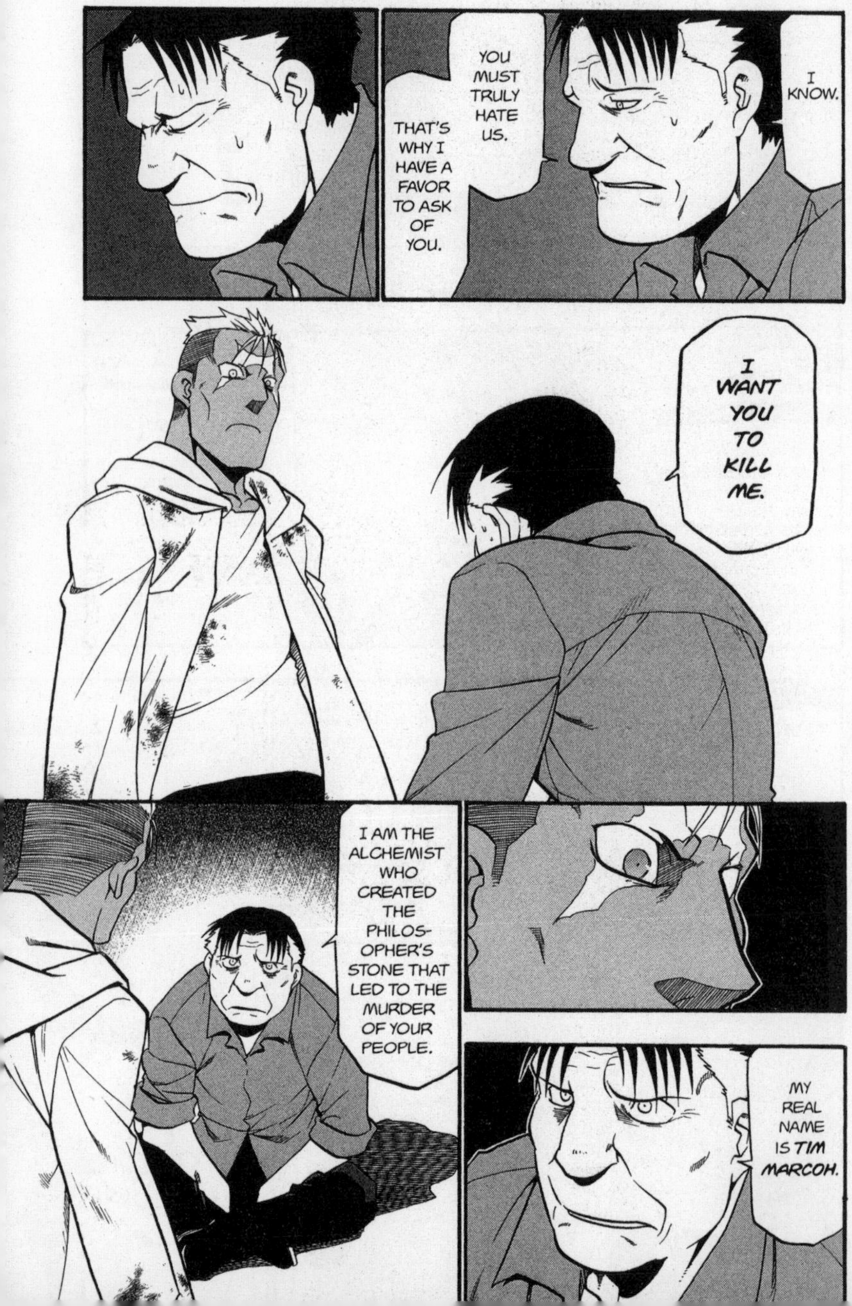
I KNOW.
YOU MUST TRULY HATE US.
THAT'S WHY I HAVE A FAVOR TO ASK OF YOU.
I WANT YOU TO KILL ME.
MY REAL NAME IS TIM MARCOH.
I AM THE ALCHEMIST WHO CREATED THE PHILOSOPHER'S STONE THAT LED TO THE MURDER OF YOUR PEOPLE.

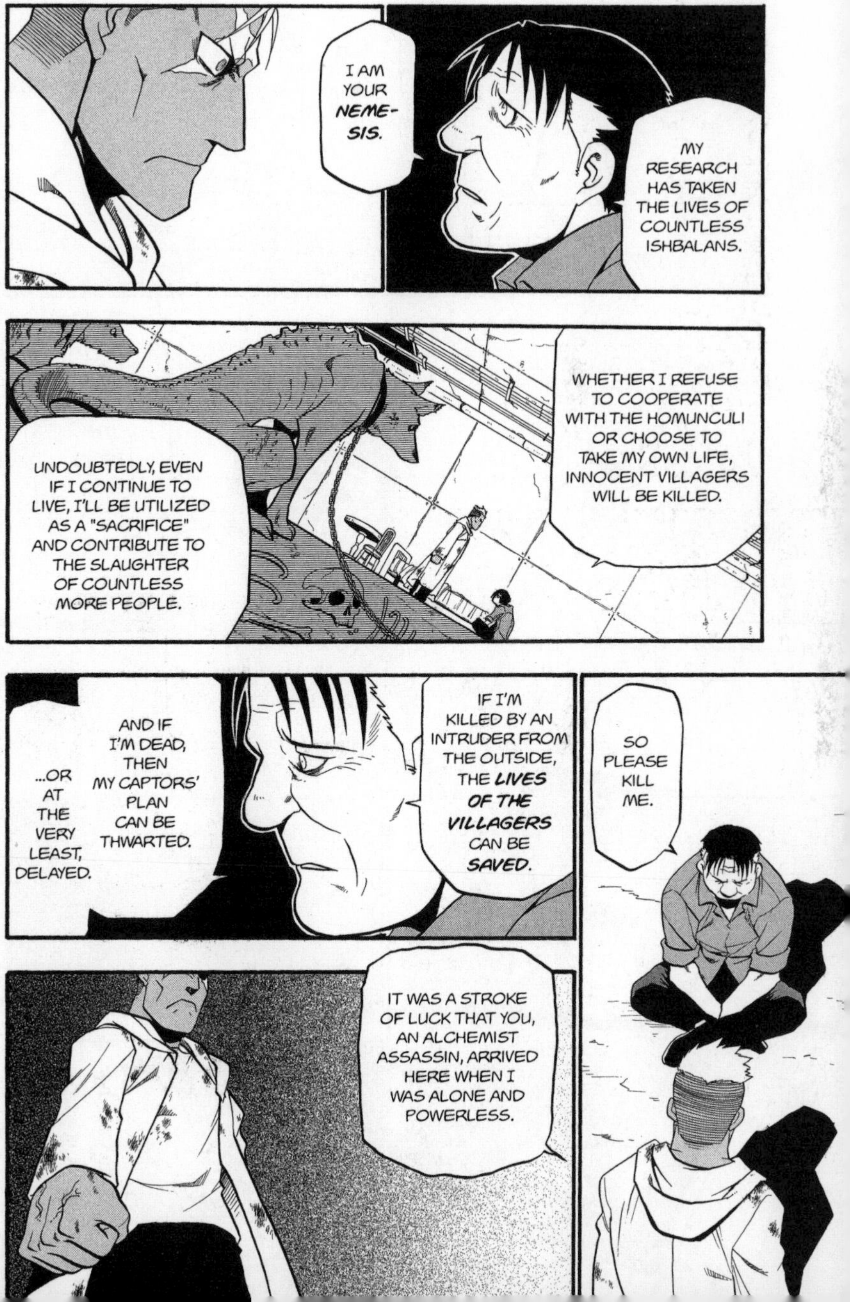
MY RESEARCH HAS TAKEN THE LIVES OF COUNTLESS ISHBALANS.
I AM YOUR *NEMESIS.*
WHETHER I REFUSE TO COOPERATE WITH THE HOMUNCULI OR CHOOSE TO TAKE MY OWN LIFE, INNOCENT VILLAGERS WILL BE KILLED.
UNDOUBTEDLY, EVEN IF I CONTINUE TO LIVE, I'LL BE UTILIZED AS A "SACRIFICE" AND CONTRIBUTE TO THE SLAUGHTER OF COUNTLESS MORE PEOPLE.
SO PLEASE KILL ME.
IF I'M KILLED BY AN INTRUDER FROM THE OUTSIDE, THE ***LIVES OF THE VILLAGERS*** CAN BE ***SAVED.***
AND IF I'M DEAD, THEN MY CAPTORS' PLAN CAN BE THWARTED.
...OR AT THE VERY LEAST, DELAYED.
IT WAS A STROKE OF LUCK THAT YOU, AN ALCHEMIST ASSASSIN, ARRIVED HERE WHEN I WAS ALONE AND POWERLESS.

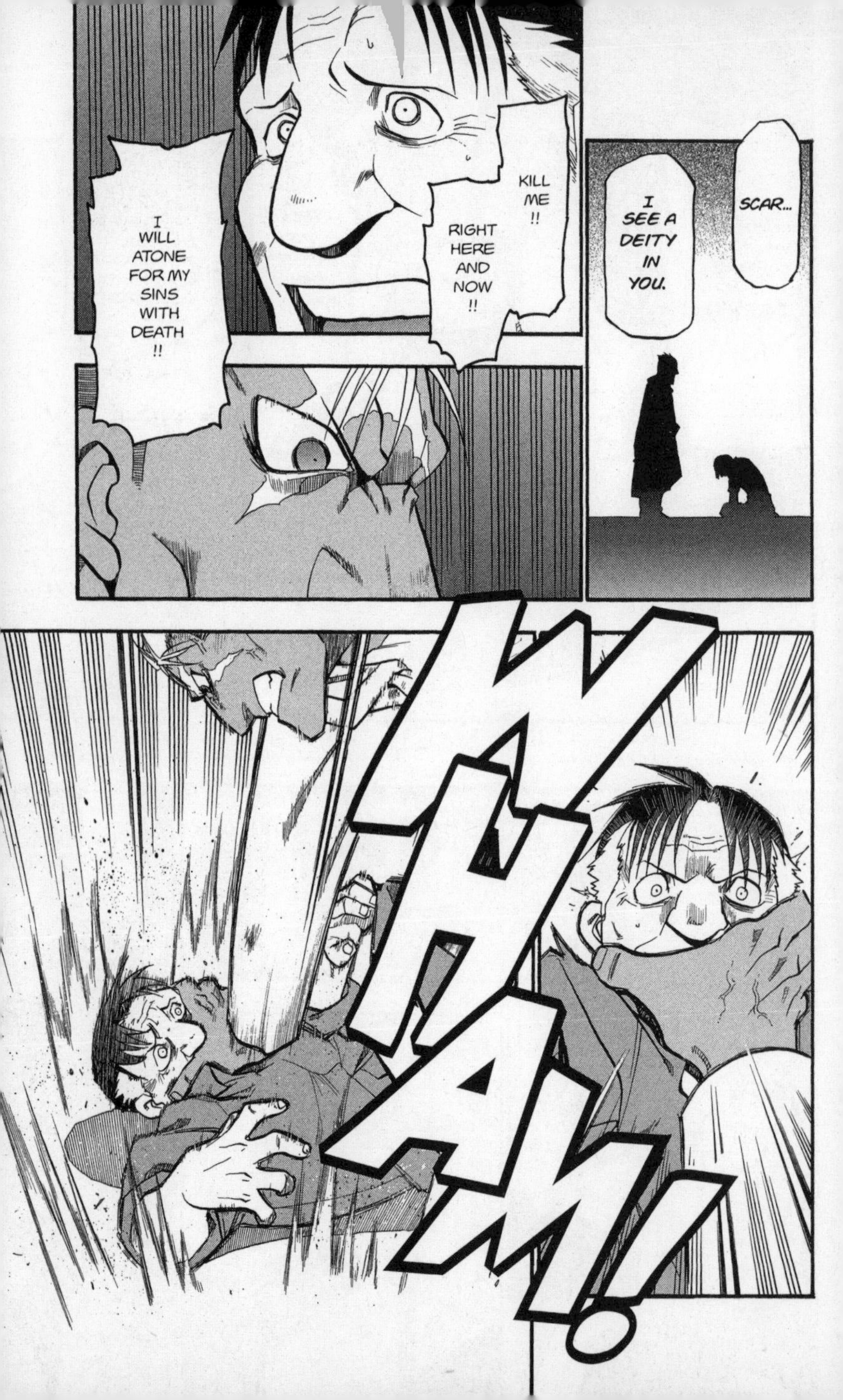
SCAR...
I SEE A DEITY IN YOU.
KILL ME !!
RIGHT HERE AND NOW !!
I WILL ATONE FOR MY SINS WITH DEATH !!
WHAM!

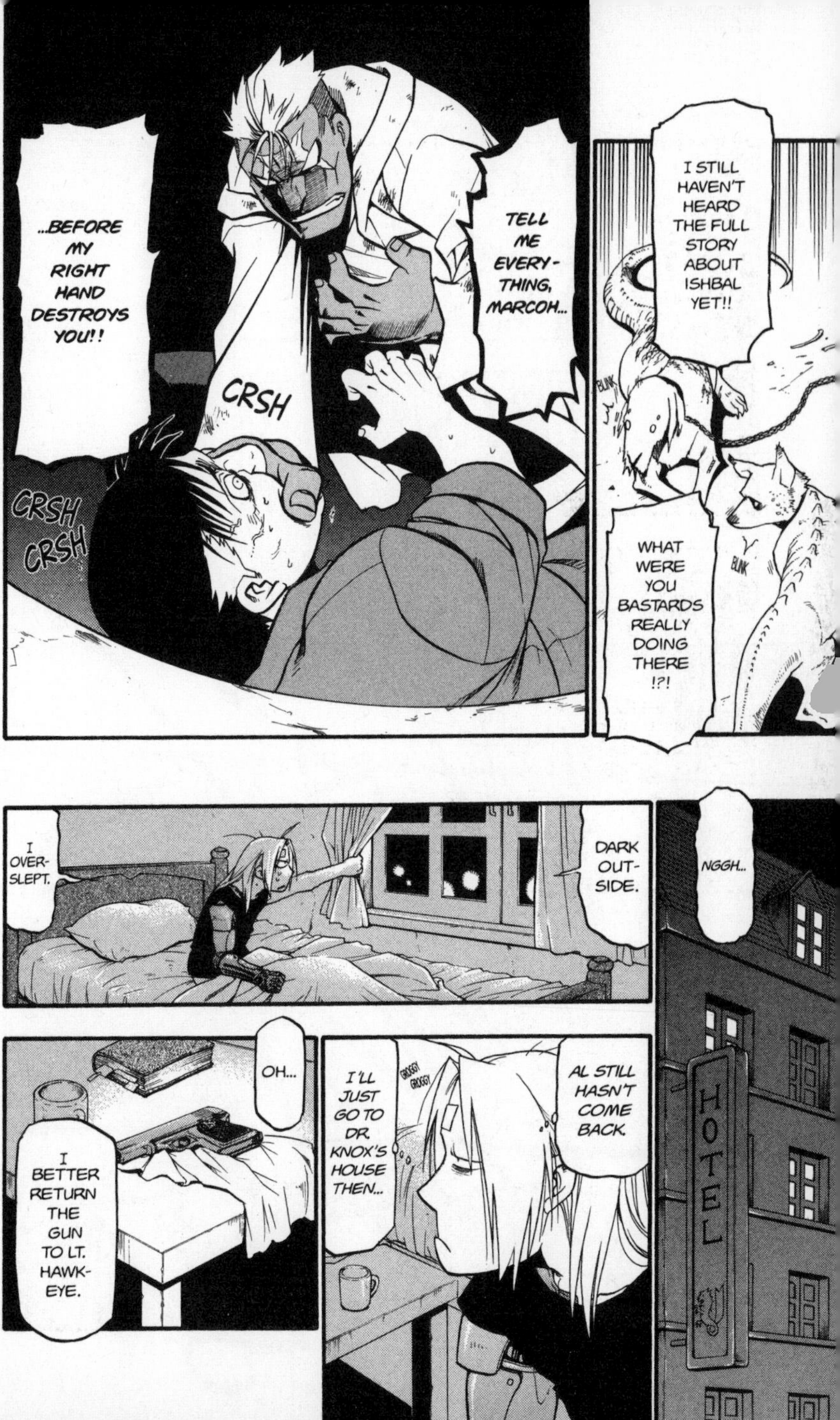
I STILL HAVEN'T HEARD THE FULL STORY ABOUT ISHBAL YET!!
BLINK
BLINK
WHAT WERE YOU BASTARDS REALLY DOING THERE!?!
TELL ME EVERY-THING, MARCOH...
...BEFORE MY RIGHT HAND DESTROYS YOU!!
CRSH
CRSH CRSH
NGGH...
HOTEL
DARK OUT-SIDE.
I OVER-SLEPT.
AL STILL HASN'T COME BACK.
GROGGY GROGGY
I'LL JUST GO TO DR. KNOX'S HOUSE THEN...
OH...
I BETTER RETURN THE GUN TO LT. HAWK-EYE.

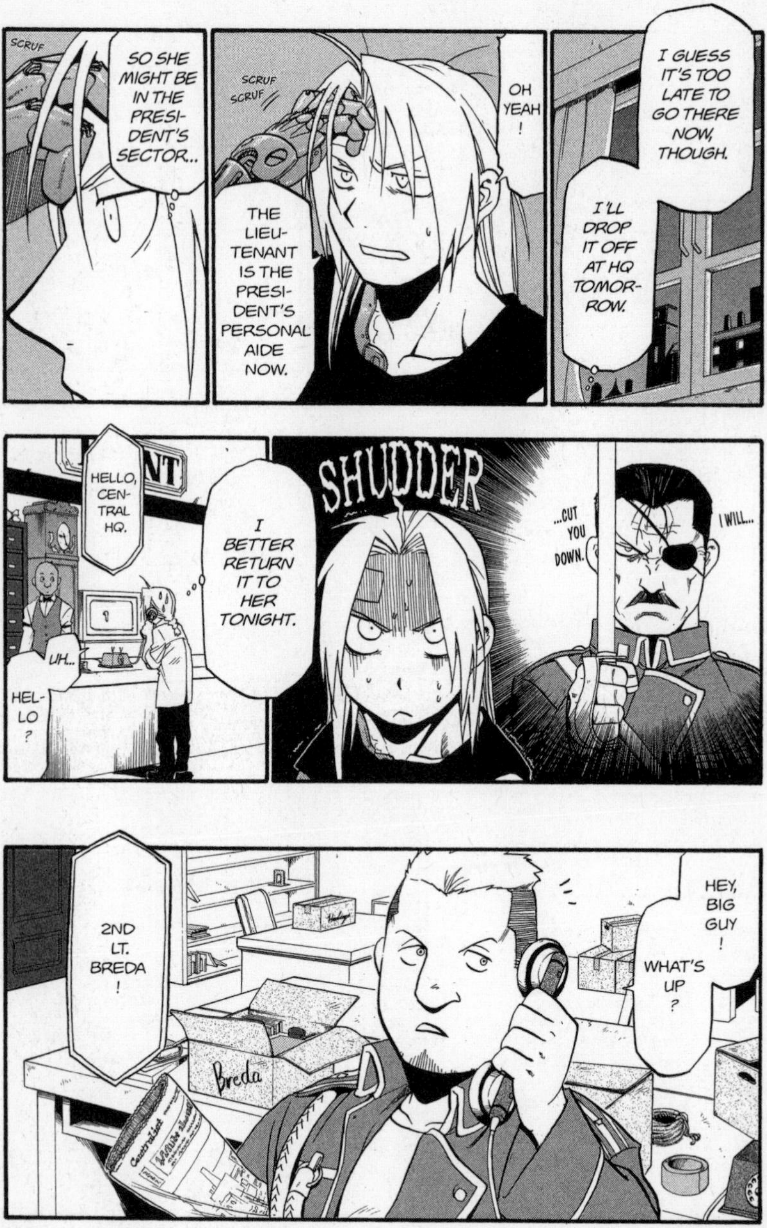
I GUESS IT'S TOO LATE TO GO THERE NOW, THOUGH.
I'LL DROP IT OFF AT HQ TOMORROW.
OH YEAH!
SCRUF SCRUF
THE LIEUTENANT IS THE PRESIDENT'S PERSONAL AIDE NOW.
SCRUF
SO SHE MIGHT BE IN THE PRESIDENT'S SECTOR...
I WILL...
...CUT YOU DOWN.
SHUDDER
I BETTER RETURN IT TO HER TONIGHT.
HELLO, CENTRAL HQ.
UH...
HELLO?
HEY, BIG GUY!
WHAT'S UP?
2ND LT. BREDA!
Breda

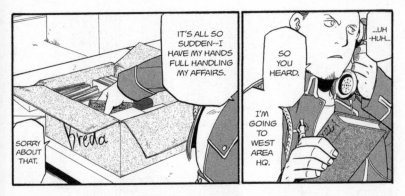

...UH -HUH...
SO YOU HEARD.
I'M GOING TO WEST AREA HQ.
IT'S ALL SO SUDDEN--I HAVE MY HANDS FULL HANDLING MY AFFAIRS.
Breda
SORRY ABOUT THAT.
STARTING TOMORROW, THE LIEUTENANT HAS TO BABY-SIT THE OLD GEEZER.
Hawkeye
NO, SHE LEFT ALREADY.
IS IT UR-GENT?
I THINK HER ADDRESS IS...
BAZAAR
NOK
NOK
HEL-LO?

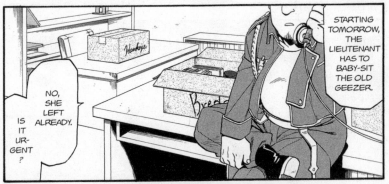

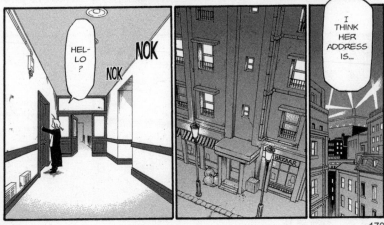

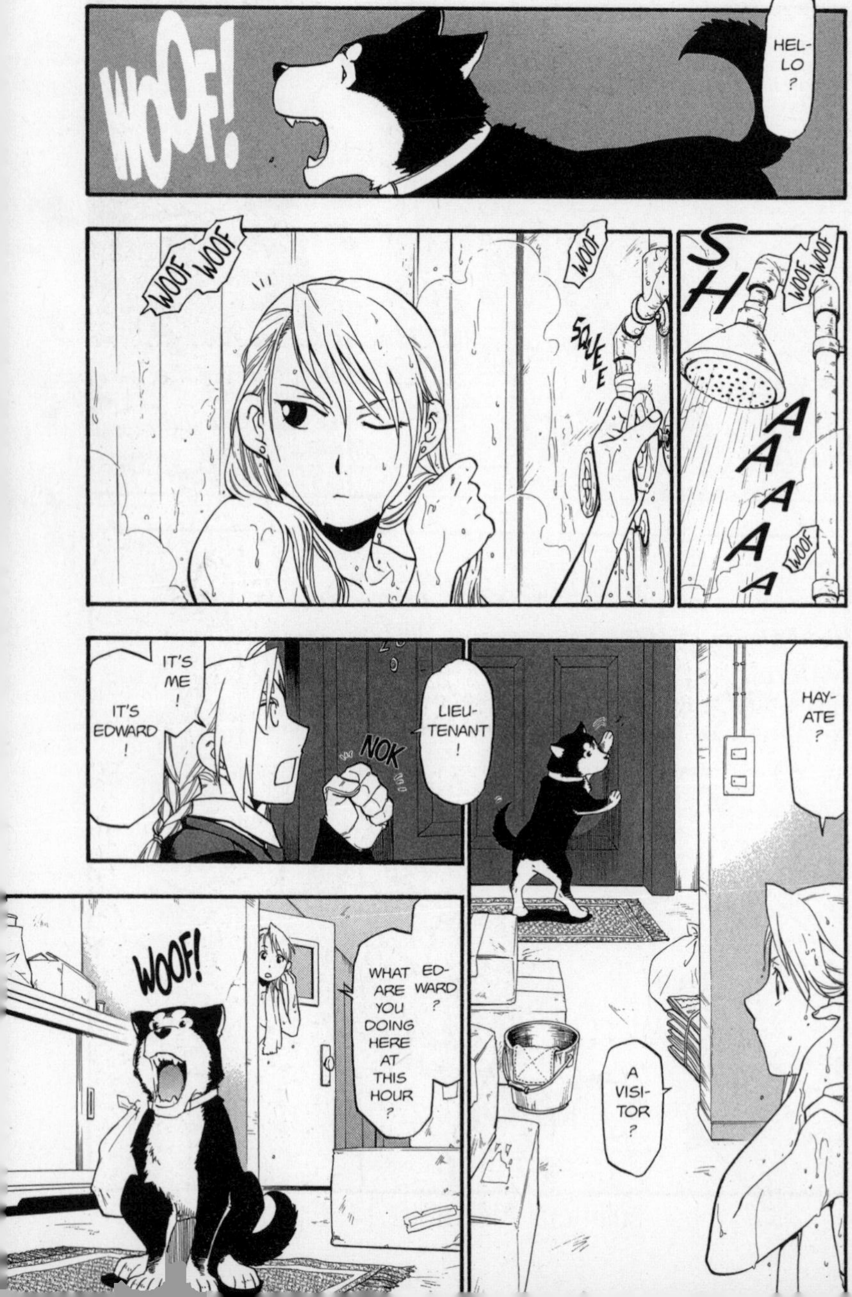
HEL-LO?
WOOF!
SHAAAAAA
WOOF WOOF
WOOF
WOOF
SQUEE
WOOF WOOF
HAY-ATE?
A VISI-TOR?
LIEU-TENANT!
NOK
IT'S ME!
IT'S EDWARD!
ED-WARD?
WHAT ARE YOU DOING HERE AT THIS HOUR?
WOOF!

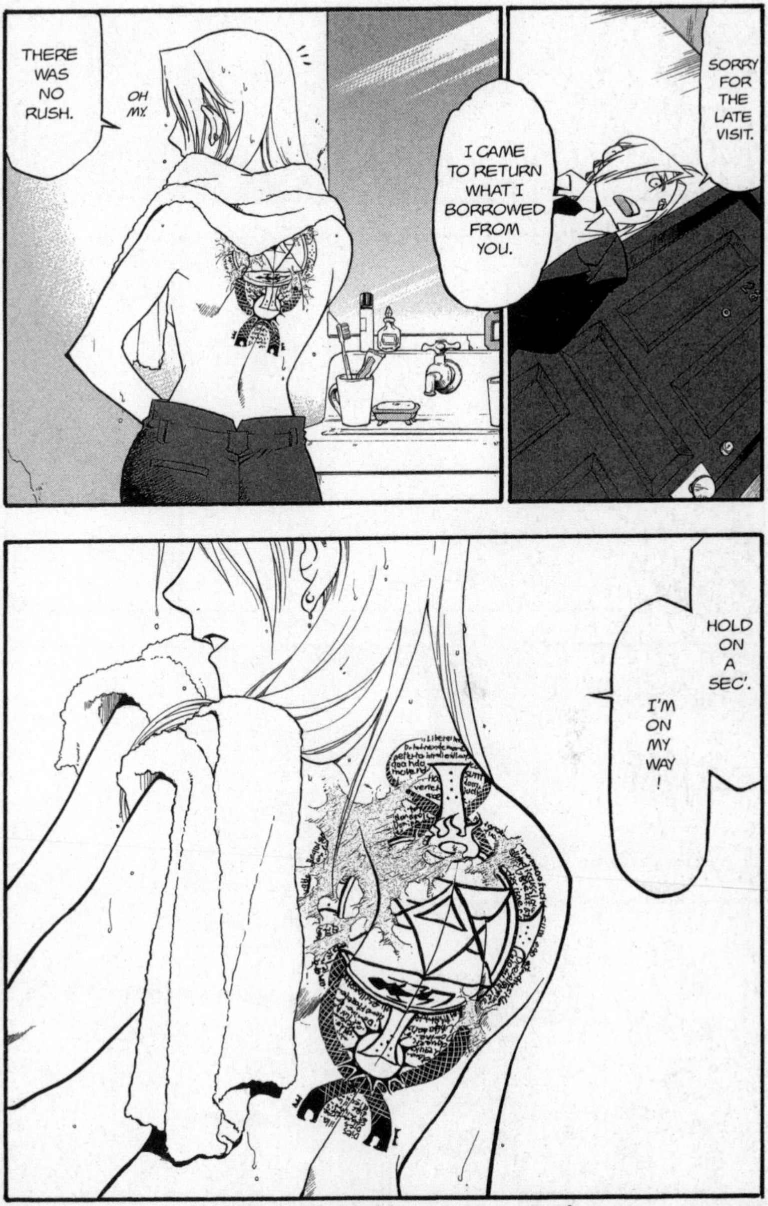
SORRY FOR THE LATE VISIT.
I CAME TO RETURN WHAT I BORROWED FROM YOU.
OH MY.
THERE WAS NO RUSH.
HOLD ON A SEC'.
I'M ON MY WAY!

Fullmetal Alchemist 14 End

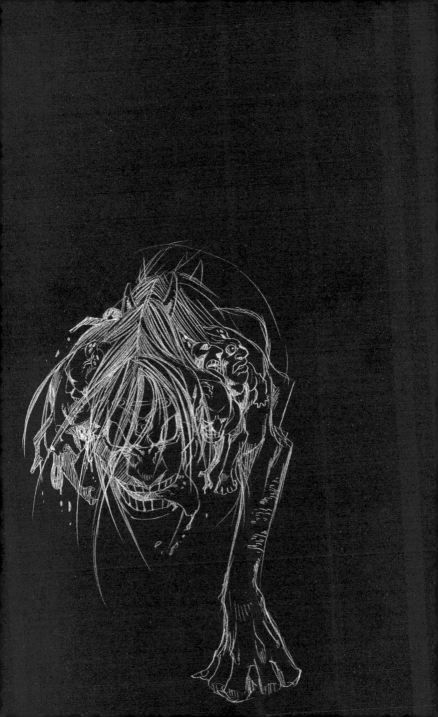

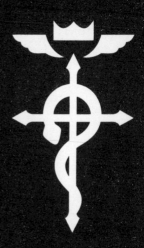

FULLMETAL
ALCHEMIST

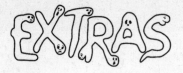

EXTRAS

Chapter 54   Change one sound effect and it's a disaster.

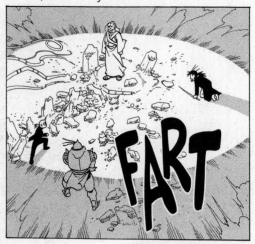

FART

What a huge fart.

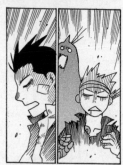

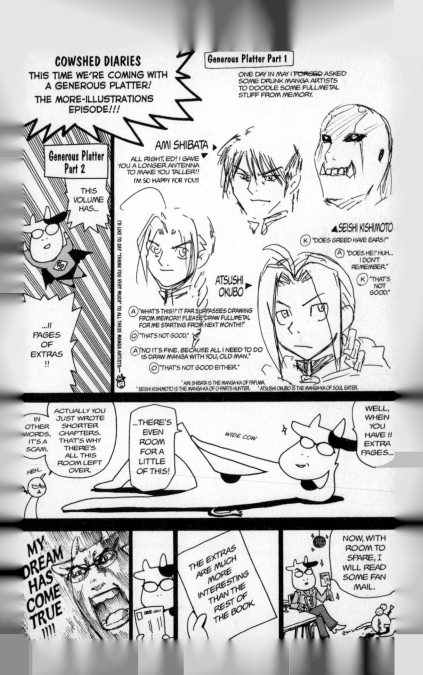

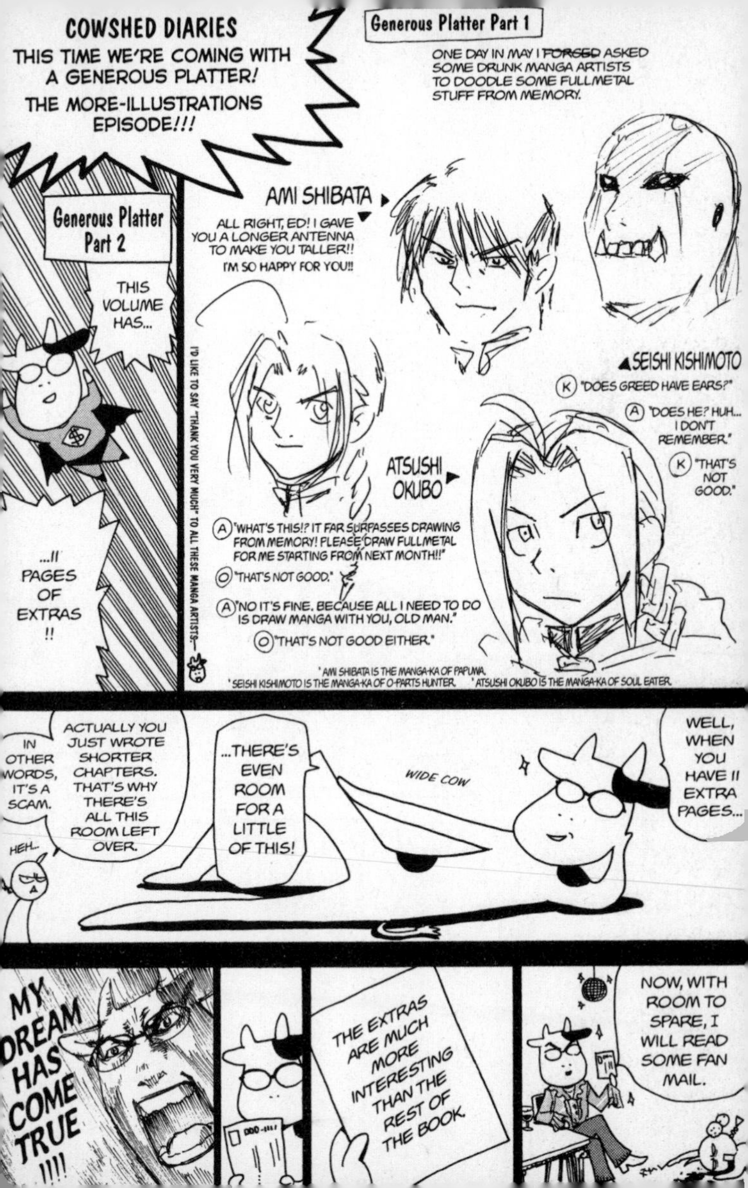
COWSHED DIARIES
THIS TIME WE'RE COMING WITH A GENEROUS PLATTER!
THE MORE-ILLUSTRATIONS EPISODE!!!
Generous Platter Part 1
ONE DAY IN MAY I ~~FORCED~~ ASKED SOME DRUNK MANGA ARTISTS TO DOODLE SOME FULLMETAL STUFF FROM MEMORY.
AMI SHIBATA
ALL RIGHT, ED! I GAVE YOU A LONGER ANTENNA TO MAKE YOU TALLER!! I'M SO HAPPY FOR YOU!!
SEISHI KISHIMOTO
K "DOES GREED HAVE EARS?"
A "DOES HE? HUH... I DON'T REMEMBER."
K "THAT'S NOT GOOD."
ATSUSHI OKUBO
A "WHAT'S THIS!? IT FAR SURPASSES DRAWING FROM MEMORY! PLEASE DRAW FULLMETAL FOR ME STARTING FROM NEXT MONTH!!"
O "THAT'S NOT GOOD."
A "NO IT'S FINE. BECAUSE ALL I NEED TO DO IS DRAW MANGA WITH YOU, OLD MAN."
O "THAT'S NOT GOOD EITHER."
* AMI SHIBATA IS THE MANGA-KA OF PAPUWA.
* SEISHI KISHIMOTO IS THE MANGA-KA OF O-PARTS HUNTER.
* ATSUSHI OKUBO IS THE MANGA-KA OF SOUL EATER.
I'D LIKE TO SAY "THANK YOU VERY MUCH" TO ALL THESE MANGA ARTISTS.
Generous Platter Part 2
THIS VOLUME HAS...
...11 PAGES OF EXTRAS!!
WELL, WHEN YOU HAVE 11 EXTRA PAGES...
...THERE'S EVEN ROOM FOR A LITTLE OF THIS!
WIDE COW
ACTUALLY YOU JUST WROTE SHORTER CHAPTERS. THAT'S WHY THERE'S ALL THIS ROOM LEFT OVER.
IN OTHER WORDS, IT'S A SCAM.
HEH..
NOW, WITH ROOM TO SPARE, I WILL READ SOME FAN MAIL.
THE EXTRAS ARE MUCH MORE INTERESTING THAN THE REST OF THE BOOK.
MY DREAM HAS COME TRUE!!!!

My Brother 60 Years Younger

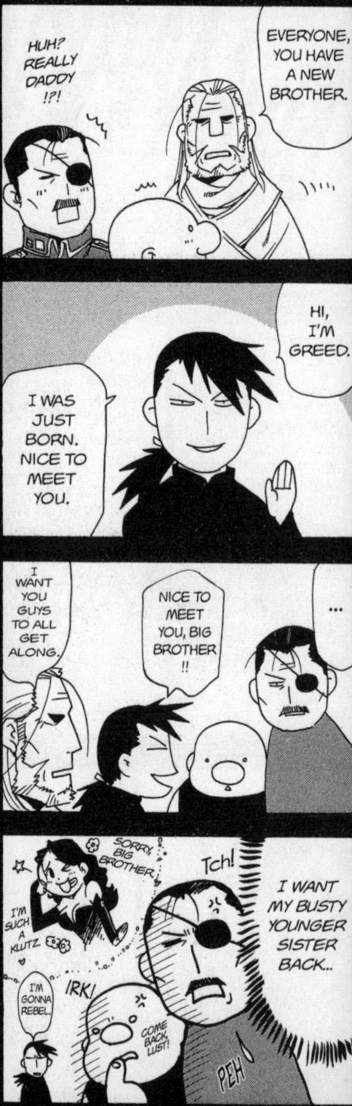
EVERYONE, YOU HAVE A NEW BROTHER.
HUH? REALLY DADDY !?!
HI, I'M GREED.
I WAS JUST BORN. NICE TO MEET YOU.
...
NICE TO MEET YOU, BIG BROTHER !!
I WANT YOU GUYS TO ALL GET ALONG.
I WANT MY BUSTY YOUNGER SISTER BACK..
Tch!
SORRY, BIG BROTHER.
I'M SUCH A KLUTZ.
IRK!
COME BACK LUST!
I'M GONNA REBEL.
PEH

Do They Still Sell Shower Caps?

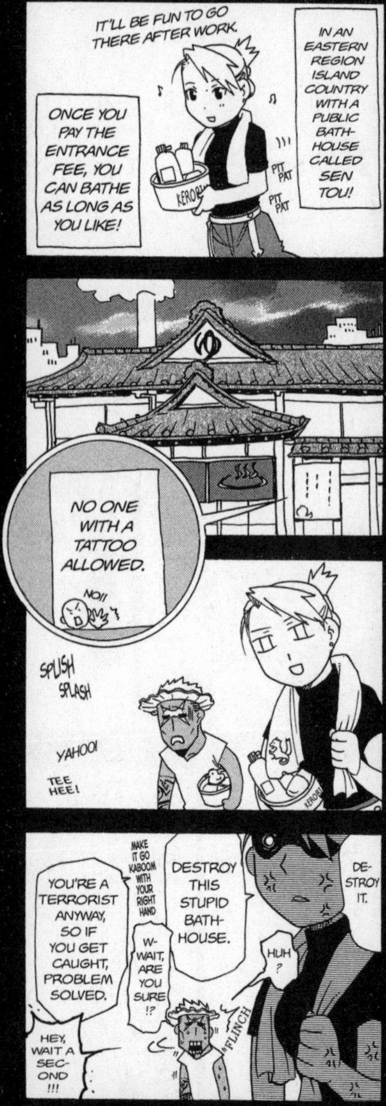
IN AN EASTERN REGION ISLAND COUNTRY WITH A PUBLIC BATH-HOUSE CALLED SEN TOU!
IT'LL BE FUN TO GO THERE AFTER WORK.
PIT PAT
PIT PAT
KERORI
ONCE YOU PAY THE ENTRANCE FEE, YOU CAN BATHE AS LONG AS YOU LIKE!
NO ONE WITH A TATTOO ALLOWED.
NO!!
SPLISH
SPLASH
YAHOO!
TEE HEE!
KERORI
DE-STROY IT.
HUH ?
DESTROY THIS STUPID BATH-HOUSE.
MAKE IT GO KABOOM WITH YOUR RIGHT HAND
W-WAIT, ARE YOU SURE !?
YOU'RE A TERRORIST ANYWAY, SO IF YOU GET CAUGHT, PROBLEM SOLVED.
FLINCH
HEY, WAIT A SEC-OND !!!

SHORT STORY

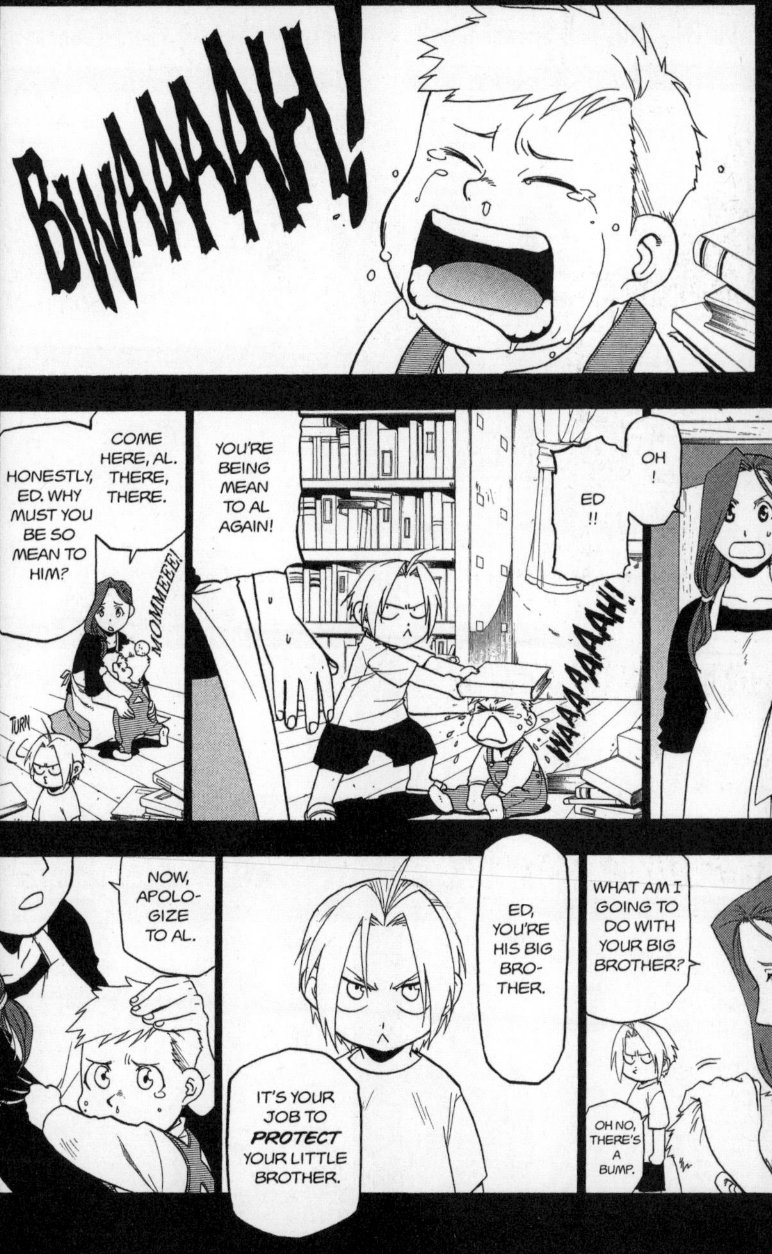
BWAAAAH!
OH! ED!!
YOU'RE BEING MEAN TO AL AGAIN!
WAAAAAAAH!
COME HERE, AL. THERE, THERE.
HONESTLY, ED. WHY MUST YOU BE SO MEAN TO HIM?
MOMMEEE!
TURN
WHAT AM I GOING TO DO WITH YOUR BIG BROTHER?
OH NO, THERE'S A BUMP.
ED, YOU'RE HIS BIG BROTHER.
IT'S YOUR JOB TO PROTECT YOUR LITTLE BROTHER.
NOW, APOLOGIZE TO AL.

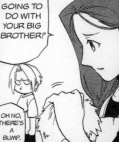

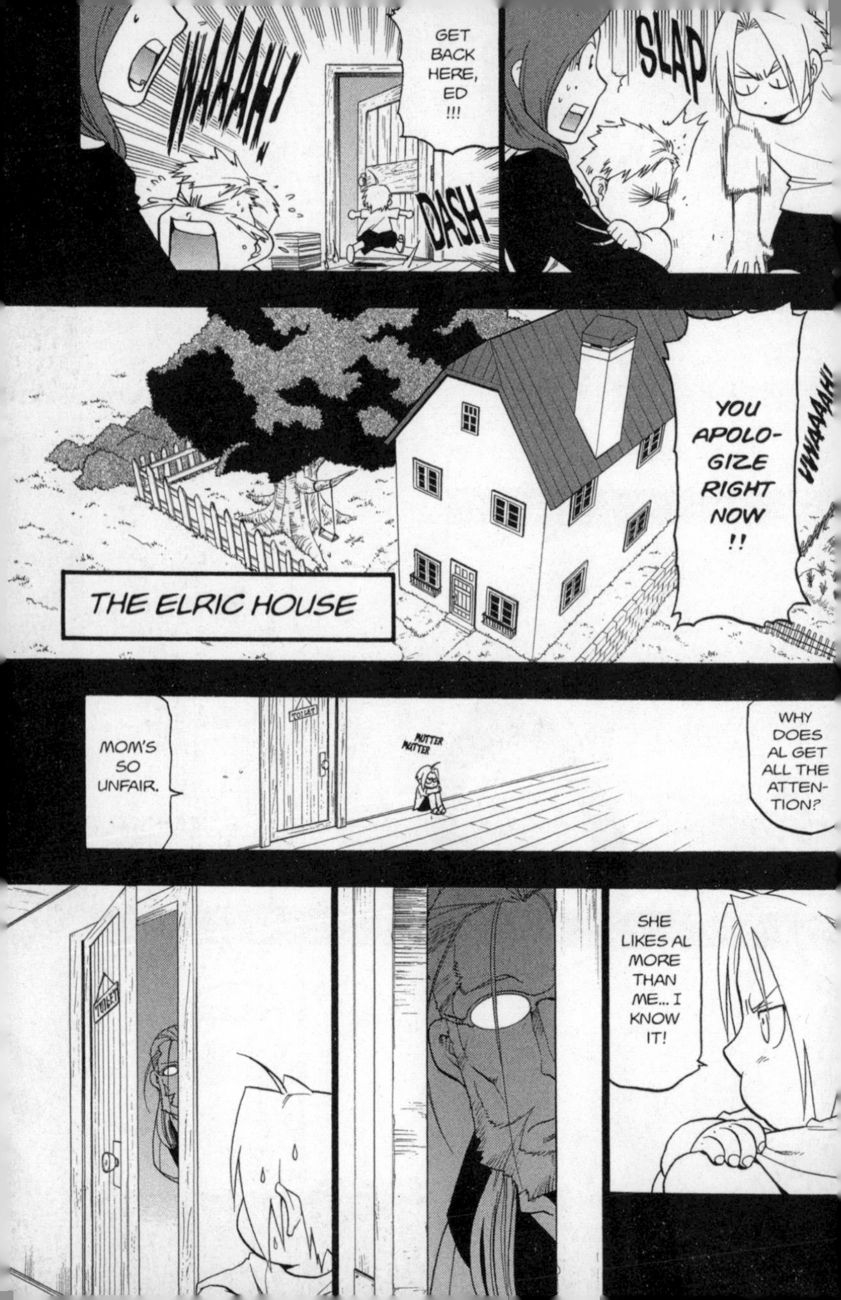
SLAP
GET BACK HERE, ED!!!
WAAAH!
DASH
WAAAAH!
YOU APOLOGIZE RIGHT NOW!!
THE ELRIC HOUSE
WHY DOES AL GET ALL THE ATTENTION?
MUTTER MUTTER
MOM'S SO UNFAIR.
SHE LIKES AL MORE THAN ME... I KNOW IT!

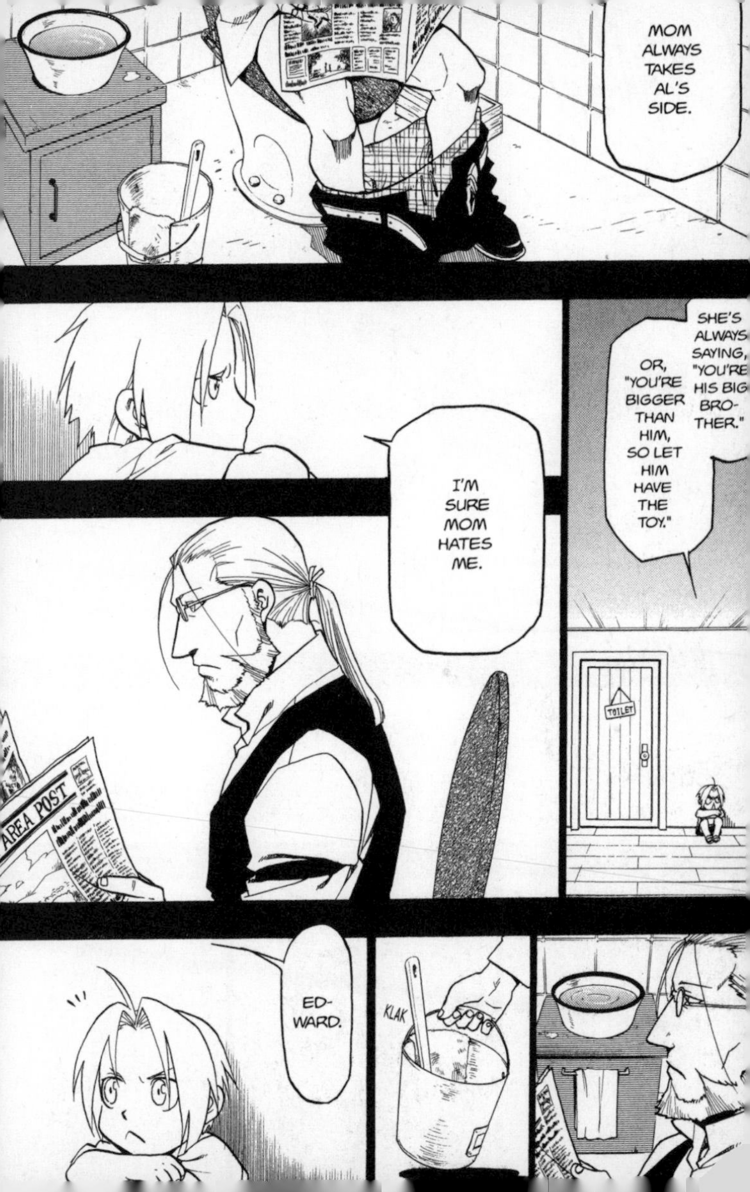
MOM ALWAYS TAKES AL'S SIDE.
SHE'S ALWAYS SAYING, "YOU'RE HIS BIG BROTHER."
OR, "YOU'RE BIGGER THAN HIM, SO LET HIM HAVE THE TOY."
TOILET
I'M SURE MOM HATES ME.
AREA POST
KLAK
ED-WARD.

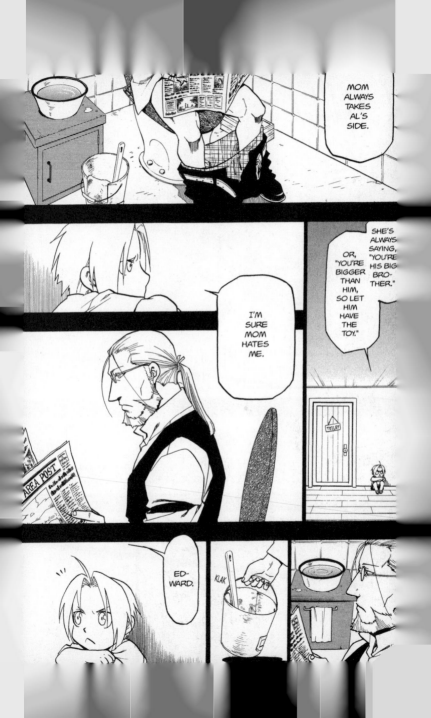

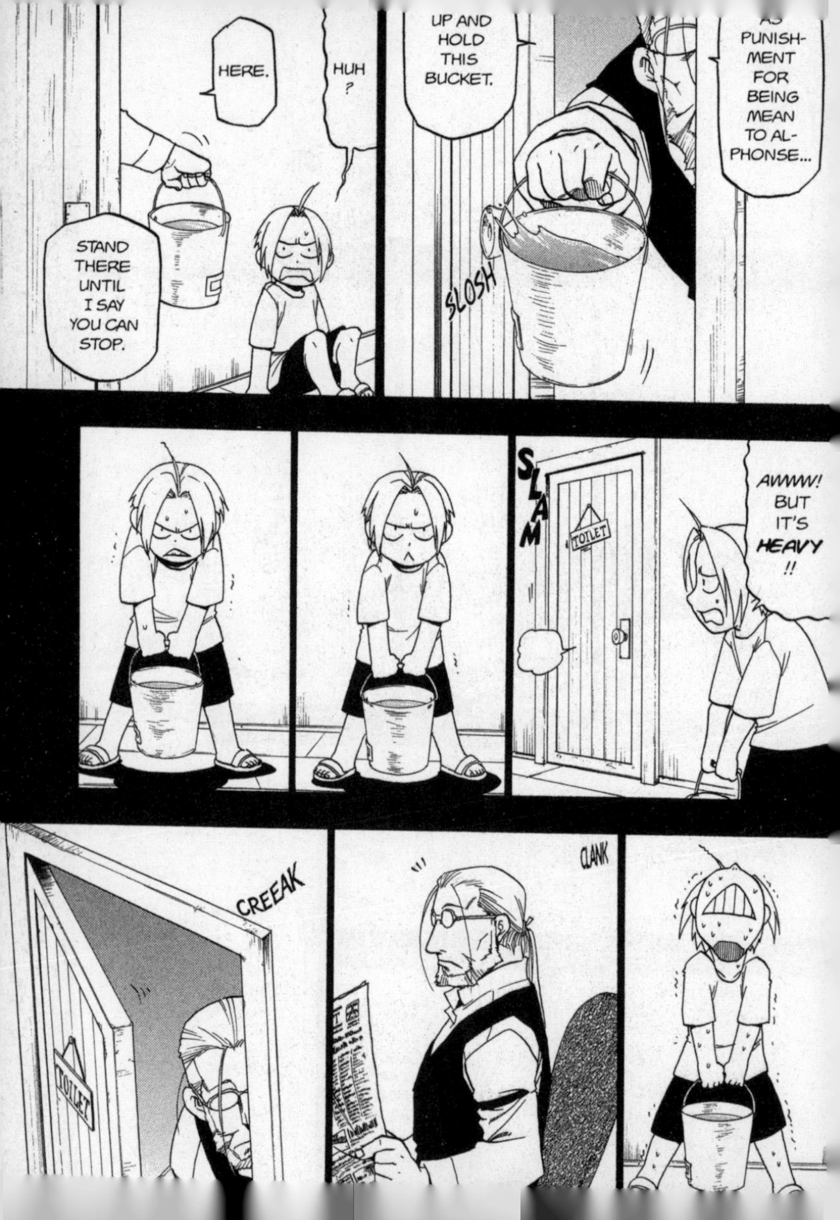
PUNISH-MENT FOR BEING MEAN TO AL-PHONSE...
UP AND HOLD THIS BUCKET.
SLOSH
HERE.
HUH?
STAND THERE UNTIL I SAY YOU CAN STOP.
AWWW! BUT IT'S HEAVY!!
SLAM
TOILET
CLANK
CREEAK
TOILET

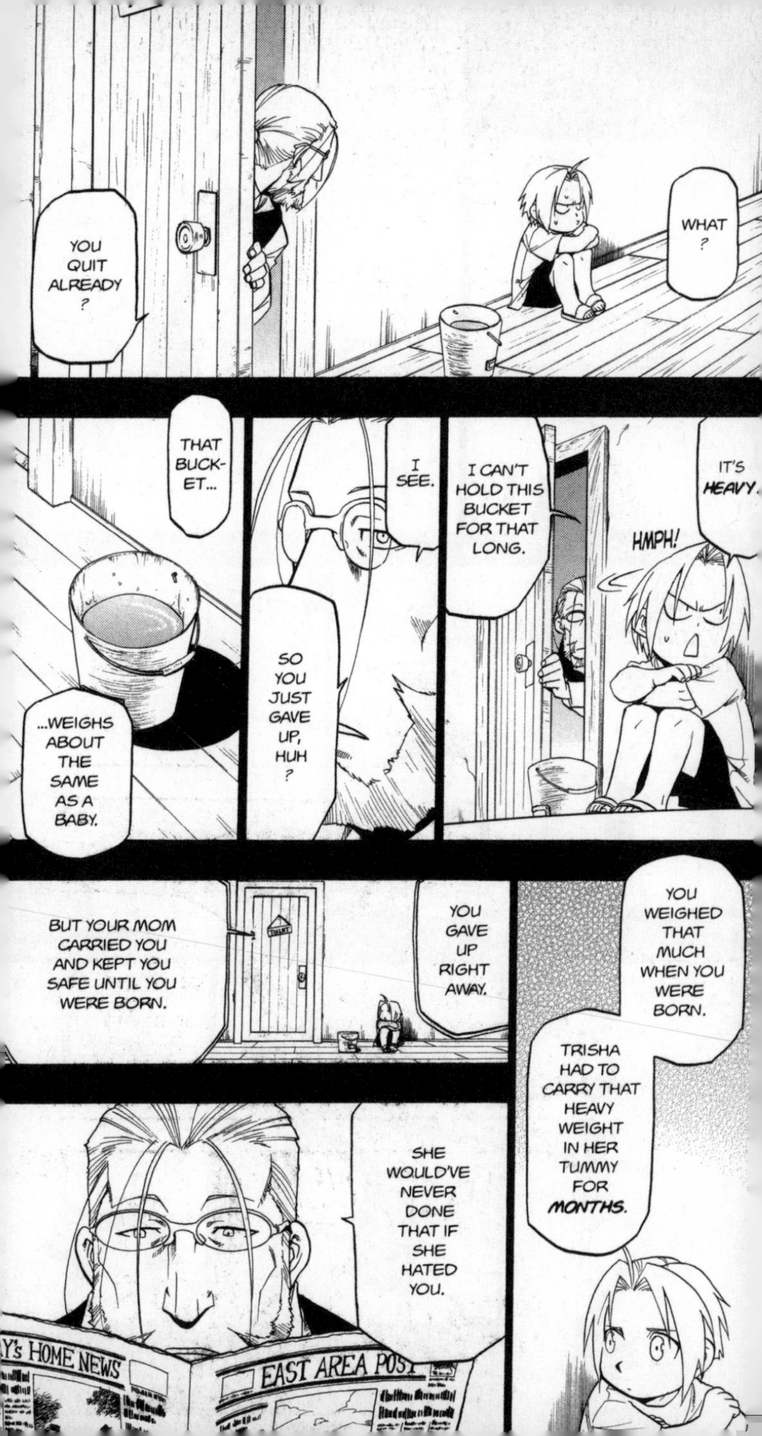
WHAT ?
YOU QUIT ALREADY ?
IT'S *HEAVY*.
HMPH!
I CAN'T HOLD THIS BUCKET FOR THAT LONG.
I SEE.
SO YOU JUST GAVE UP, HUH ?
THAT BUCK-ET...
...WEIGHS ABOUT THE SAME AS A BABY.
YOU WEIGHED THAT MUCH WHEN YOU WERE BORN.
TRISHA HAD TO CARRY THAT HEAVY WEIGHT IN HER TUMMY FOR *MONTHS*.
YOU GAVE UP RIGHT AWAY.
BUT YOUR MOM CARRIED YOU AND KEPT YOU SAFE UNTIL YOU WERE BORN.
SHE WOULD'VE NEVER DONE THAT IF SHE HATED YOU.
EAST AREA POST

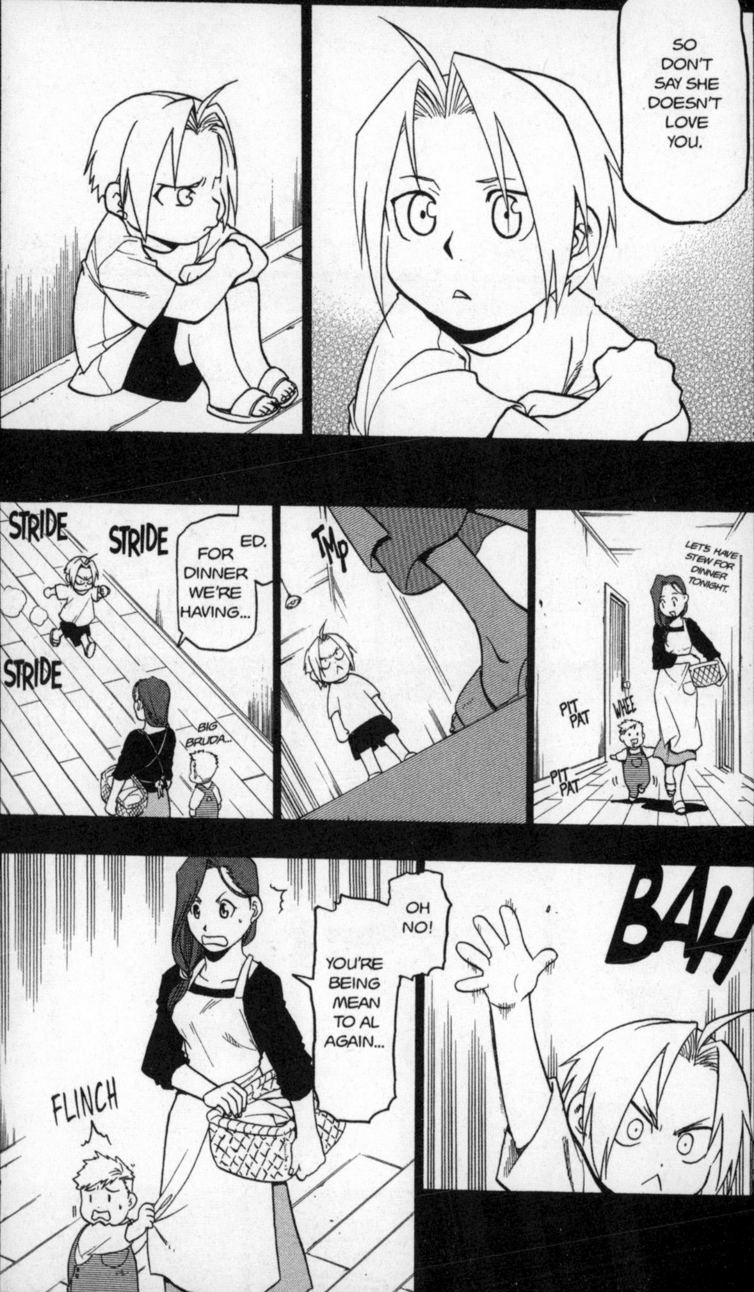
SO DON'T SAY SHE DOESN'T LOVE YOU.
LET'S HAVE STEW FOR DINNER TONIGHT.
PIT PAT
WHEE
PIT PAT
TMP
STRIDE
STRIDE
ED. FOR DINNER WE'RE HAVING...
STRIDE
BIG BRUDA...
BAH
OH NO!
YOU'RE BEING MEAN TO AL AGAIN...
FLINCH

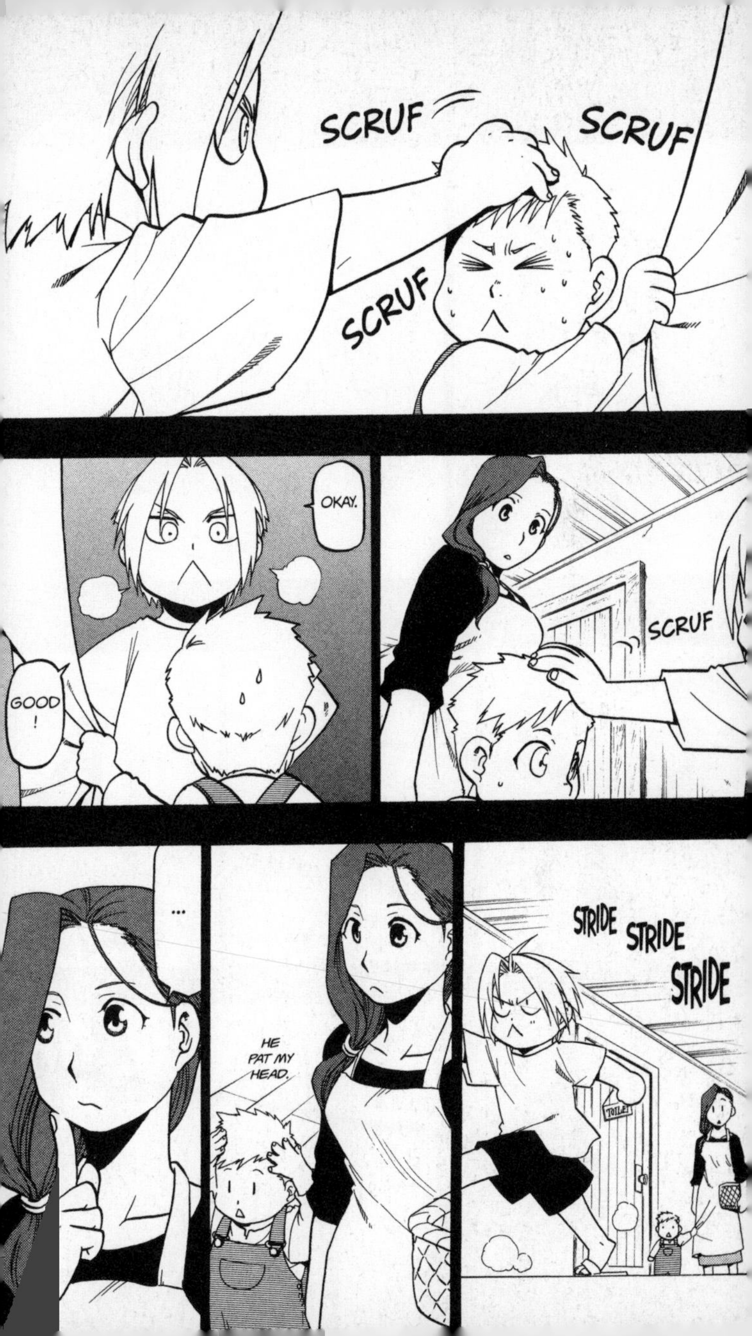
SCRUF
SCRUF
SCRUF
SCRUF
OKAY.
GOOD!
STRIDE STRIDE STRIDE
HE PAT MY HEAD.
...

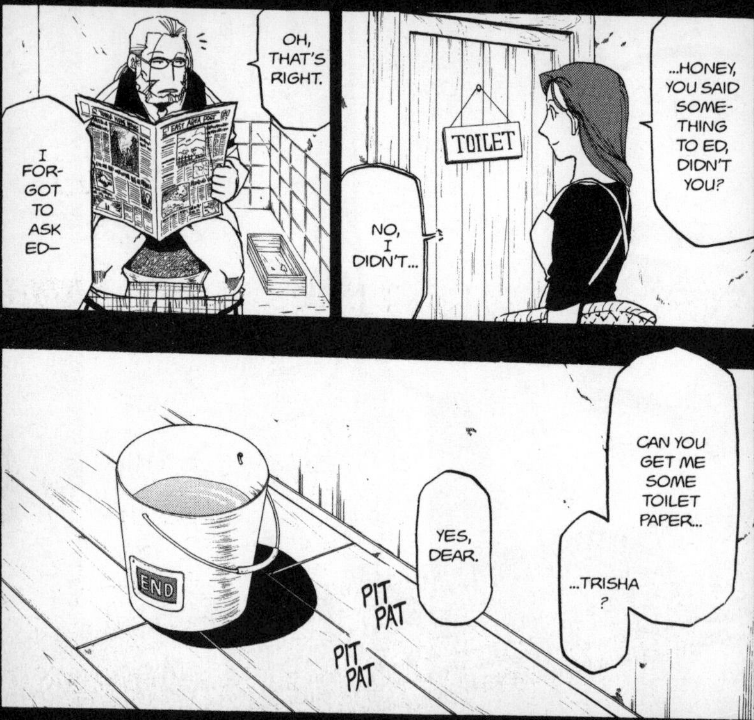
...HONEY, YOU SAID SOMETHING TO ED, DIDN'T YOU?
TOILET
NO, I DIDN'T...
OH, THAT'S RIGHT.
I FORGOT TO ASK ED—
CAN YOU GET ME SOME TOILET PAPER... ...TRISHA?
YES, DEAR.
PIT PAT
PIT PAT
END

FULLMETAL ALCHEMIST 14

SPECIAL THANKS

CONTRIBUTING ARTISTS
ON MEMORY DOODLES
ATSUSHI OKUBO
SEICHI KISHIMOTO
AMI SHIBATA

EDITOR YOICHI SHIMOMURA

KEISUI TAKAEDA
SANKICHI HINODEYA
JUN TOKO
AIYABALL
NONO
BIG BROTHER YOICHI KAMITONO
MASASHI MIZUTANI

DEN'S STUFFED ANIMAL ON
COVER INSIDE FLAP CREATED BY
HISAE IWAOKA

AND YOU!!

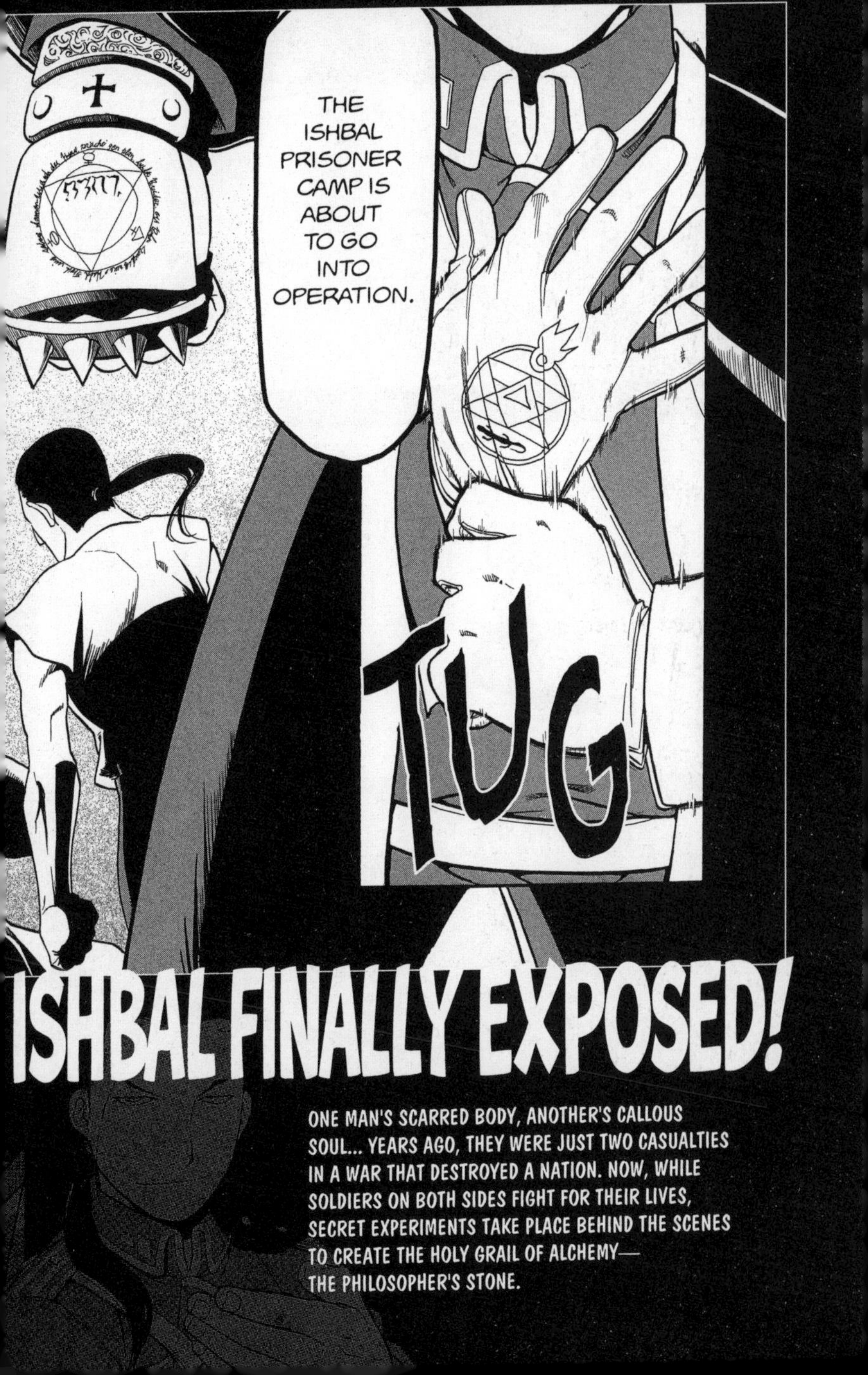
THE ISHBAL PRISONER CAMP IS ABOUT TO GO INTO OPERATION.
TUG

ISHBAL FINALLY EXPOSED!

ONE MAN'S SCARRED BODY, ANOTHER'S CALLOUS SOUL... YEARS AGO, THEY WERE JUST TWO CASUALTIES IN A WAR THAT DESTROYED A NATION. NOW, WHILE SOLDIERS ON BOTH SIDES FIGHT FOR THEIR LIVES, SECRET EXPERIMENTS TAKE PLACE BEHIND THE SCENES TO CREATE THE HOLY GRAIL OF ALCHEMY—THE PHILOSOPHER'S STONE.

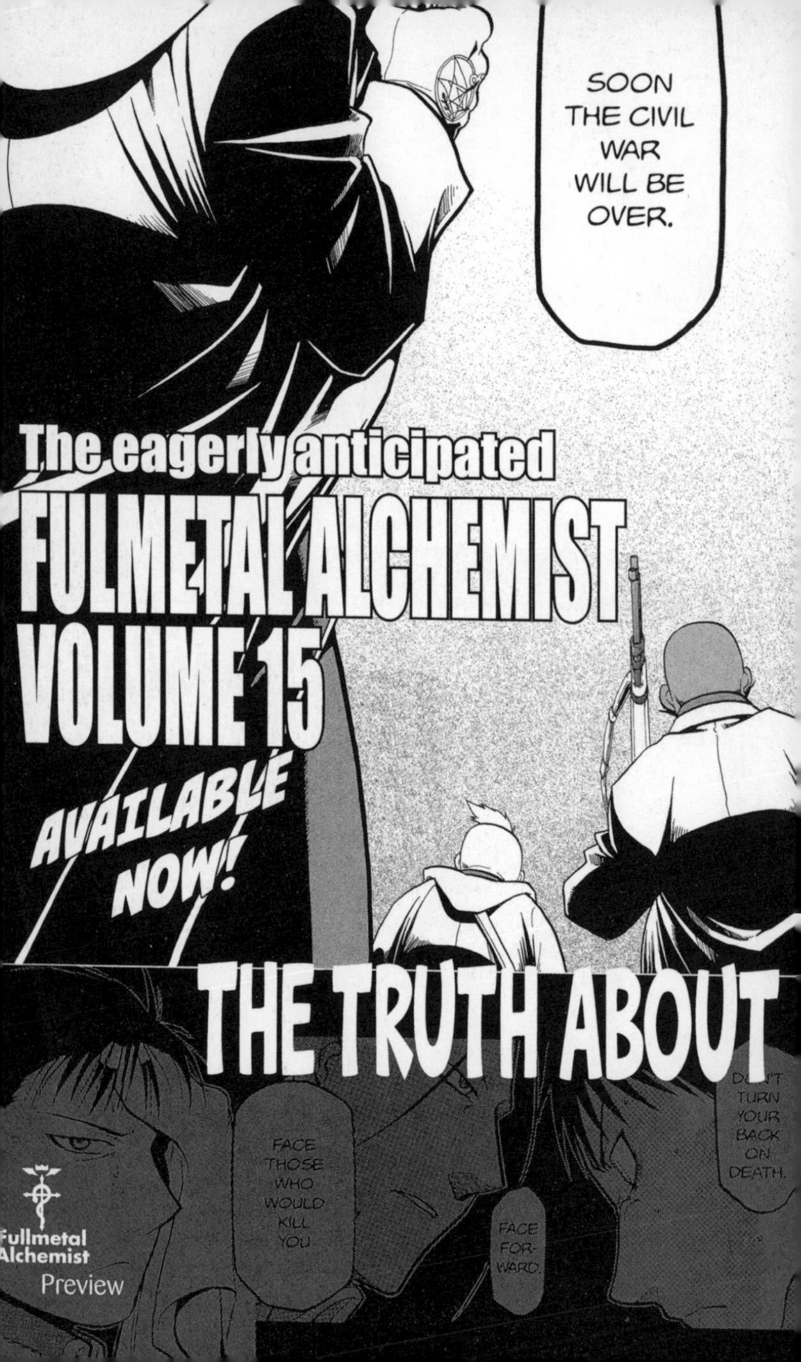
SOON THE CIVIL WAR WILL BE OVER.
The eagerly anticipated
FULMETAL ALCHEMIST VOLUME 15
AVAILABLE NOW!
THE TRUTH ABOUT
DON'T TURN YOUR BACK ON DEATH.
FACE FOR-WARD.
FACE THOSE WHO WOULD KILL YOU.
Fullmetal Alchemist
Preview

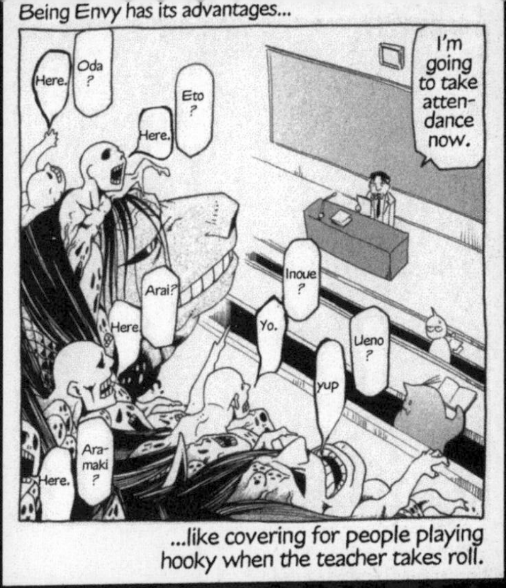
Being Envy has its advantages...
I'm going to take attendance now.
Eto?
Here.
Oda?
Here.
Inoue?
Yo.
Arai?
Here
Ueno?
yup
Aramaki?
Here.
...like covering for people playing hooky when the teacher takes roll.

Volume 10, Chapter 43

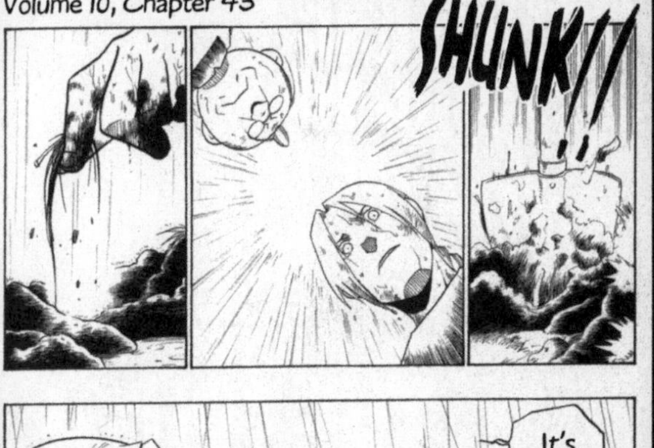
SHUNK!!
It's the colonel!!

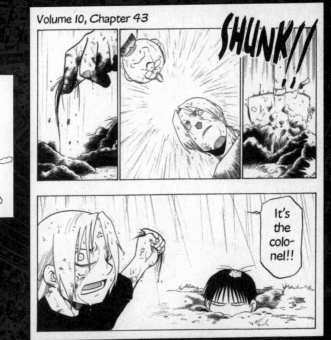

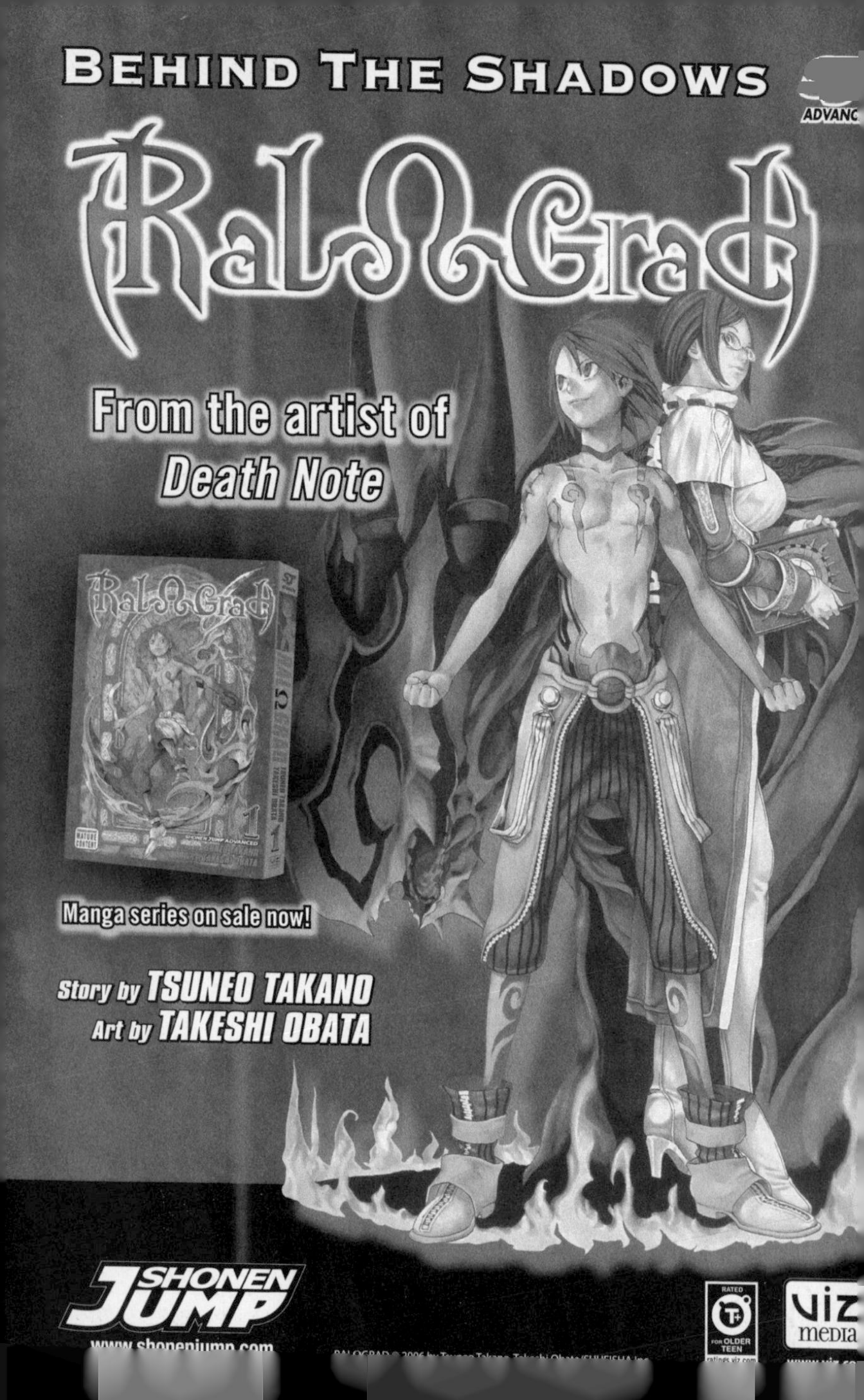

BEHIND THE SHADOWS
ADVANC
RalΩGrad
From the artist of
Death Note
Manga series on sale now!
Story by TSUNEO TAKANO
Art by TAKESHI OBATA
SHONEN JUMP
RATED
T+
FOR OLDER TEEN
viz media

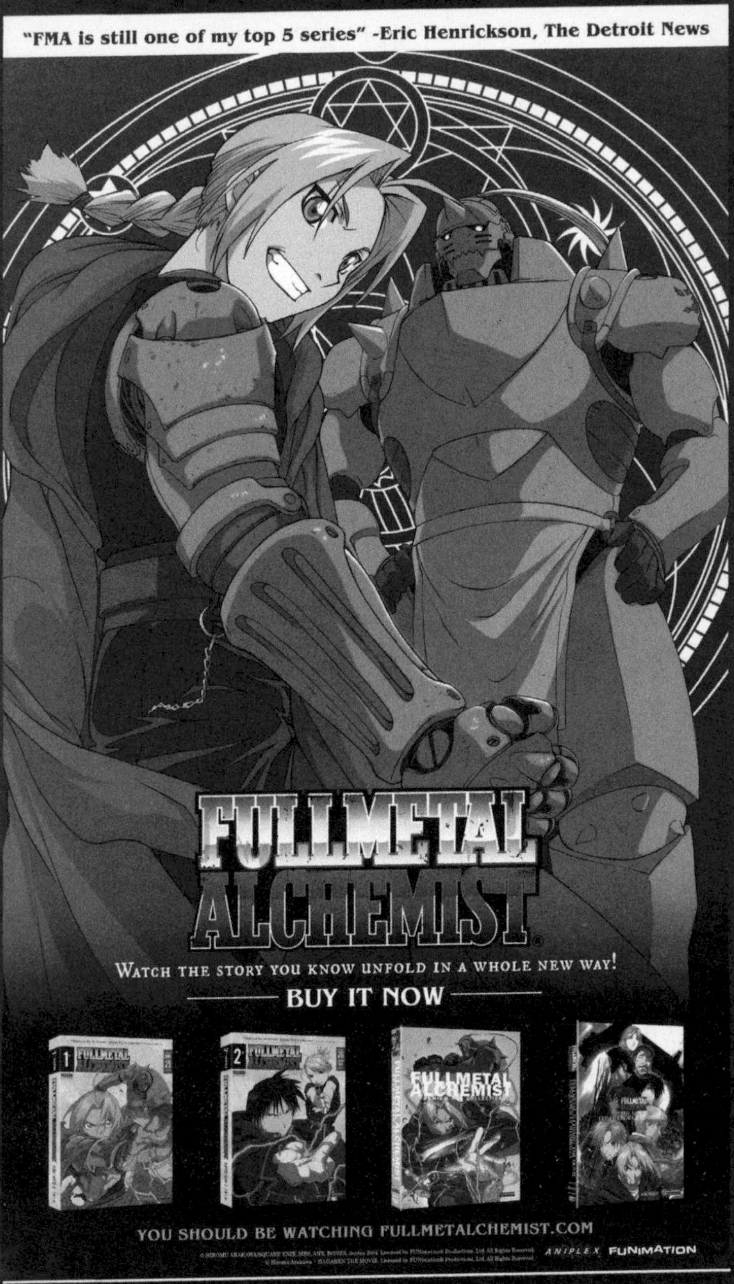
"FMA is still one of my top 5 series" -Eric Henrickson, The Detroit News
FULLMETAL ALCHEMIST®
WATCH THE STORY YOU KNOW UNFOLD IN A WHOLE NEW WAY!
BUY IT NOW
YOU SHOULD BE WATCHING FULLMETALCHEMIST.COM
ANIPLEX
FUNIMATION

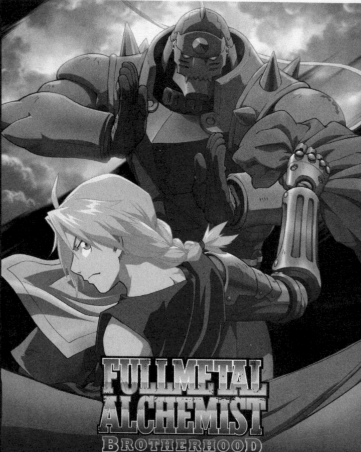

FROM THE STUDIO THAT BROUGHT YOU *COWBOY BEBOP: THE MOVIE* AND *SOUL EATER*

FULLMETAL ALCHEMIST
BROTHERHOOD

YOU'VE SEEN FULLMETAL ALCHEMIST. NOW SEE IT THE WAY THE CREATOR INTENDED.
ADD *FULLMETAL ALCHEMIST: BROTHERHOOD* TO YOUR LIBRARY.

BUY TODAY!

YOU SHOULD BE WATCHING FULLMETALALCHEMIST.COM

© Hiromu Arakawa/FA Project, MBS. Licensed by FUNimation Productions, Ltd. All Rights Reserved.
© Hiromu Arakawa/HAGAREN THE MOVIE 2011. Licensed by FUNimation Productions, Ltd. All Rights Reserved.

ANIPLEX FUNiMATION

Hey! You're Reading in the Wrong Direction!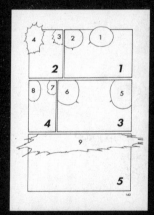

This is the **end** of this graphic novel!

To properly enjoy this VIZ graphic novel, please turn it around and begin reading from **right to left.** Unlike English, Japanese is read right to left, so Japanese comics are read in reverse order from the way English comics are typically read.

Follow the action this way

This book has been printed in the original Japanese format in order to preserve the orientation of the original artwork. Have fun with it!

FULLMETAL ALCHEMIST VOL. 14

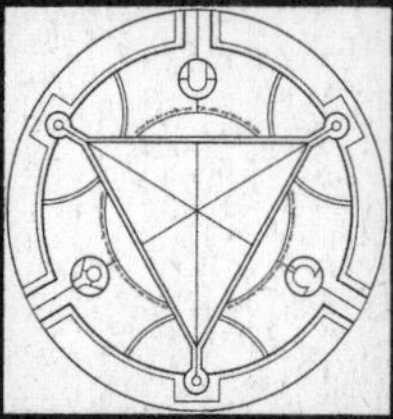

VIZ Media Edition

Story and Art by Hiromu Arakawa

Translation/Akira Watanabe
English Adaptation/Jake Forbes
Touch-up Art & Lettering/Wayne Truman
Design/Amy Martin
Editor/Annette Roman

Hagane no RenkinJutsushi vol. 14 © 2006 Hiromu Arakawa/SQUARE ENIX. First published in Japan in 2006 by SQUARE ENIX CO., LTD. English translation rights arranged with SQUARE ENIX CO., LTD. and VIZ Media, LLC.

The stories, characters and incidents mentioned in this publication are entirely fictional.

No portion of this book may be reproduced or transmitted in any form or by any means without written permission from the copyright holders.

Printed in the U.S.A.

Published by VIZ Media, LLC
P.O. Box 77010
San Francisco, CA 94107

10 9
First printing, August 2007
Ninth printing, December 2014

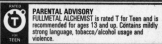

PARENTAL ADVISORY
FULLMETAL ALCHEMIST is rated T for Teen and is recommended for ages 13 and up. Contains mildly strong language, tobacco/alcohol usage and violence.
ratings.viz.com

www.viz.com

...seconds till beef...

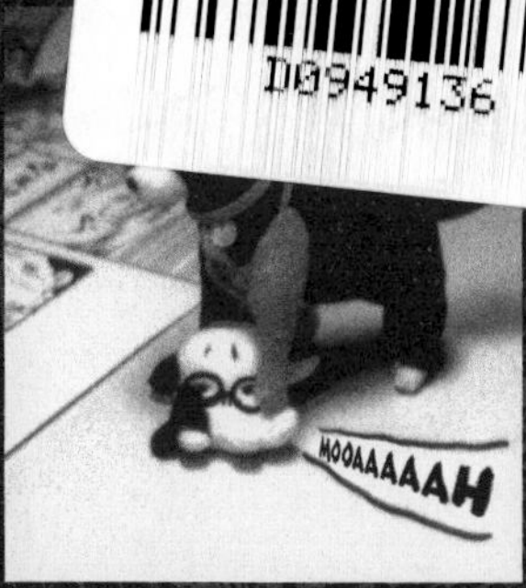

Hiromu Arakawa, 2006

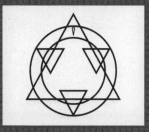

HOOAAAAAH

Born in Hokkaido (northern Japan), Hiromu Arakawa first attracted national attention in 1999 with her award-winning manga *Stray Dog*. Her series *Fullmetal Alchemist* debuted in 2001 in Square Enix's monthly manga anthology *Shonen Gangan*.

D0949136